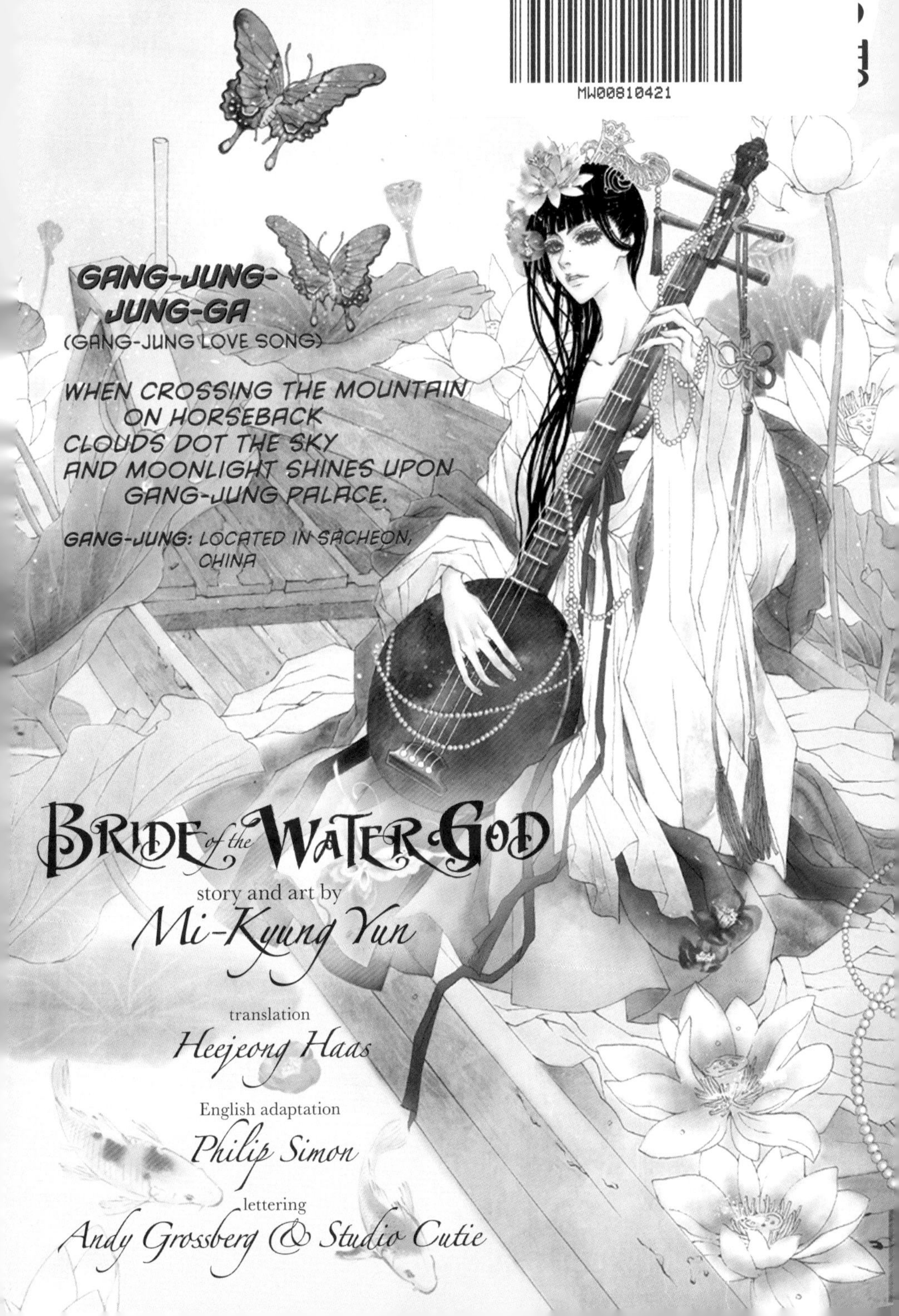
GANG-JUNG-JUNG-GA
(GANG-JUNG LOVE SONG)
WHEN CROSSING THE MOUNTAIN
ON HORSEBACK
CLOUDS DOT THE SKY
AND MOONLIGHT SHINES UPON
GANG-JUNG PALACE.
GANG-JUNG: LOCATED IN SACHEON, CHINA

BRIDE of the WATER GOD

story and art by

Mi-Kyung Yun

translation

Heejeong Haas

English adaptation

Philip Simon

lettering

Andy Grossberg & Studio Cutie

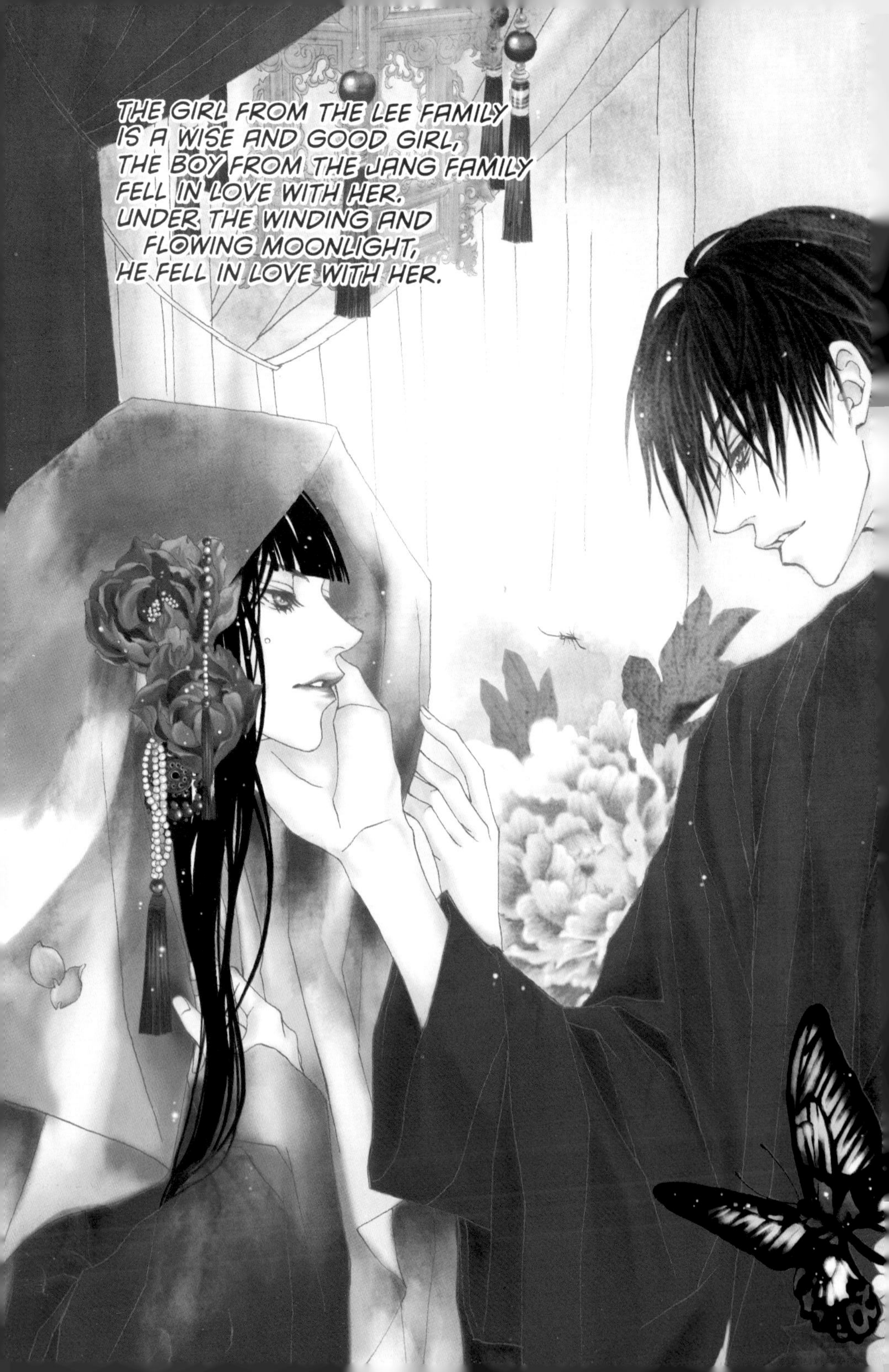
THE GIRL FROM THE LEE FAMILY
IS A WISE AND GOOD GIRL,
THE BOY FROM THE JANG FAMILY
FELL IN LOVE WITH HER.
UNDER THE WINDING AND
FLOWING MOONLIGHT,
HE FELL IN LOVE WITH HER.

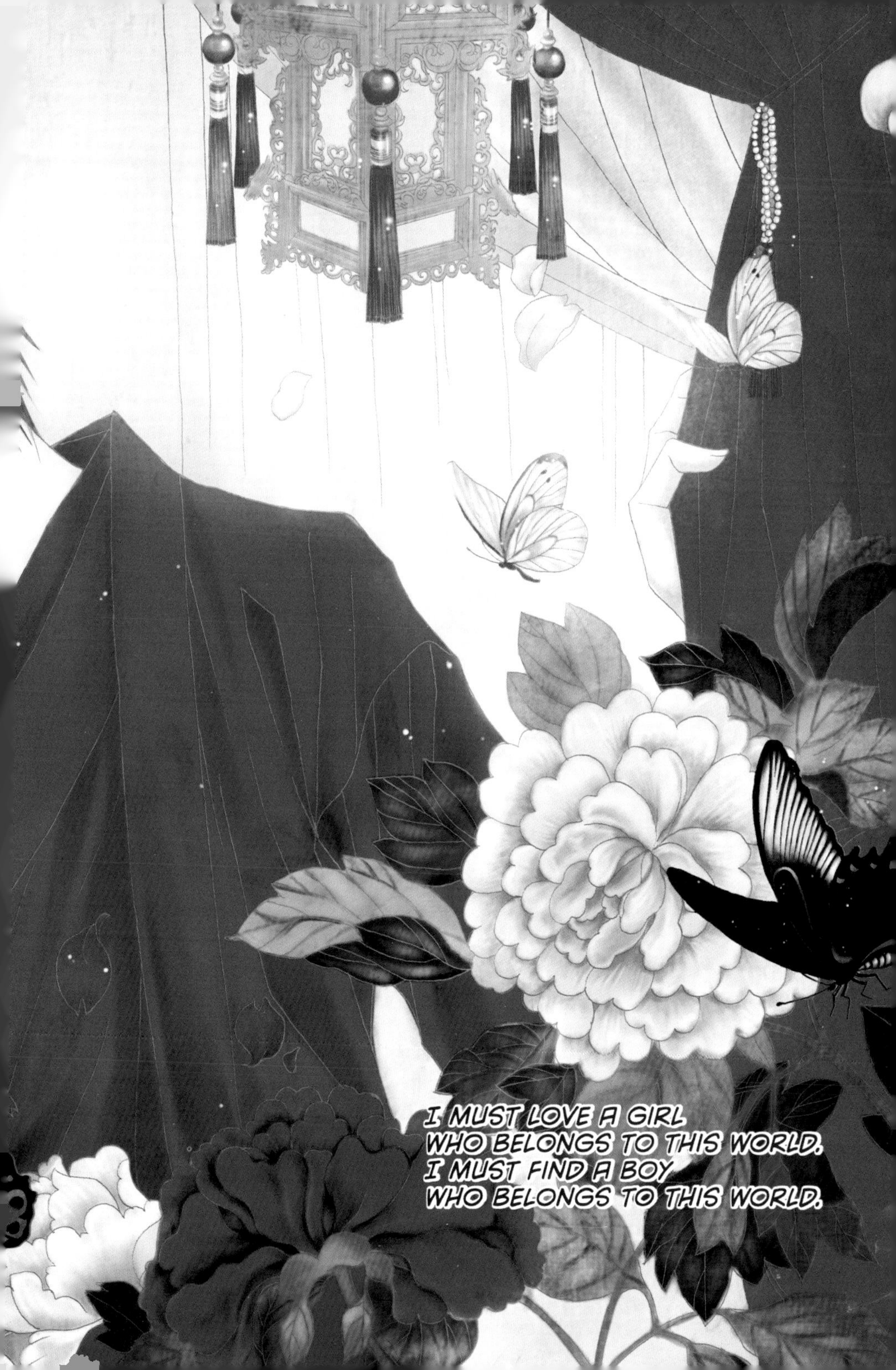
I MUST LOVE A GIRL
WHO BELONGS TO THIS WORLD.
I MUST FIND A BOY
WHO BELONGS TO THIS WORLD.

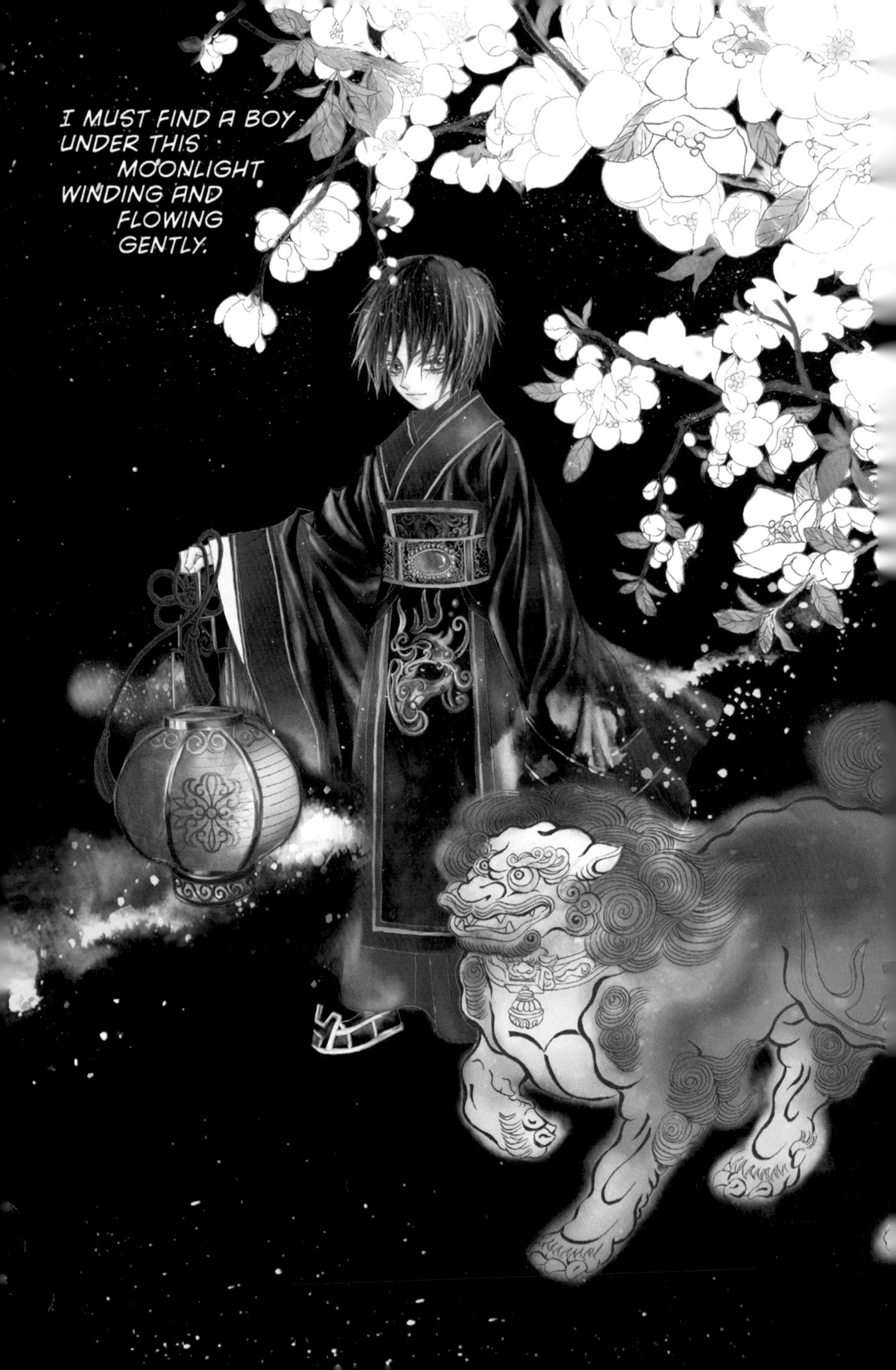
I MUST FIND A BOY UNDER THIS MOONLIGHT WINDING AND FLOWING GENTLY.

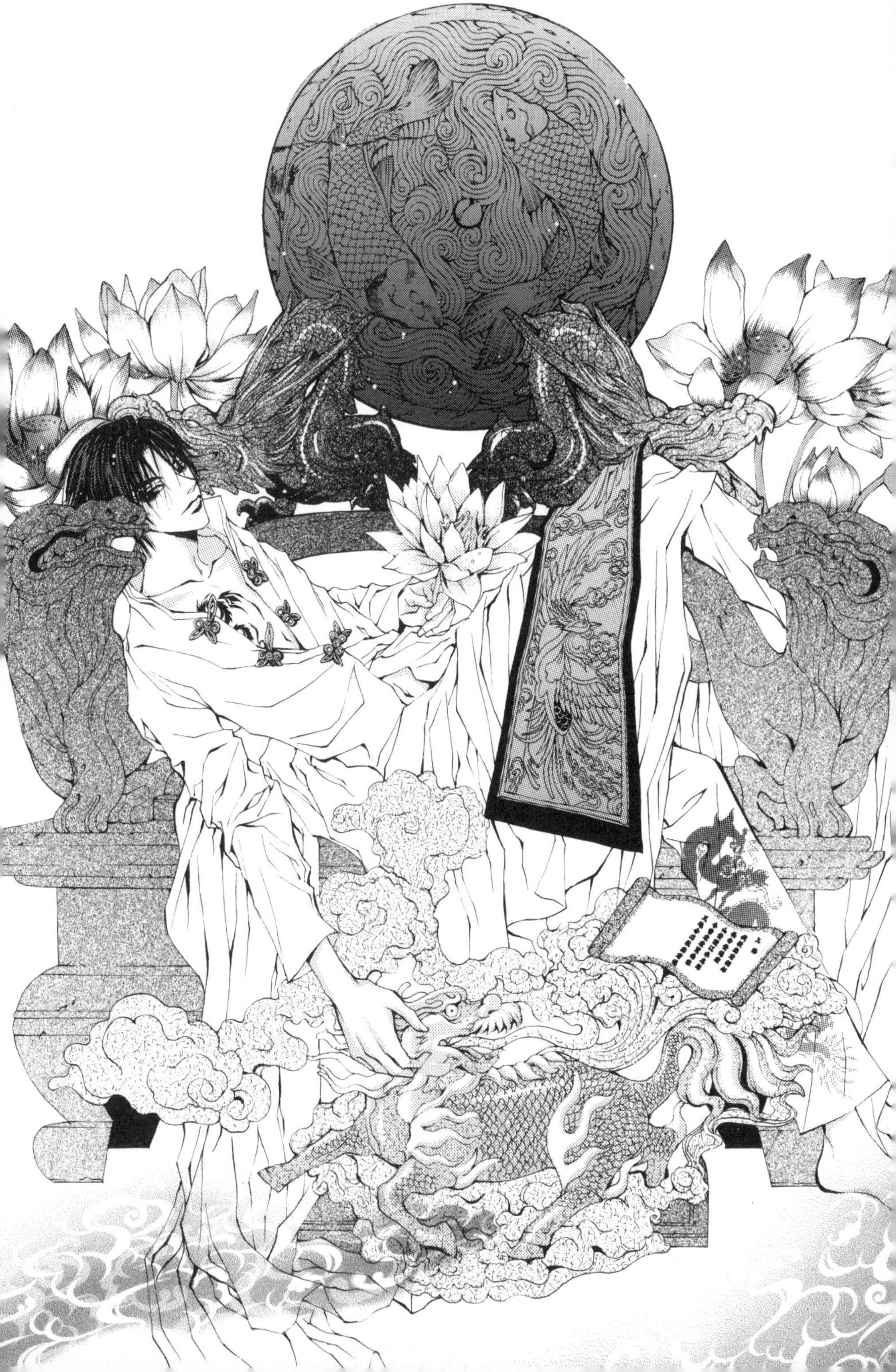

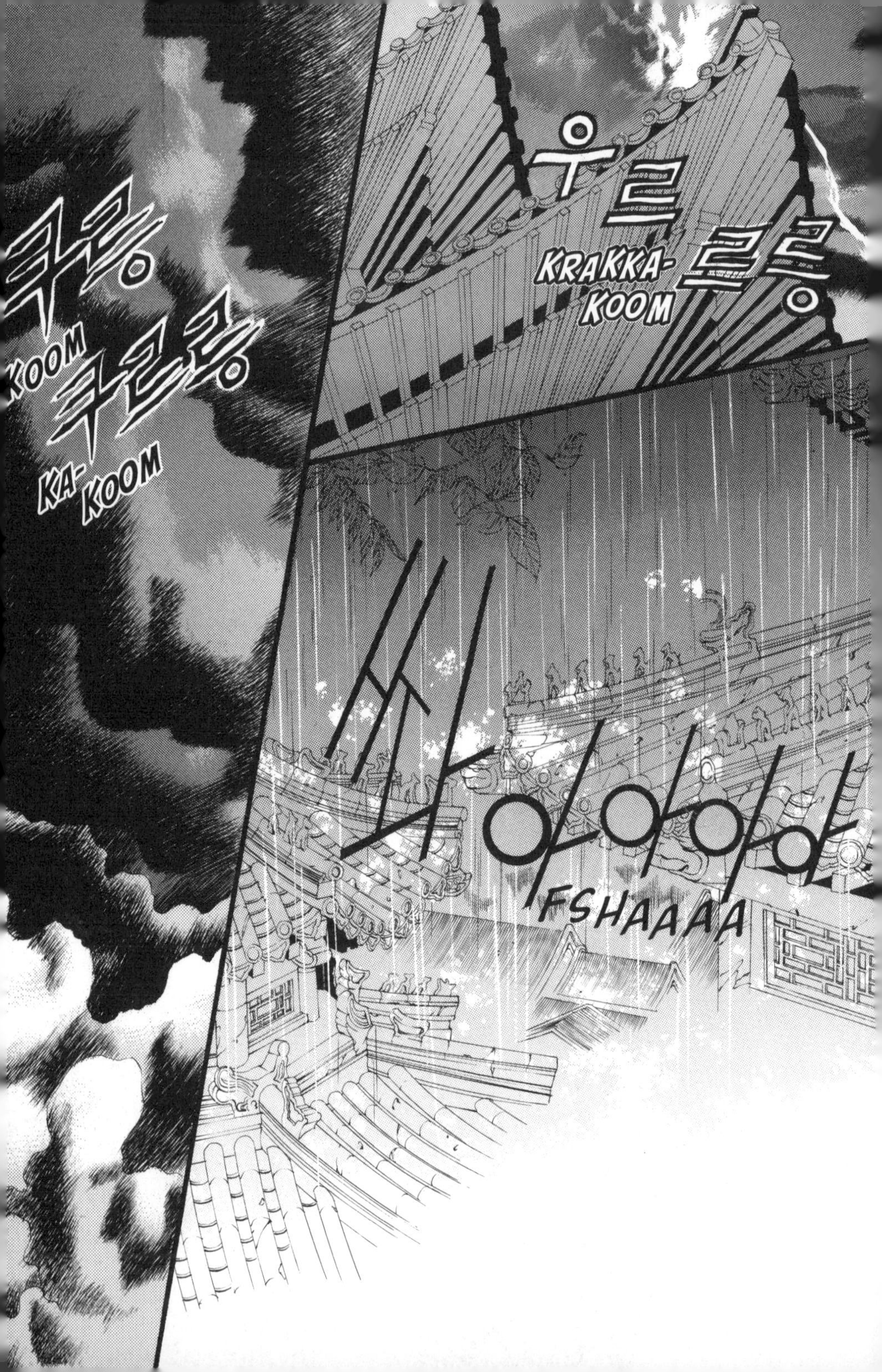
쿠릉
KOOM
쿠르릉
KA-KOOM
우르르릉
KRAKKA-KOOM
쏴아아아아
FSHAAAAA

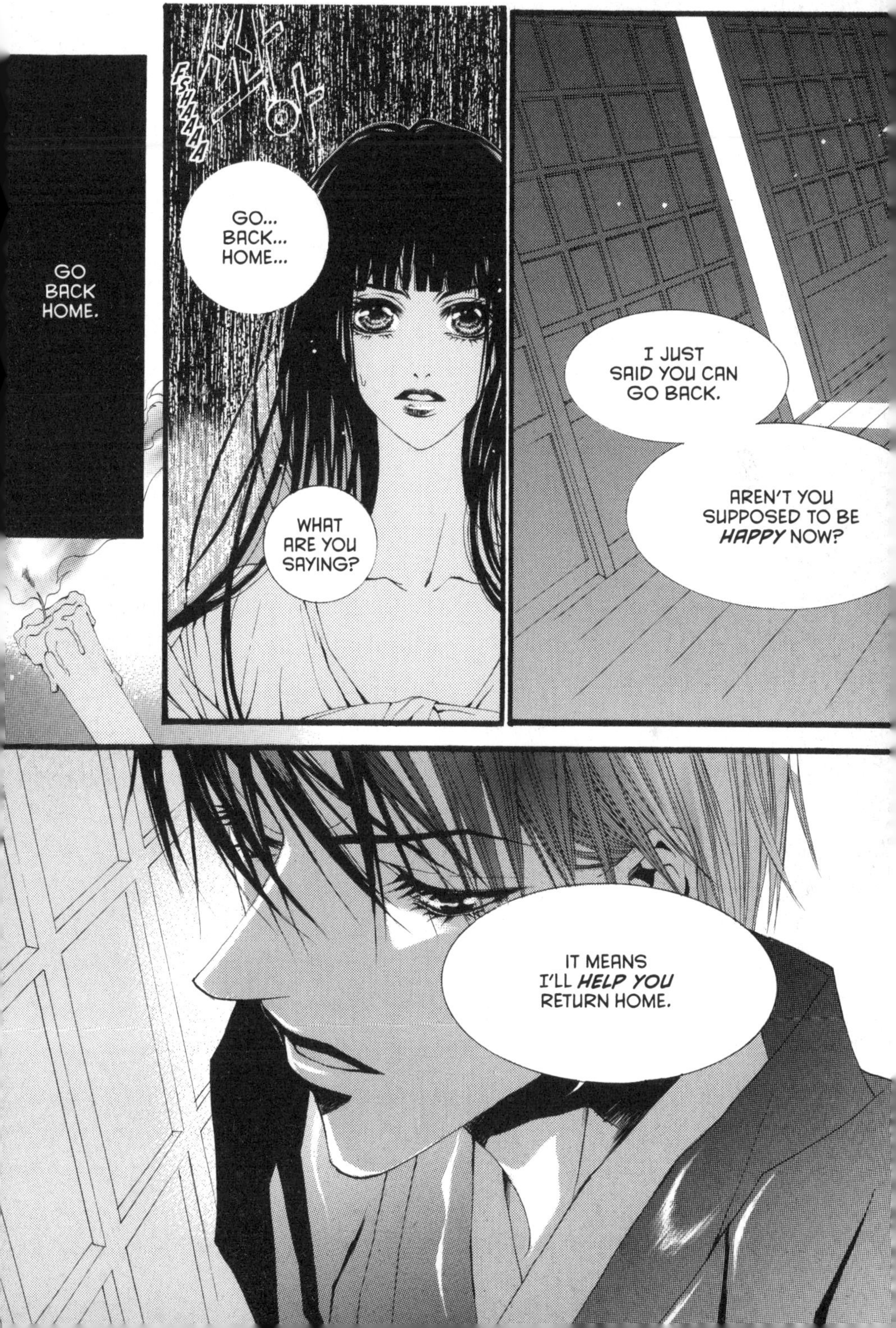
GO BACK HOME.
FSHAAAA
GO... BACK... HOME...
WHAT ARE YOU SAYING?
I JUST SAID YOU CAN GO BACK.
AREN'T YOU SUPPOSED TO BE *HAPPY* NOW?
IT MEANS I'LL *HELP YOU* RETURN HOME.

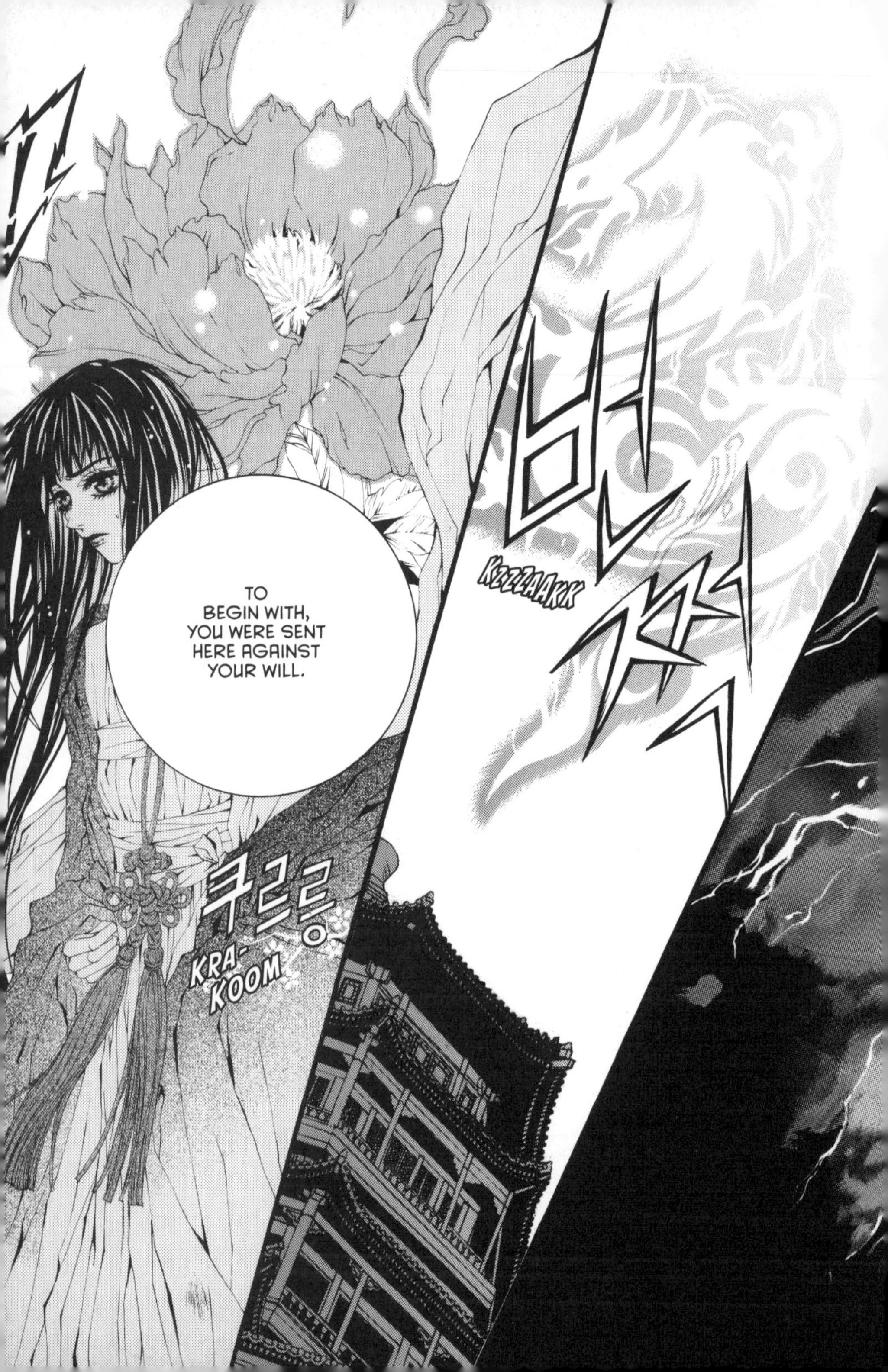
TO BEGIN WITH, YOU WERE SENT HERE AGAINST YOUR WILL.
번쩍
KZZZAAKK
쿠르릉
KRA-KOOM

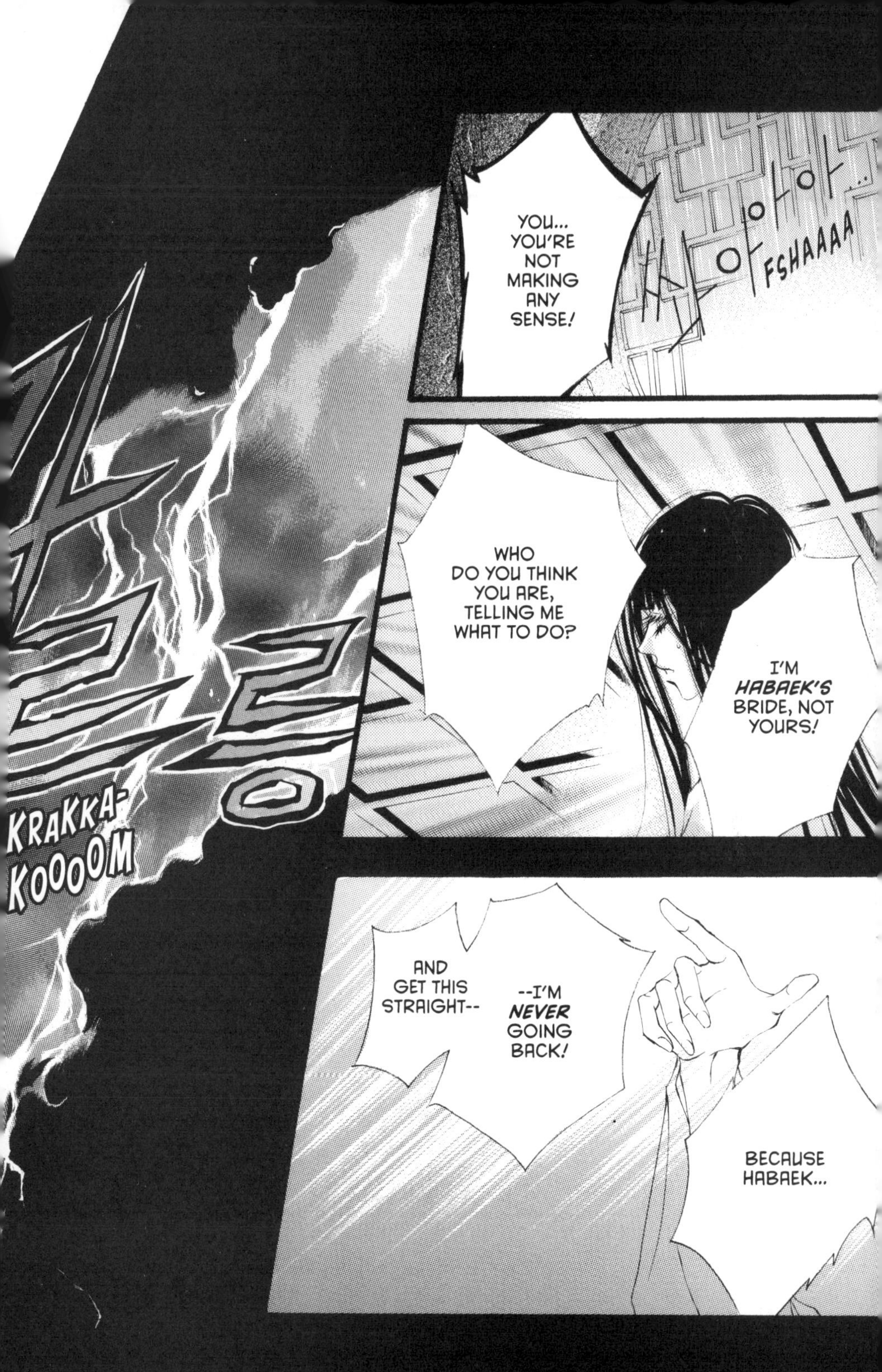
KRAKKA-KOOOOM
FSHAAAA
YOU... YOU'RE NOT MAKING ANY SENSE!
WHO DO YOU THINK YOU ARE, TELLING ME WHAT TO DO?
I'M ***HABAEK'S*** BRIDE, NOT YOURS!
AND GET THIS STRAIGHT--
--I'M ***NEVER*** GOING BACK!
BECAUSE HABAEK...

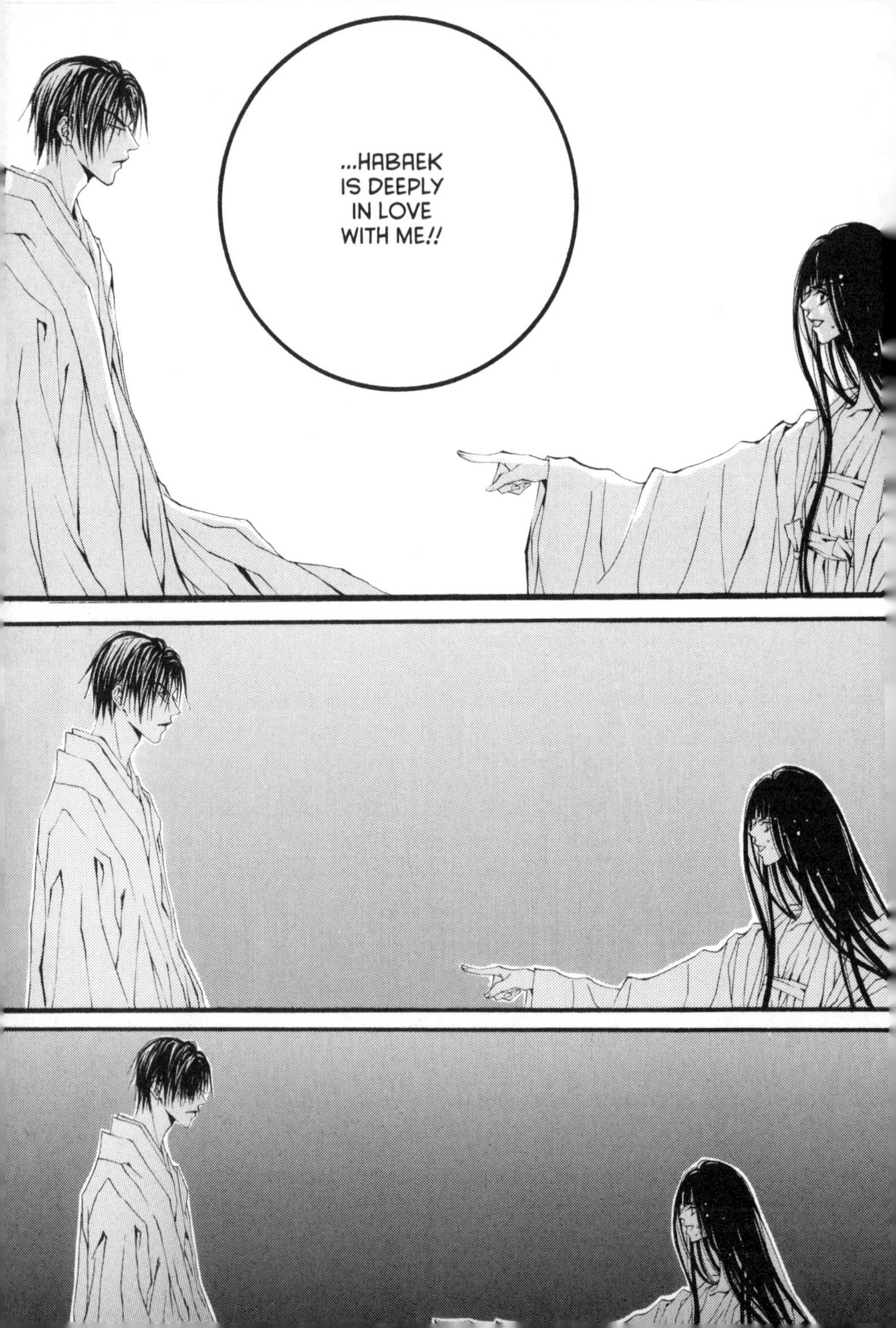
...HABAEK IS DEEPLY IN LOVE WITH ME!!

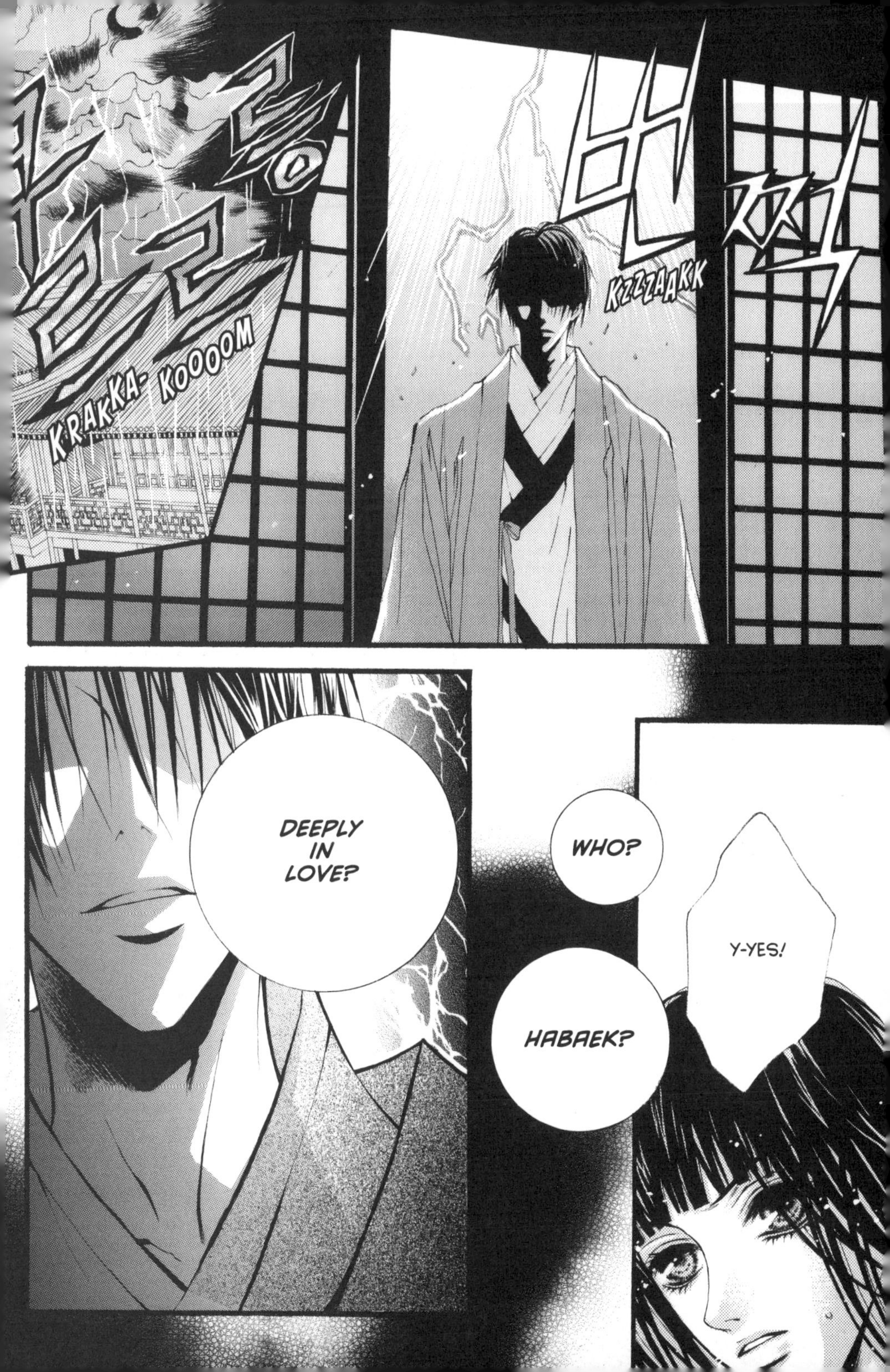
KRAKKA- KOOOOM
KZZZAAKK
DEEPLY IN LOVE?
WHO?
HABAEK?
Y-YES!

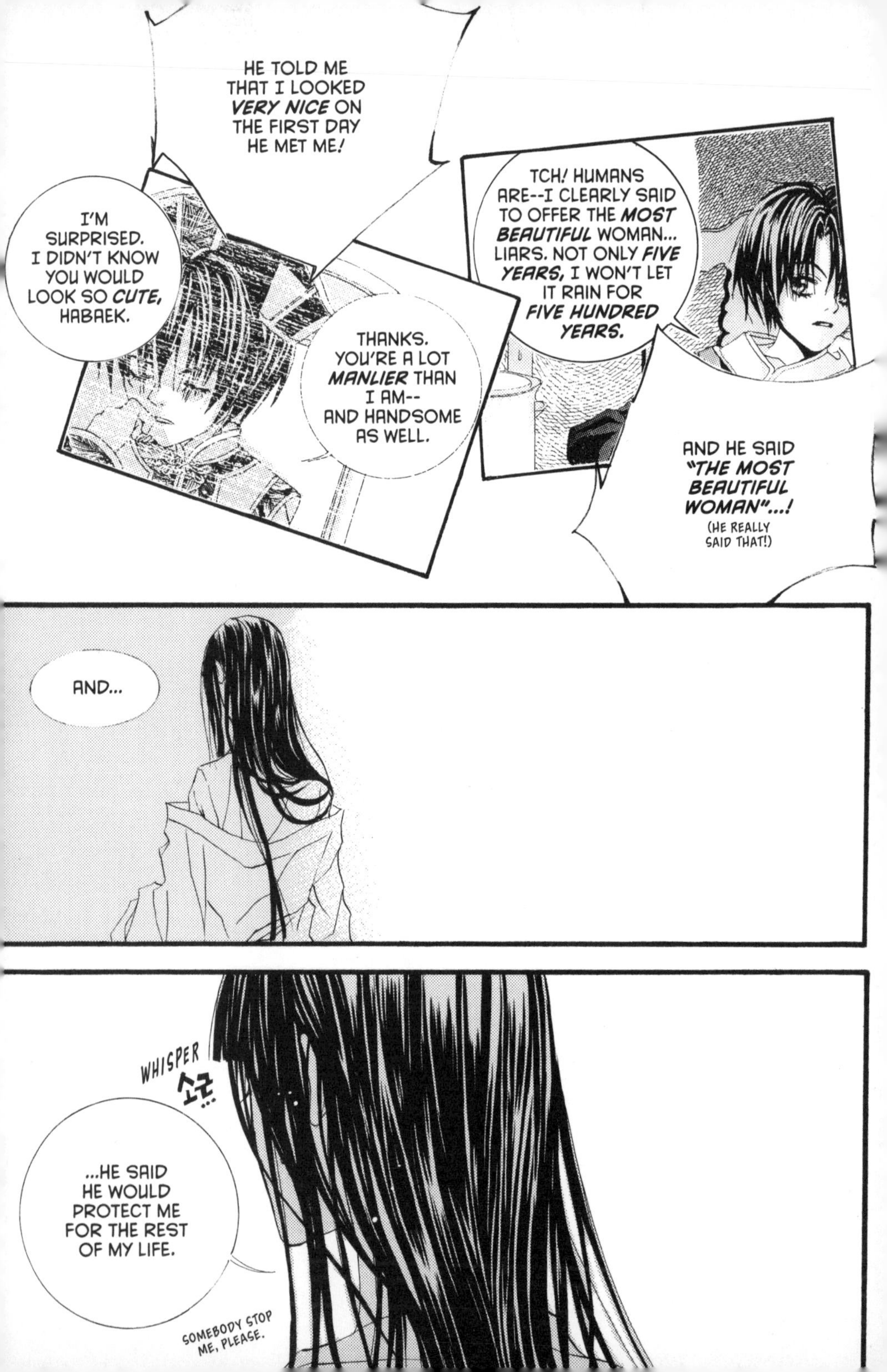
HE TOLD ME THAT I LOOKED *VERY NICE* ON THE FIRST DAY HE MET ME!
I'M SURPRISED. I DIDN'T KNOW YOU WOULD LOOK SO *CUTE,* HABAEK.
THANKS. YOU'RE A LOT *MANLIER* THAN I AM-- AND HANDSOME AS WELL.
TCH! HUMANS ARE--I CLEARLY SAID TO OFFER THE *MOST BEAUTIFUL* WOMAN... LIARS. NOT ONLY *FIVE YEARS,* I WON'T LET IT RAIN FOR *FIVE HUNDRED YEARS.*
AND HE SAID *"THE MOST BEAUTIFUL WOMAN"...!*
(HE REALLY SAID THAT!)
AND...
WHISPER
소곤...
...HE SAID HE WOULD PROTECT ME FOR THE REST OF MY LIFE.
SOMEBODY STOP ME, PLEASE.

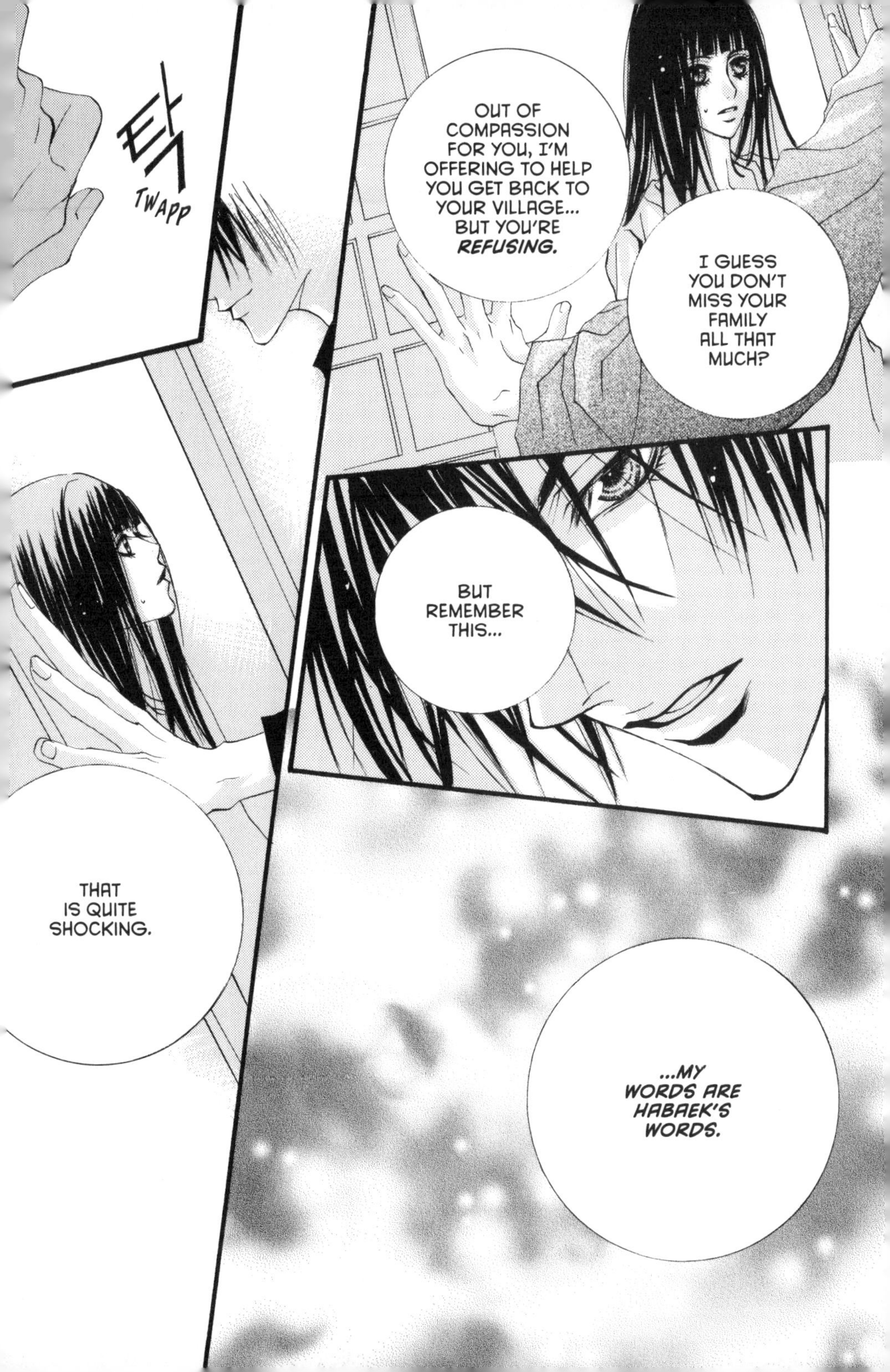
탁
TWAPP
OUT OF COMPASSION FOR YOU, I'M OFFERING TO HELP YOU GET BACK TO YOUR VILLAGE... BUT YOU'RE *REFUSING.*
I GUESS YOU DON'T MISS YOUR FAMILY ALL THAT MUCH?
THAT IS QUITE SHOCKING.
BUT REMEMBER THIS...
...MY WORDS ARE HABAEK'S WORDS.

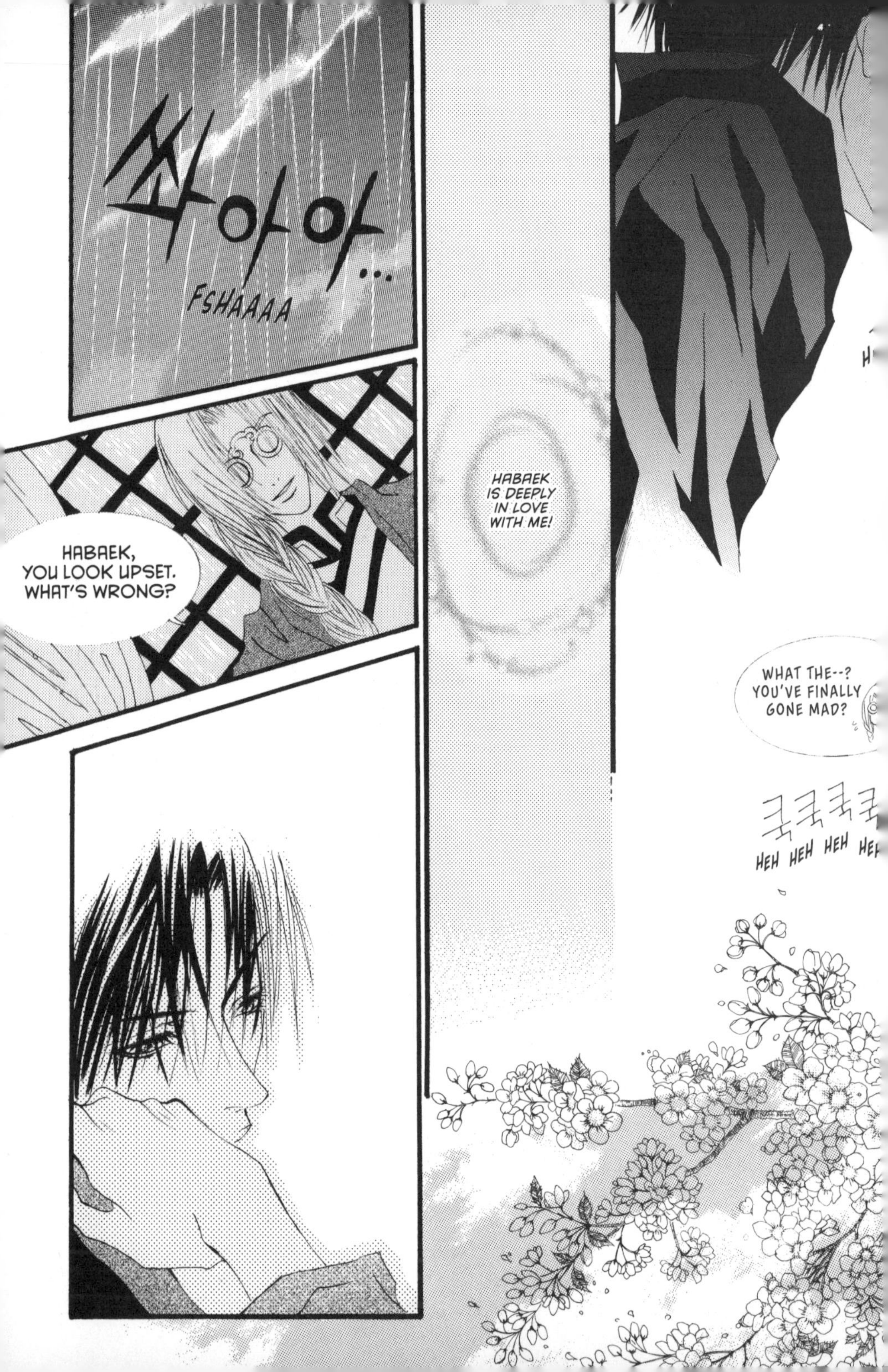

쏴아아...
FSHAAAA
HABAEK, YOU LOOK UPSET. WHAT'S WRONG?
HABAEK IS DEEPLY IN LOVE WITH ME!
WHAT THE--? YOU'VE FINALLY GONE MAD?
쿡쿡쿡
HEH HEH HEH

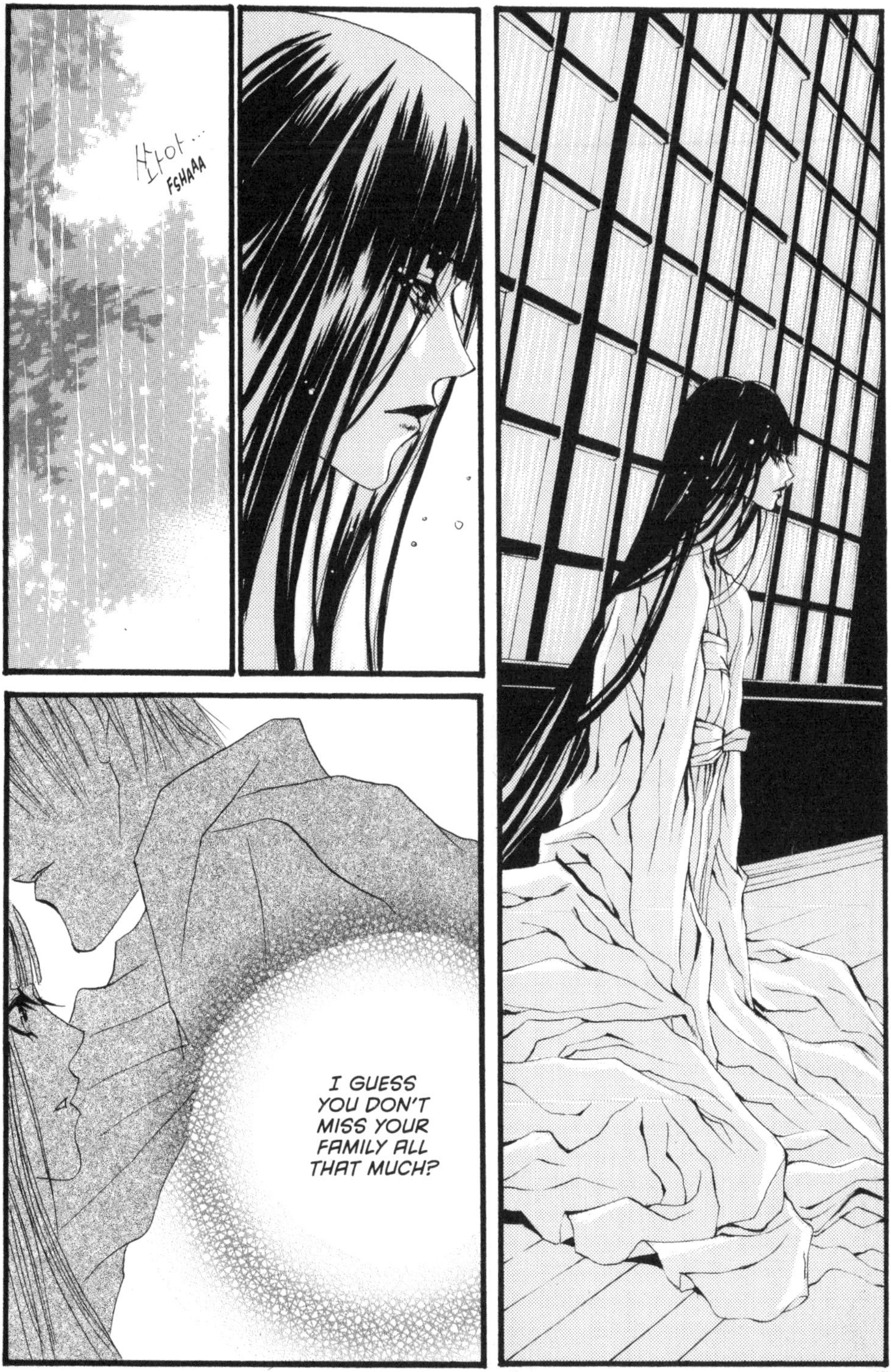
FSHAAA
I GUESS YOU DON'T MISS YOUR FAMILY ALL THAT MUCH?

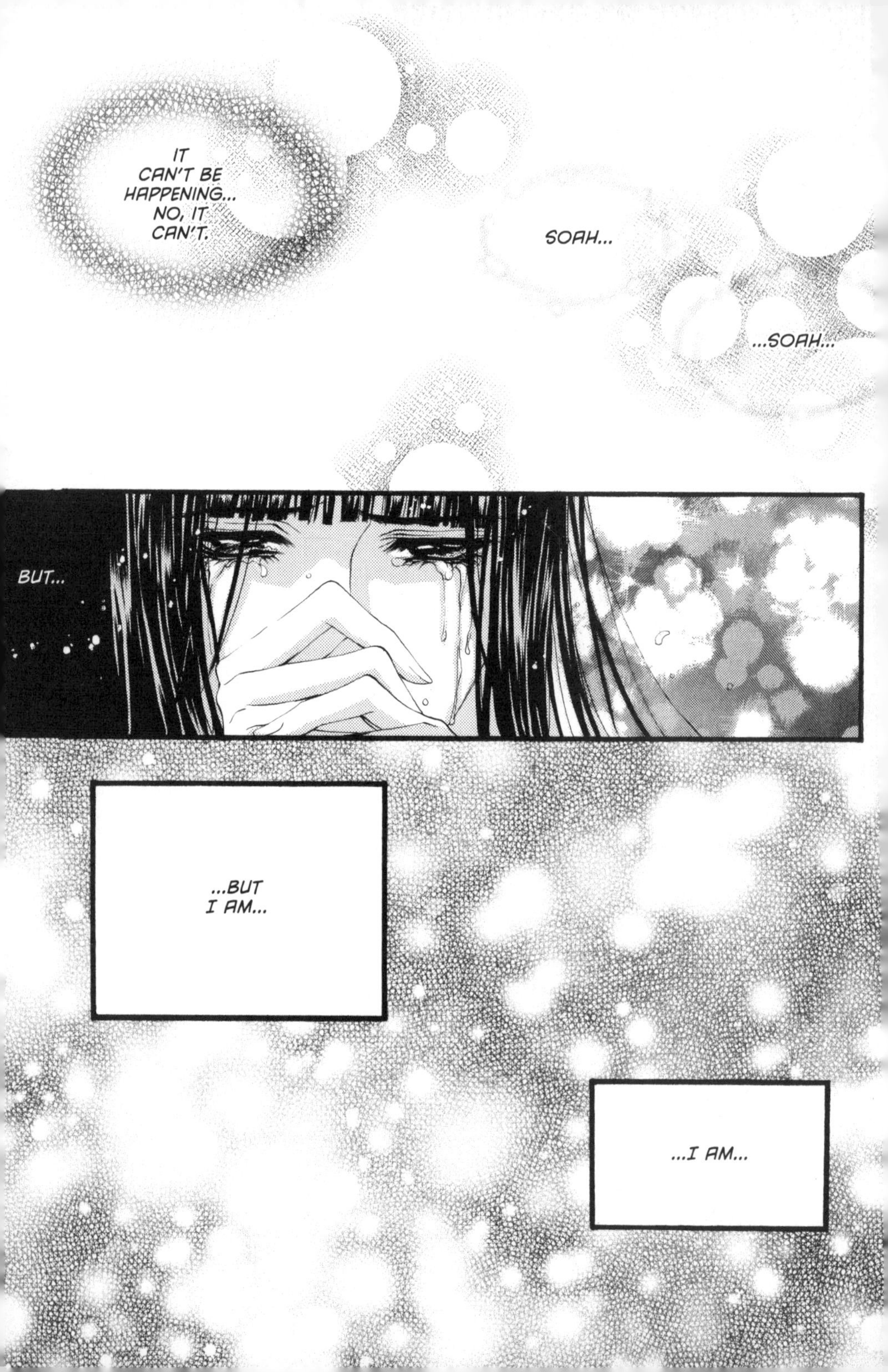
IT CAN'T BE HAPPENING... NO, IT CAN'T.
SOAH...
...SOAH...
BUT...
...BUT I AM...
...I AM...

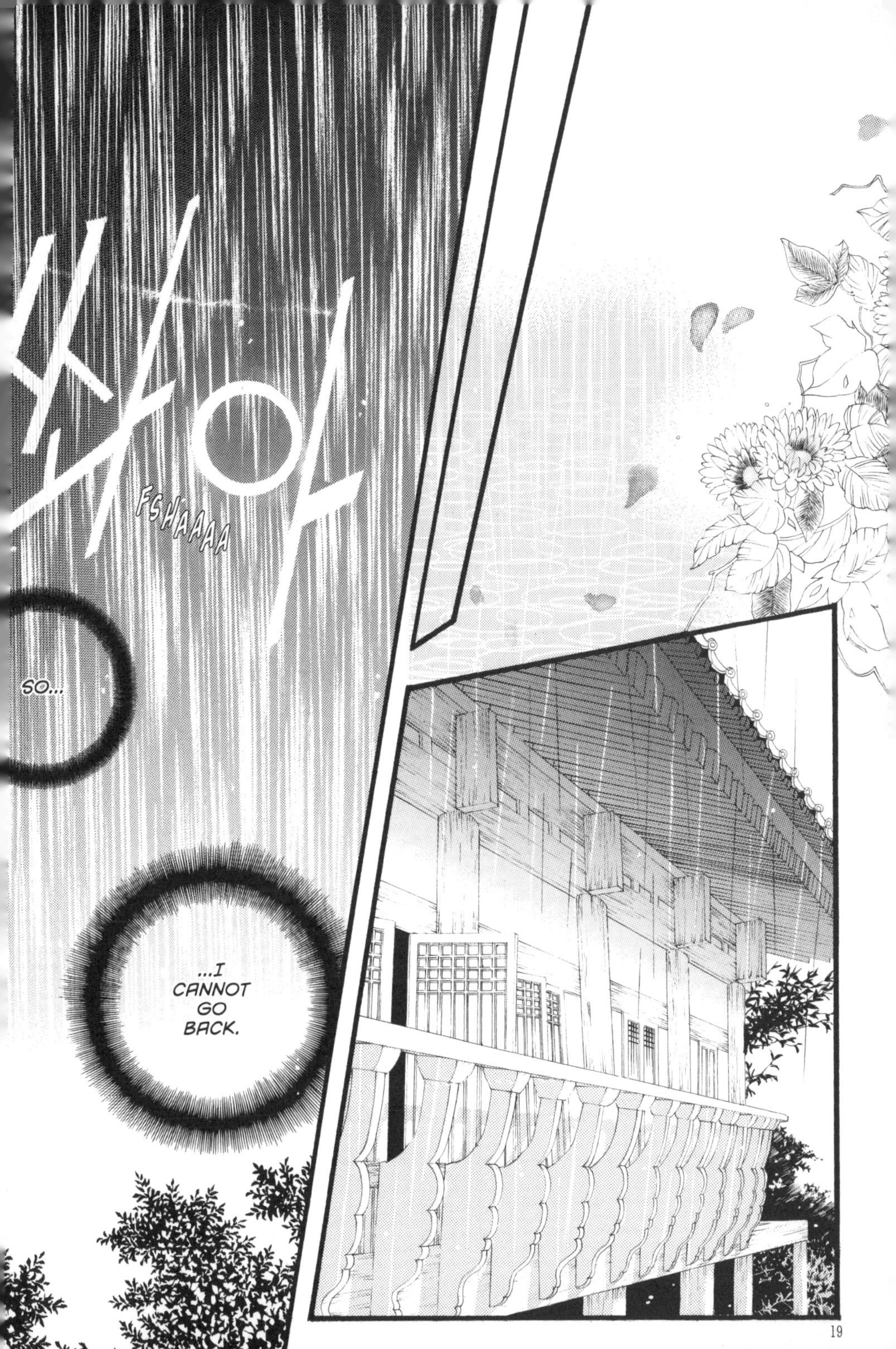
FSHAAAA
SO...
...I CANNOT GO BACK.

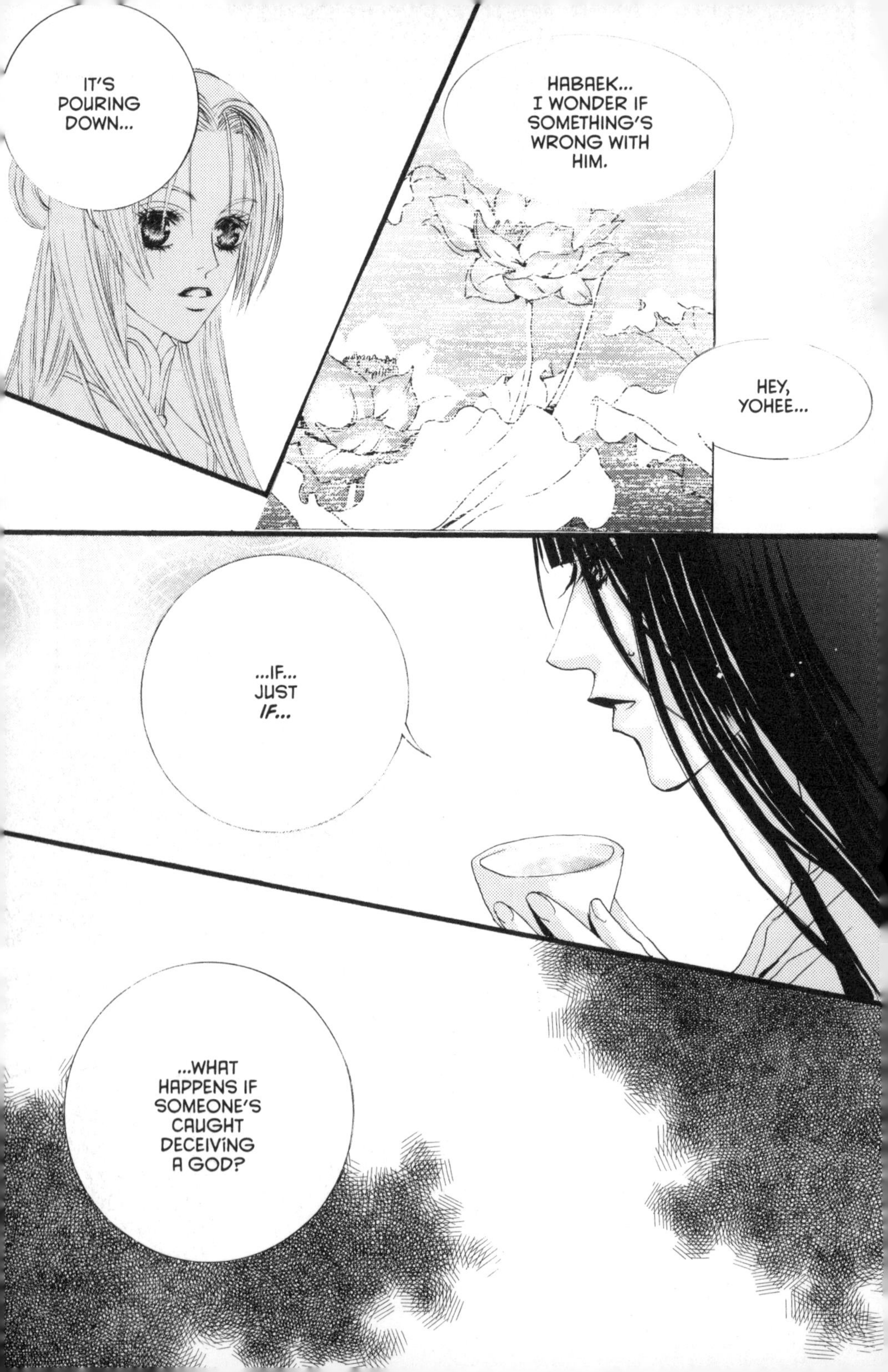
IT'S POURING DOWN...
HABAEK... I WONDER IF SOMETHING'S WRONG WITH HIM.
HEY, YOHEE...
...IF... JUST *IF...*
...WHAT HAPPENS IF SOMEONE'S CAUGHT DECEIVING A GOD?

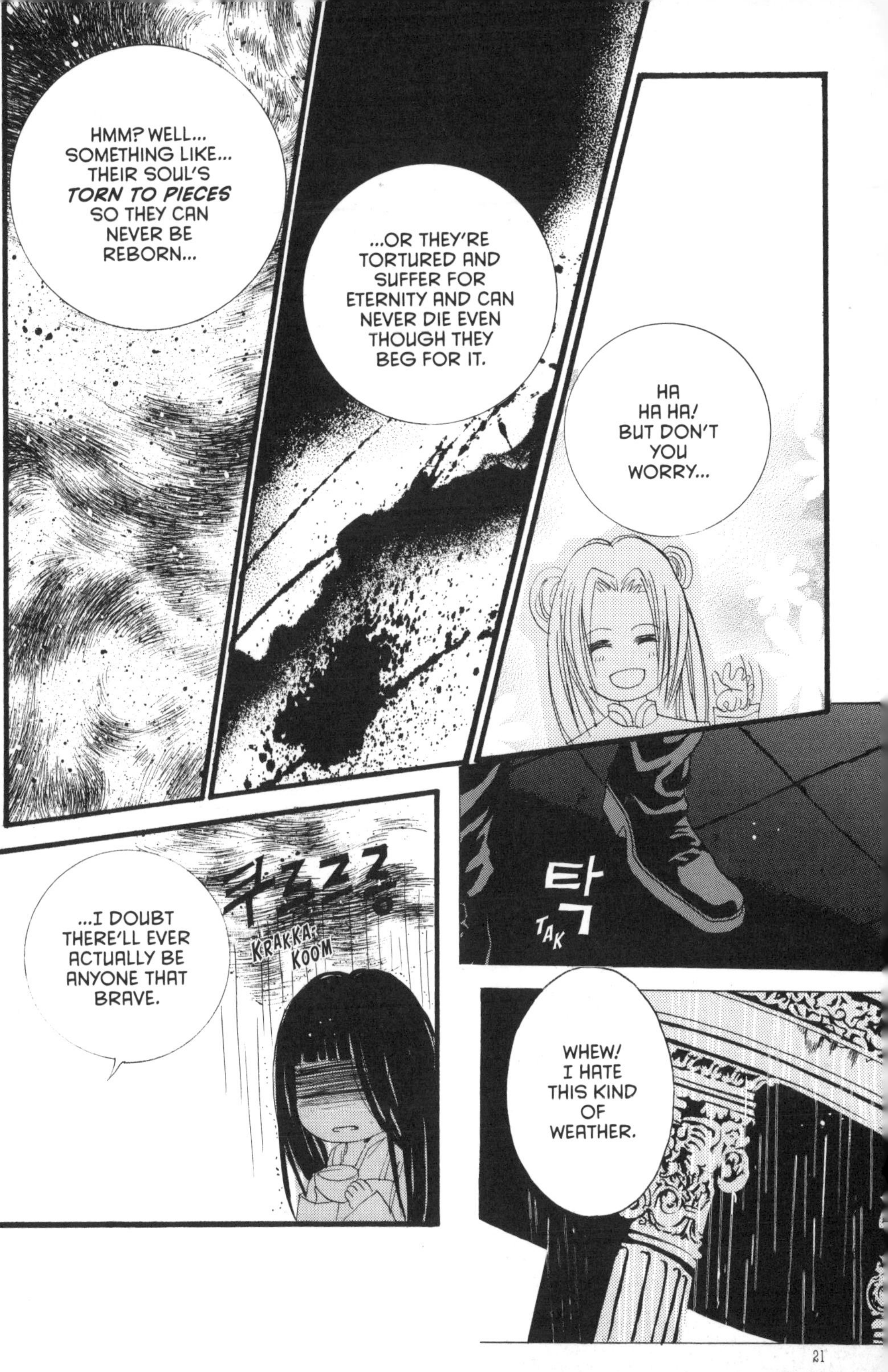

HMM? WELL... SOMETHING LIKE... THEIR SOUL'S *TORN TO PIECES* SO THEY CAN NEVER BE REBORN...
...OR THEY'RE TORTURED AND SUFFER FOR ETERNITY AND CAN NEVER DIE EVEN THOUGH THEY BEG FOR IT.
HA HA HA! BUT DON'T YOU WORRY...
타ㄱ
TAK
...I DOUBT THERE'LL EVER ACTUALLY BE ANYONE THAT BRAVE.
KRAKKA-KOOM
WHEW! I HATE THIS KIND OF WEATHER.

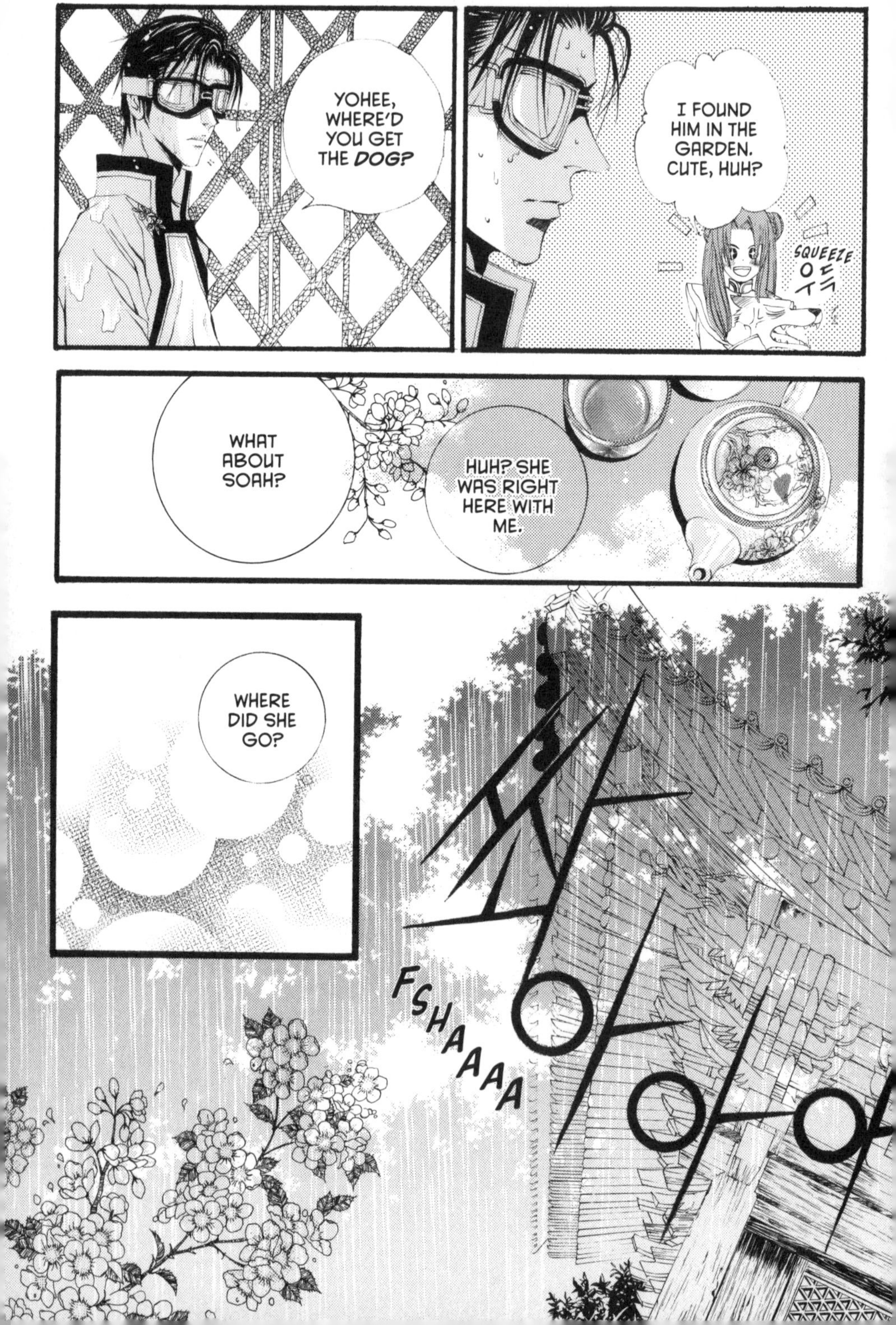
YOHEE, WHERE'D YOU GET THE DOG?
I FOUND HIM IN THE GARDEN. CUTE, HUH?
SQUEEZE
WHAT ABOUT SOAH?
HUH? SHE WAS RIGHT HERE WITH ME.
WHERE DID SHE GO?
FSHAAAAA

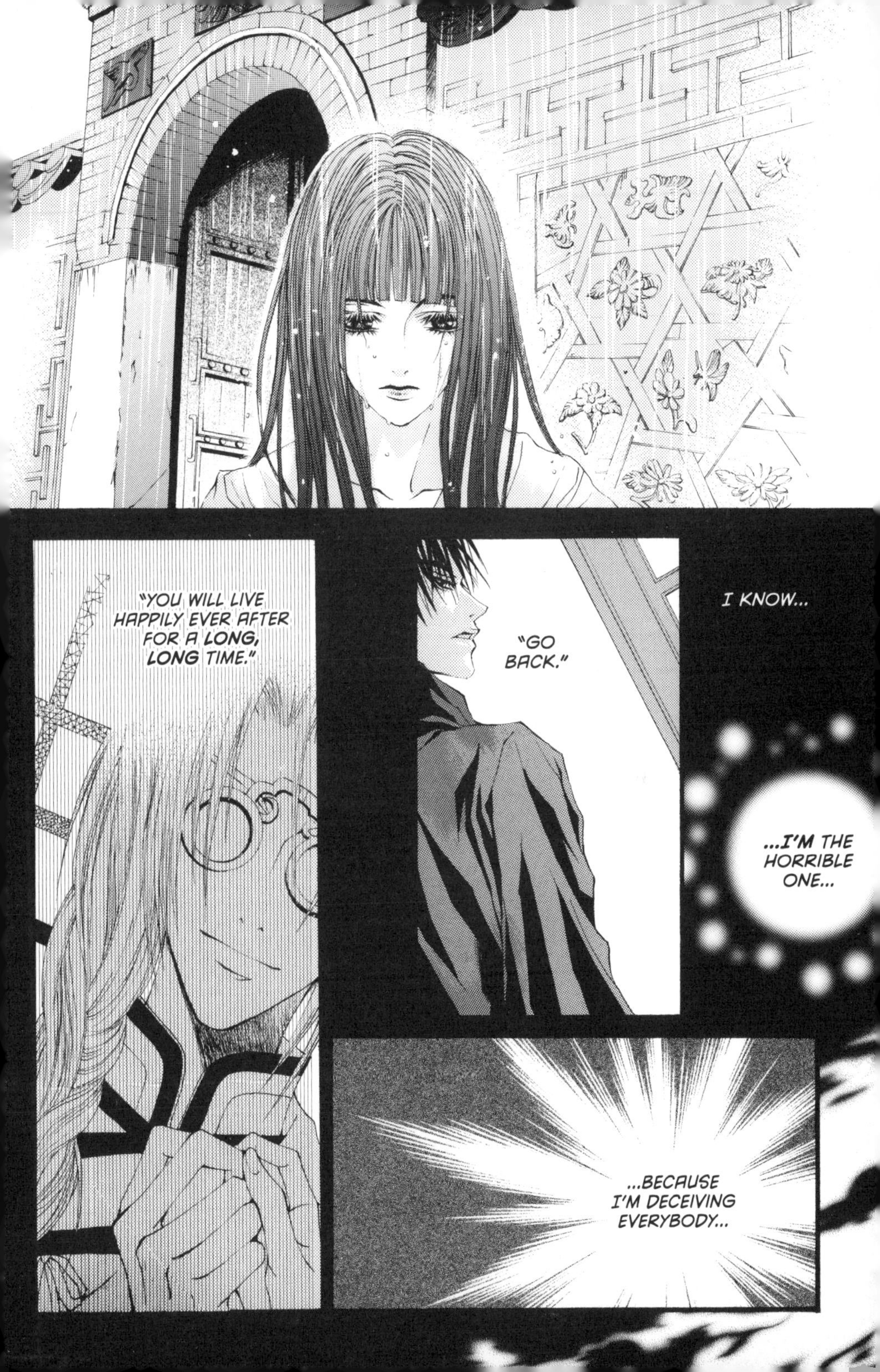
I KNOW...
"GO BACK."
...I'M THE HORRIBLE ONE...
"YOU WILL LIVE HAPPILY EVER AFTER FOR A LONG, LONG TIME."
...BECAUSE I'M DECEIVING EVERYBODY...

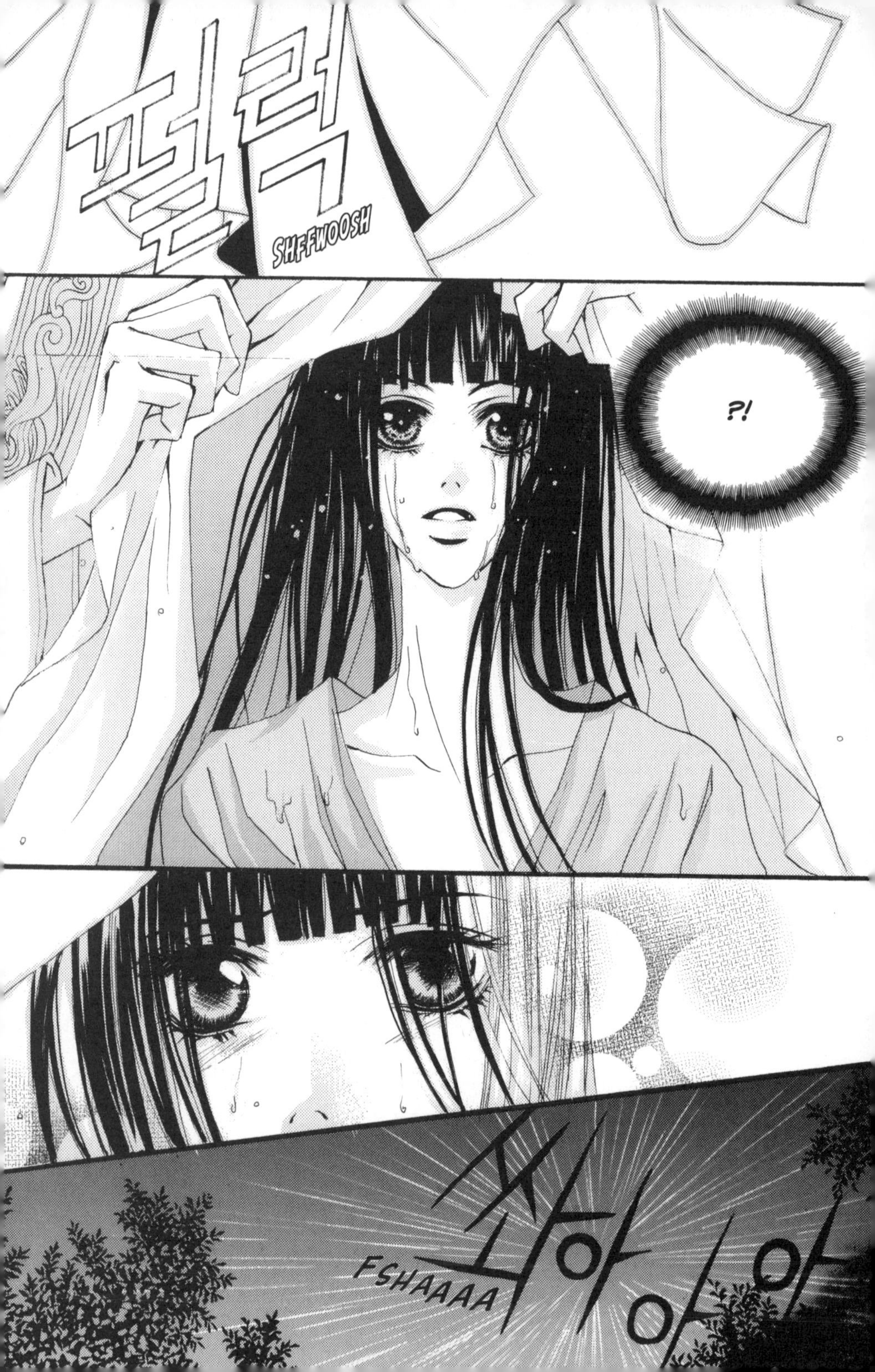
펄럭
SHFFWOOSH
?!
쏴아아아
FSHAAAA

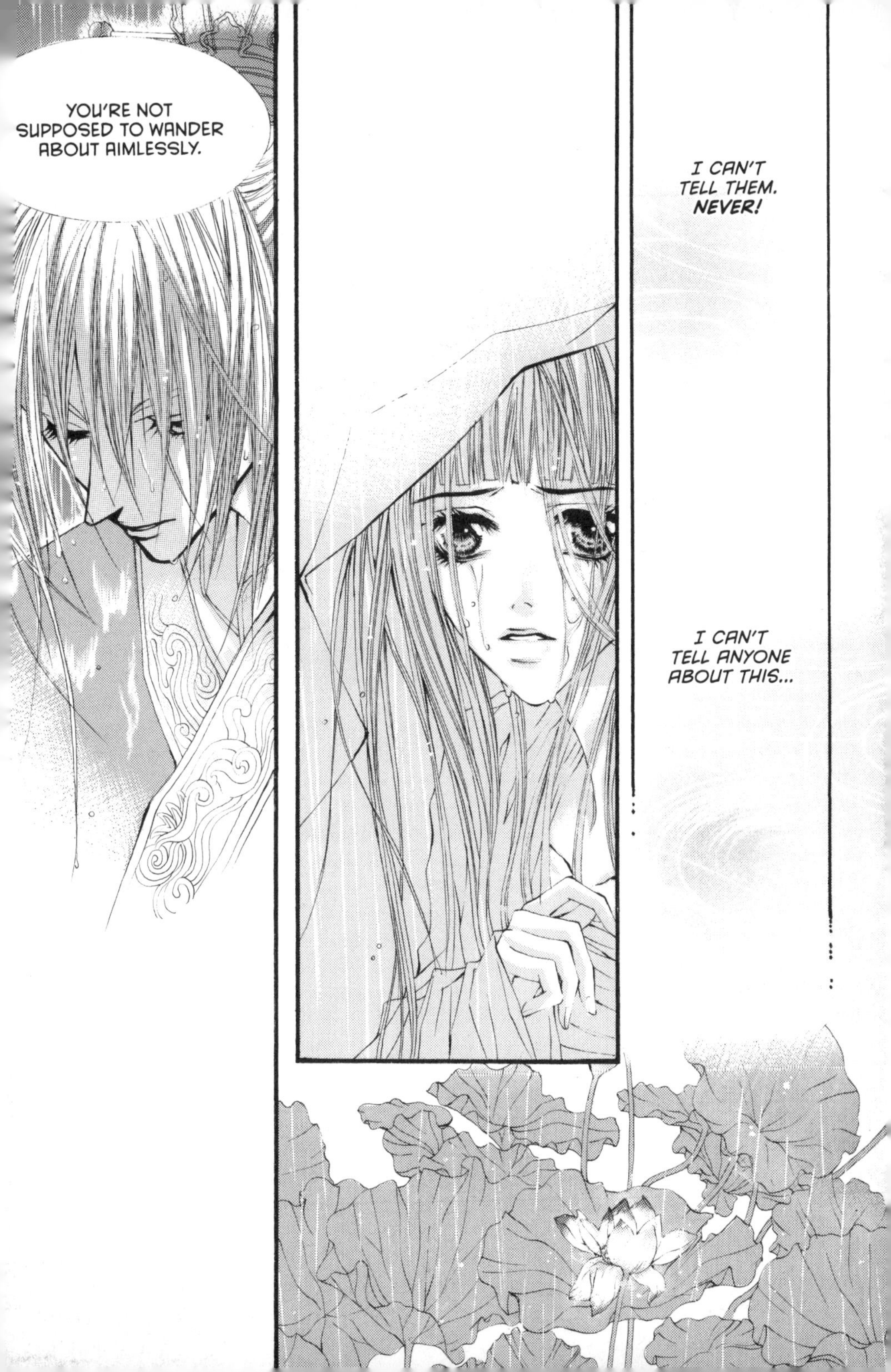
I CAN'T TELL THEM. NEVER!
I CAN'T TELL ANYONE ABOUT THIS...
YOU'RE NOT SUPPOSED TO WANDER ABOUT AIMLESSLY.

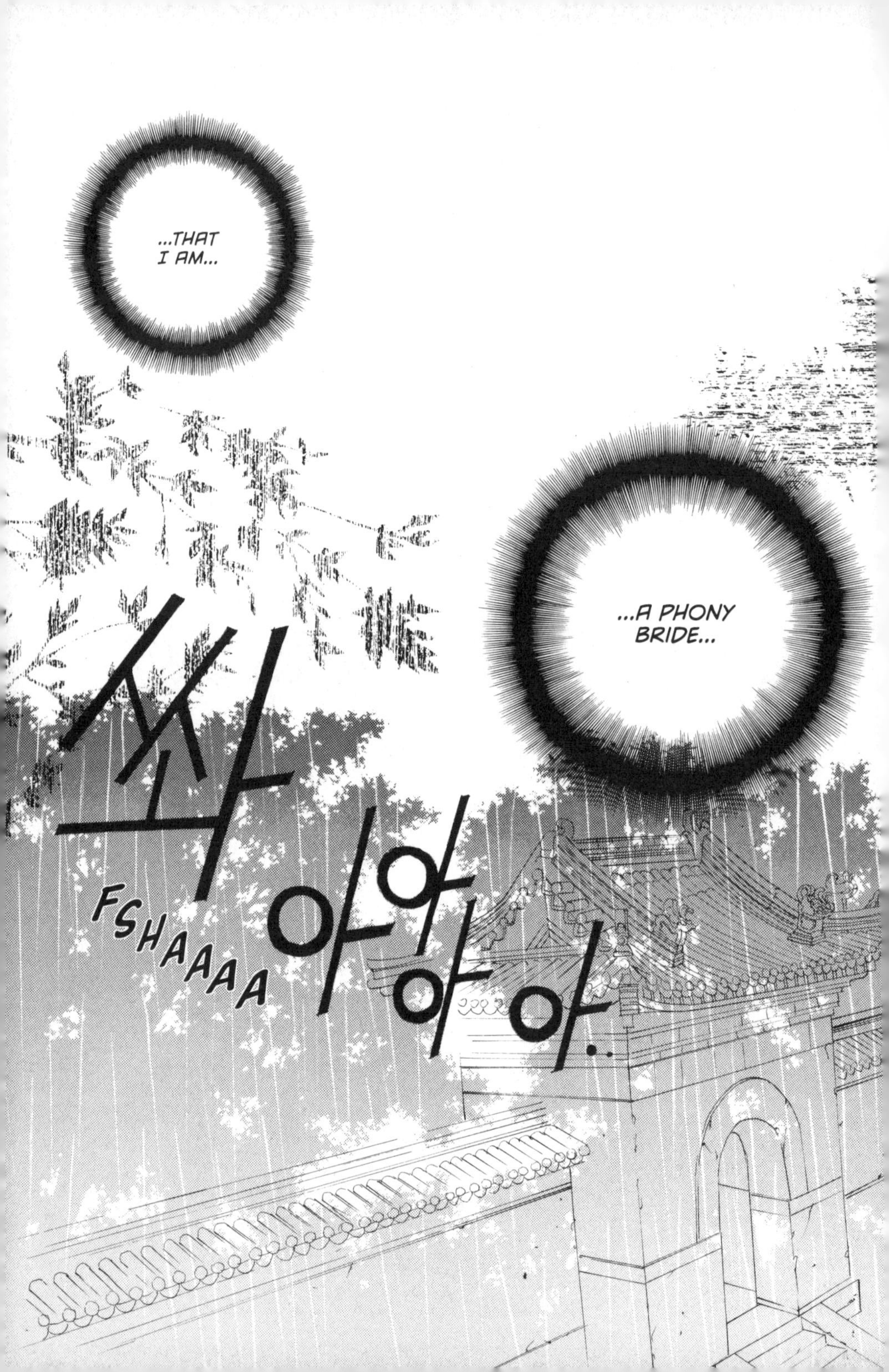
...THAT I AM...
...A PHONY BRIDE...
쏴아아아아..
FSHAAAAA

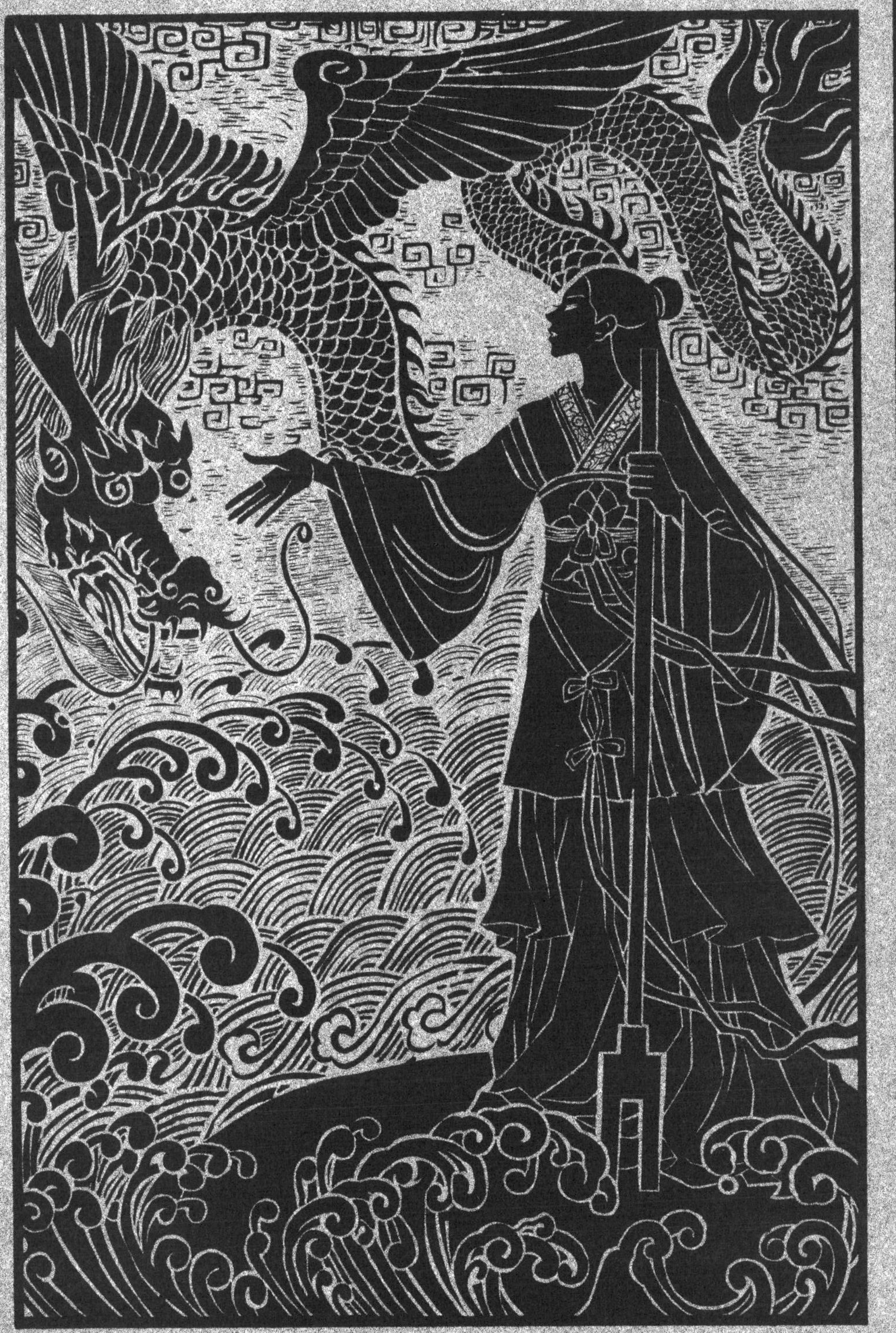

WOULD YOU TAKE ME TO THE OTHER SIDE?

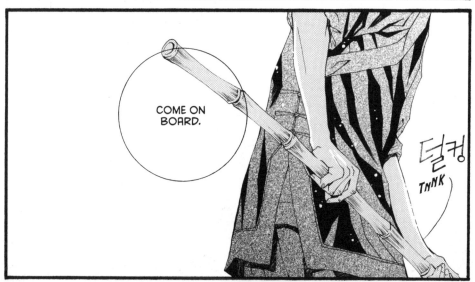

COME ON BOARD.

덜컹
TNNK

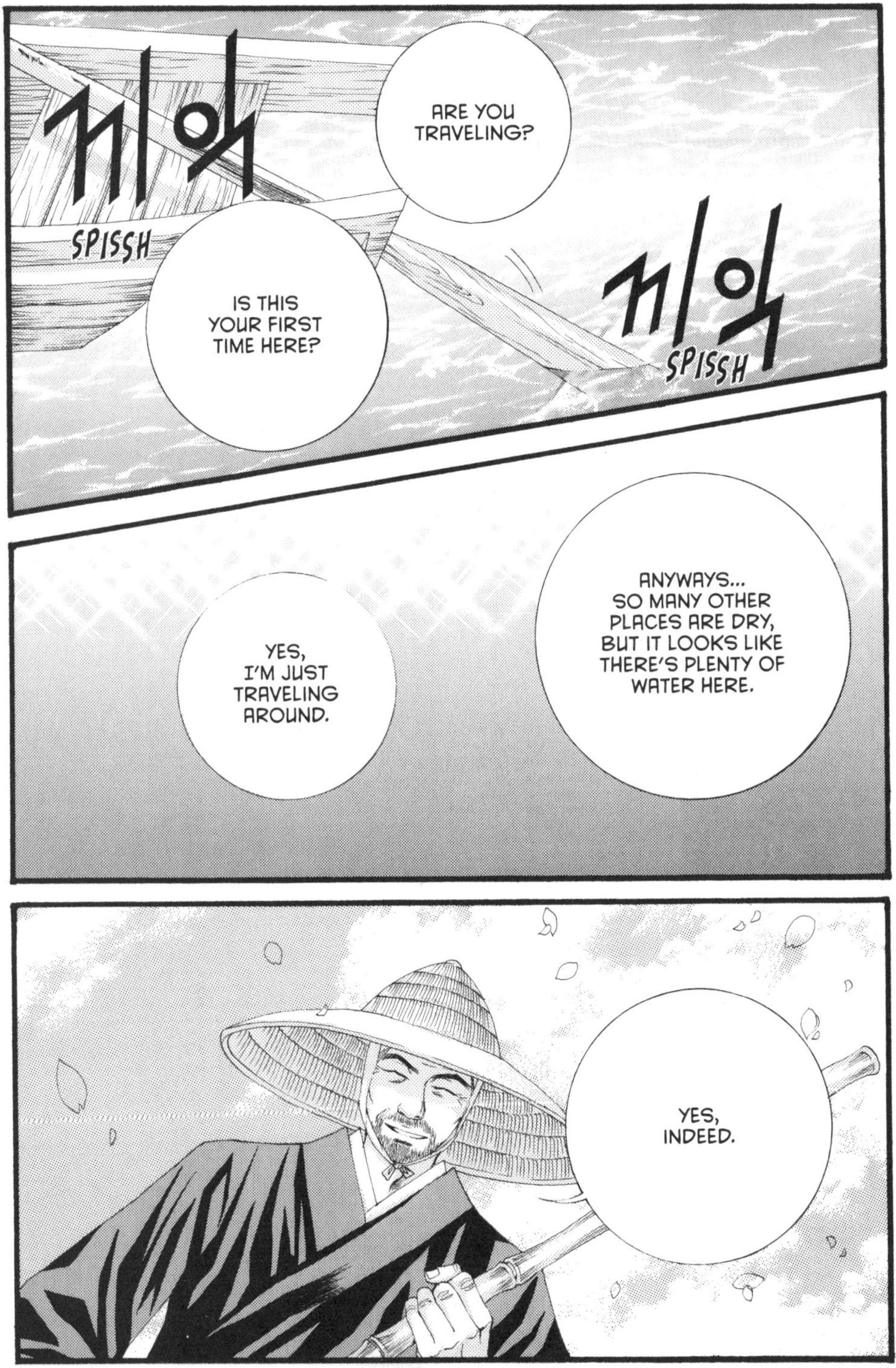

끼익
SPISSH
ARE YOU TRAVELING?
IS THIS YOUR FIRST TIME HERE?
끼익
SPISSH
ANYWAYS... SO MANY OTHER PLACES ARE DRY, BUT IT LOOKS LIKE THERE'S PLENTY OF WATER HERE.
YES, I'M JUST TRAVELING AROUND.
YES, INDEED.

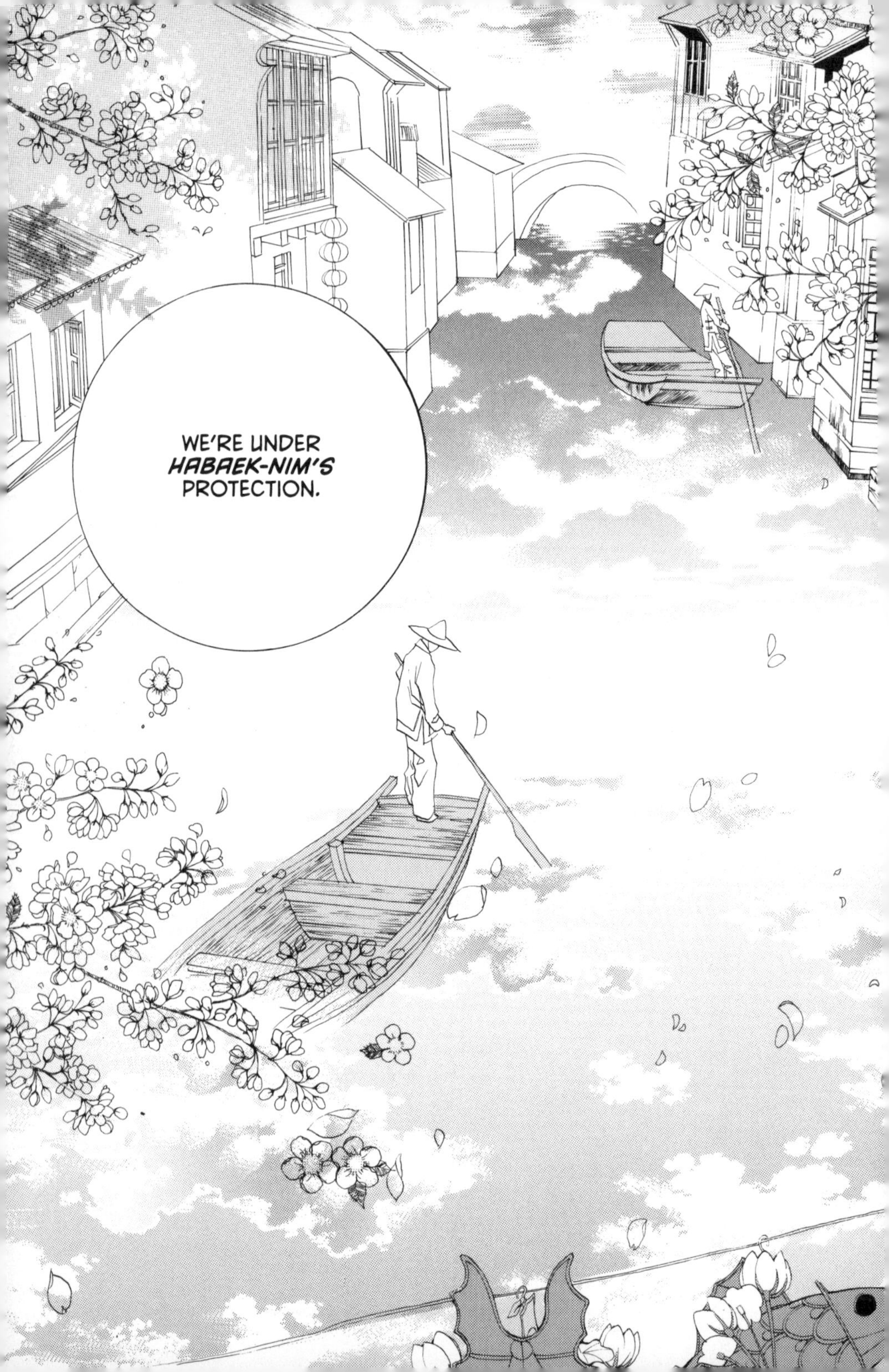
WE'RE UNDER *HABAEK-NIM'S* PROTECTION.

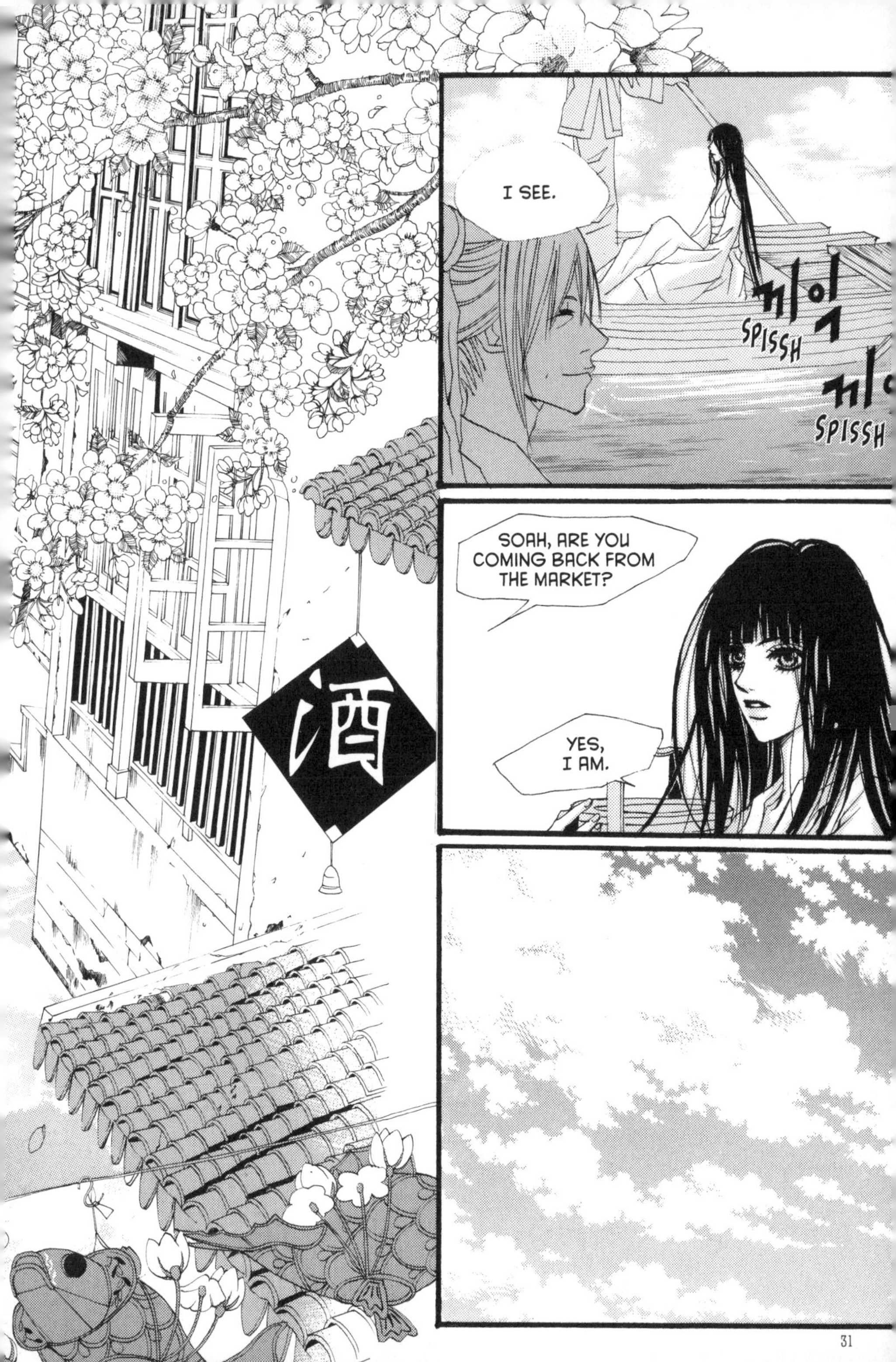

酒
I SEE.
SPISSH
SPISSH
SOAH, ARE YOU COMING BACK FROM THE MARKET?
YES, I AM.

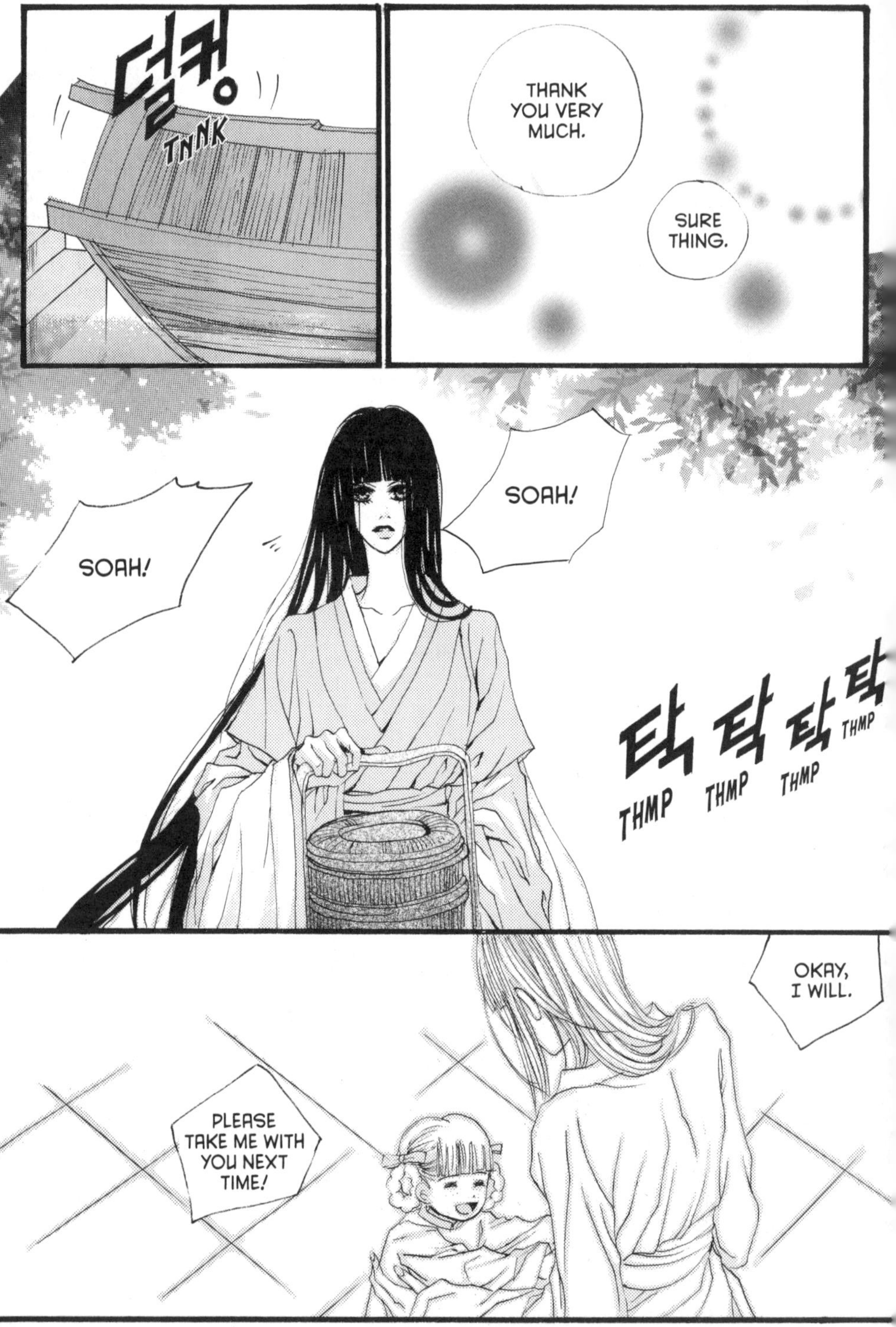
덜컹
TNNK
THANK YOU VERY MUCH.
SURE THING.
SOAH!
SOAH!
탁 탁 탁 탁
THMP THMP THMP THMP
PLEASE TAKE ME WITH YOU NEXT TIME!
OKAY, I WILL.

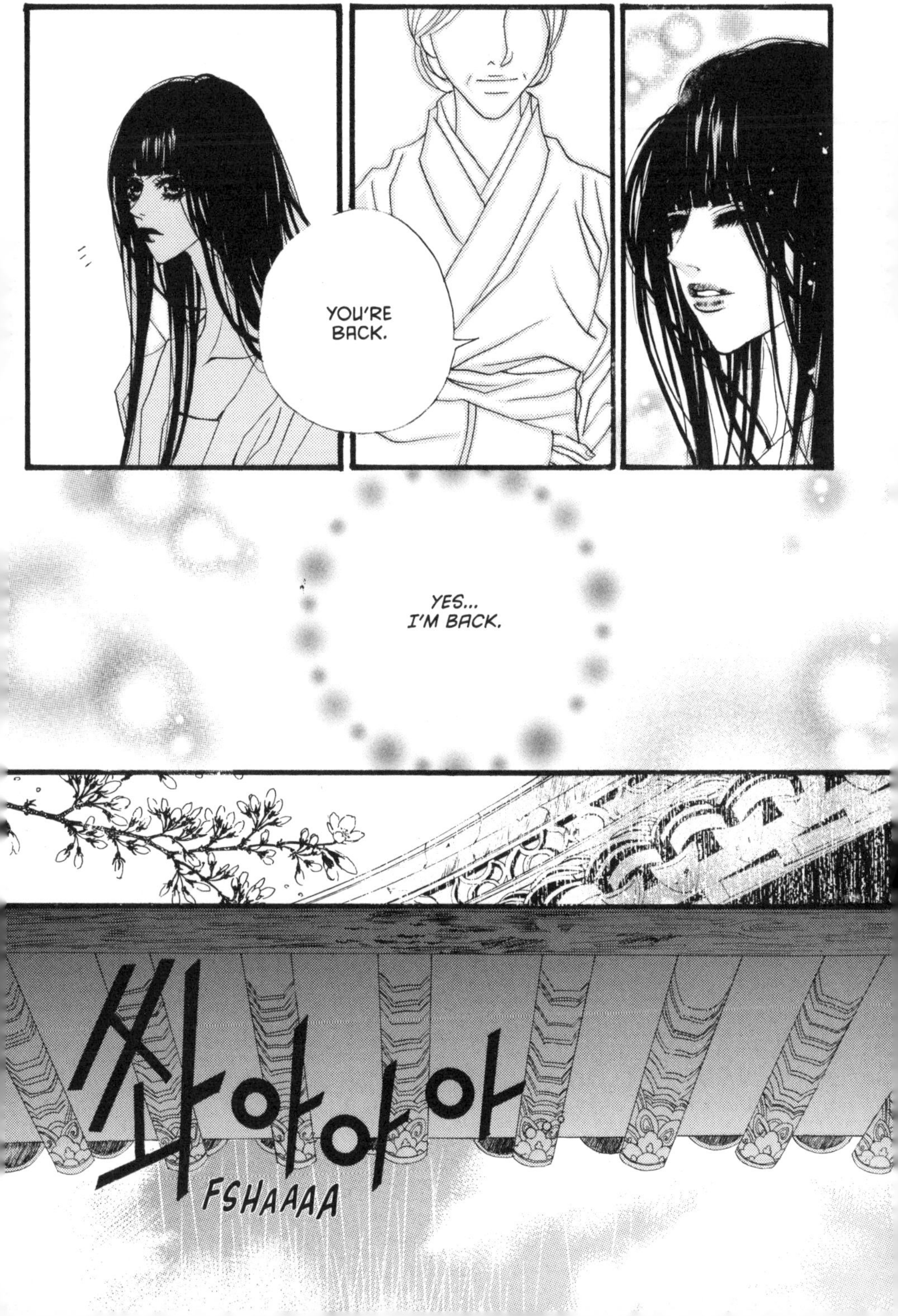
YOU'RE BACK.
YES... I'M BACK.
쏴아아아
FSHAAAA

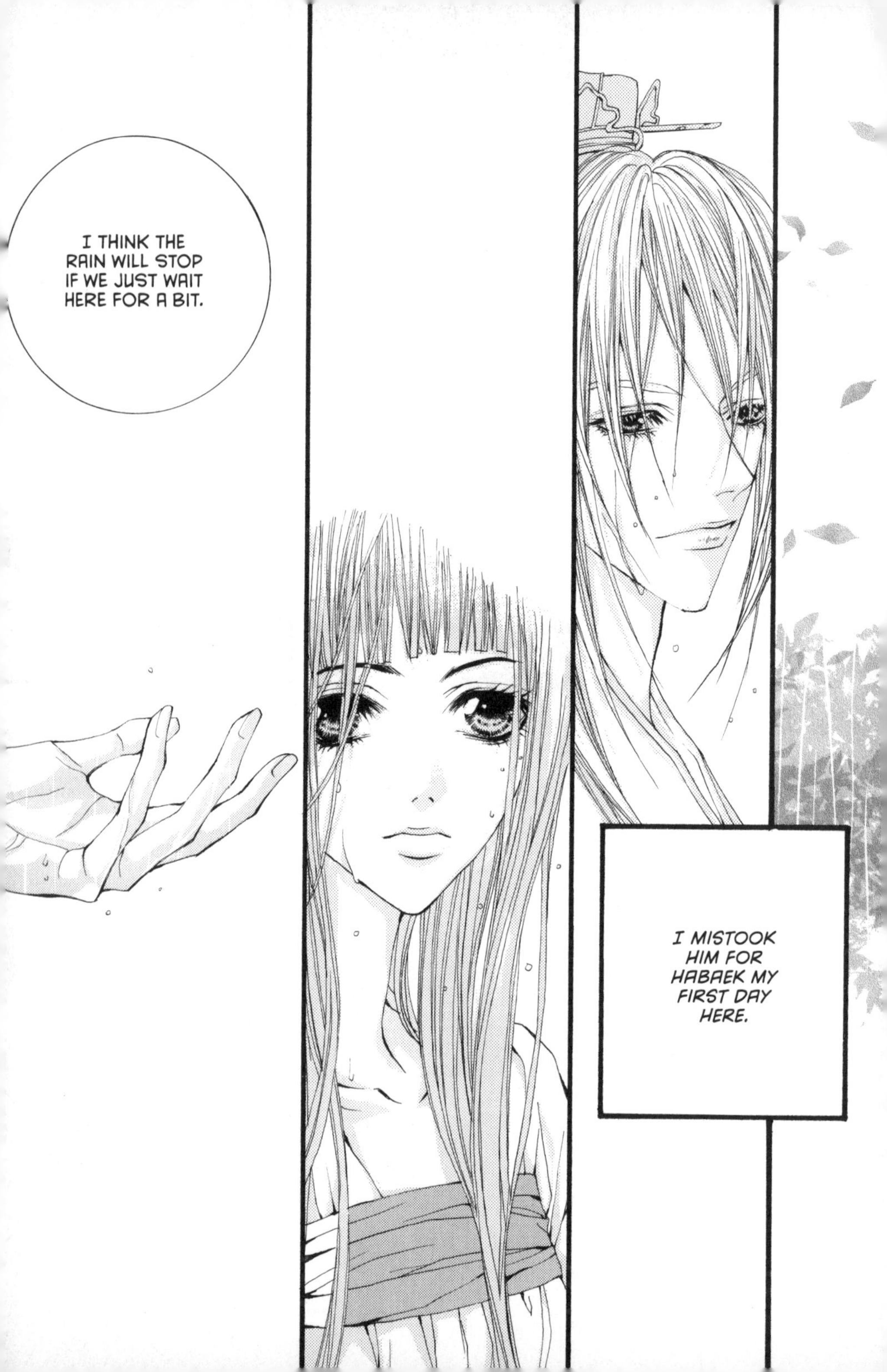

I THINK THE RAIN WILL STOP IF WE JUST WAIT HERE FOR A BIT.
I MISTOOK HIM FOR HABAEK MY FIRST DAY HERE.

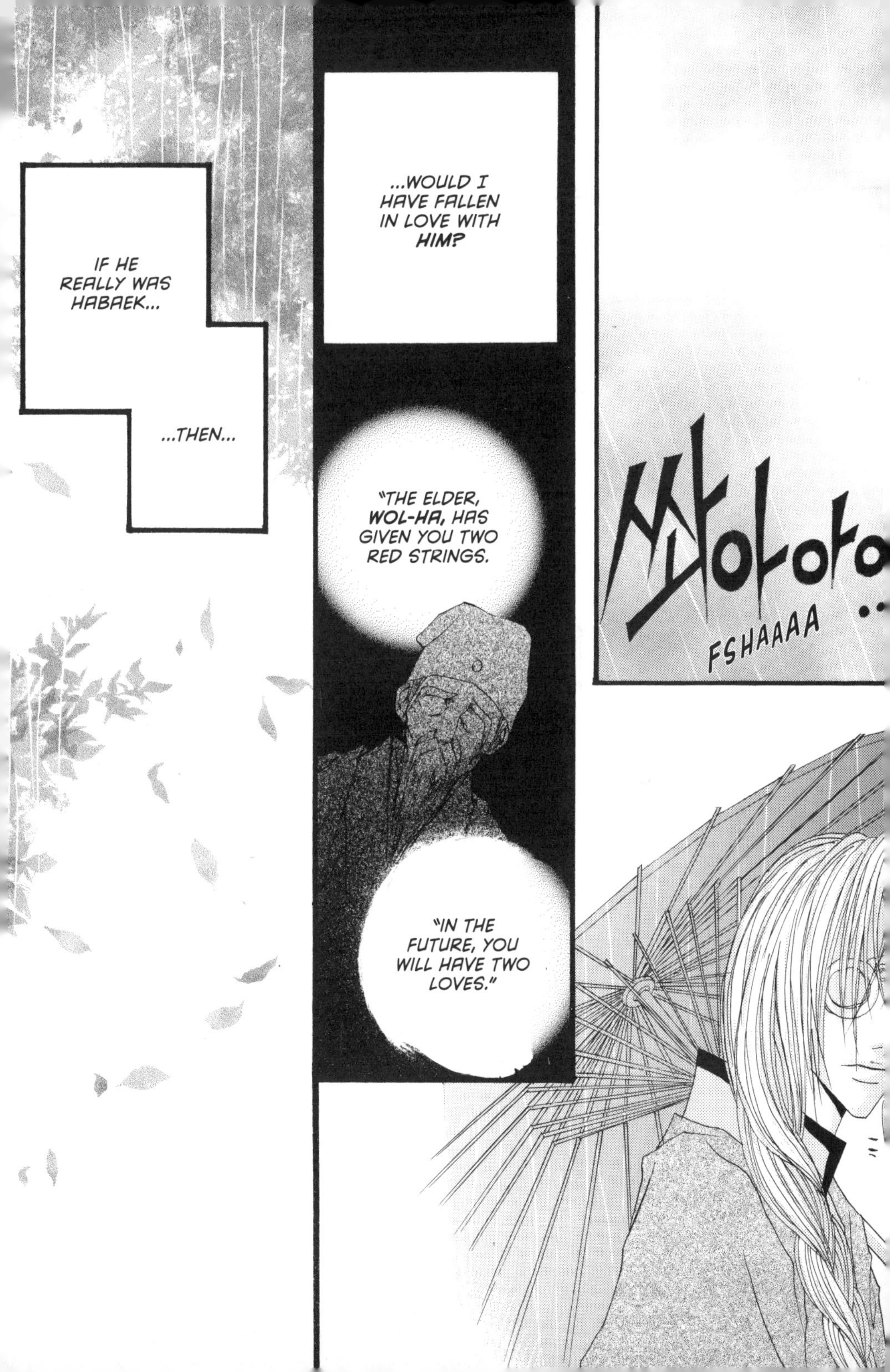
IF HE REALLY WAS HABAEK...
...THEN...
...WOULD I HAVE FALLEN IN LOVE WITH HIM?
"THE ELDER, WOL-HA, HAS GIVEN YOU TWO RED STRINGS.
"IN THE FUTURE, YOU WILL HAVE TWO LOVES."
FSHAAAA

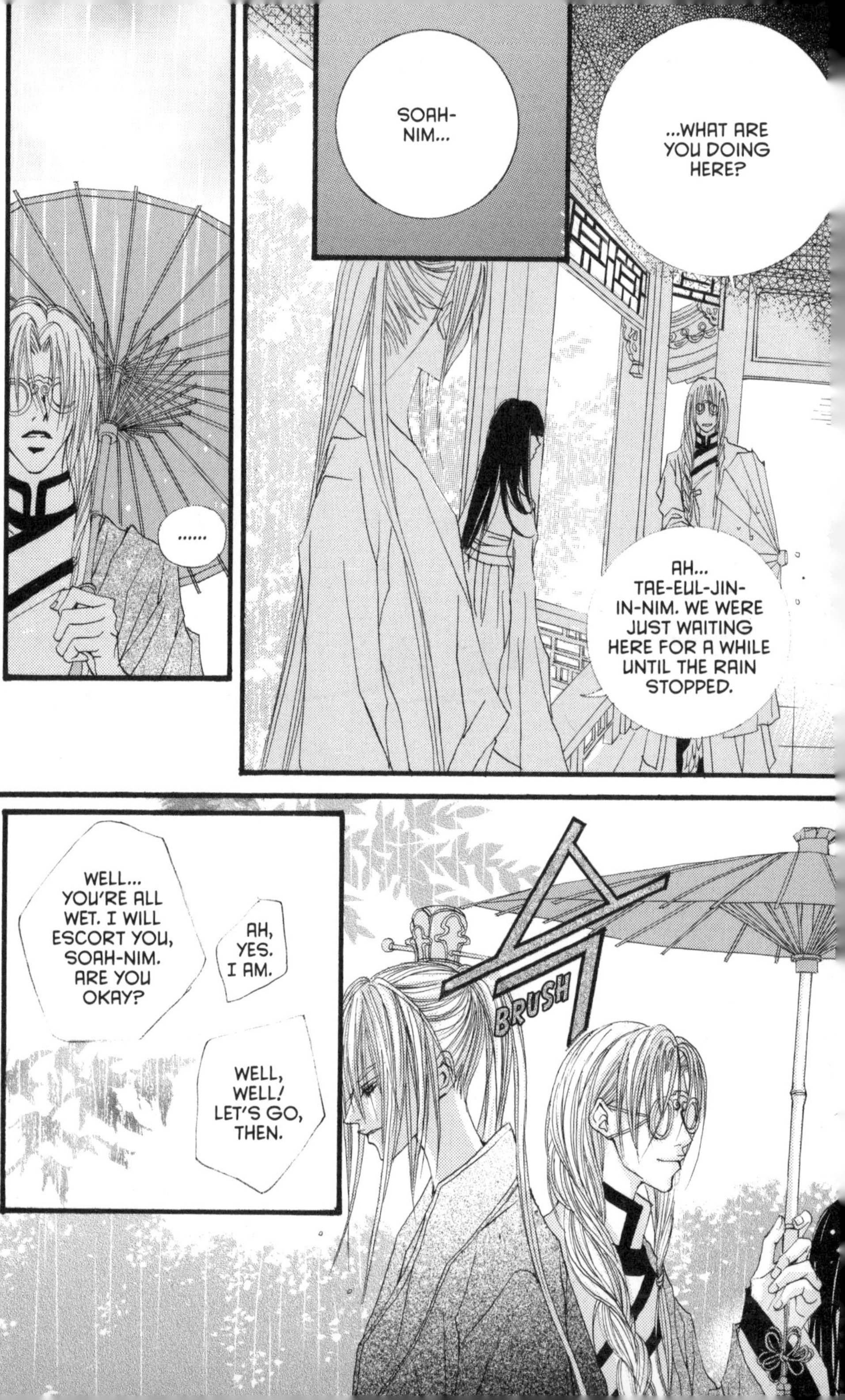
......
SOAH-NIM...
...WHAT ARE YOU DOING HERE?
AH... TAE-EUL-JIN-IN-NIM. WE WERE JUST WAITING HERE FOR A WHILE UNTIL THE RAIN STOPPED.
WELL... YOU'RE ALL WET. I WILL ESCORT YOU, SOAH-NIM. ARE YOU OKAY?
AH, YES. I AM.
WELL, WELL! LET'S GO, THEN.
BRUSH

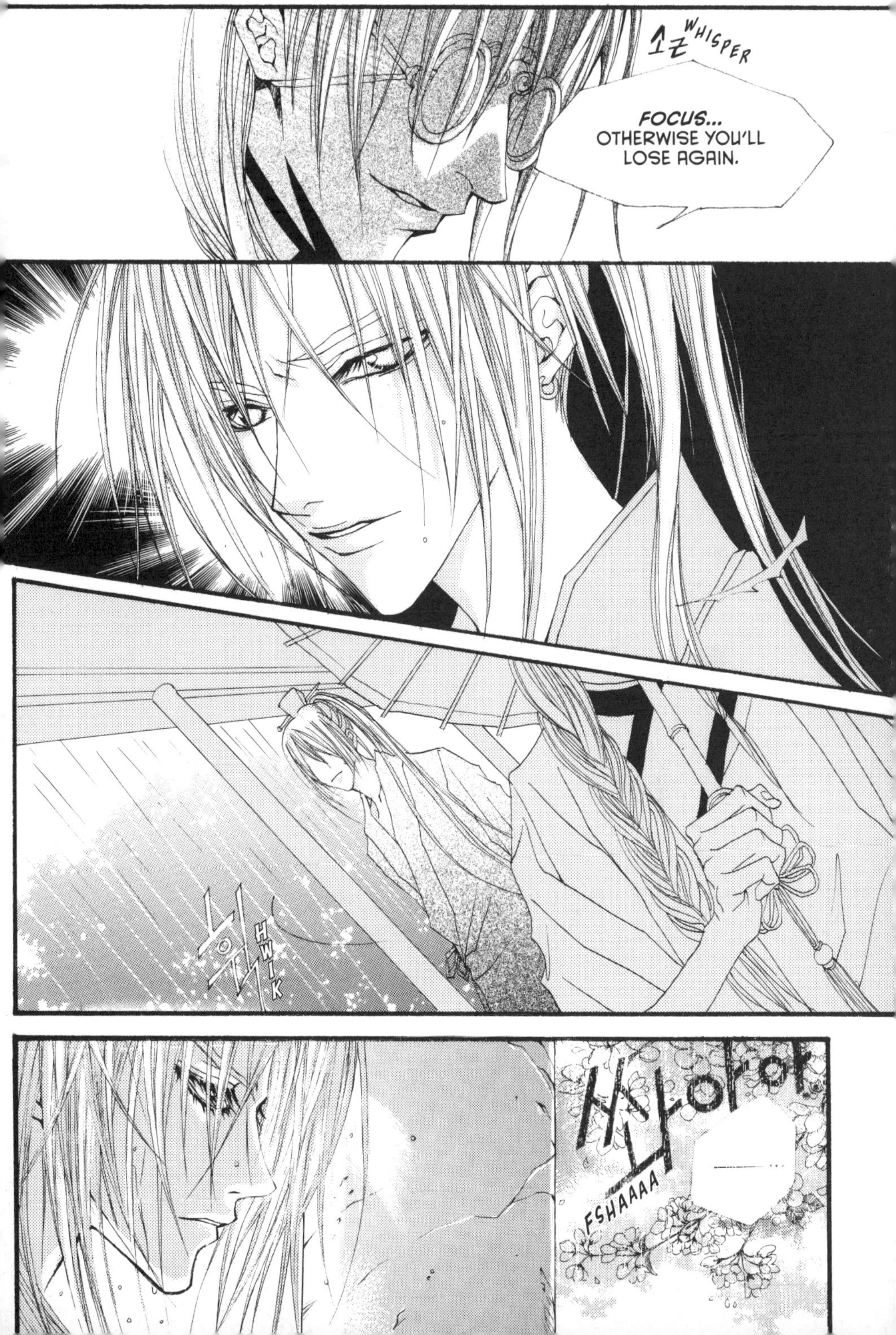
WHISPER
FOCUS... OTHERWISE YOU'LL LOSE AGAIN.
HWIK
FSHAAAA
——...

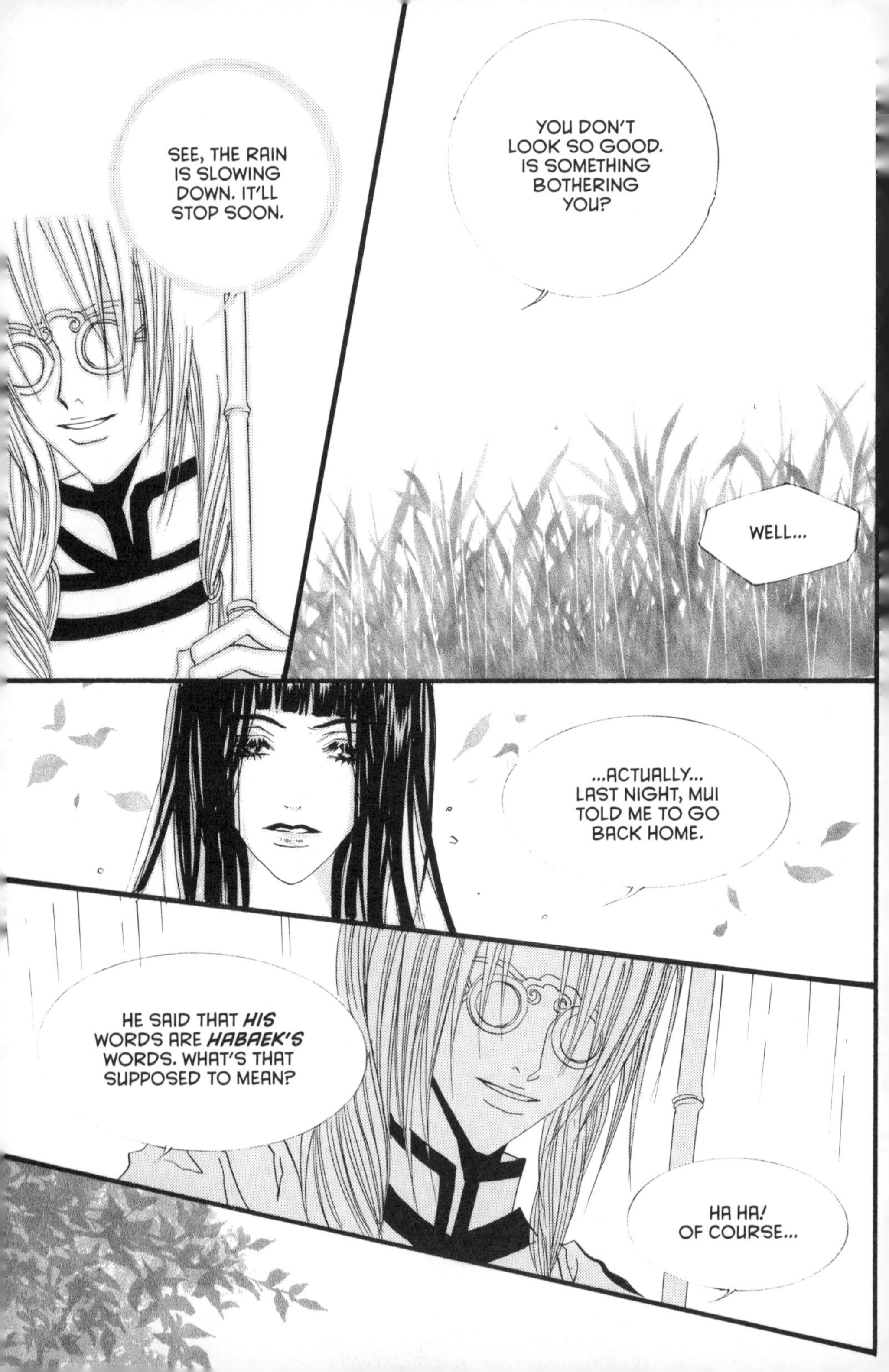

YOU DON'T LOOK SO GOOD. IS SOMETHING BOTHERING YOU?
SEE, THE RAIN IS SLOWING DOWN. IT'LL STOP SOON.
WELL...
...ACTUALLY... LAST NIGHT, MUI TOLD ME TO GO BACK HOME.
HE SAID THAT *HIS* WORDS ARE *HABAEK'S* WORDS. WHAT'S THAT SUPPOSED TO MEAN?
HA HA! OF COURSE...

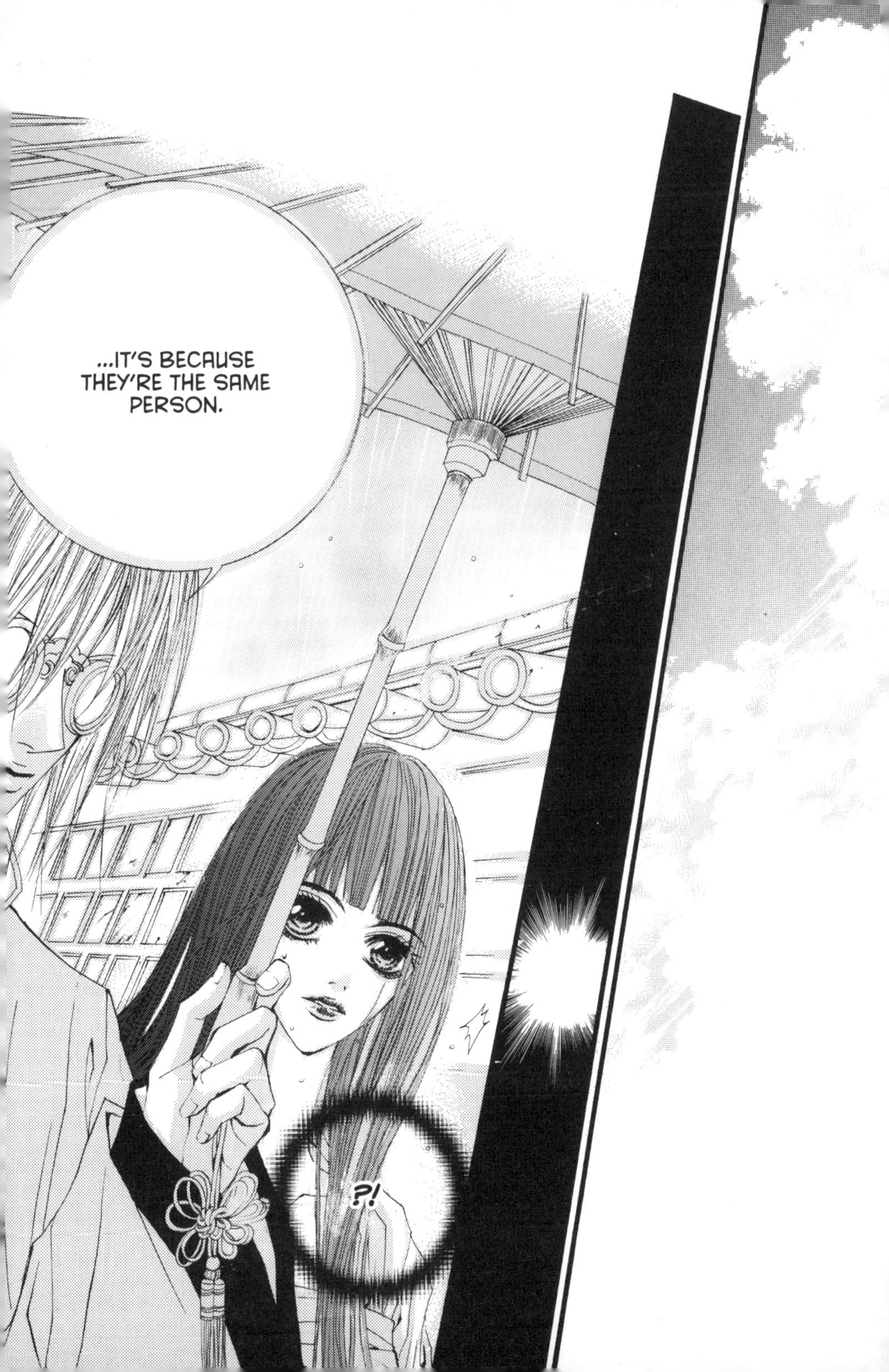
...IT'S BECAUSE THEY'RE THE SAME PERSON.
?!

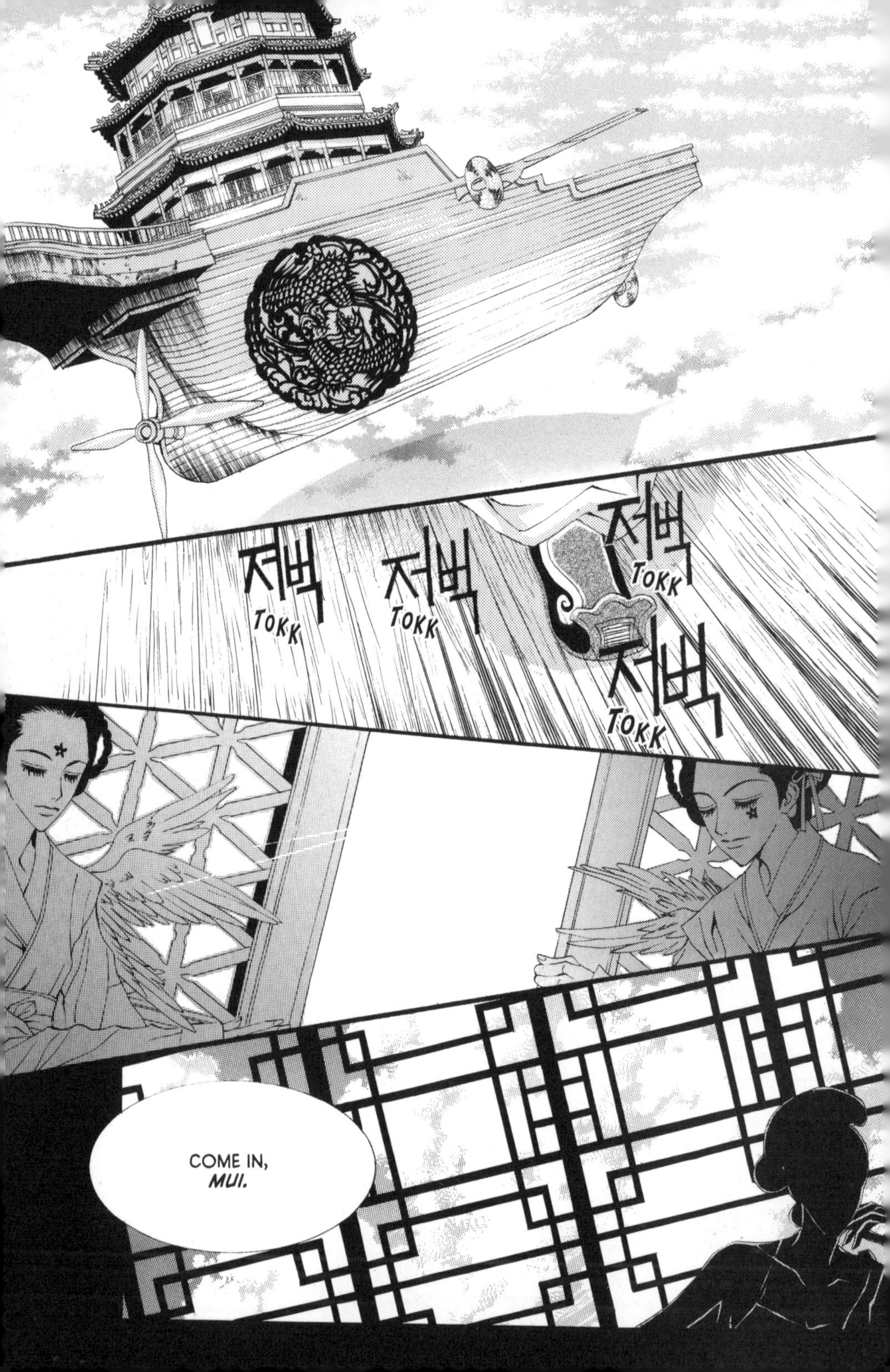

저벅
TOKK
저벅
TOKK
저벅
TOKK
저벅
TOKK
COME IN,
MUI.

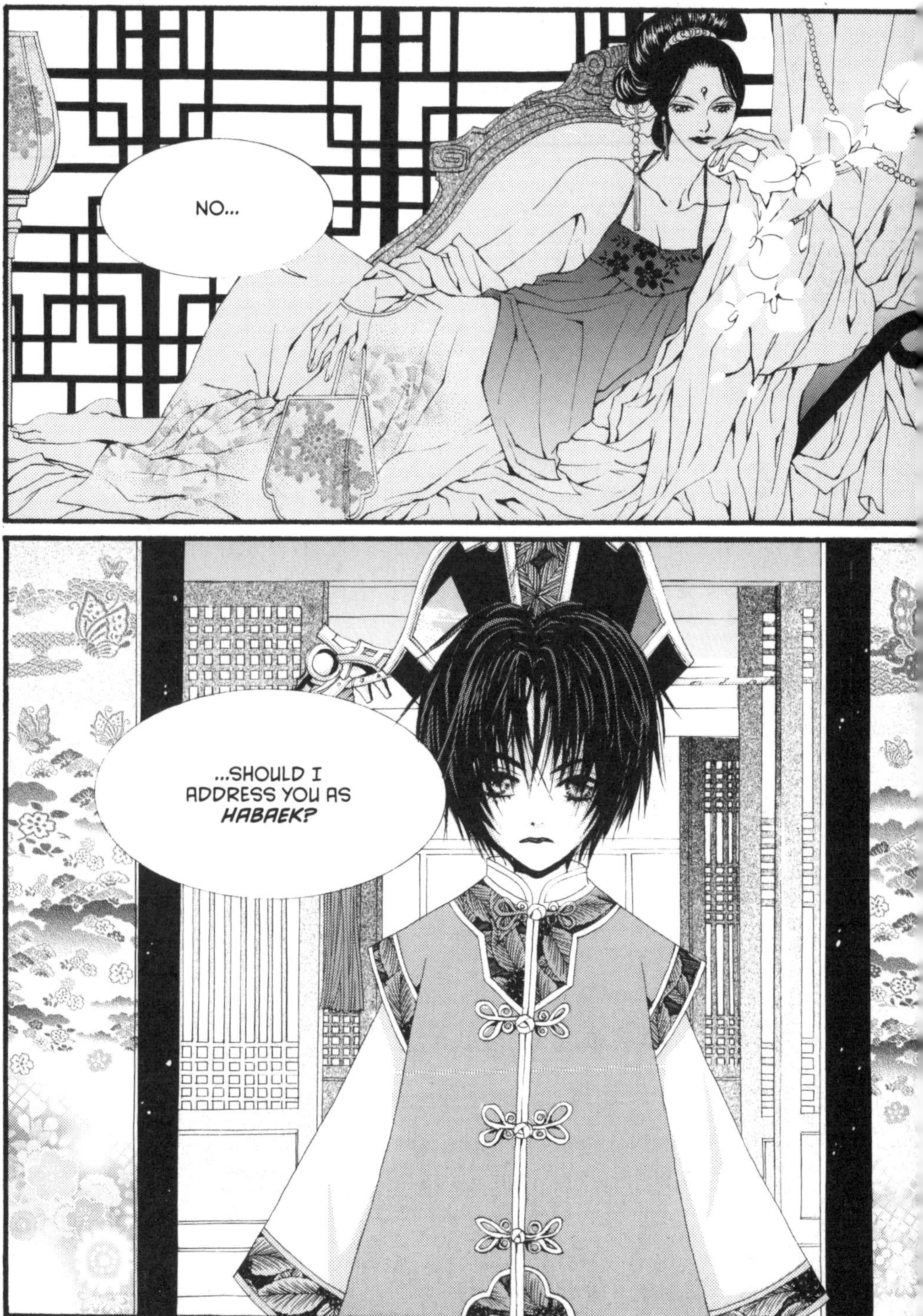
NO...
...SHOULD I ADDRESS YOU AS *HABAEK?*

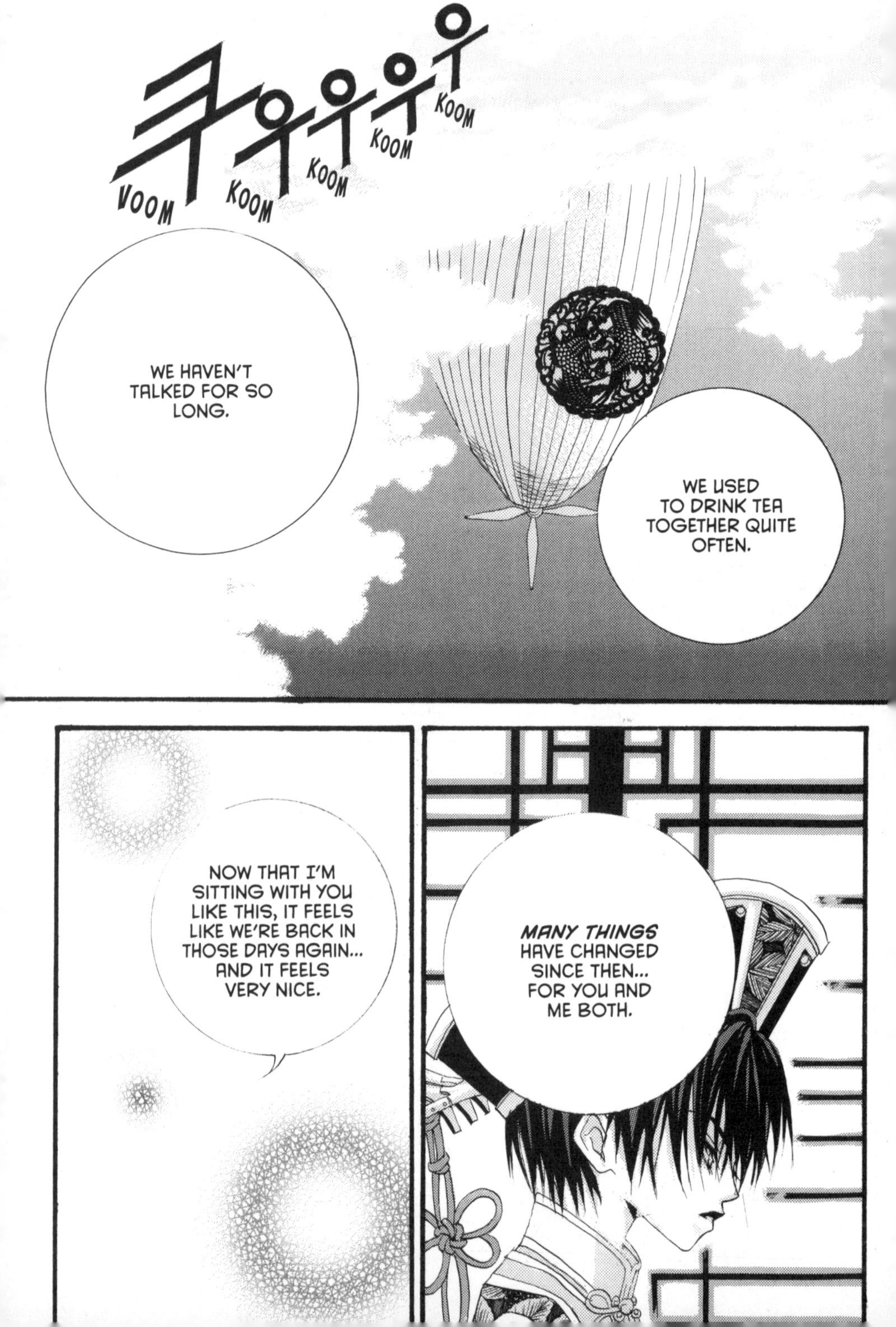
쿠우우우우
VOOM KOOM KOOM KOOM KOOM
WE HAVEN'T TALKED FOR SO LONG.
WE USED TO DRINK TEA TOGETHER QUITE OFTEN.
NOW THAT I'M SITTING WITH YOU LIKE THIS, IT FEELS LIKE WE'RE BACK IN THOSE DAYS AGAIN... AND IT FEELS VERY NICE.
MANY THINGS HAVE CHANGED SINCE THEN... FOR YOU AND ME BOTH.

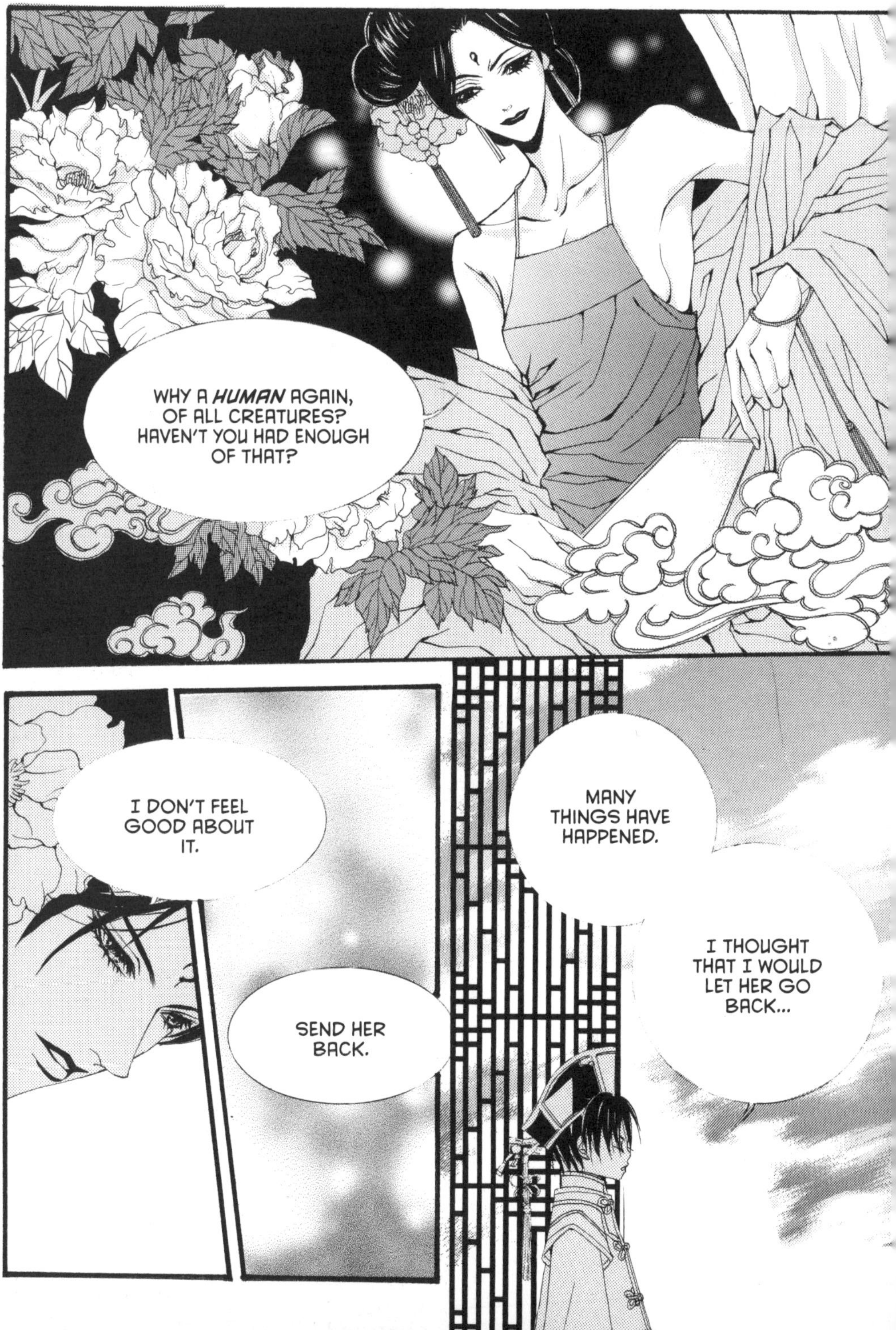

WHY A *HUMAN* AGAIN, OF ALL CREATURES? HAVEN'T YOU HAD ENOUGH OF THAT?
I DON'T FEEL GOOD ABOUT IT.
SEND HER BACK.
MANY THINGS HAVE HAPPENED.
I THOUGHT THAT I WOULD LET HER GO BACK...

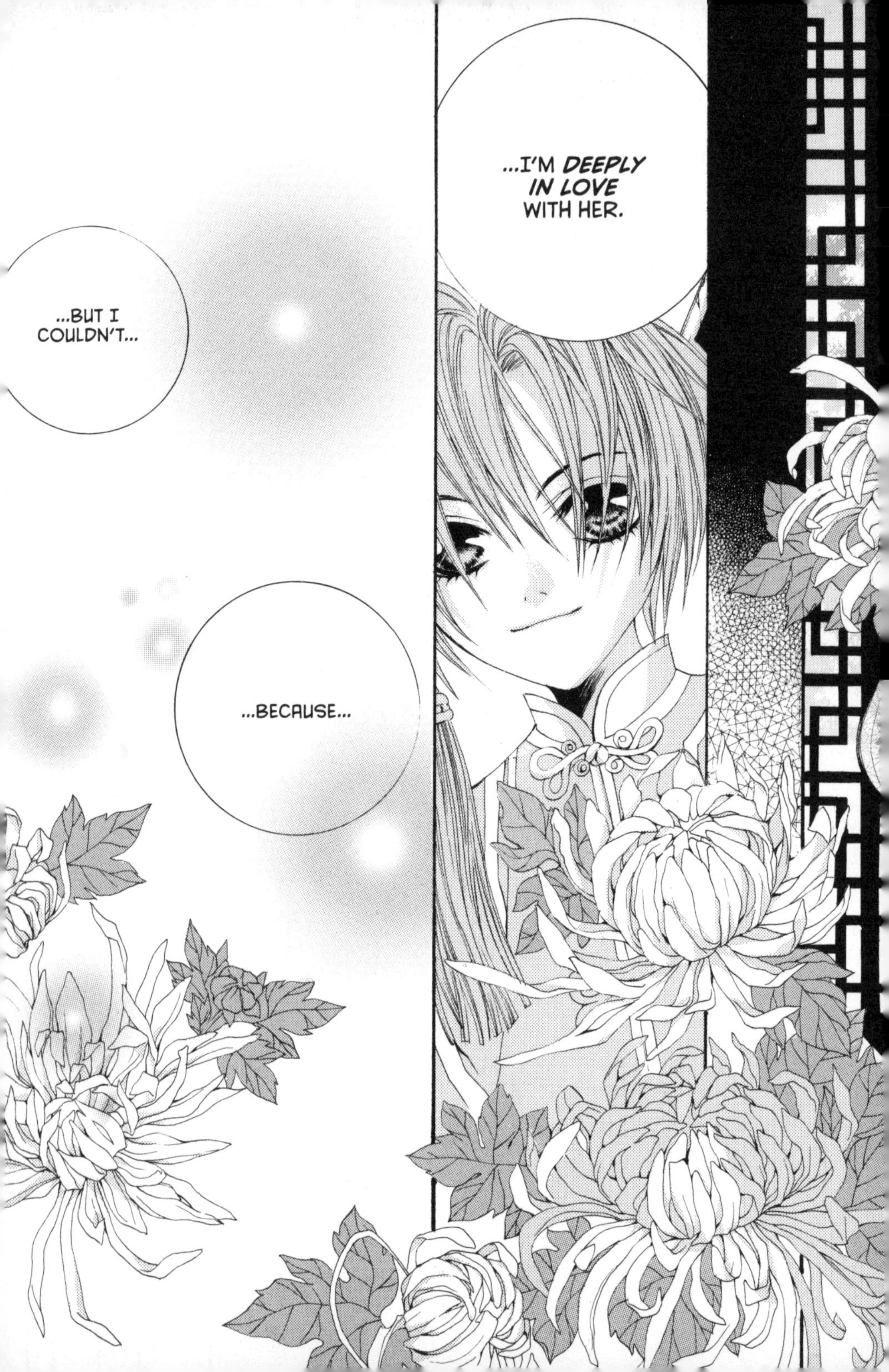
...BUT I COULDN'T...
...BECAUSE...
...I'M *DEEPLY IN LOVE* WITH HER.

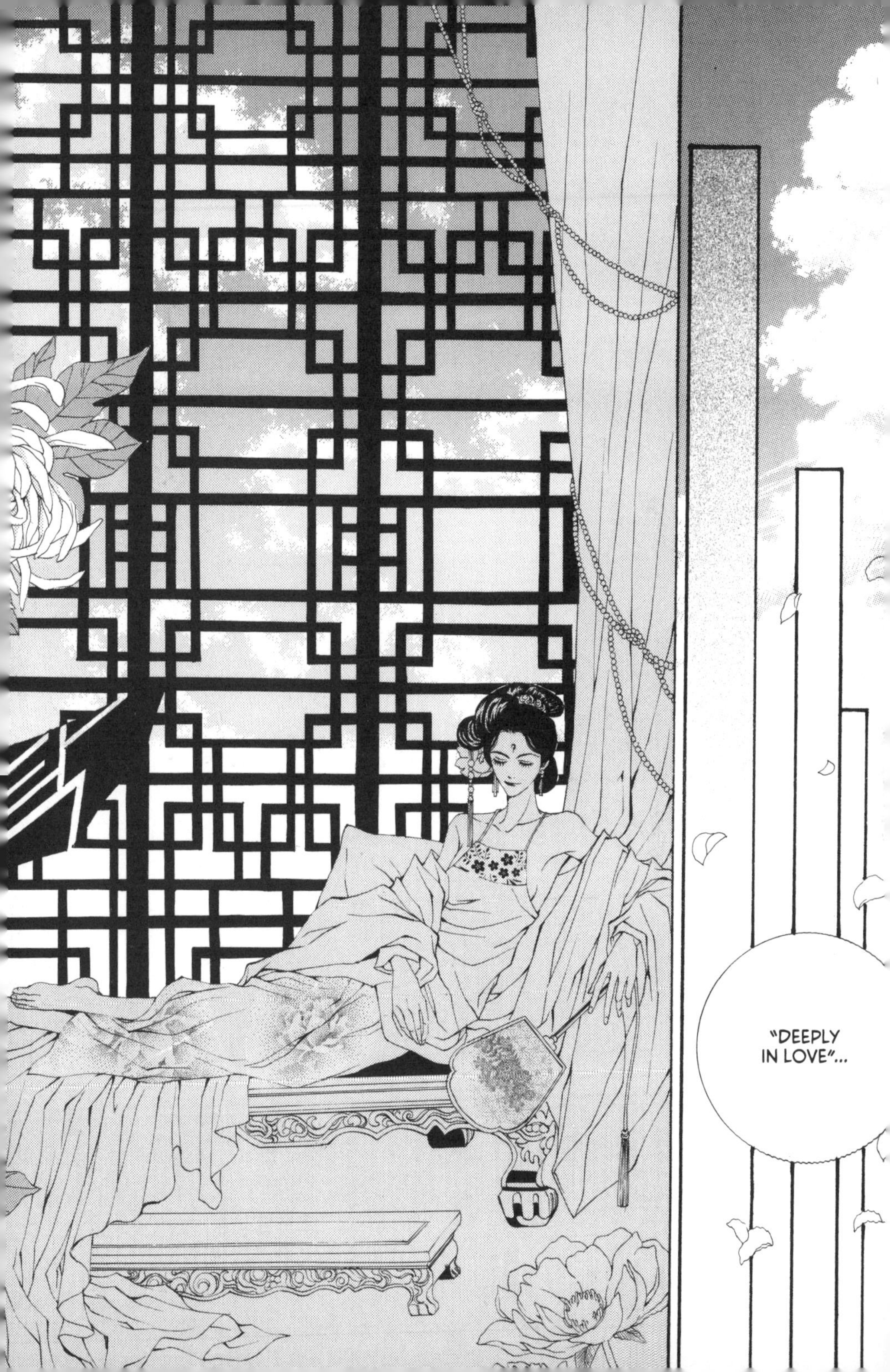
"DEEPLY IN LOVE"...

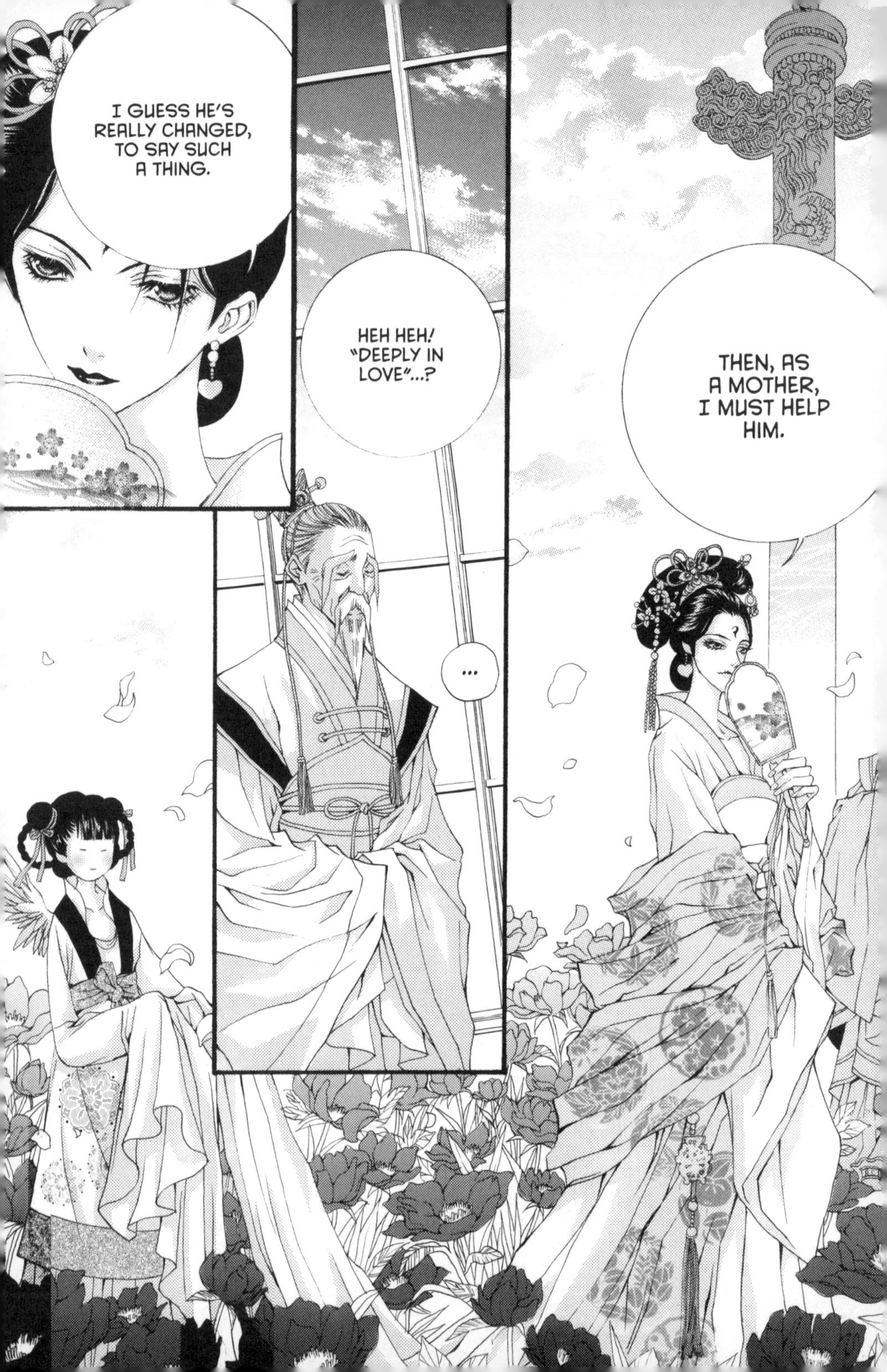
I GUESS HE'S REALLY CHANGED, TO SAY SUCH A THING.
HEH HEH! "DEEPLY IN LOVE"...?
THEN, AS A MOTHER, I MUST HELP HIM.
...

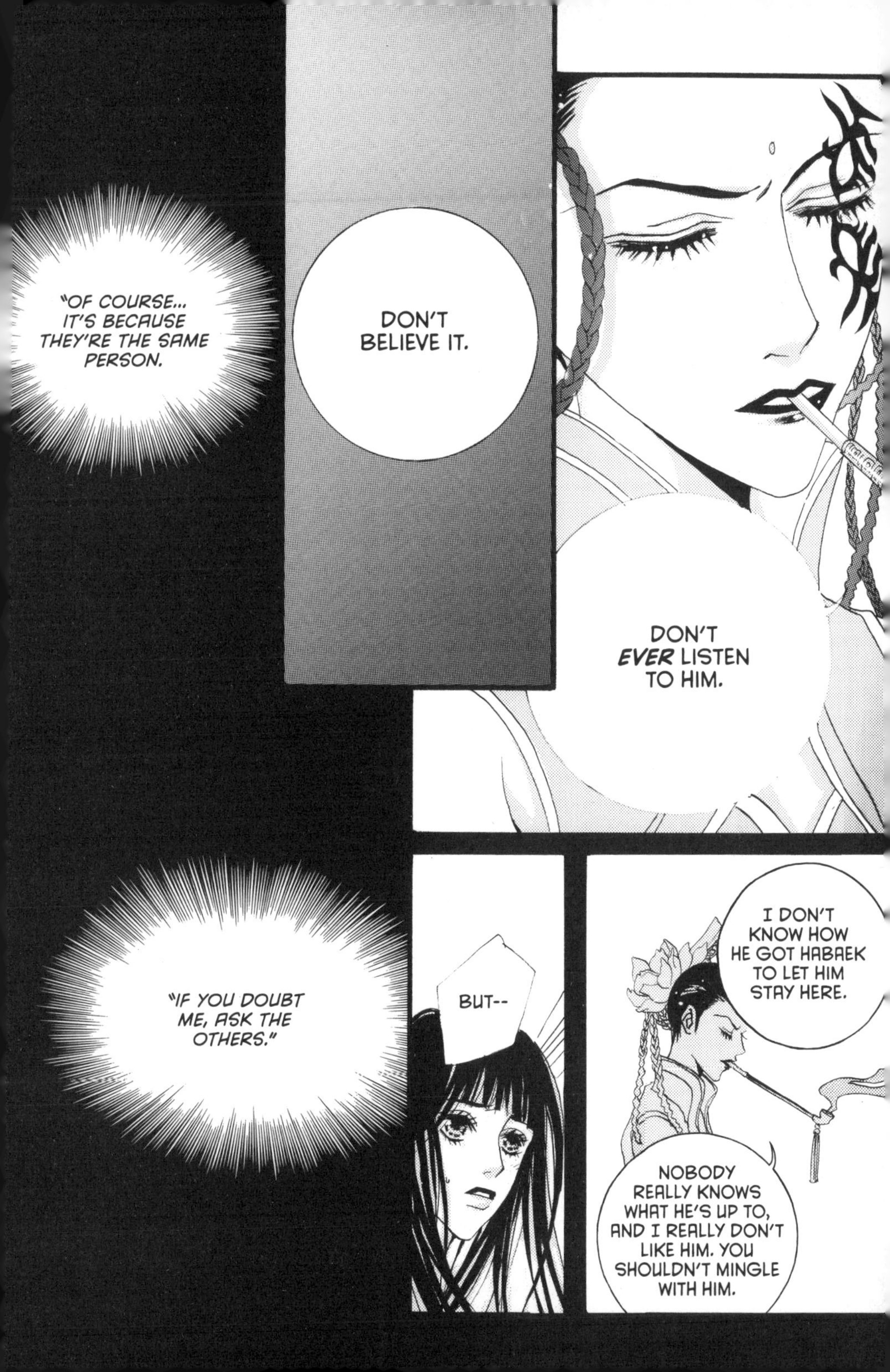
"OF COURSE... IT'S BECAUSE THEY'RE THE SAME PERSON.
DON'T BELIEVE IT.
DON'T EVER LISTEN TO HIM.
"IF YOU DOUBT ME, ASK THE OTHERS."
BUT--
I DON'T KNOW HOW HE GOT HABAEK TO LET HIM STAY HERE.
NOBODY REALLY KNOWS WHAT HE'S UP TO, AND I REALLY DON'T LIKE HIM. YOU SHOULDN'T MINGLE WITH HIM.

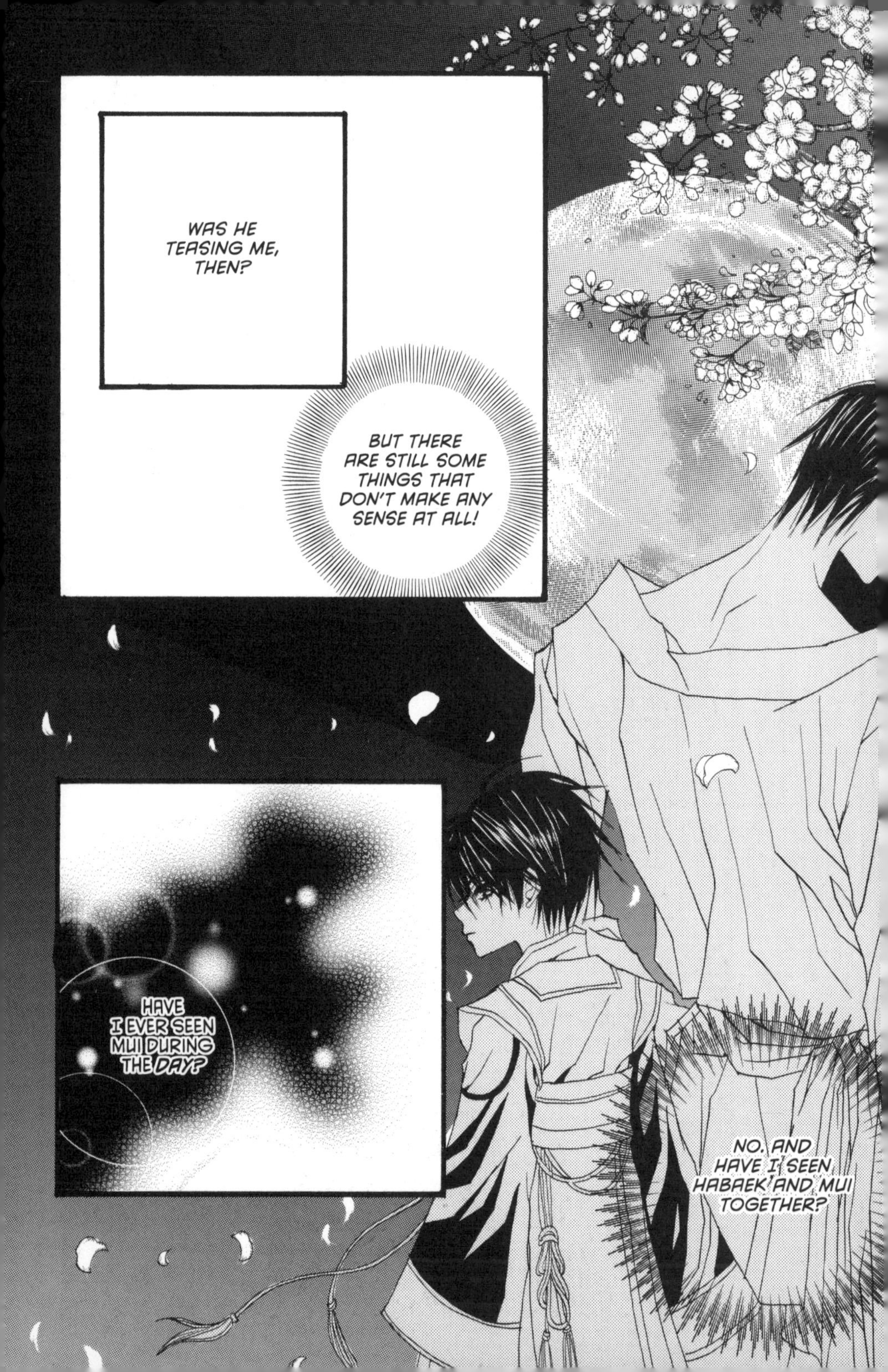
WAS HE TEASING ME, THEN?
BUT THERE ARE STILL SOME THINGS THAT DON'T MAKE ANY SENSE AT ALL!
HAVE I EVER SEEN MUI DURING THE DAY?
NO. AND HAVE I SEEN HABAEK AND MUI TOGETHER?

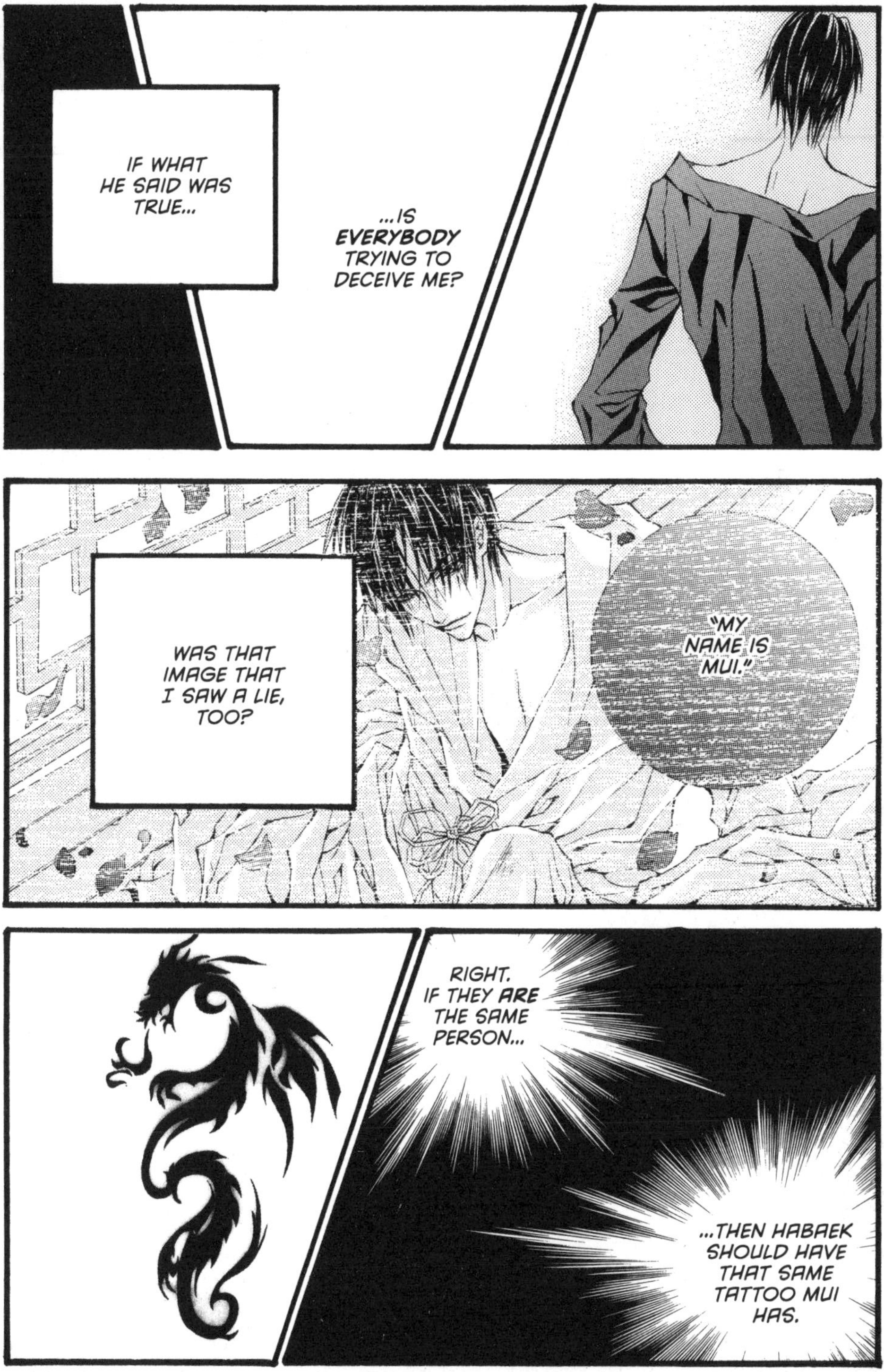

IF WHAT HE SAID WAS TRUE...
...IS EVERYBODY TRYING TO DECEIVE ME?
WAS THAT IMAGE THAT I SAW A LIE, TOO?
"MY NAME IS MUI."
RIGHT. IF THEY ARE THE SAME PERSON...
...THEN HABAEK SHOULD HAVE THAT SAME TATTOO MUI HAS.

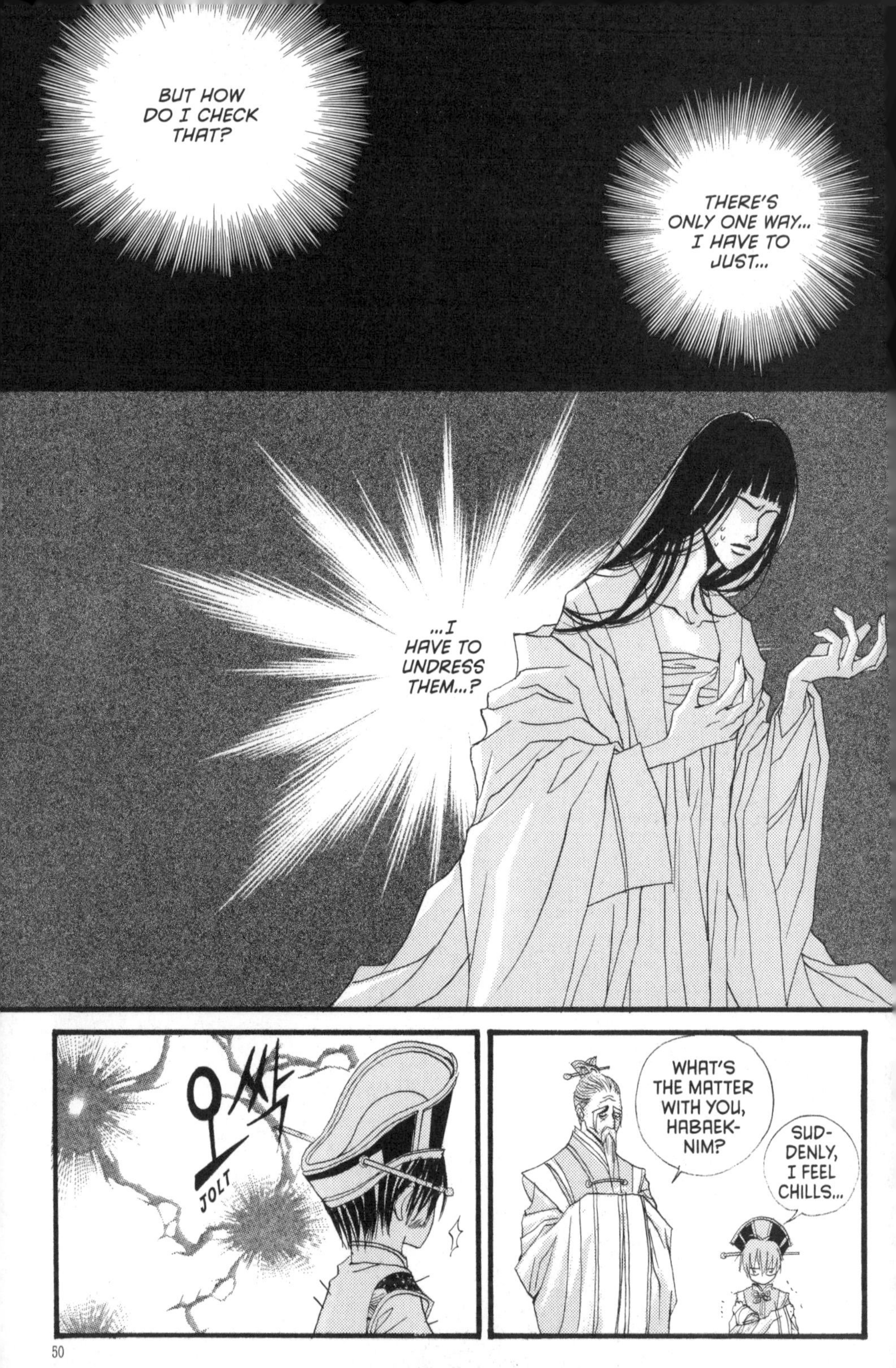
BUT HOW DO I CHECK THAT?
THERE'S ONLY ONE WAY... I HAVE TO JUST...
...I HAVE TO UNDRESS THEM...?
오싹
JOLT
WHAT'S THE MATTER WITH YOU, HABAEK-NIM?
SUD-DENLY, I FEEL CHILLS...

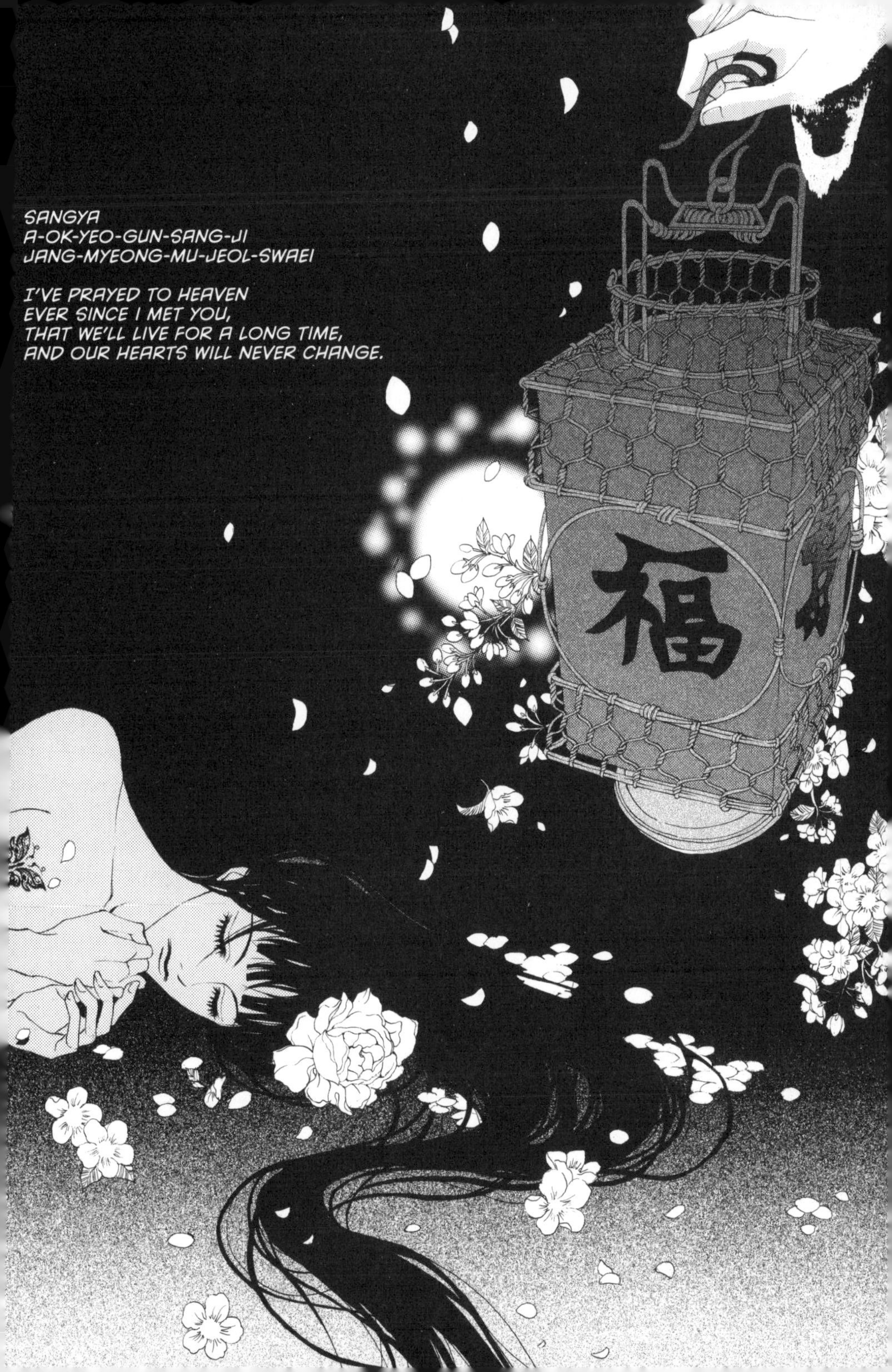
SANGYA
A-OK-YEO-GUN-SANG-JI
JANG-MYEONG-MU-JEOL-SWAEI
I'VE PRAYED TO HEAVEN
EVER SINCE I MET YOU,
THAT WE'LL LIVE FOR A LONG TIME,
AND OUR HEARTS WILL NEVER CHANGE.
福

SAN-MU-REUNG-GANG-SU-WI-GAL
DONG-RWAEI-JIN-JIN-HA-WU-SEOL
CHEON-JI-HAP-NAE-GAM-YEO-GUN-JEOL

WHEN ALL THE HILLS ARE GONE
ON THE MOUNTAIN
AND THE RIVER DRIES OUT,
AND IT THUNDERS IN THE WINTER
AND SNOWS IN THE SUMMER,
AND WHEN THE WORLD IS
FINALLY AT ITS END,
WHERE HEAVEN AND EARTH MEET,
THEN, RELUCTANTLY, WE WILL PART.

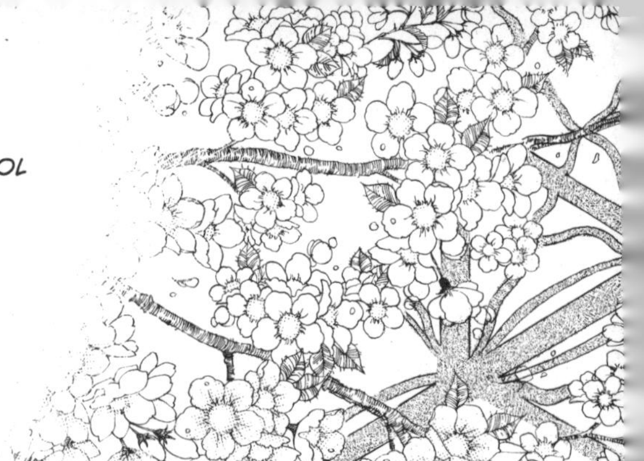

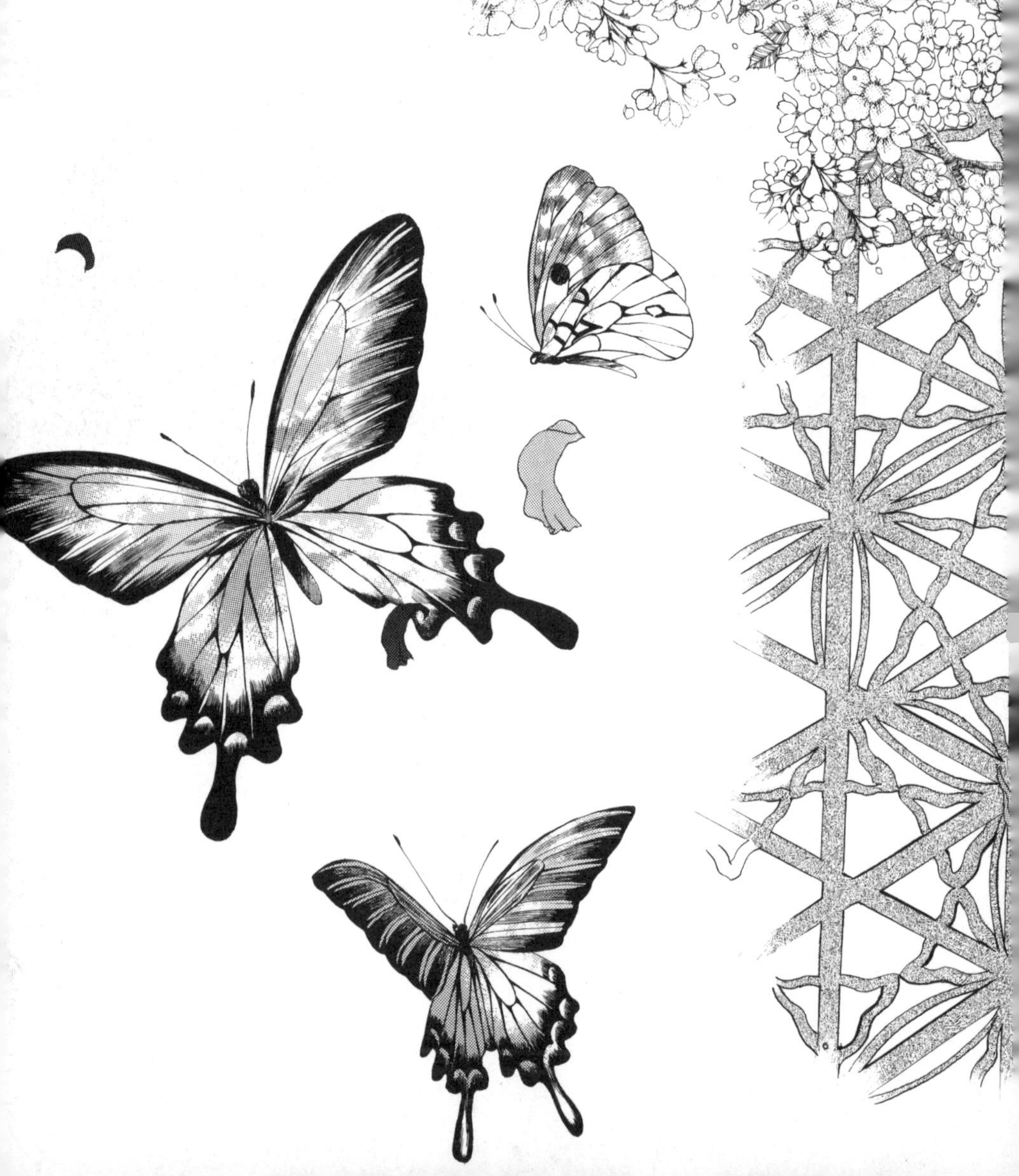

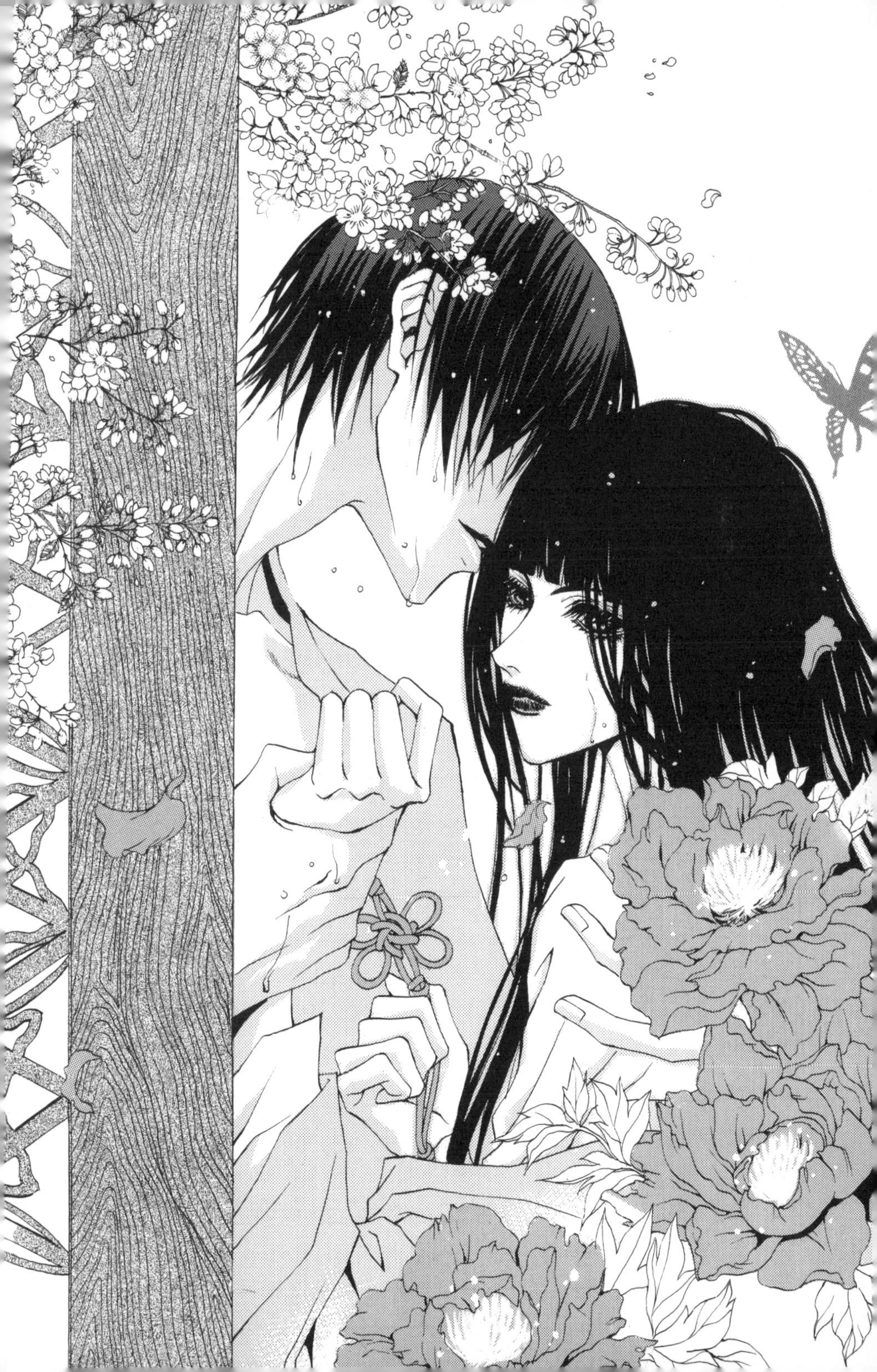

WAIT A MINUTE...WHAT DID I SAY?

...TO MUI, A FEW DAYS AGO...

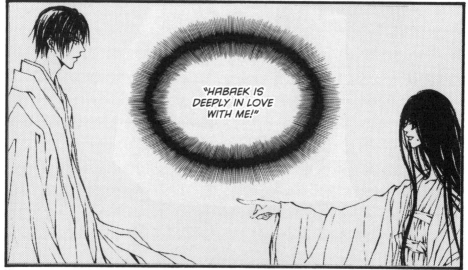

"HABAEK IS DEEPLY IN LOVE WITH ME!"

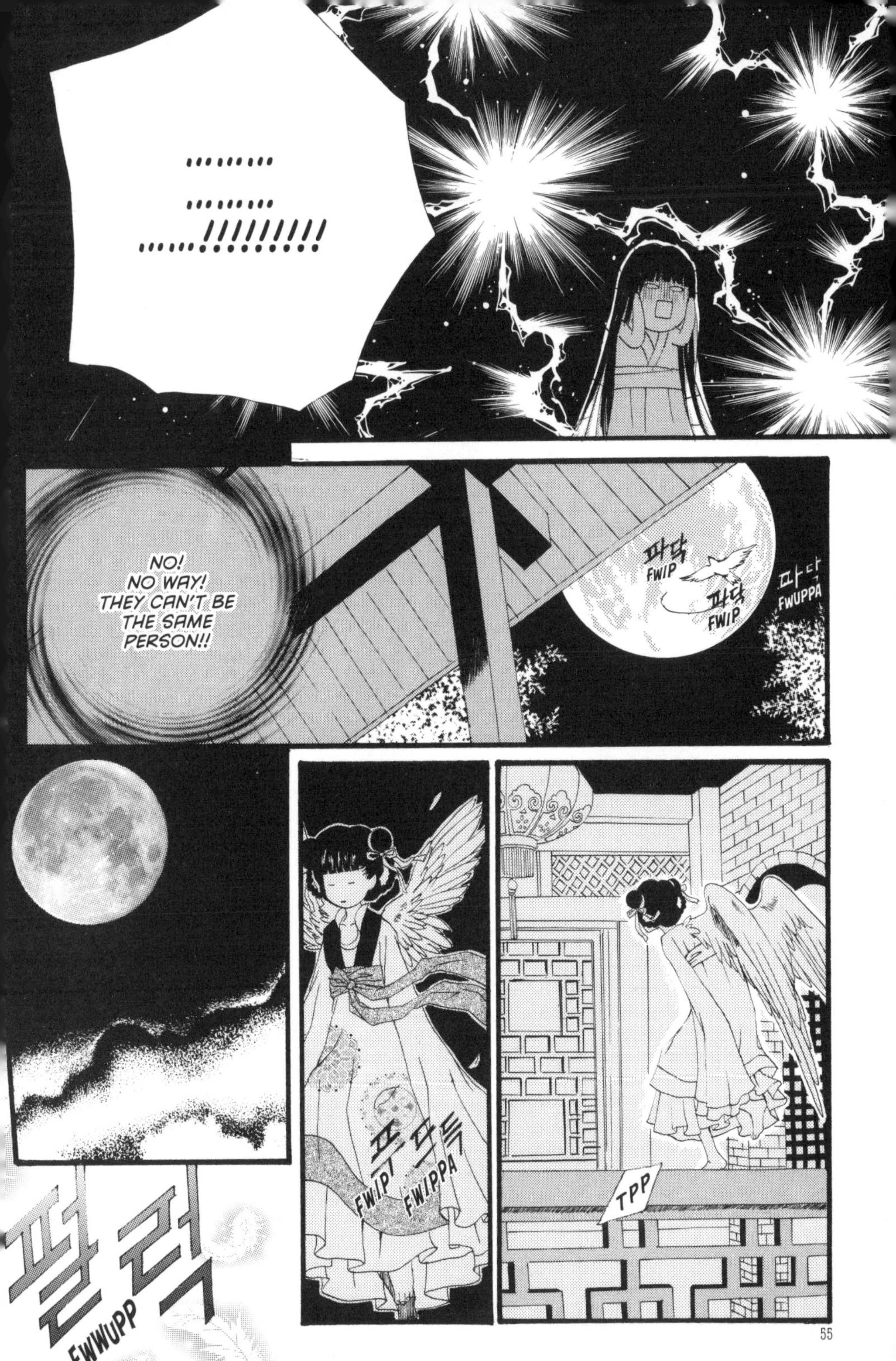
....
....
......!!!!!!!!!
NO! NO WAY! THEY CAN'T BE THE SAME PERSON!!
파닥
FWIP
파닥
FWIP
파닥
FWUPPA
펄럭
FWWUPP
푸드득
FWIP FWIPPA
TPP

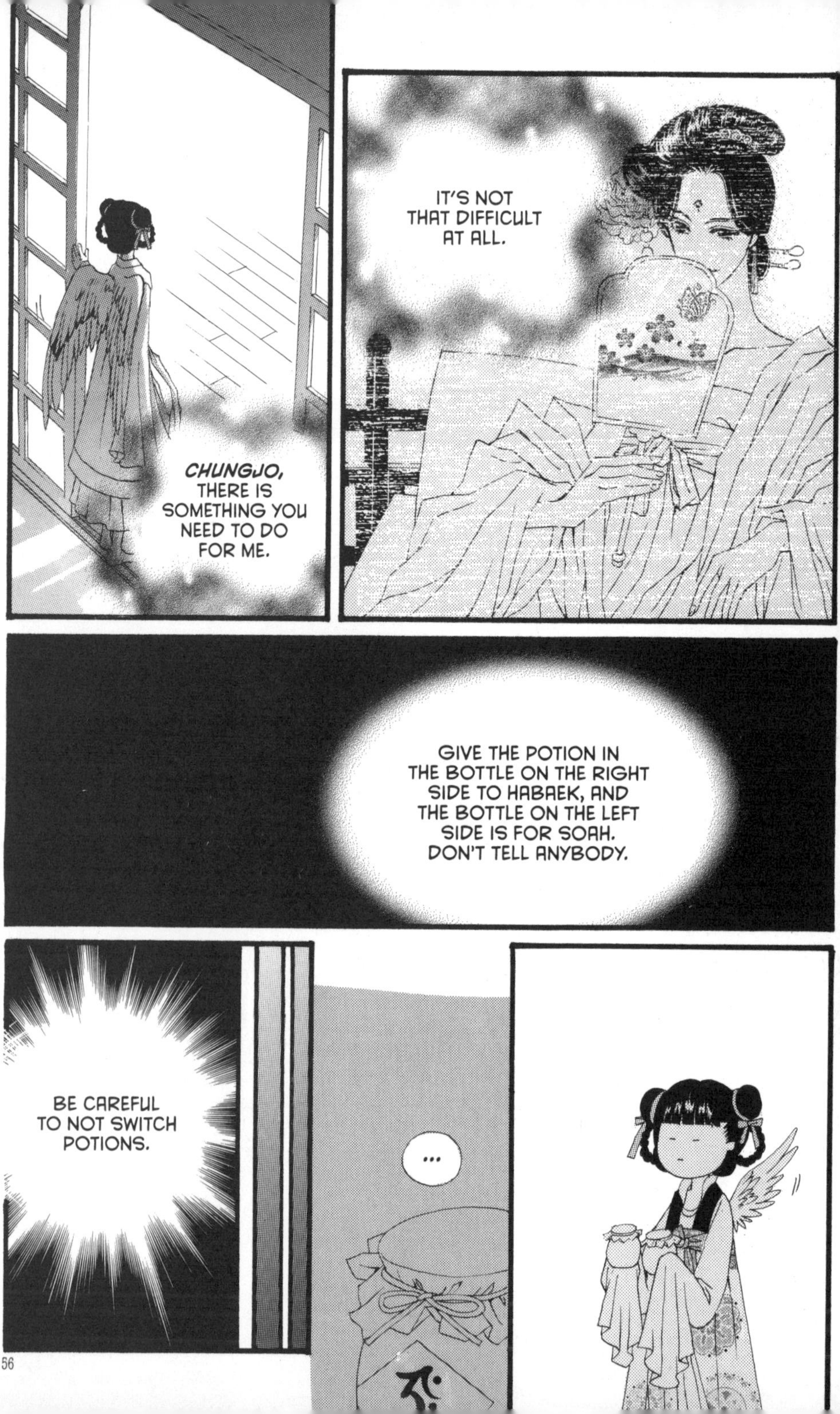
IT'S NOT THAT DIFFICULT AT ALL.
CHUNGJO, THERE IS SOMETHING YOU NEED TO DO FOR ME.
GIVE THE POTION IN THE BOTTLE ON THE RIGHT SIDE TO HABAEK, AND THE BOTTLE ON THE LEFT SIDE IS FOR SOAH. DON'T TELL ANYBODY.
BE CAREFUL TO NOT SWITCH POTIONS.
...

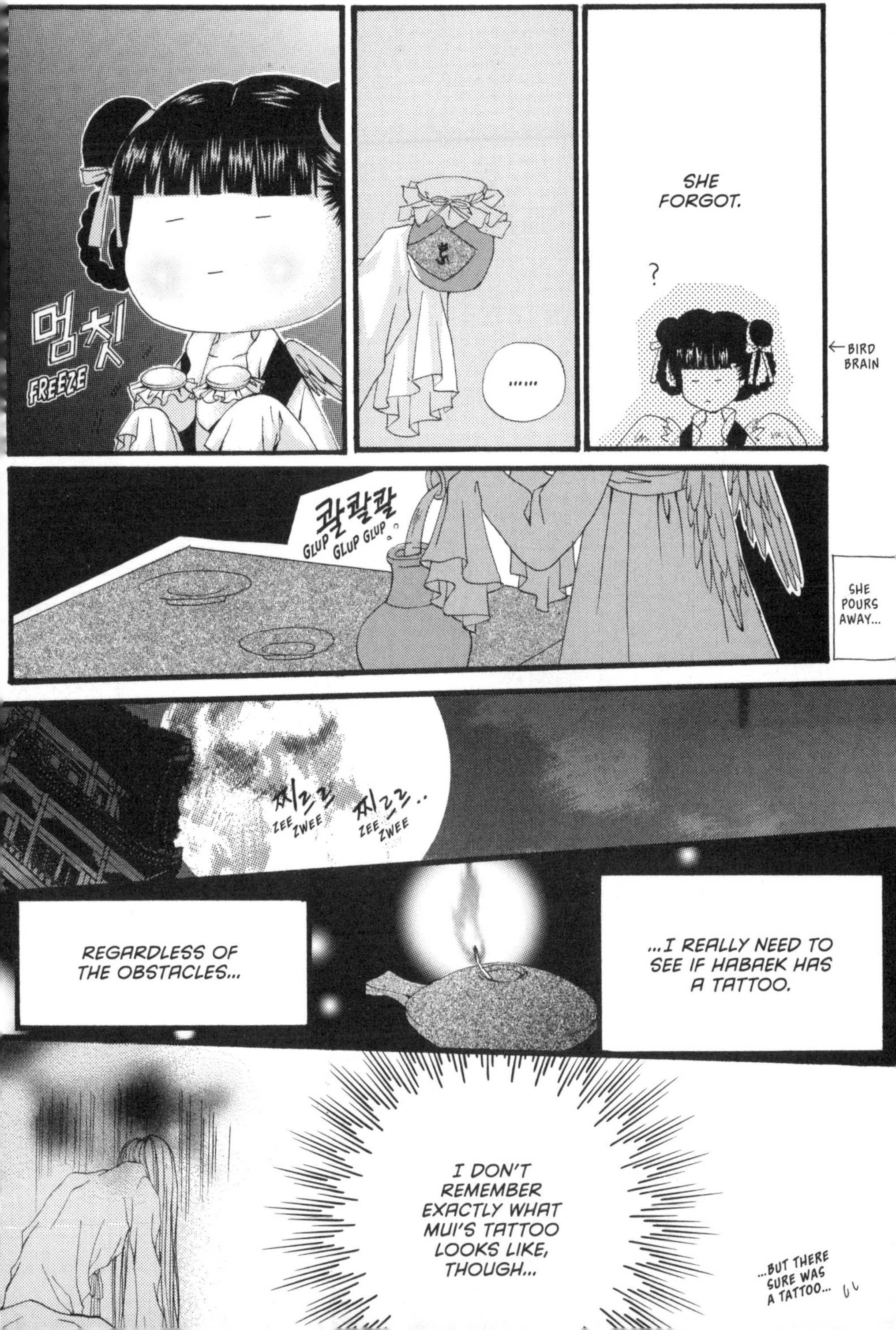
멈칫
FREEZE
......
SHE FORGOT.
?
← BIRD BRAIN
콸콸콸
GLUP GLUP GLUP
SHE POURS AWAY...
찌르르
ZEE ZWEE
찌르르..
ZEE ZWEE
REGARDLESS OF THE OBSTACLES...
...I REALLY NEED TO SEE IF HABAEK HAS A TATTOO.
I DON'T REMEMBER EXACTLY WHAT MUI'S TATTOO LOOKS LIKE, THOUGH...
...BUT THERE SURE WAS A TATTOO...

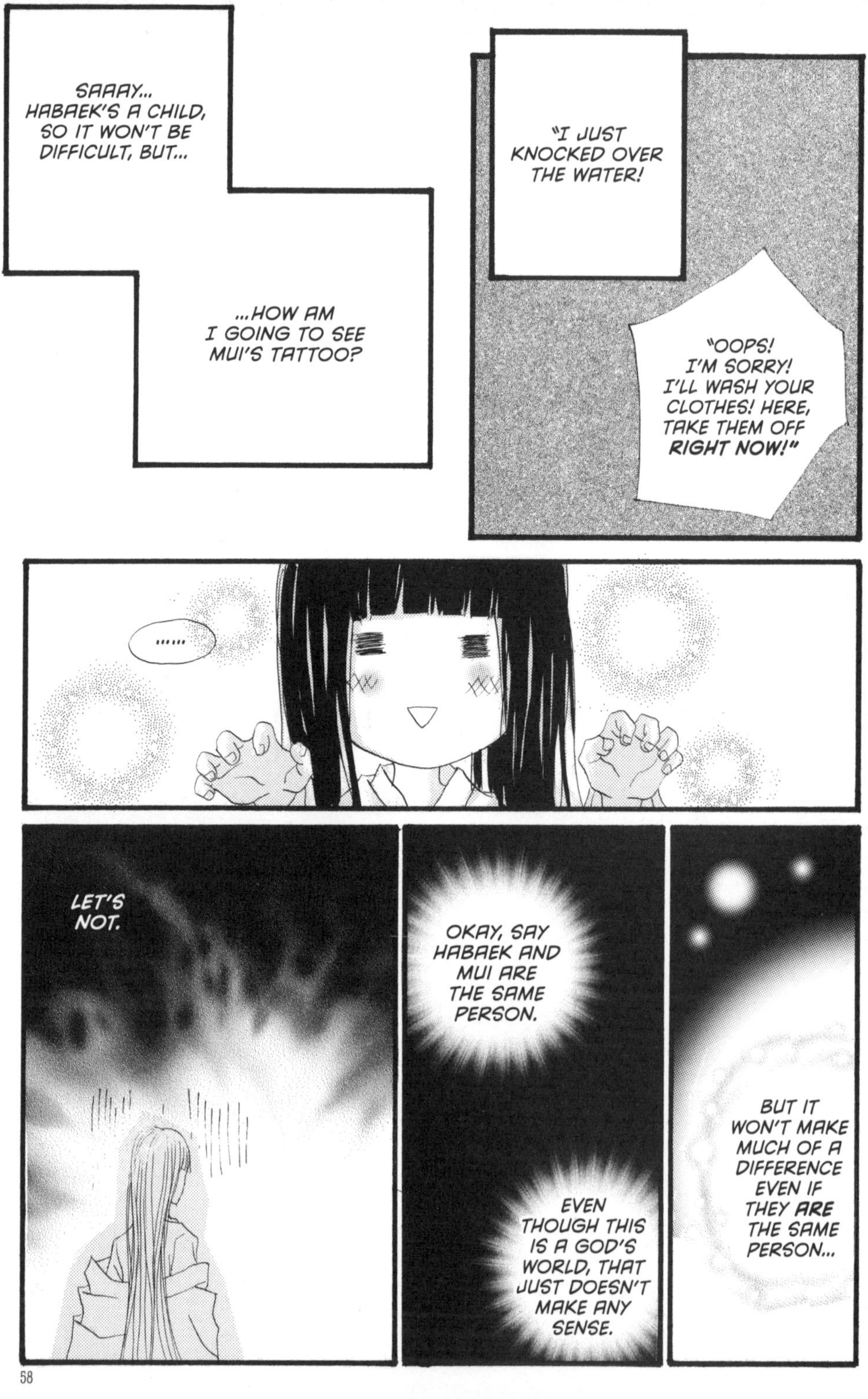
SAAAY... HABAEK'S A CHILD, SO IT WON'T BE DIFFICULT, BUT...
...HOW AM I GOING TO SEE MUI'S TATTOO?
"I JUST KNOCKED OVER THE WATER!
"OOPS! I'M SORRY! I'LL WASH YOUR CLOTHES! HERE, TAKE THEM OFF **RIGHT NOW!**"
......
LET'S NOT.
OKAY, SAY HABAEK AND MUI ARE THE SAME PERSON.
EVEN THOUGH THIS IS A GOD'S WORLD, THAT JUST DOESN'T MAKE ANY SENSE.
BUT IT WON'T MAKE MUCH OF A DIFFERENCE EVEN IF THEY **ARE** THE SAME PERSON...

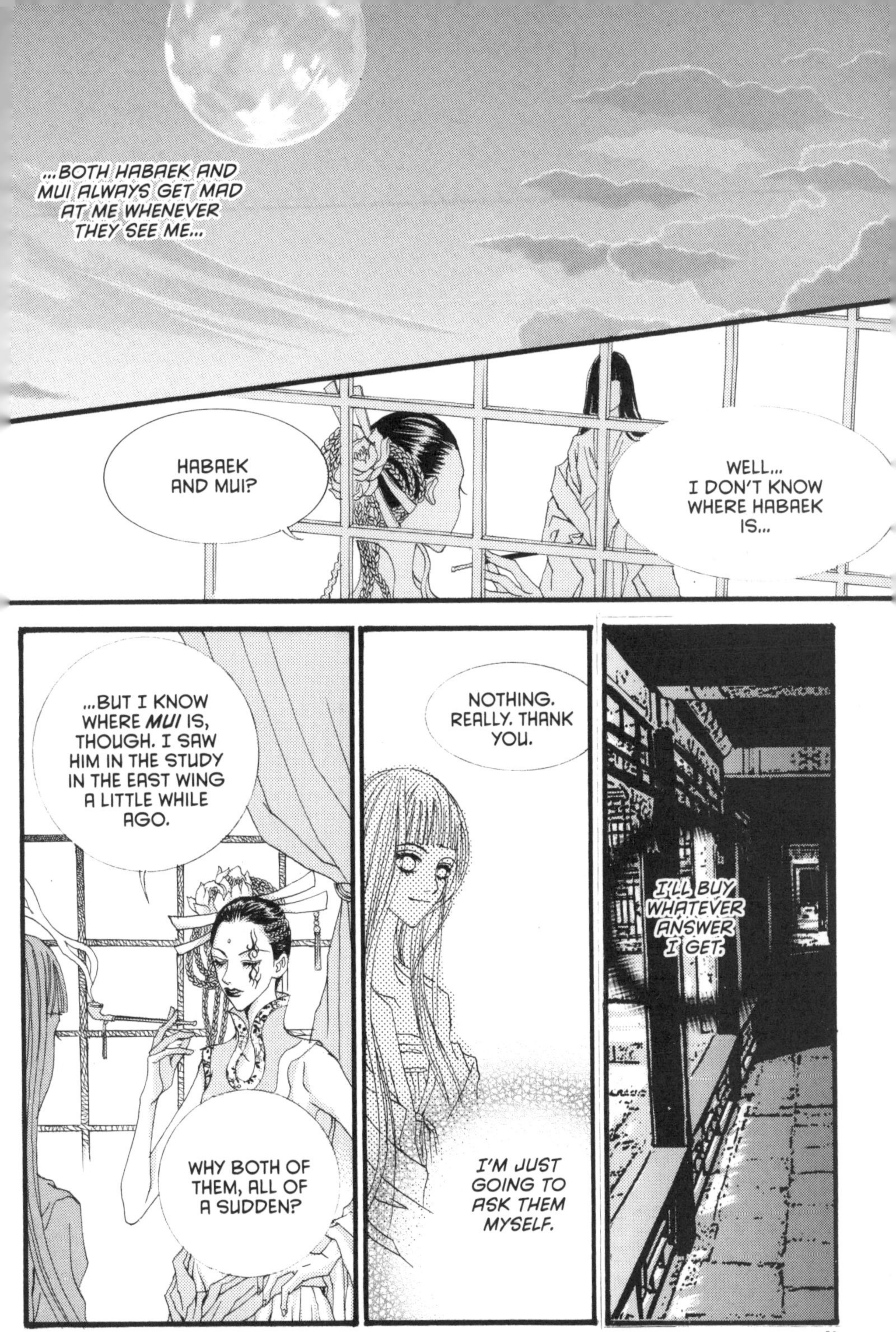

...BOTH HABAEK AND MUI ALWAYS GET MAD AT ME WHENEVER THEY SEE ME...
HABAEK AND MUI?
WELL... I DON'T KNOW WHERE HABAEK IS...
...BUT I KNOW WHERE MUI IS, THOUGH. I SAW HIM IN THE STUDY IN THE EAST WING A LITTLE WHILE AGO.
WHY BOTH OF THEM, ALL OF A SUDDEN?
NOTHING. REALLY. THANK YOU.
I'M JUST GOING TO ASK THEM MYSELF.
I'LL BUY WHATEVER ANSWER I GET.

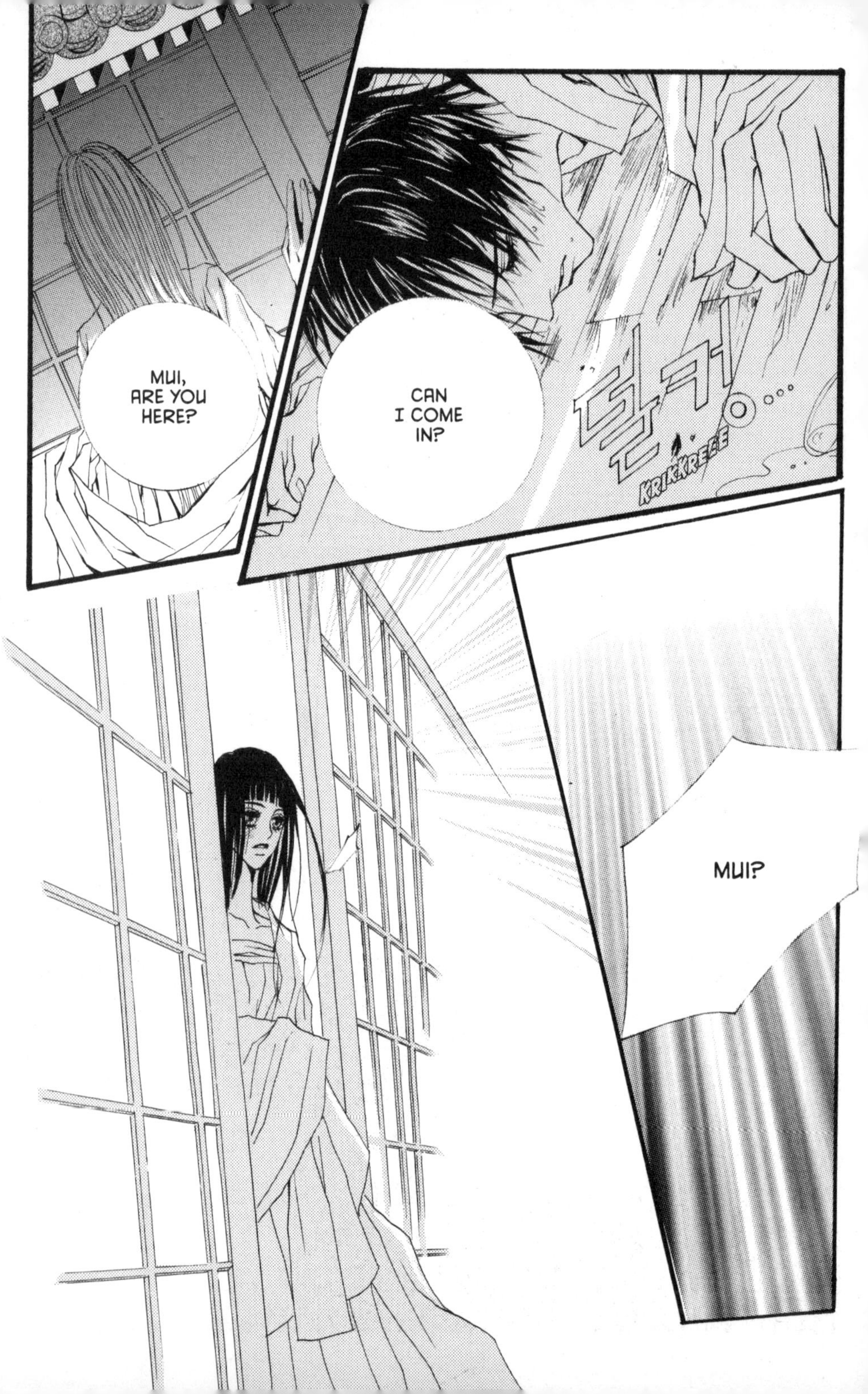
MUI, ARE YOU HERE?
CAN I COME IN?
KRIKKREEE
MUI?

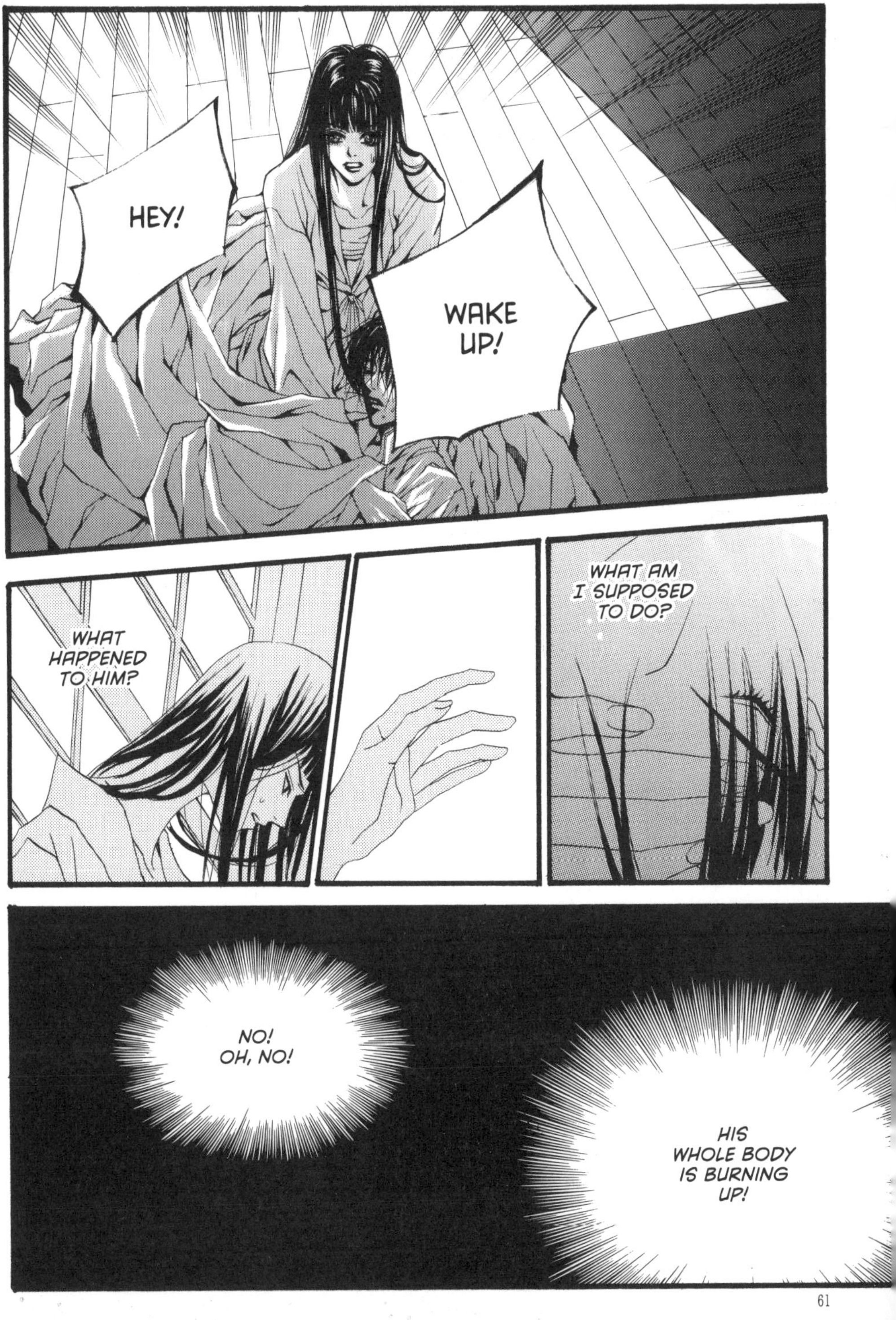
HEY!
WAKE UP!
WHAT HAPPENED TO HIM?
WHAT AM I SUPPOSED TO DO?
NO! OH, NO!
HIS WHOLE BODY IS BURNING UP!

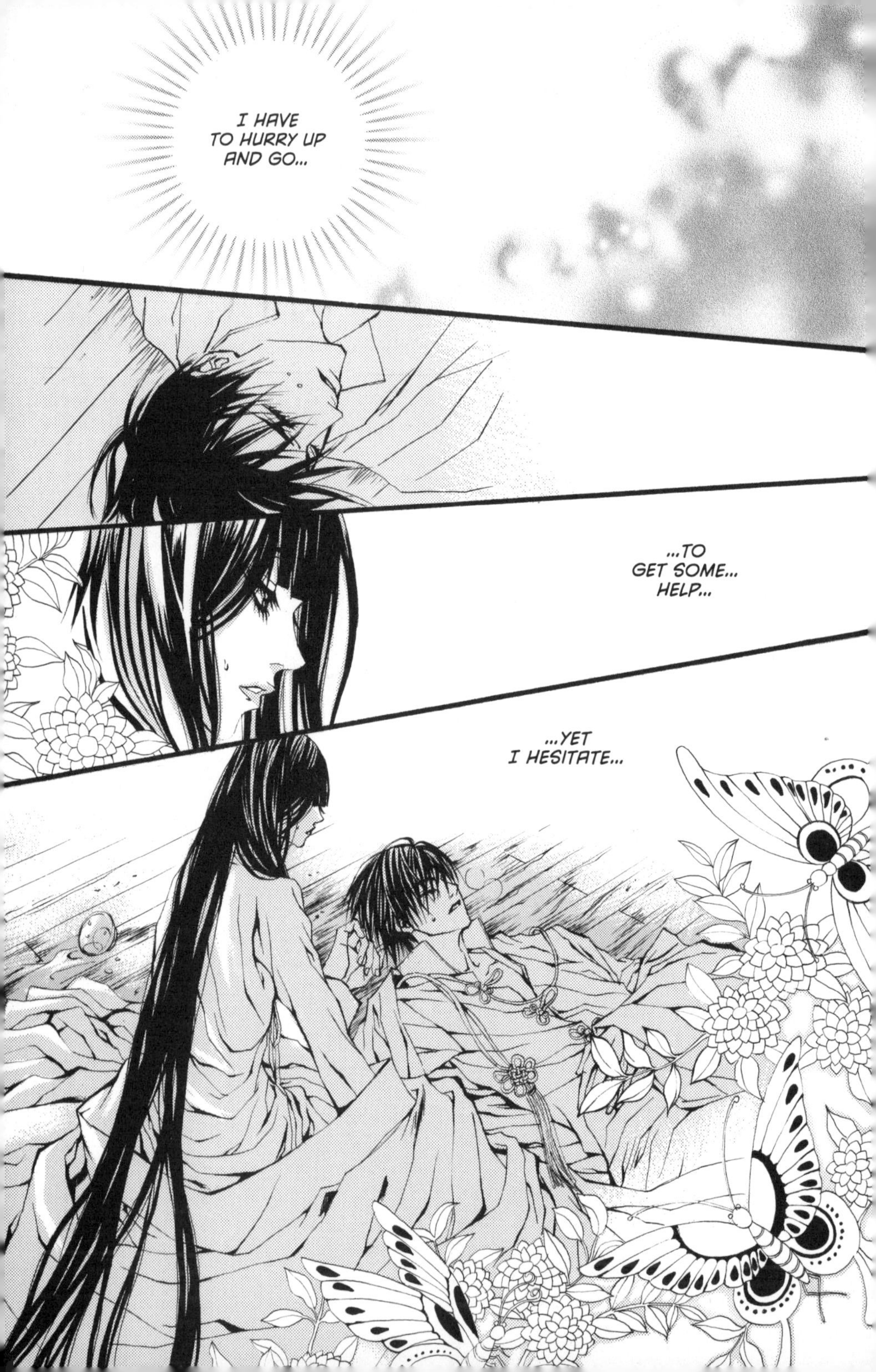
I HAVE TO HURRY UP AND GO...
...TO GET SOME... HELP...
...YET I HESITATE...

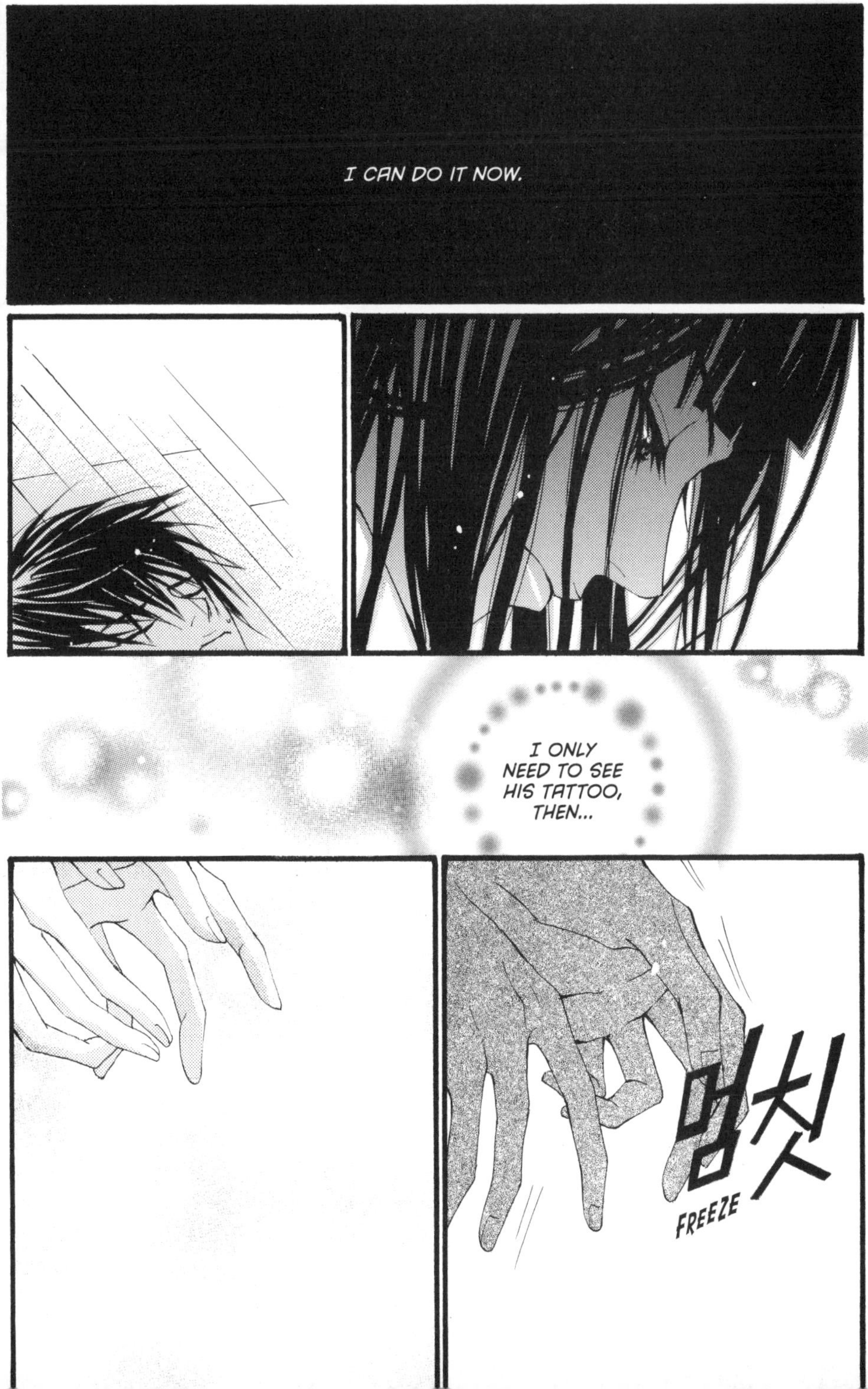
I CAN DO IT NOW.
I ONLY NEED TO SEE HIS TATTOO, THEN...
멈칫
FREEZE

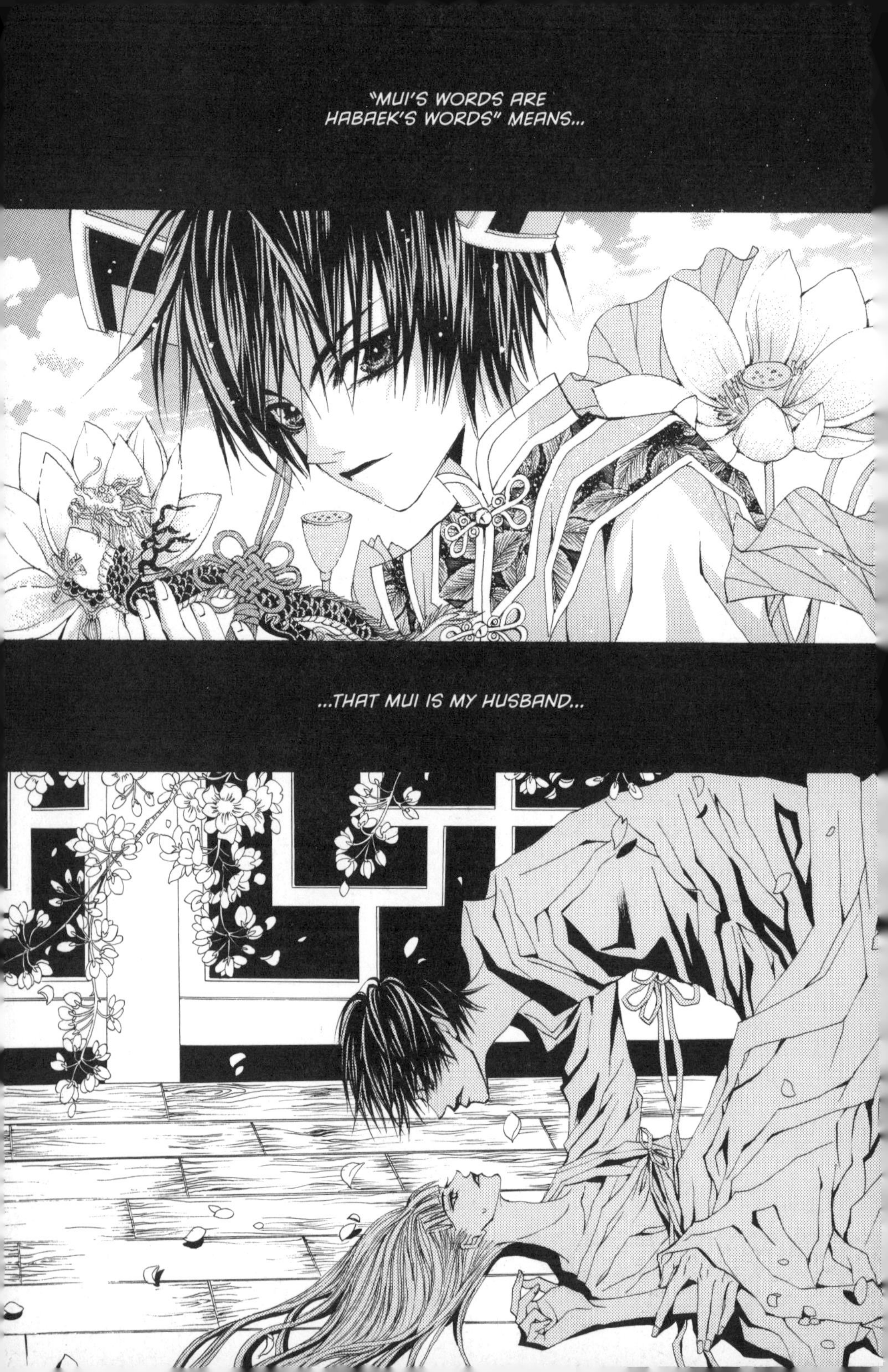
"MUI'S WORDS ARE HABAEK'S WORDS" MEANS...
...THAT MUI IS MY HUSBAND...

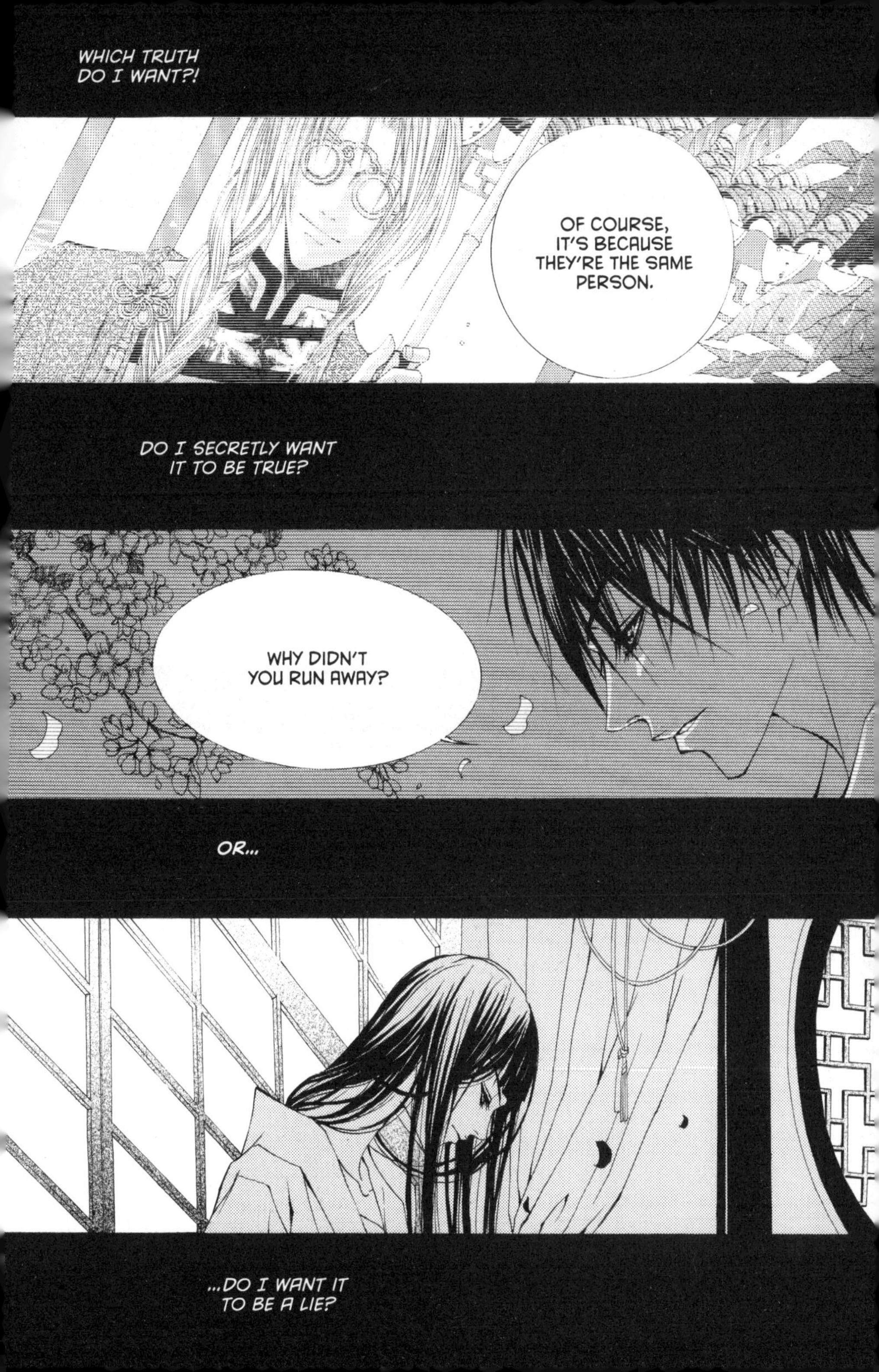
WHICH TRUTH DO I WANT?!
OF COURSE, IT'S BECAUSE THEY'RE THE SAME PERSON.
DO I SECRETLY WANT IT TO BE TRUE?
WHY DIDN'T YOU RUN AWAY?
OR...
...DO I WANT IT TO BE A LIE?

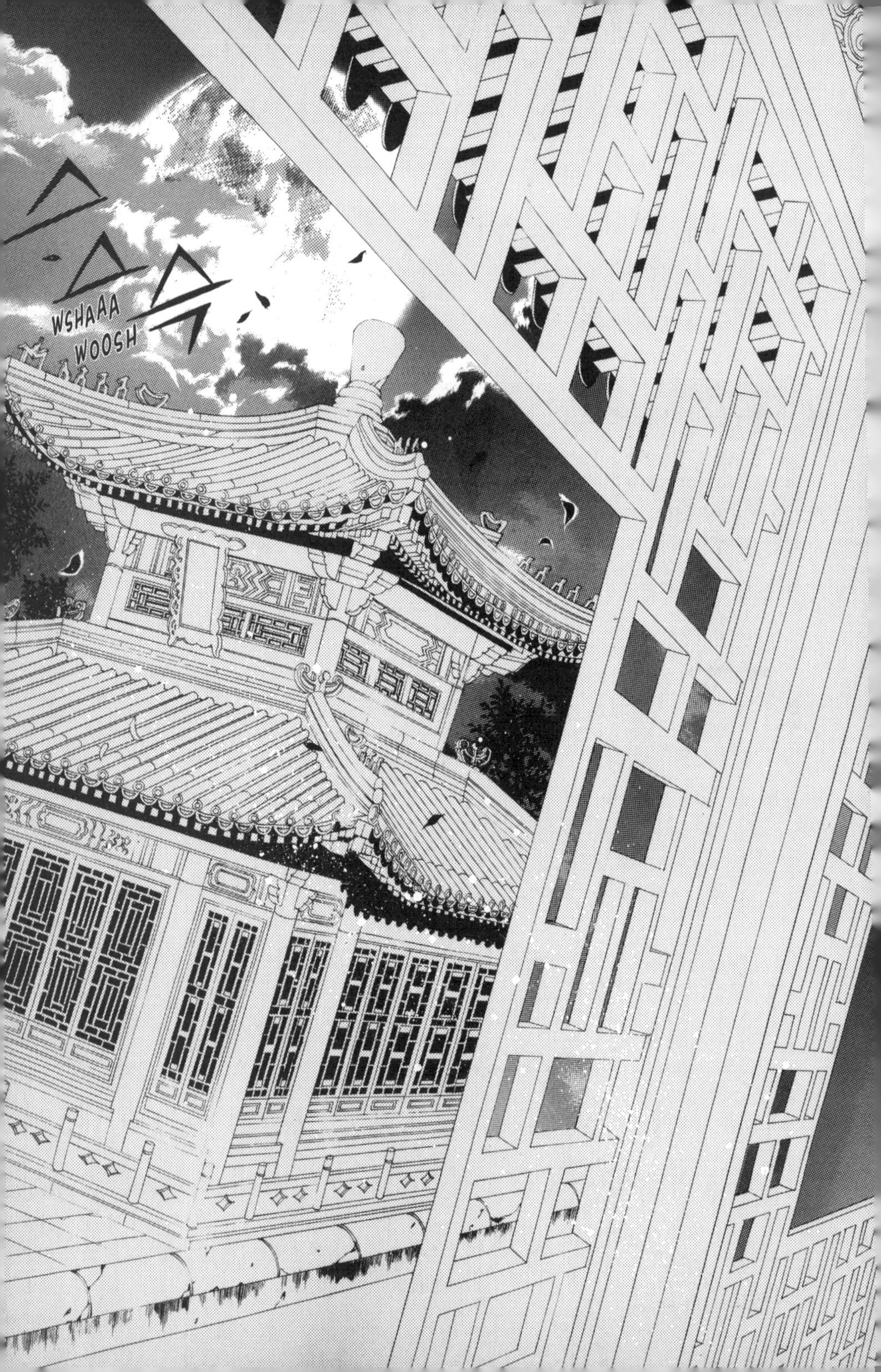
WSHAAA
WOOSH

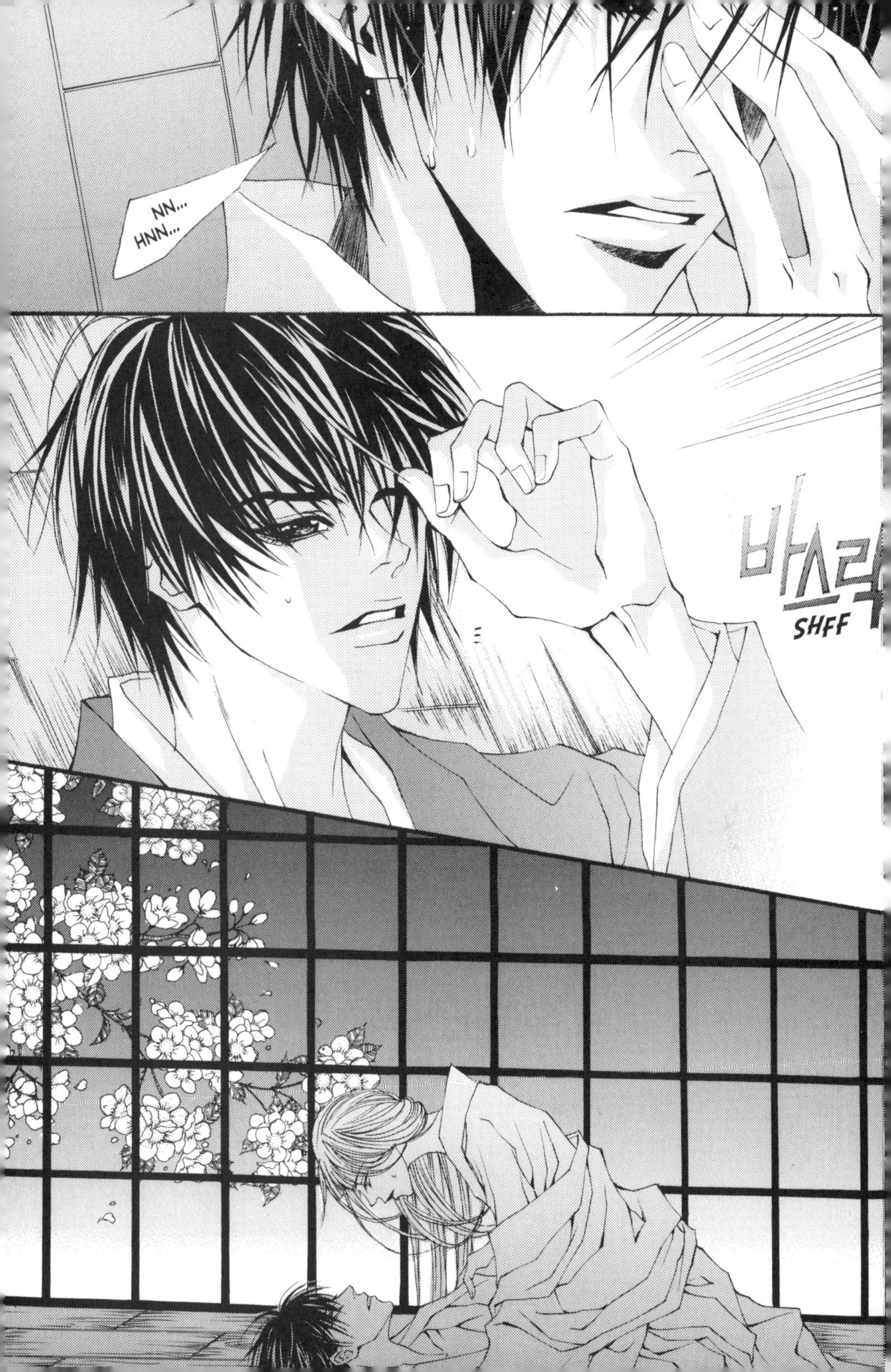
NN... HNN...
바스락
SHFF

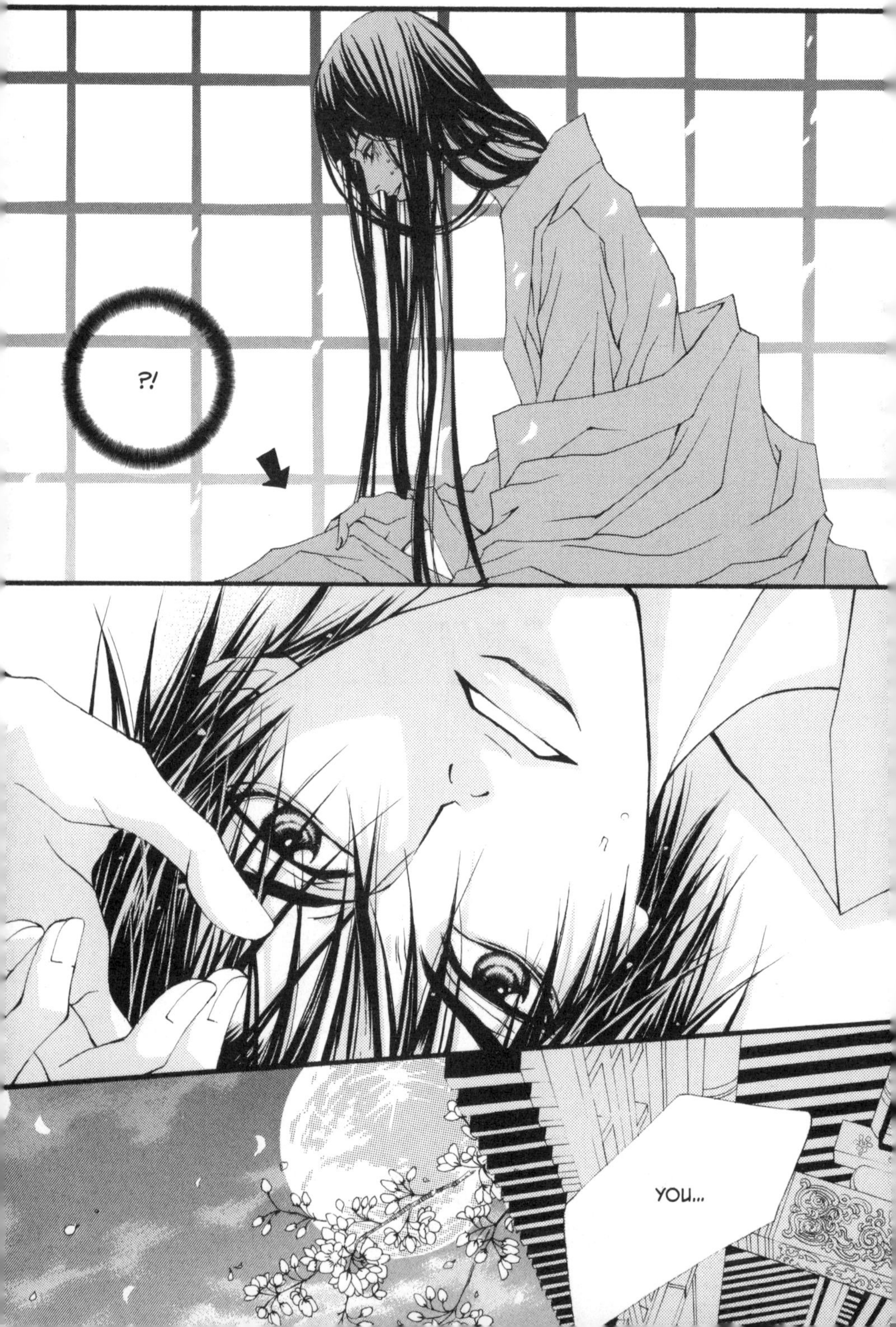
?!
YOU...

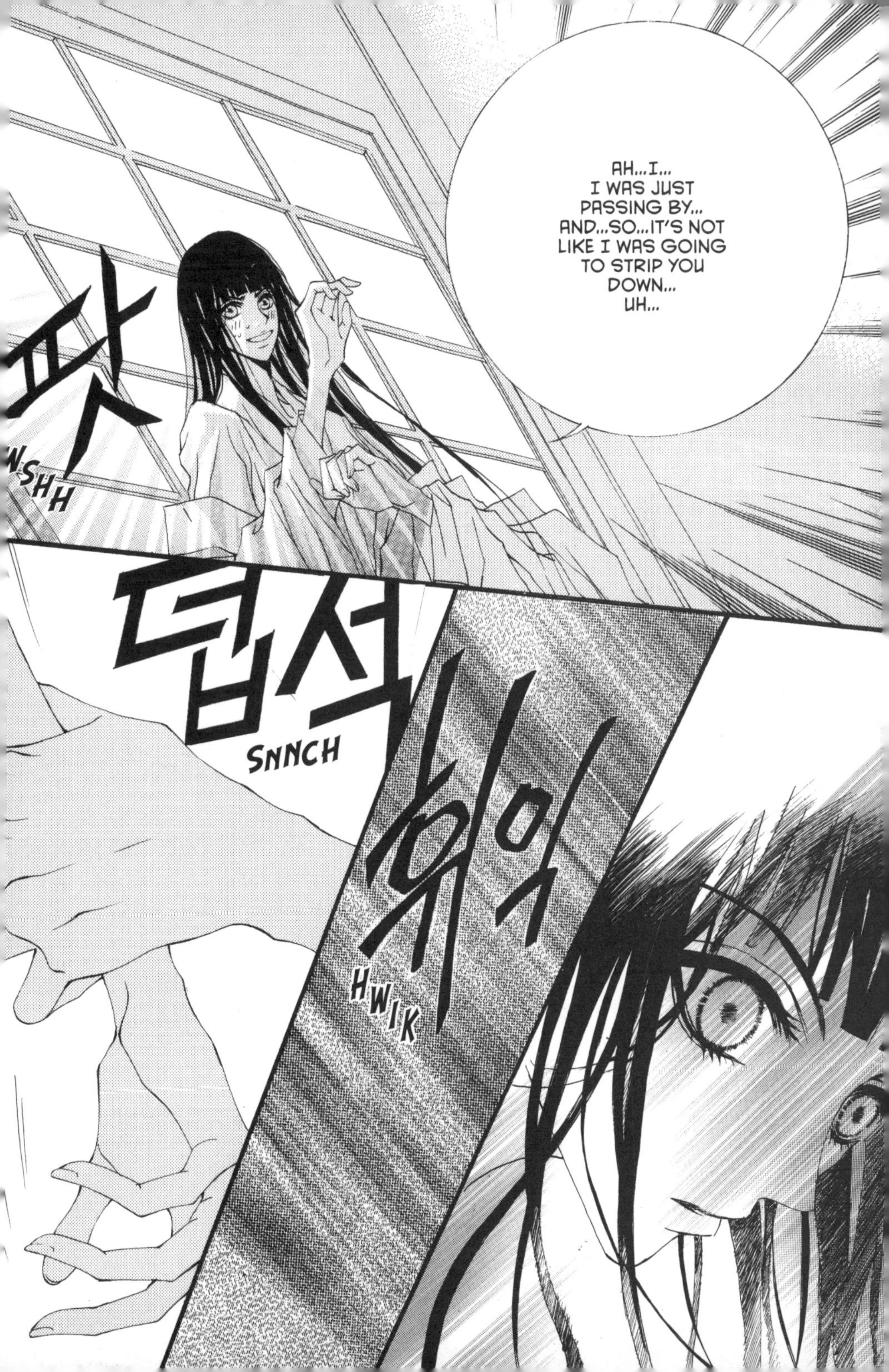

팟
NSHH
AH...I... I WAS JUST PASSING BY... AND...SO...IT'S NOT LIKE I WAS GOING TO STRIP YOU DOWN... UH...
덥석
SNNCH
휘익
HWIK

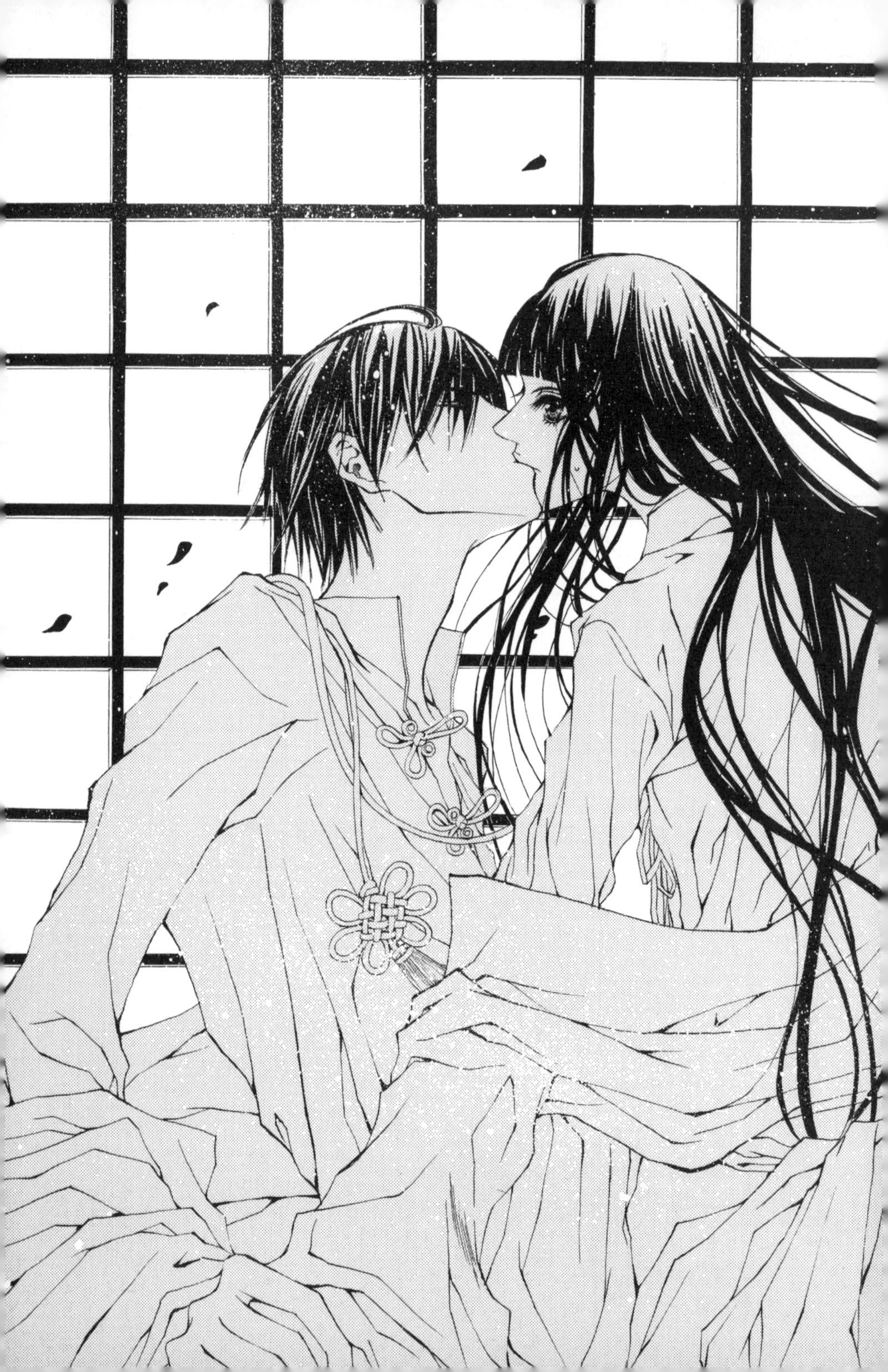

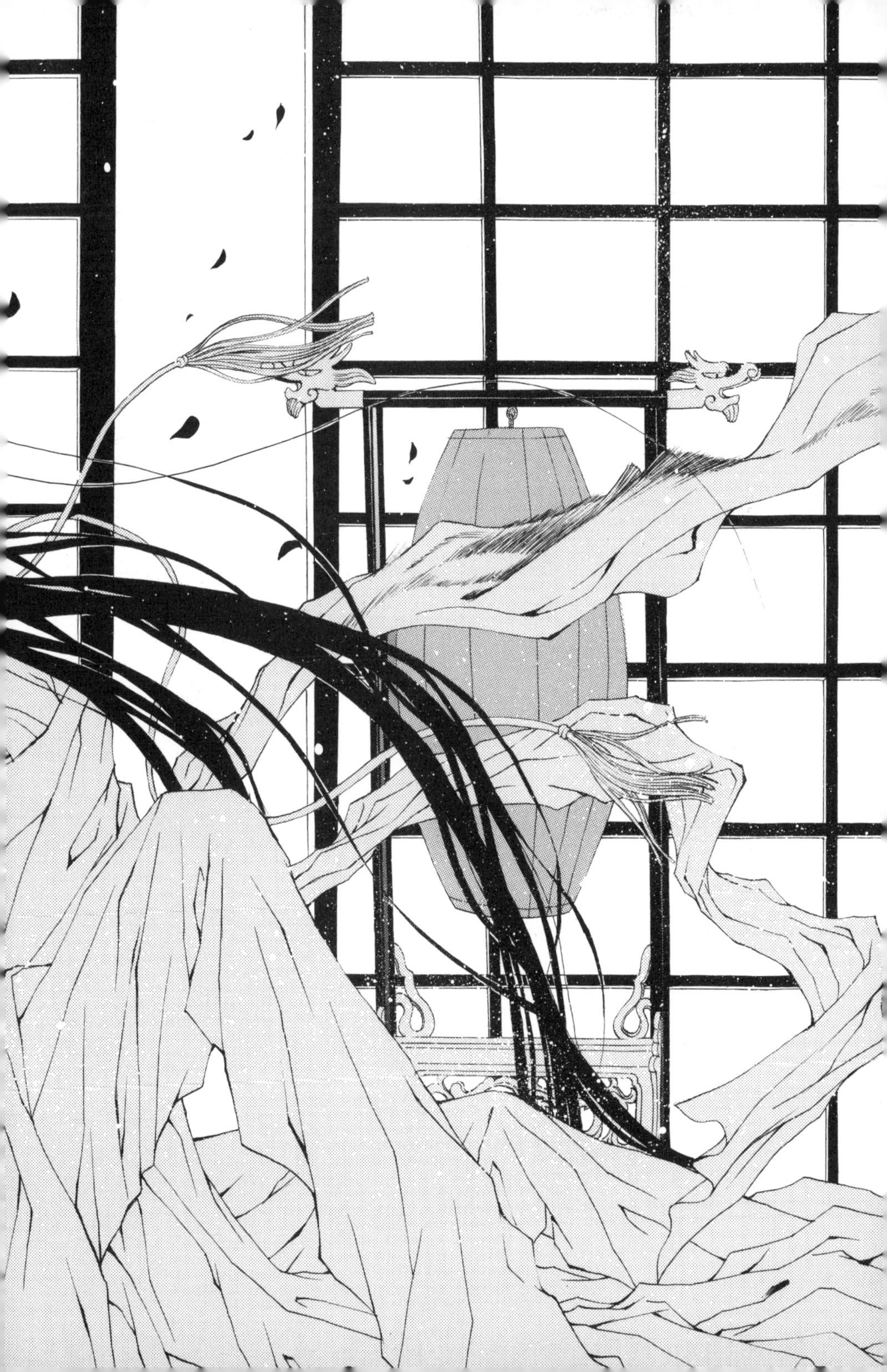

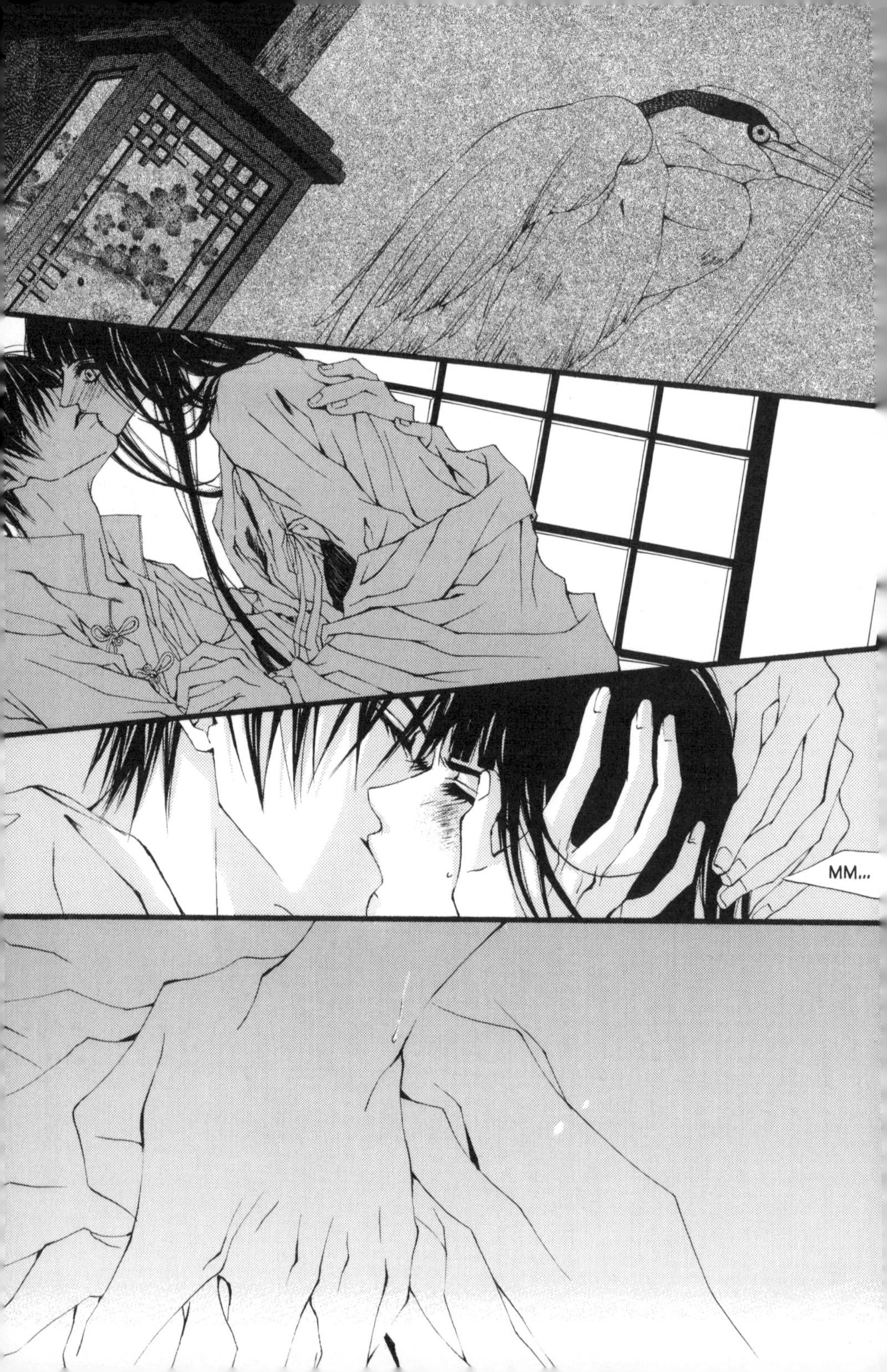
MM...

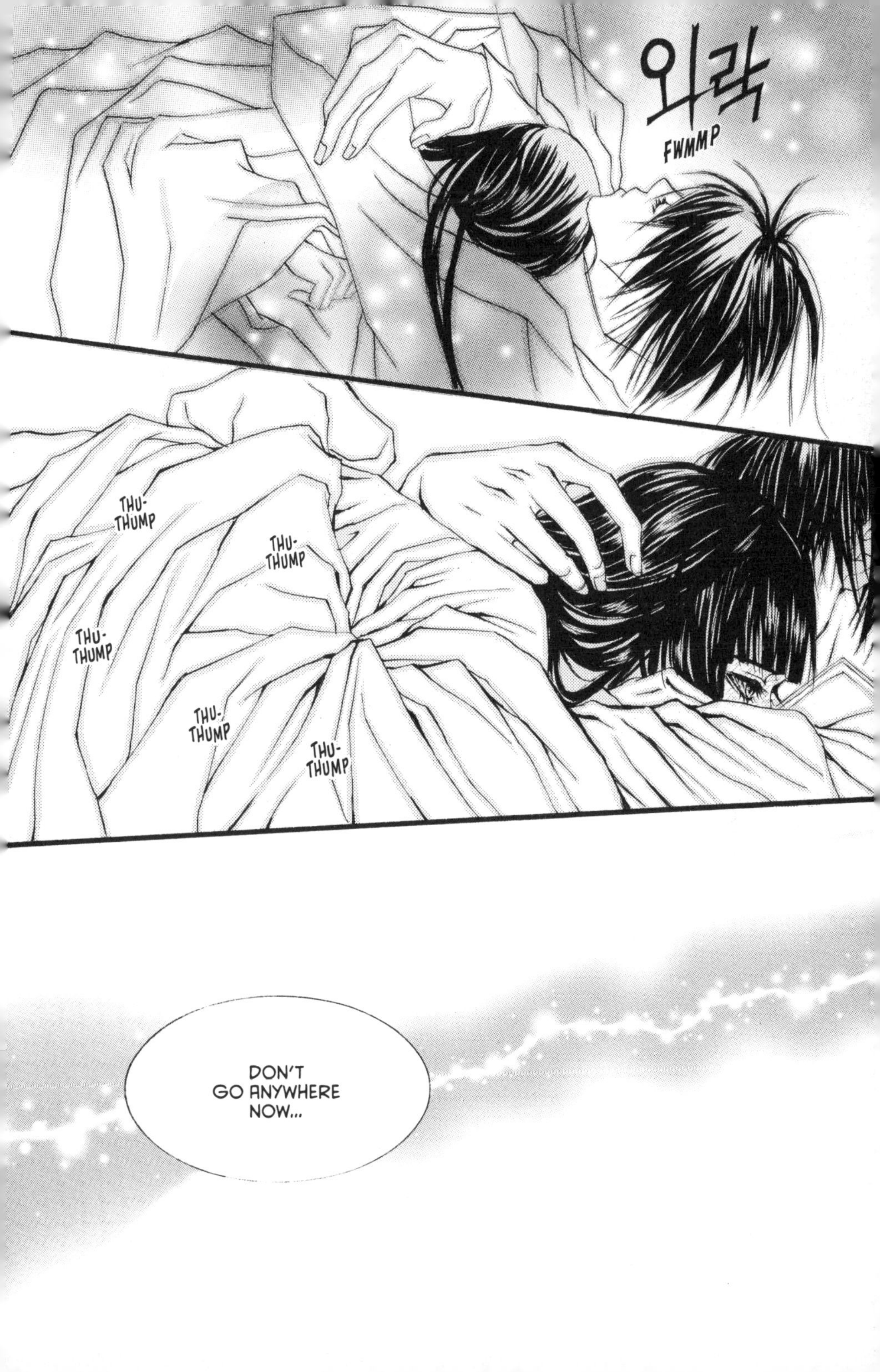

와락
FWMMP
THU-THUMP
THU-THUMP
THU-THUMP
THU-THUMP
THU-THUMP
DON'T GO ANYWHERE NOW...

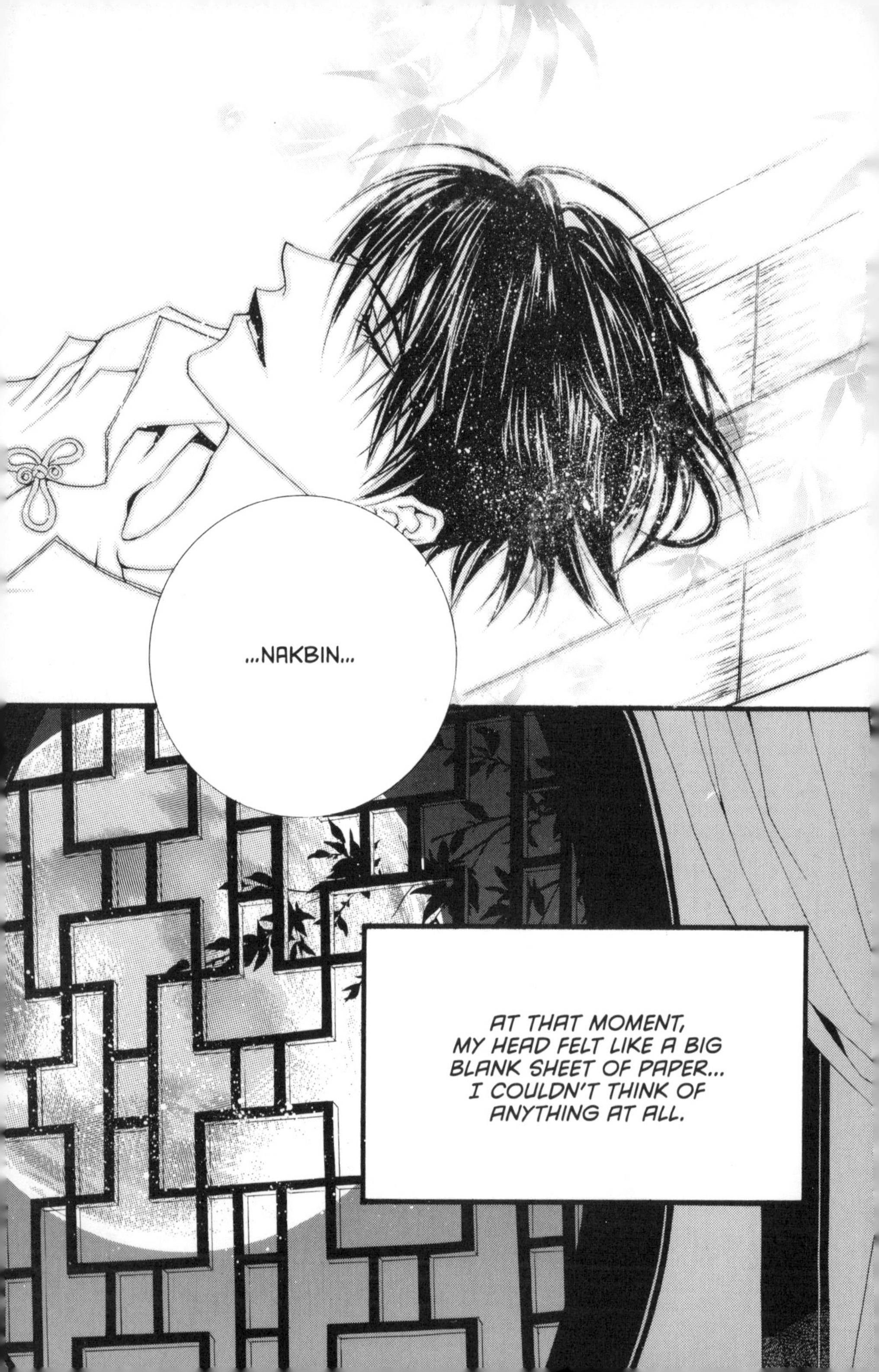
...NAKBIN...
AT THAT MOMENT, MY HEAD FELT LIKE A BIG BLANK SHEET OF PAPER... I COULDN'T THINK OF ANYTHING AT ALL.

BRIDE of the WATER GOD

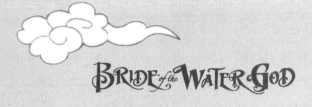

*"A man giving
a lady a comb as a gift
means he's proposing
for marriage."*

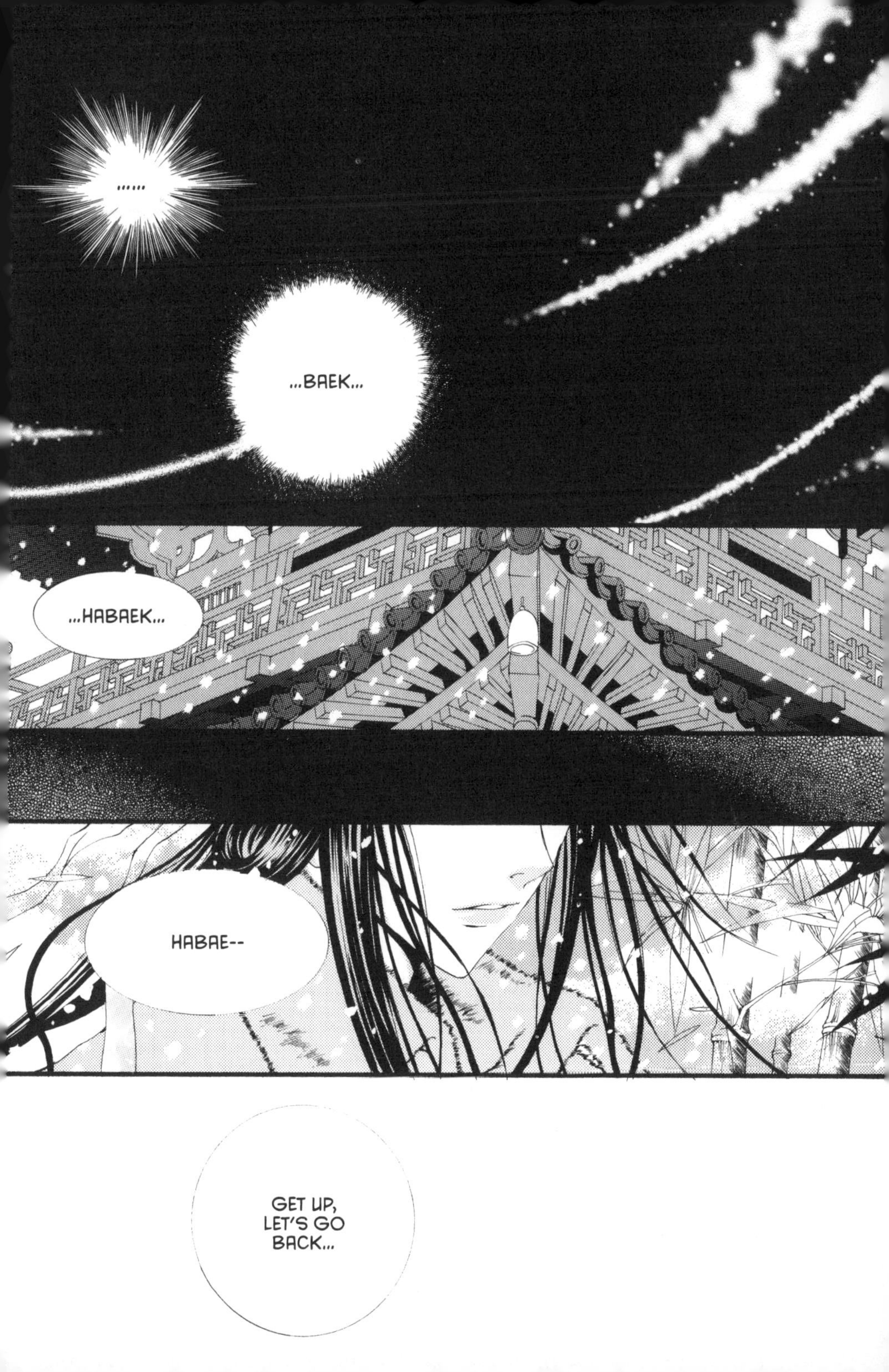
......
...BAEK...
...HABAEK...
HABAE--
GET UP, LET'S GO BACK...

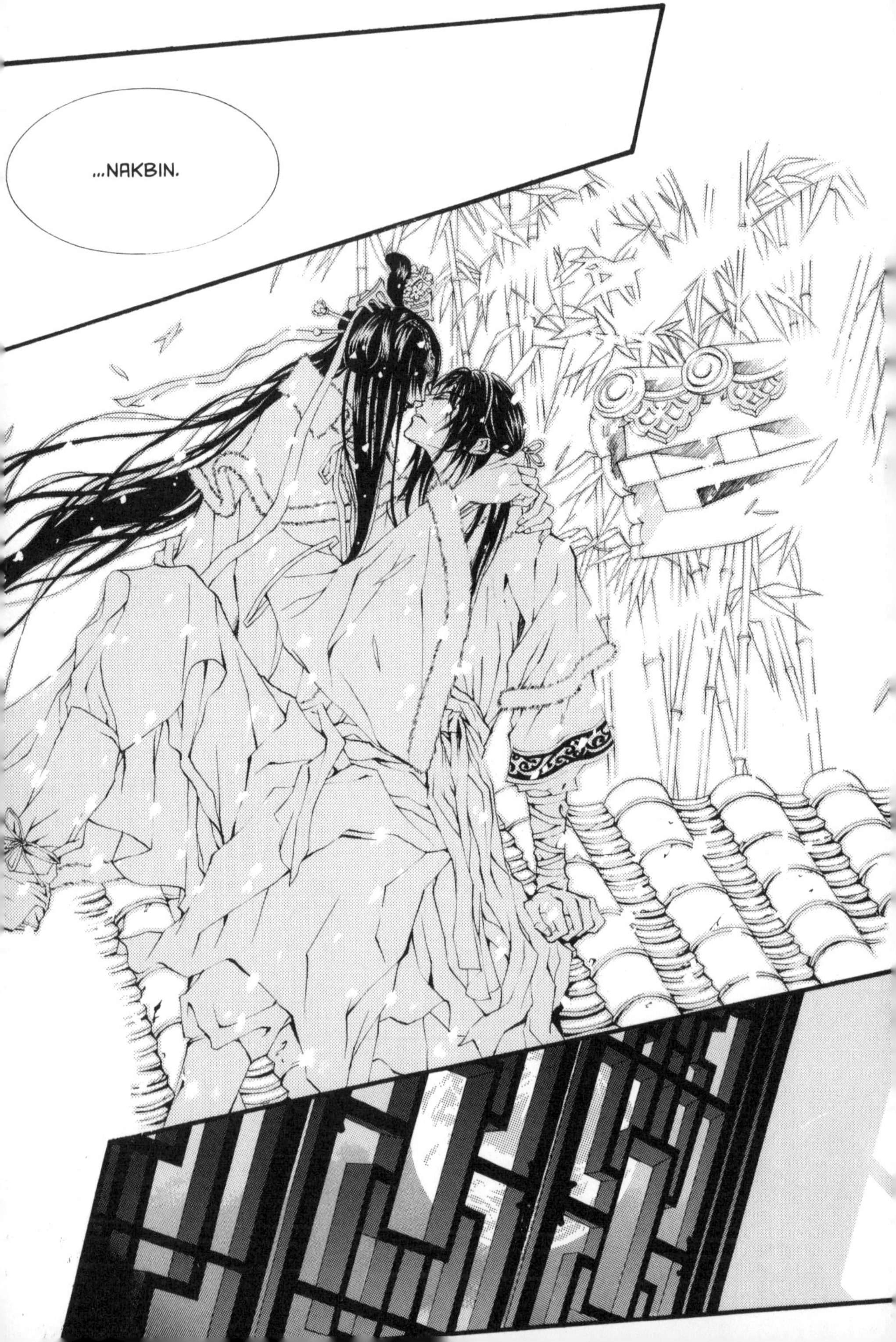
...NAKBIN.

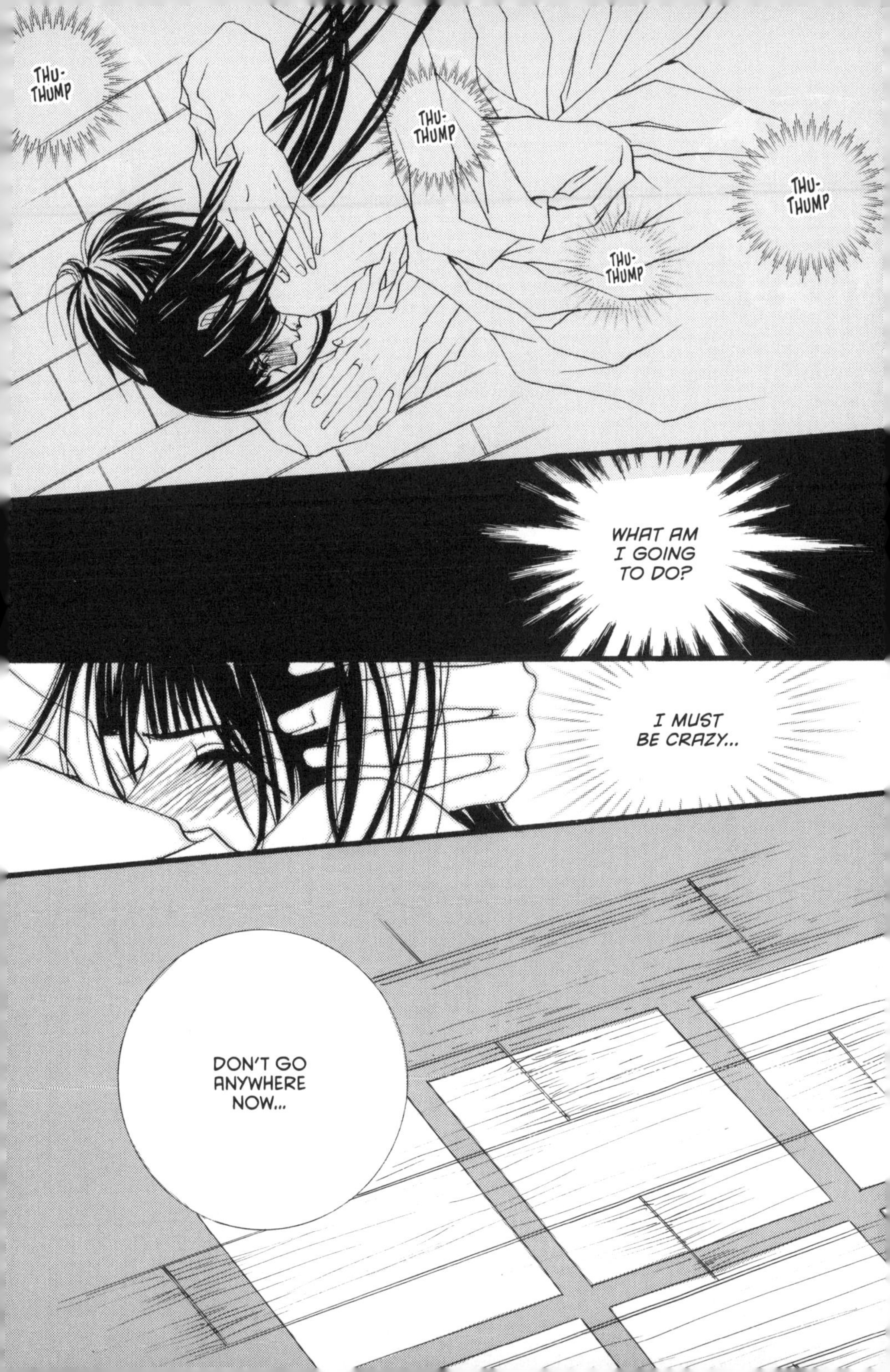
THU-THUMP
THU-THUMP
THU-THUMP
THU-THUMP
WHAT AM I GOING TO DO?
I MUST BE CRAZY...
DON'T GO ANYWHERE NOW...

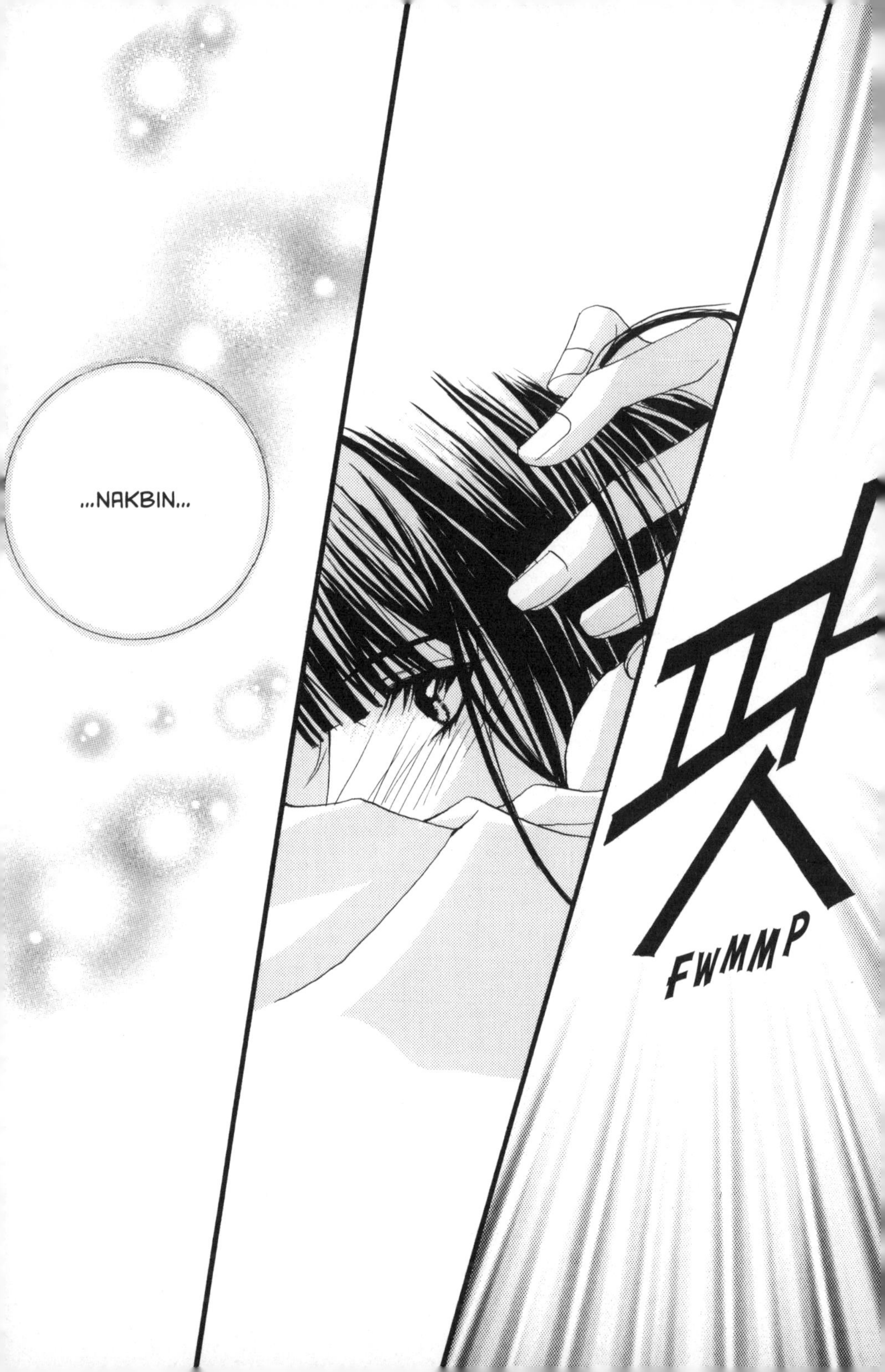
...NAKBIN...
FWMMP

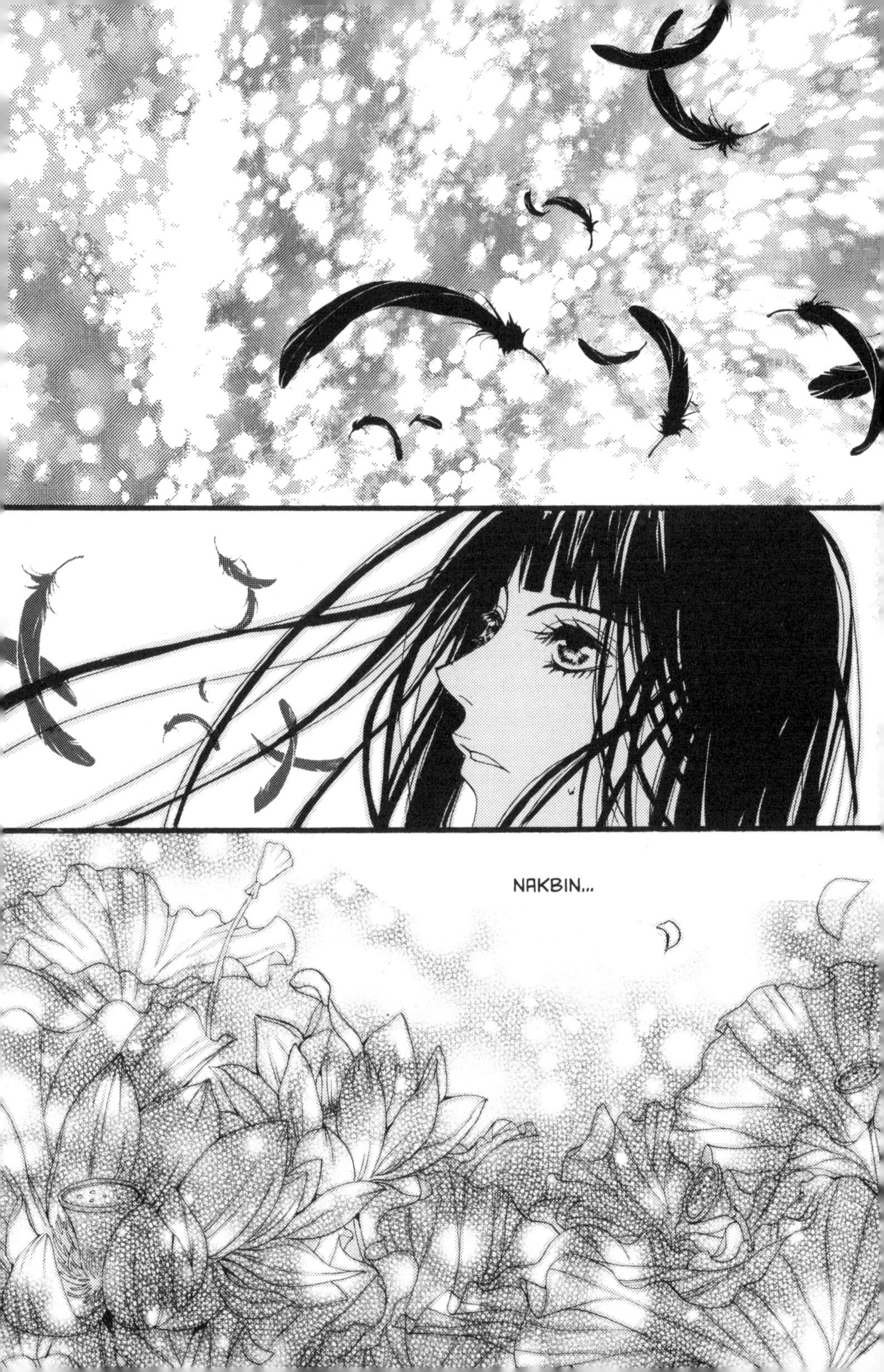
NAKBIN...

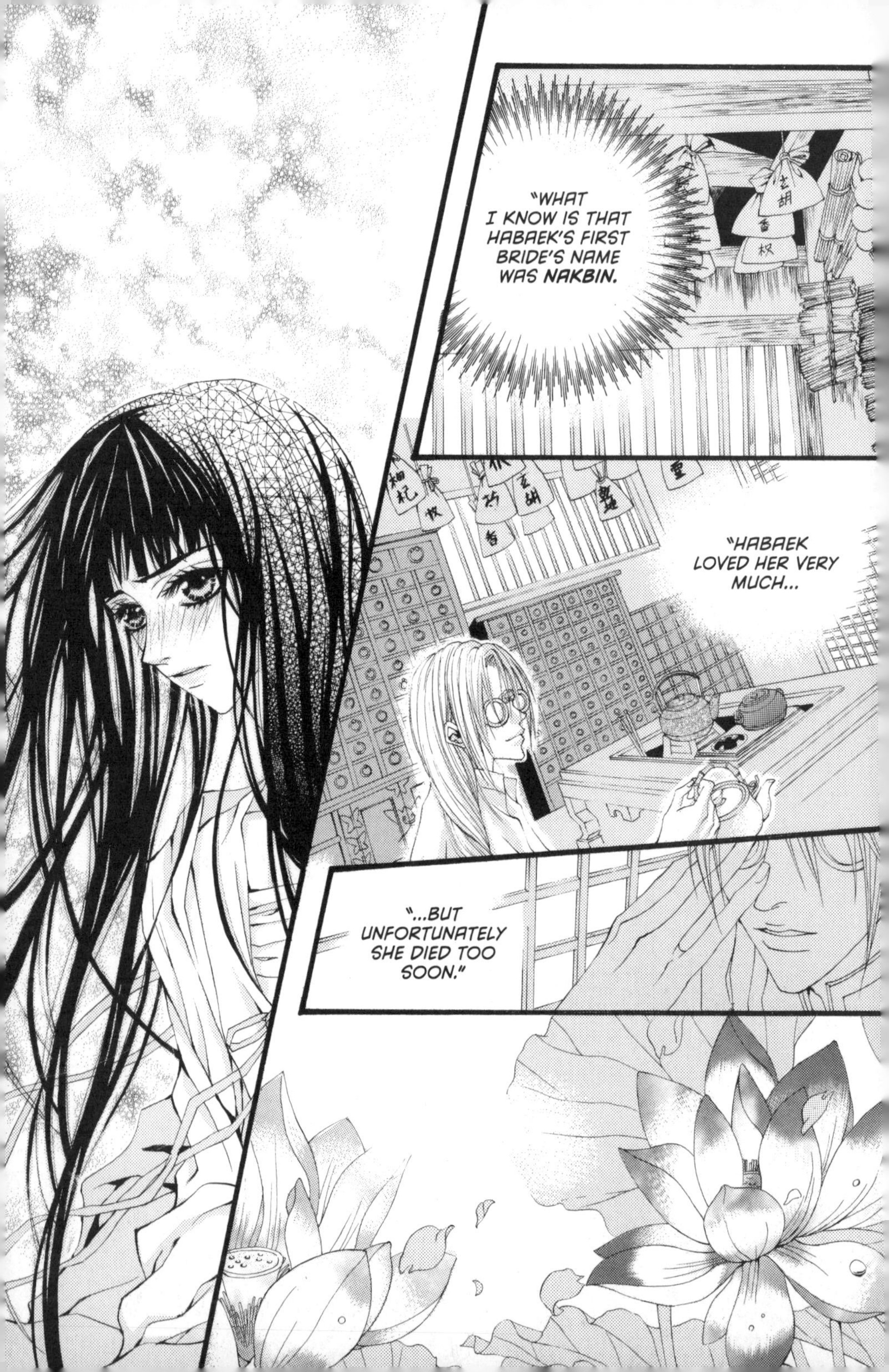
"WHAT I KNOW IS THAT HABAEK'S FIRST BRIDE'S NAME WAS NAKBIN.
"HABAEK LOVED HER VERY MUCH...
"...BUT UNFORTUNATELY SHE DIED TOO SOON."

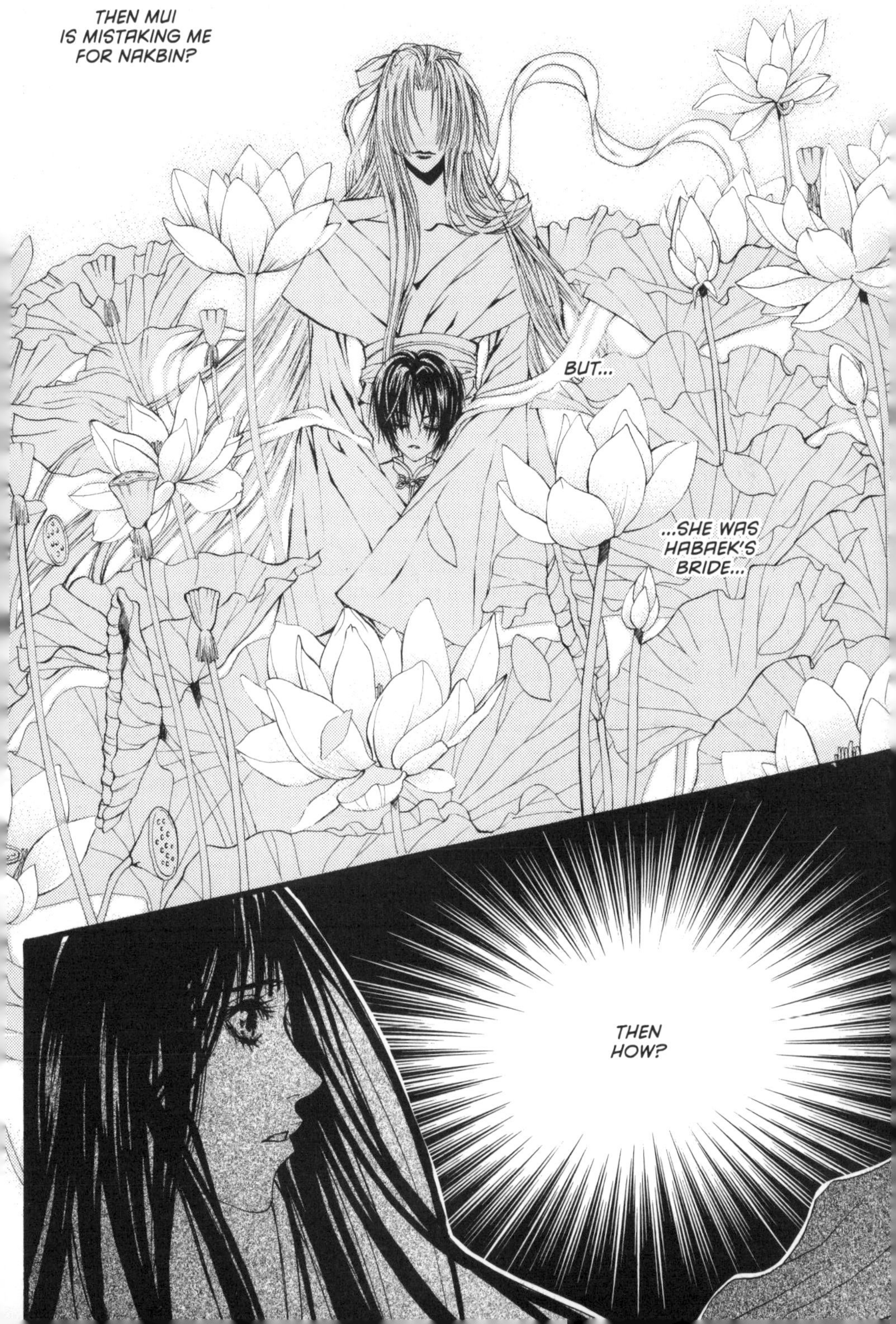
THEN MUI IS MISTAKING ME FOR NAKBIN?
BUT...
...SHE WAS HABAEK'S BRIDE...
THEN HOW?

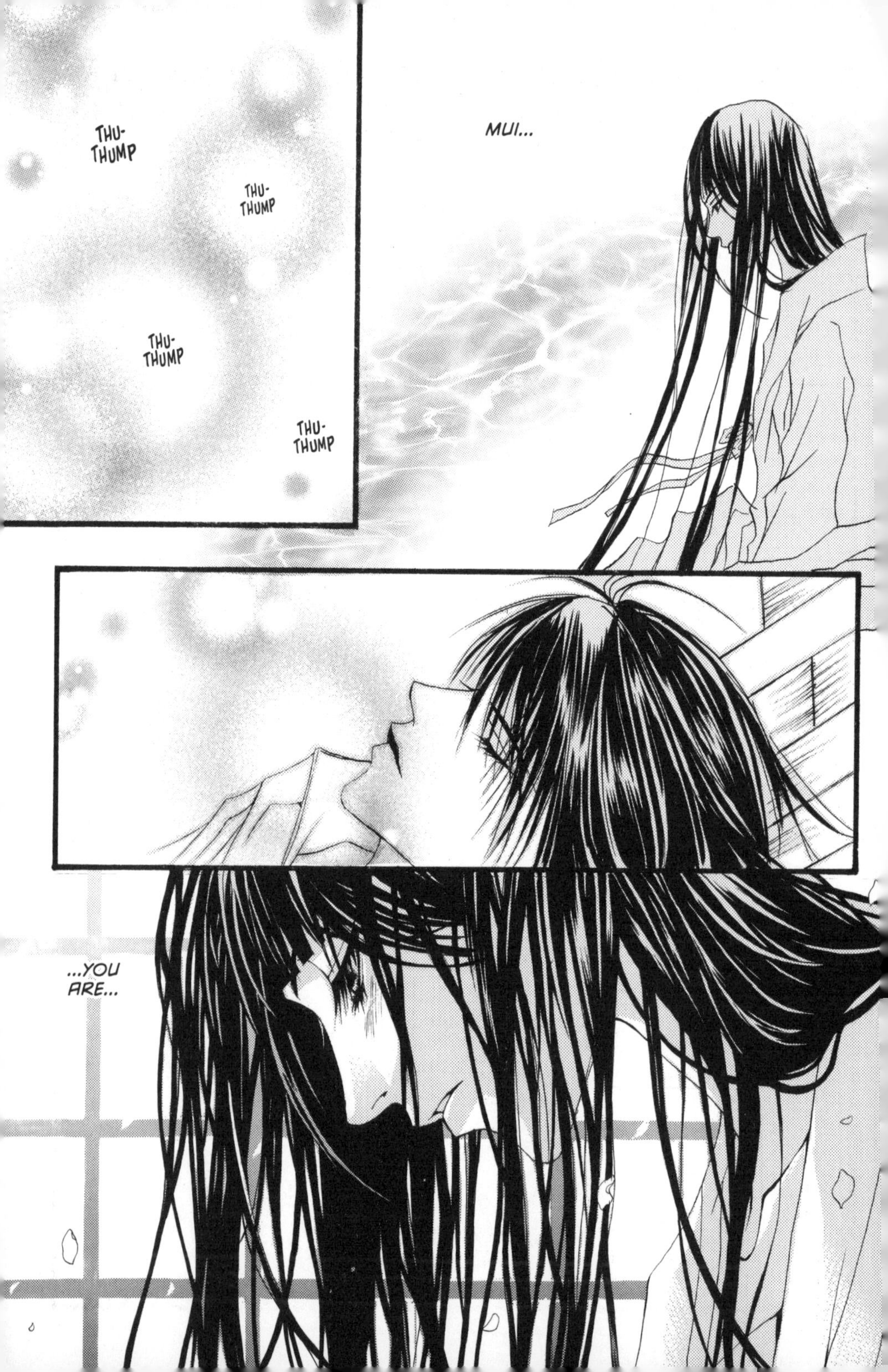
MUI...
THU-THUMP
THU-THUMP
THU-THUMP
THU-THUMP
...YOU ARE...

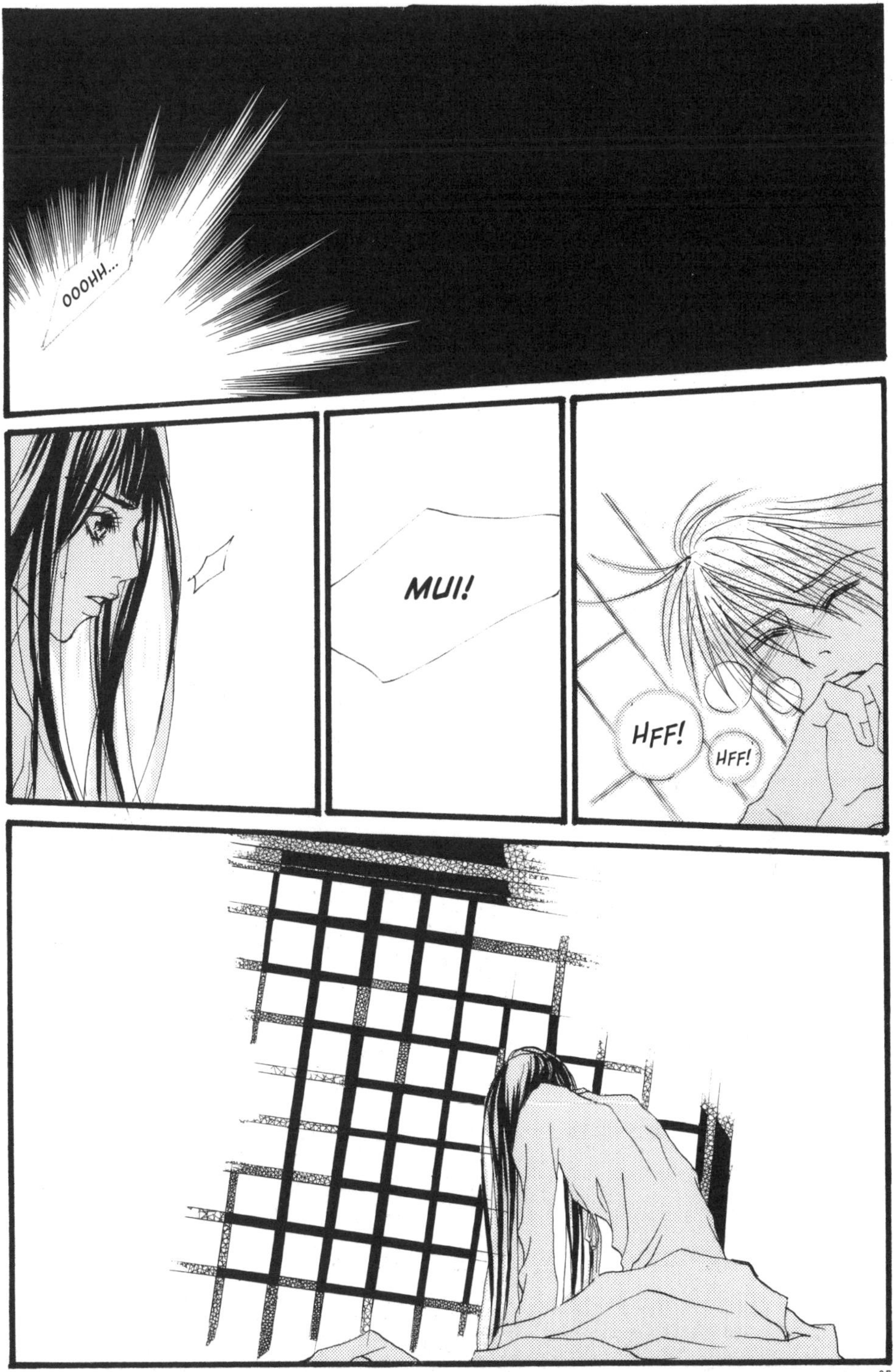
OOOHH...
MUI!
HFF!
HFF!

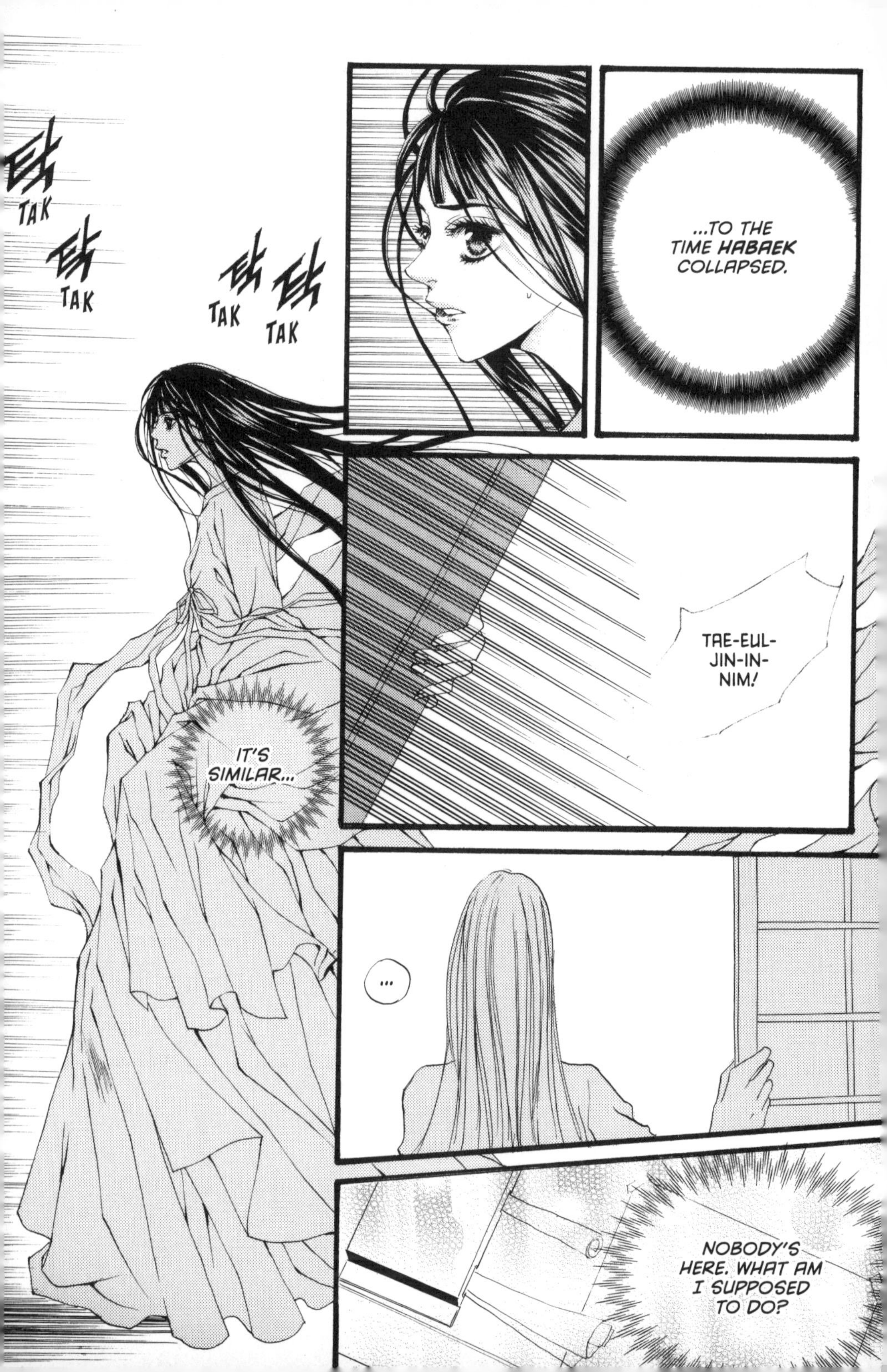

탁 TAK
탁 TAK
탁 TAK
탁 TAK
...TO THE TIME HABAEK COLLAPSED.
TAE-EUL-JIN-IN-NIM!
IT'S SIMILAR...
...
NOBODY'S HERE. WHAT AM I SUPPOSED TO DO?

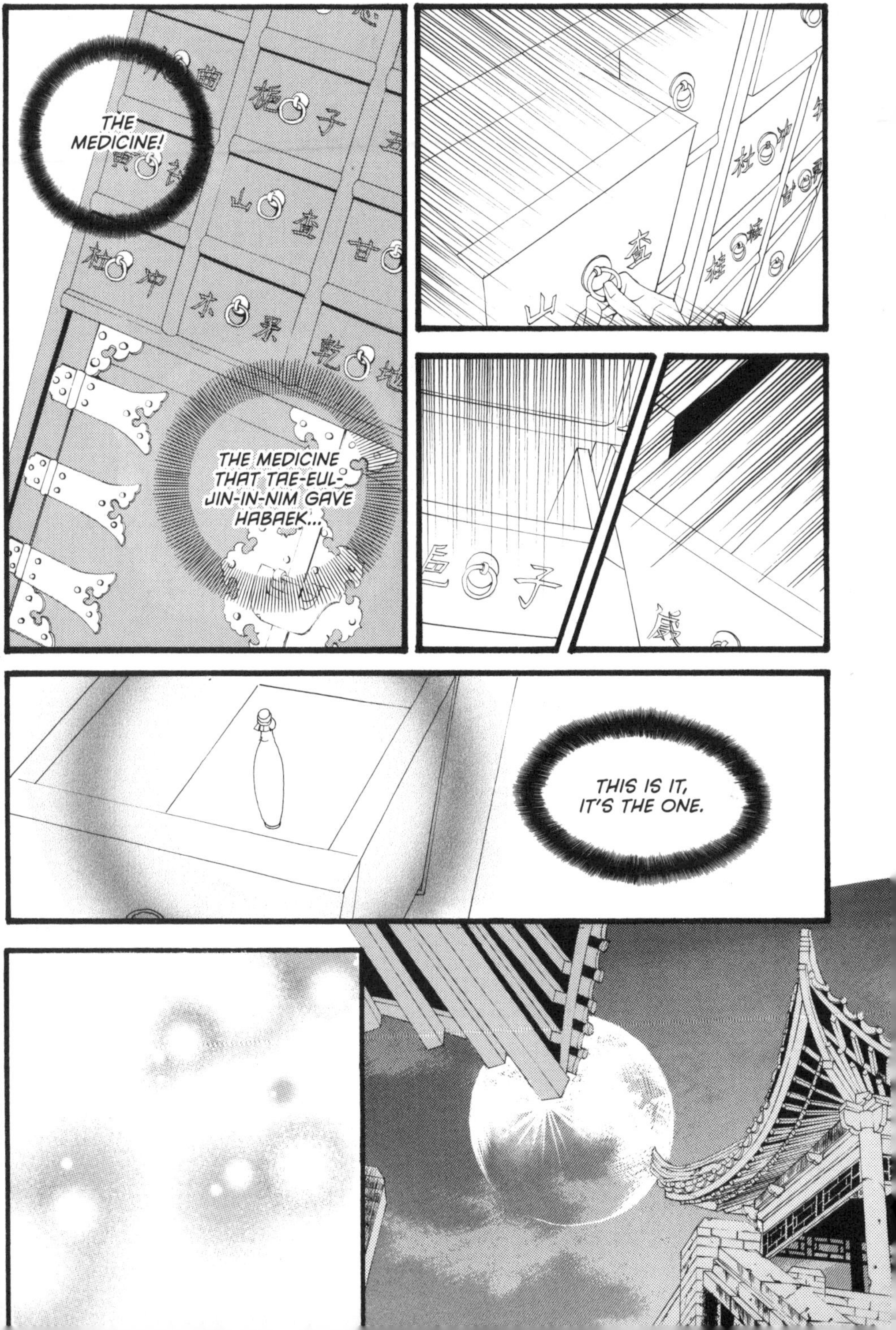
THE MEDICINE!
THE MEDICINE THAT TAE-EUL-JIN-IN-NIM GAVE HABAEK...
THIS IS IT, IT'S THE ONE.

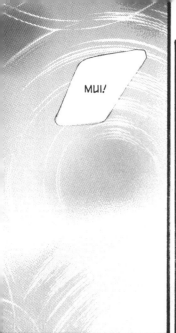

MUI!

TRY TO GET UP.

TAKE THIS.

OOH...

KクッッKクッッ

DRIBBLE

ピッ ピッ

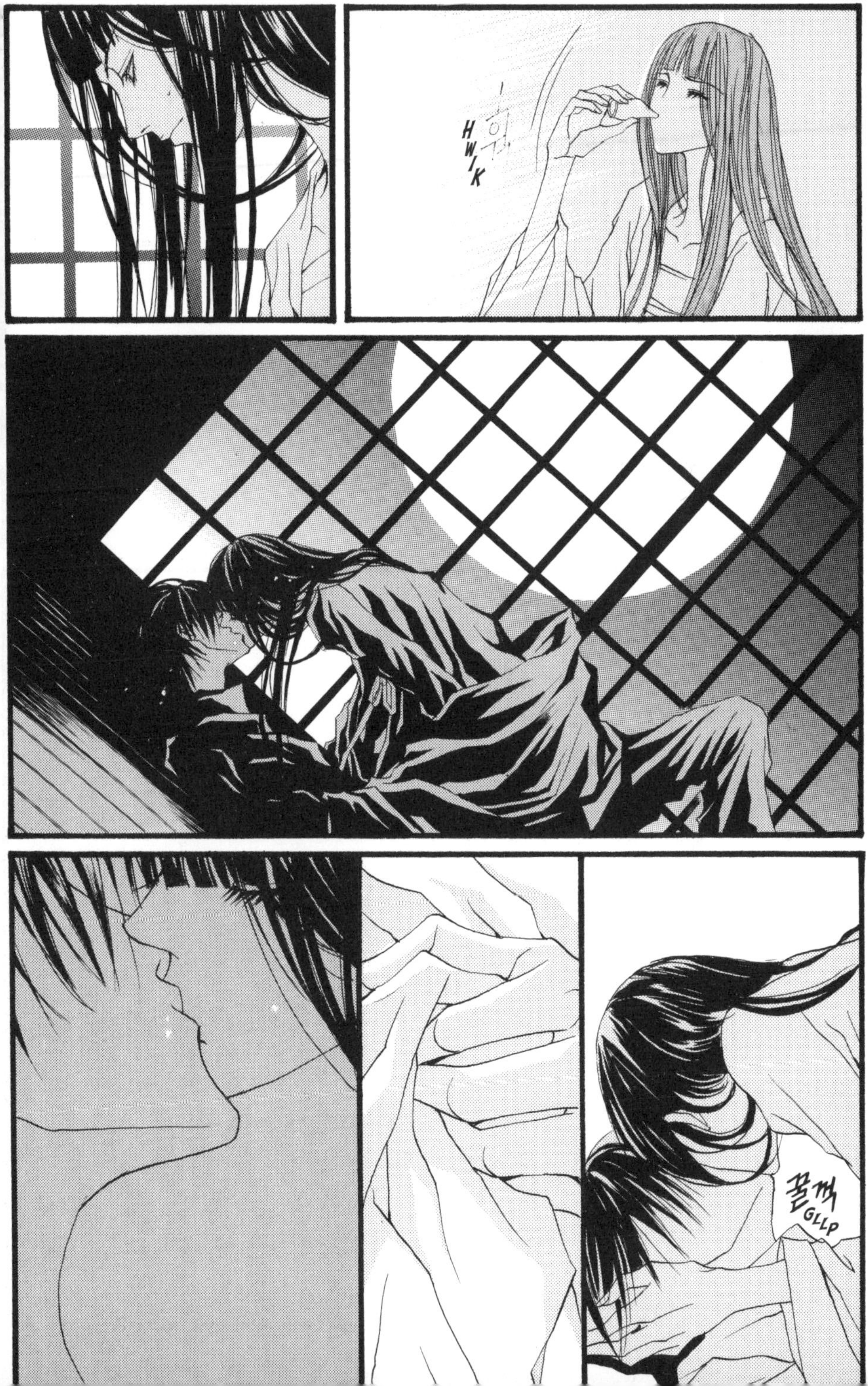
휘익
HWIK
꿀꺽
GLLP

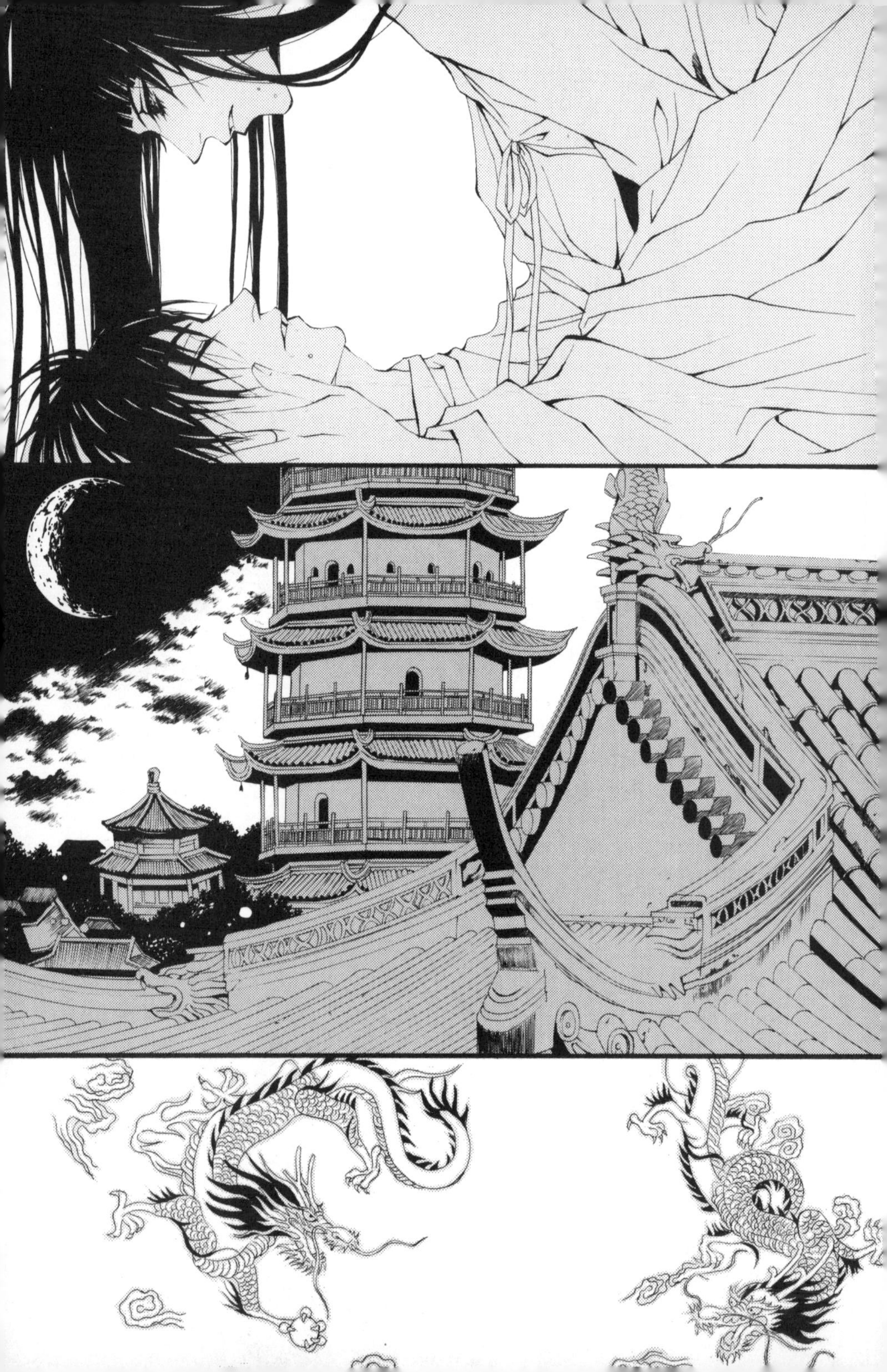

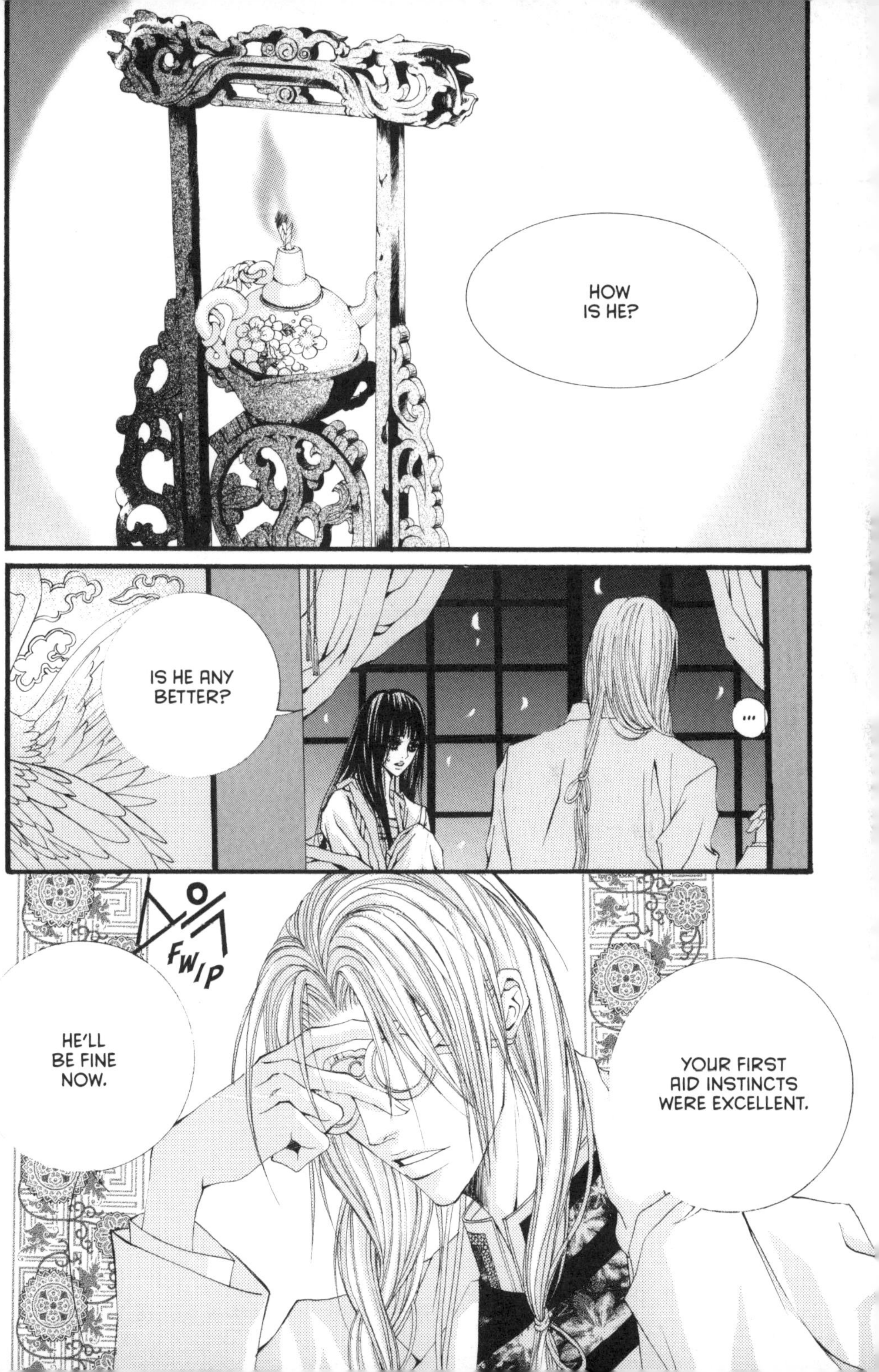
HOW IS HE?
IS HE ANY BETTER?
...
FWIP
HE'LL BE FINE NOW.
YOUR FIRST AID INSTINCTS WERE EXCELLENT.

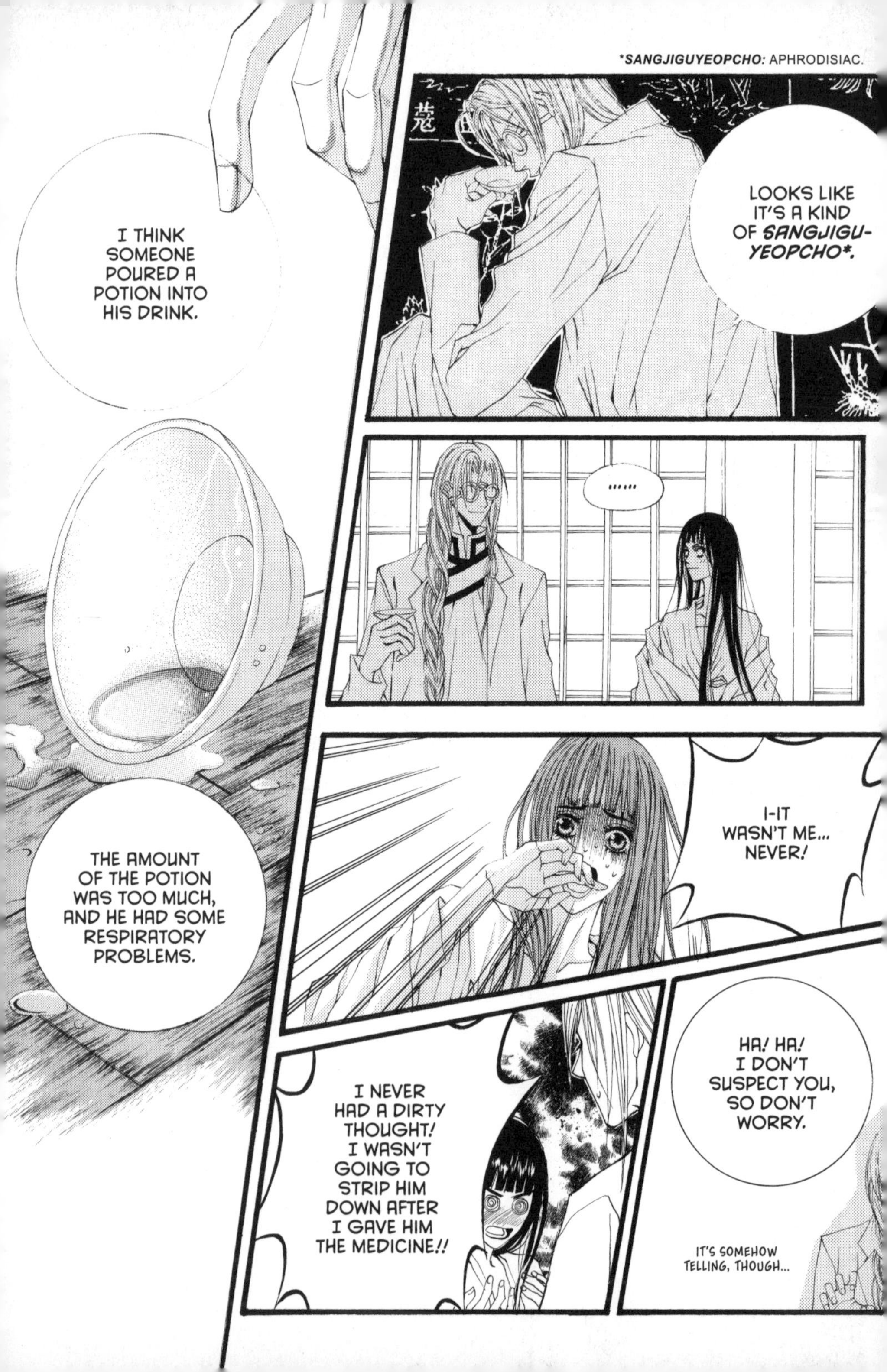
I THINK SOMEONE POURED A POTION INTO HIS DRINK.
LOOKS LIKE IT'S A KIND OF *SANGJIGU-YEOPCHO**.
......
THE AMOUNT OF THE POTION WAS TOO MUCH, AND HE HAD SOME RESPIRATORY PROBLEMS.
I-IT WASN'T ME... NEVER!
I NEVER HAD A DIRTY THOUGHT! I WASN'T GOING TO STRIP HIM DOWN AFTER I GAVE HIM THE MEDICINE!!
HA! HA! I DON'T SUSPECT YOU, SO DON'T WORRY.
IT'S SOMEHOW TELLING, THOUGH...

**SANGJIGUYEOPCHO:* APHRODISIAC.

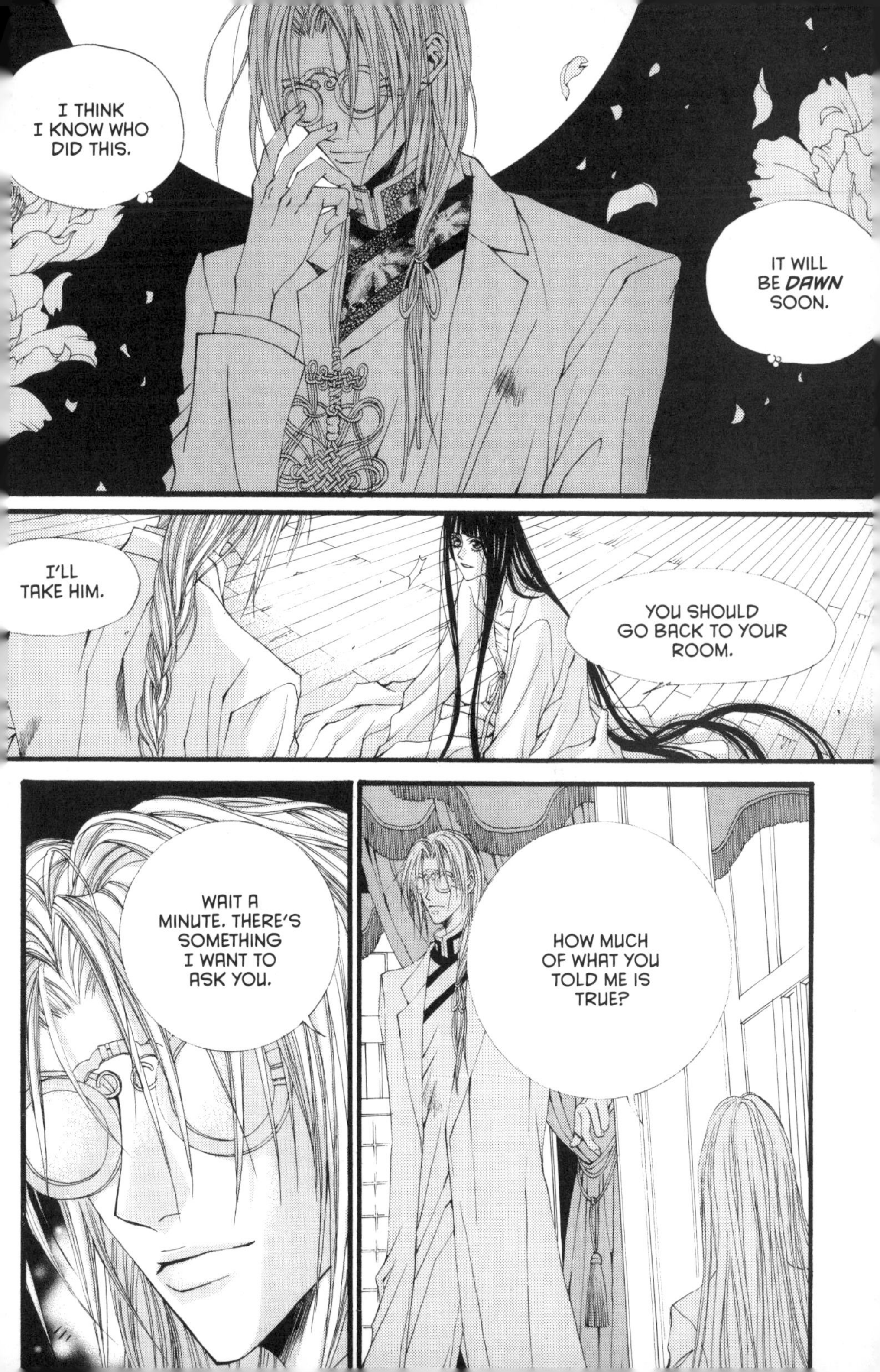
I THINK I KNOW WHO DID THIS.
IT WILL BE DAWN SOON.
I'LL TAKE HIM.
YOU SHOULD GO BACK TO YOUR ROOM.
WAIT A MINUTE. THERE'S SOMETHING I WANT TO ASK YOU.
HOW MUCH OF WHAT YOU TOLD ME IS TRUE?

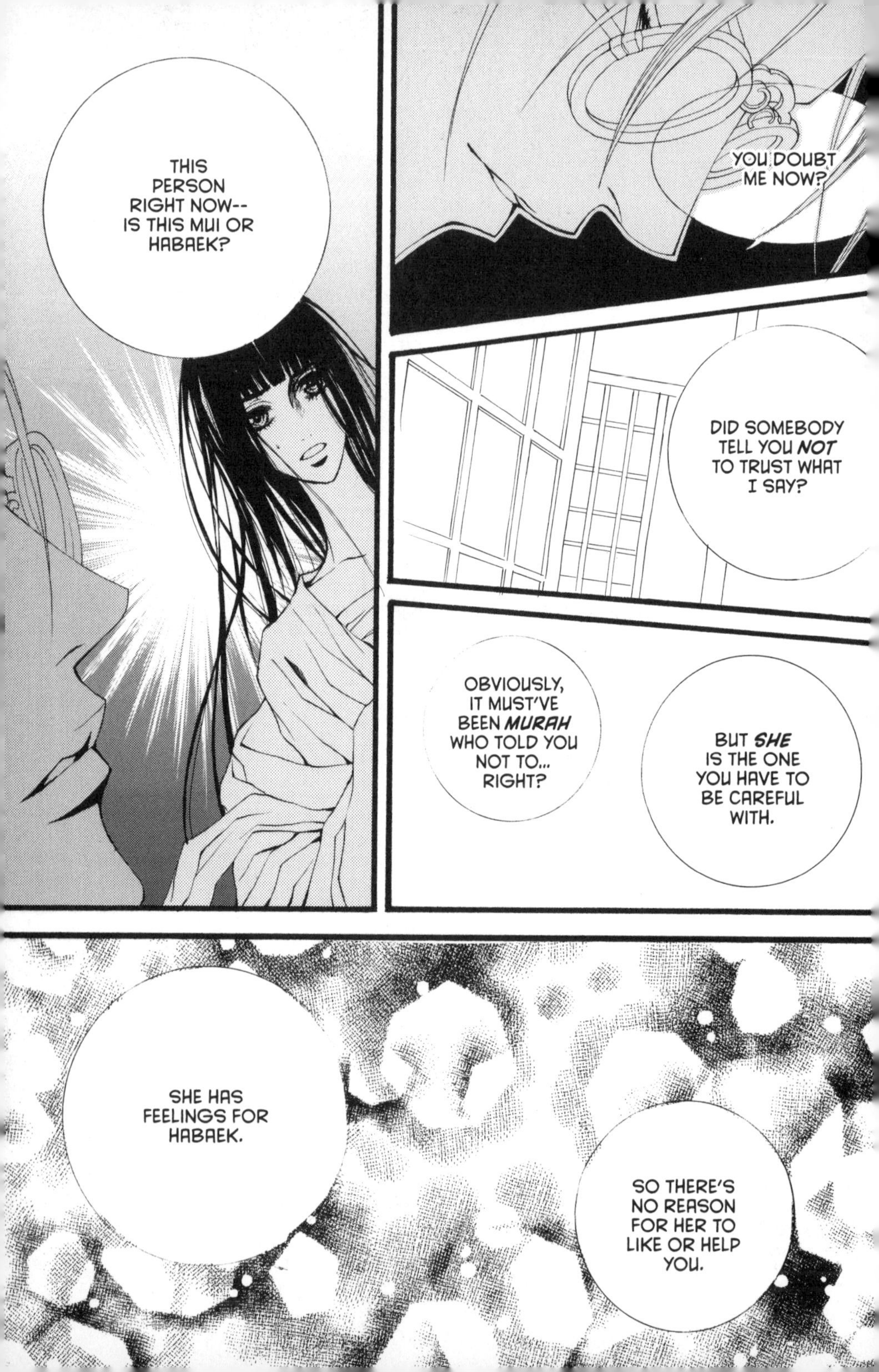
YOU DOUBT ME NOW?
THIS PERSON RIGHT NOW-- IS THIS MUI OR HABAEK?
DID SOMEBODY TELL YOU *NOT* TO TRUST WHAT I SAY?
BUT *SHE* IS THE ONE YOU HAVE TO BE CAREFUL WITH.
OBVIOUSLY, IT MUST'VE BEEN *MURAH* WHO TOLD YOU NOT TO... RIGHT?
SO THERE'S NO REASON FOR HER TO LIKE OR HELP YOU.
SHE HAS FEELINGS FOR HABAEK.

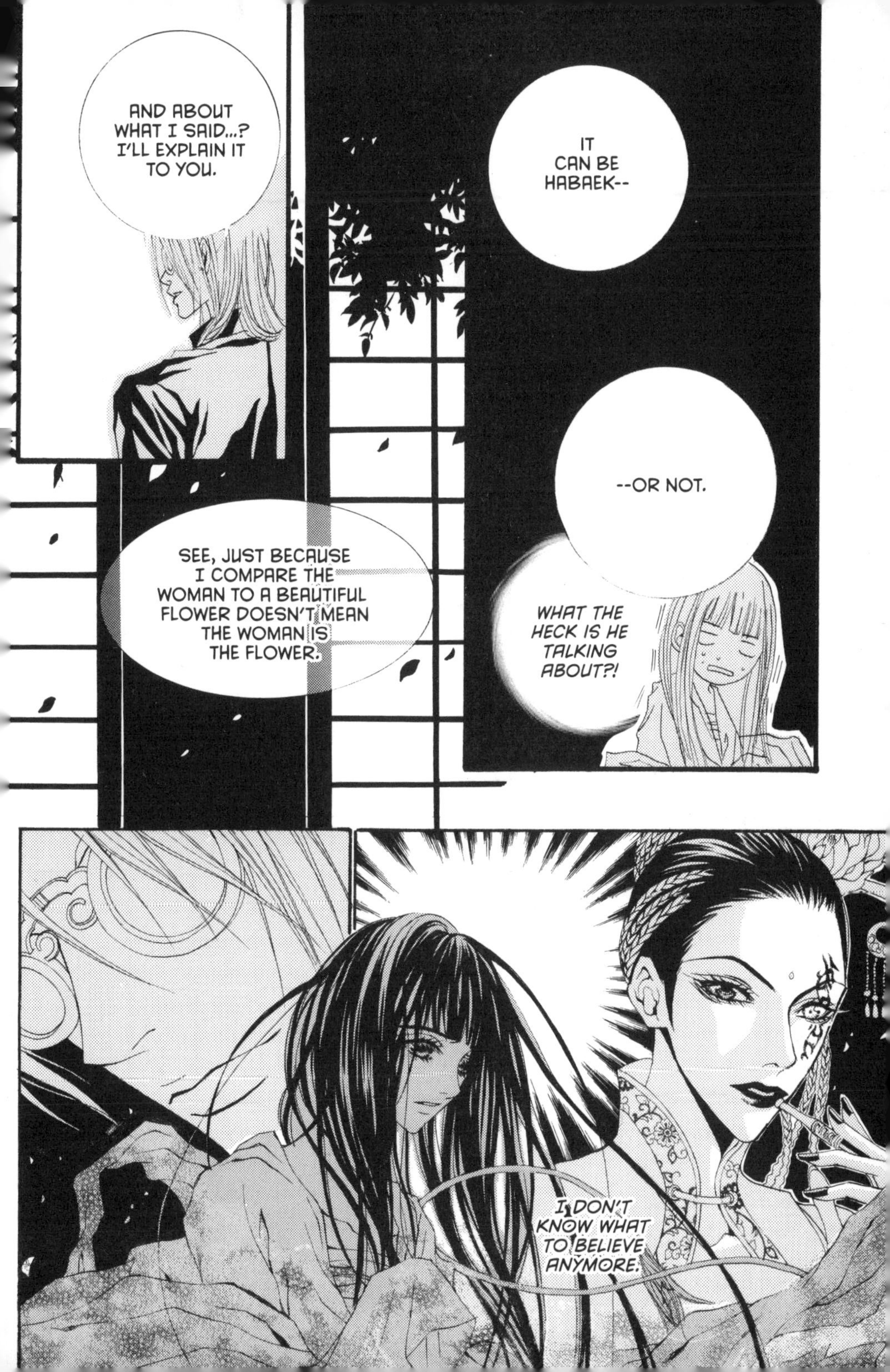
AND ABOUT WHAT I SAID...? I'LL EXPLAIN IT TO YOU.
IT CAN BE HABAEK--
--OR NOT.
SEE, JUST BECAUSE I COMPARE THE WOMAN TO A BEAUTIFUL FLOWER DOESN'T MEAN THE WOMAN IS THE FLOWER.
WHAT THE HECK IS HE TALKING ABOUT?!
I DON'T KNOW WHAT TO BELIEVE ANYMORE.

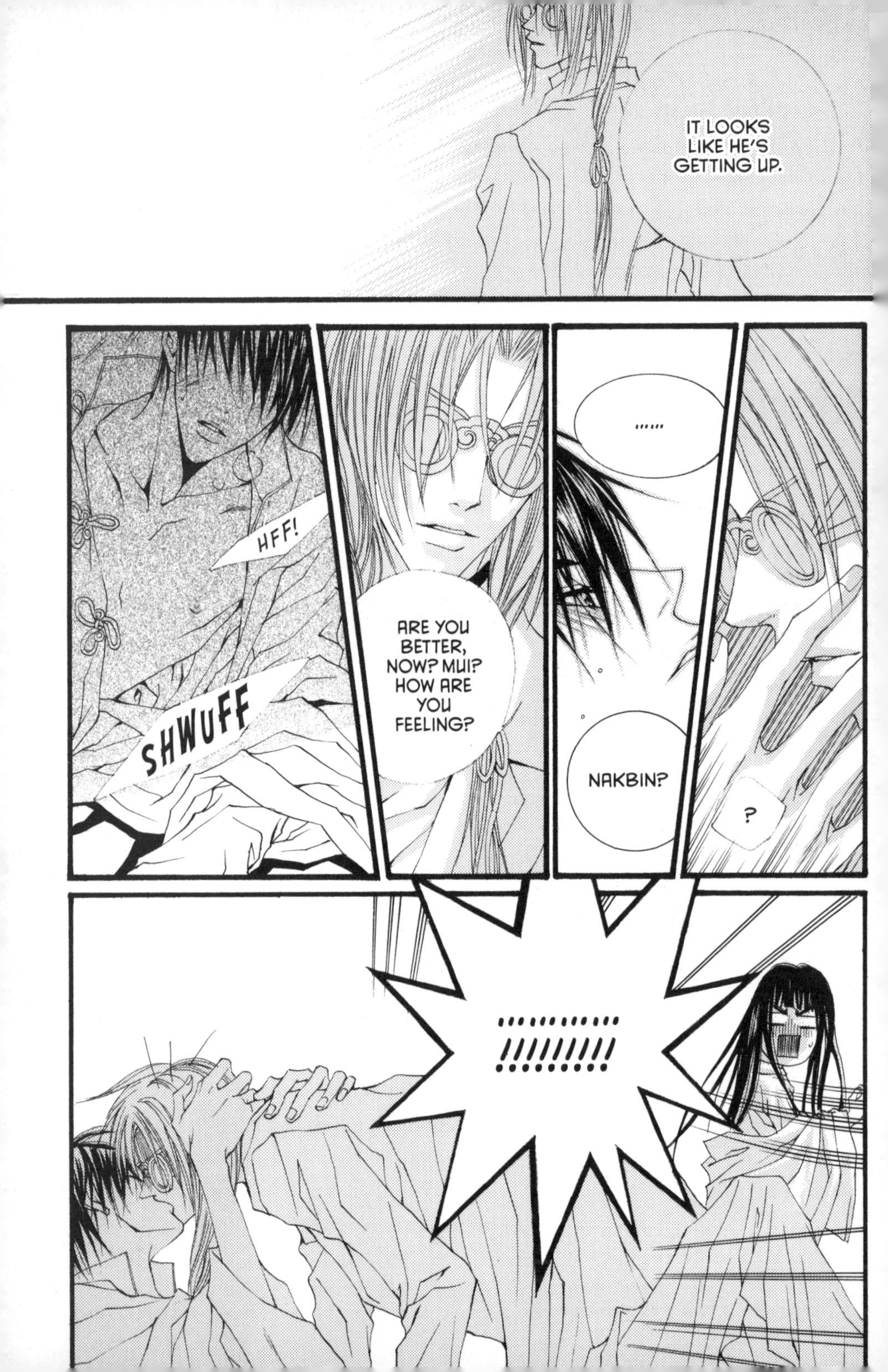
IT LOOKS LIKE HE'S GETTING UP.
?
......
NAKBIN?
ARE YOU BETTER, NOW? MUI? HOW ARE YOU FEELING?
HFF!
SHWUFF
!!!!!!!!!

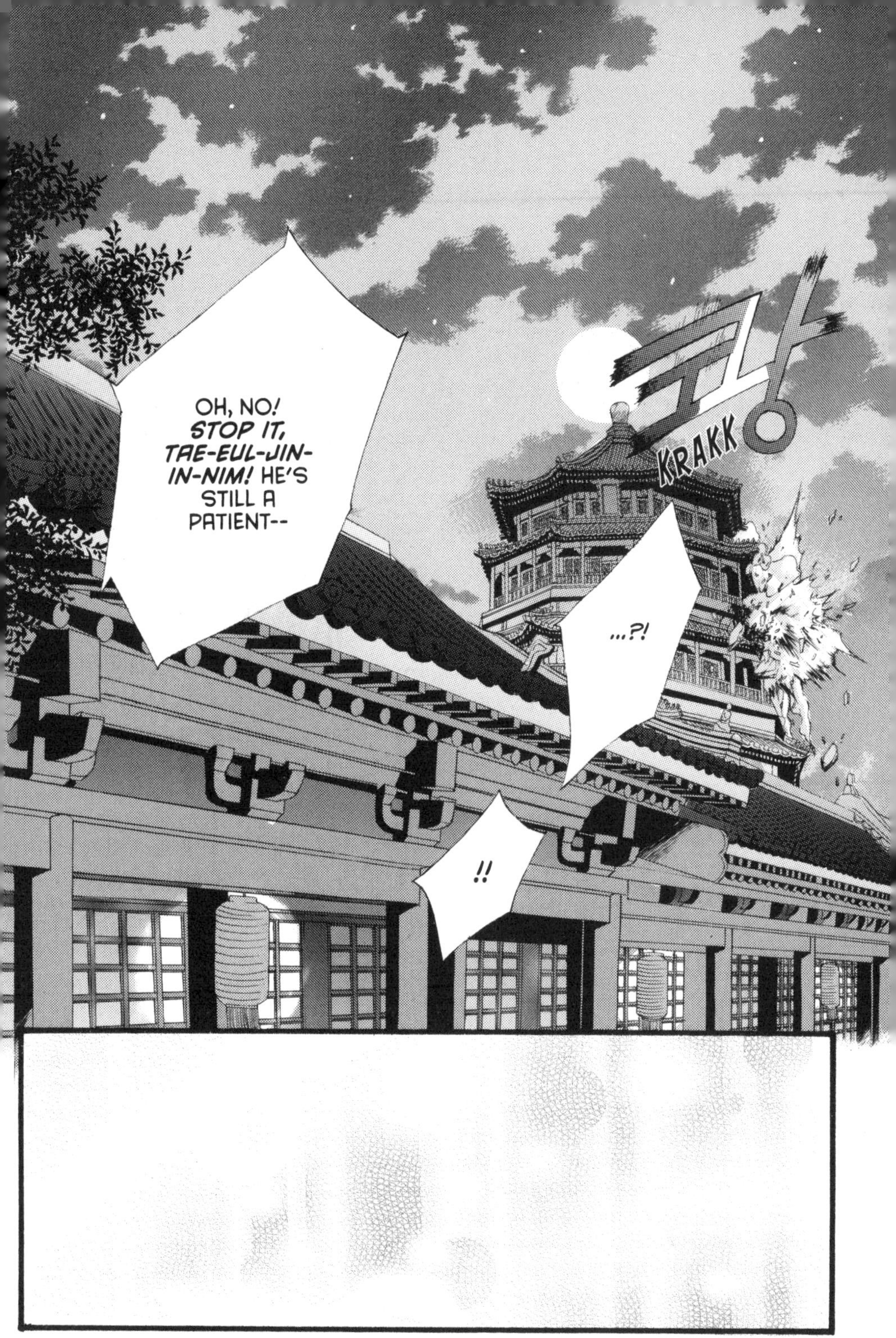
OH, NO! *STOP IT, TAE-EUL-JIN-IN-NIM!* HE'S STILL A PATIENT--
KRAKK
...?!
!!

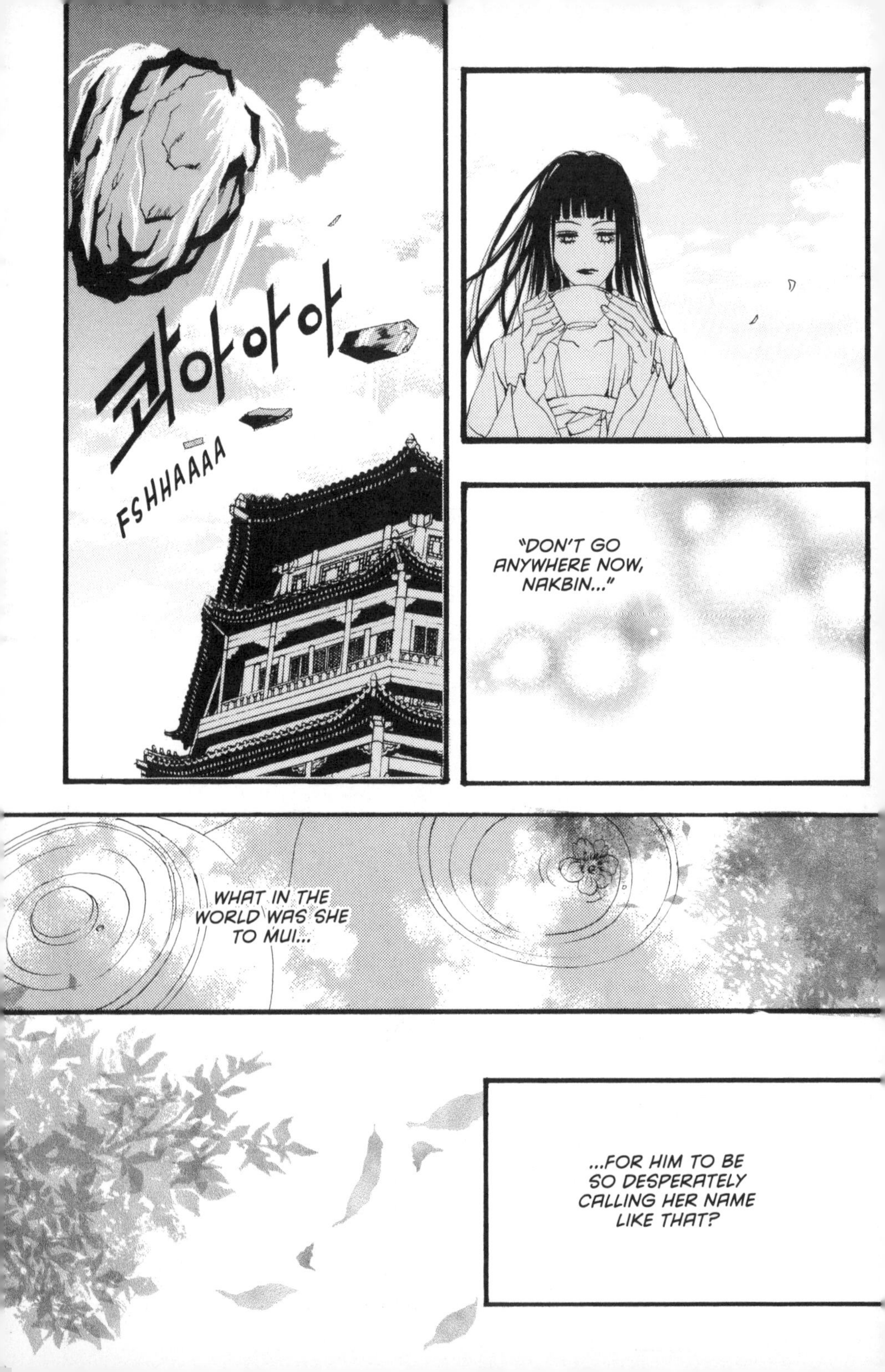
콰아아아
FSHHAAAA
"DON'T GO ANYWHERE NOW, NAKBIN..."
WHAT IN THE WORLD WAS SHE TO MUI...
...FOR HIM TO BE SO DESPERATELY CALLING HER NAME LIKE THAT?

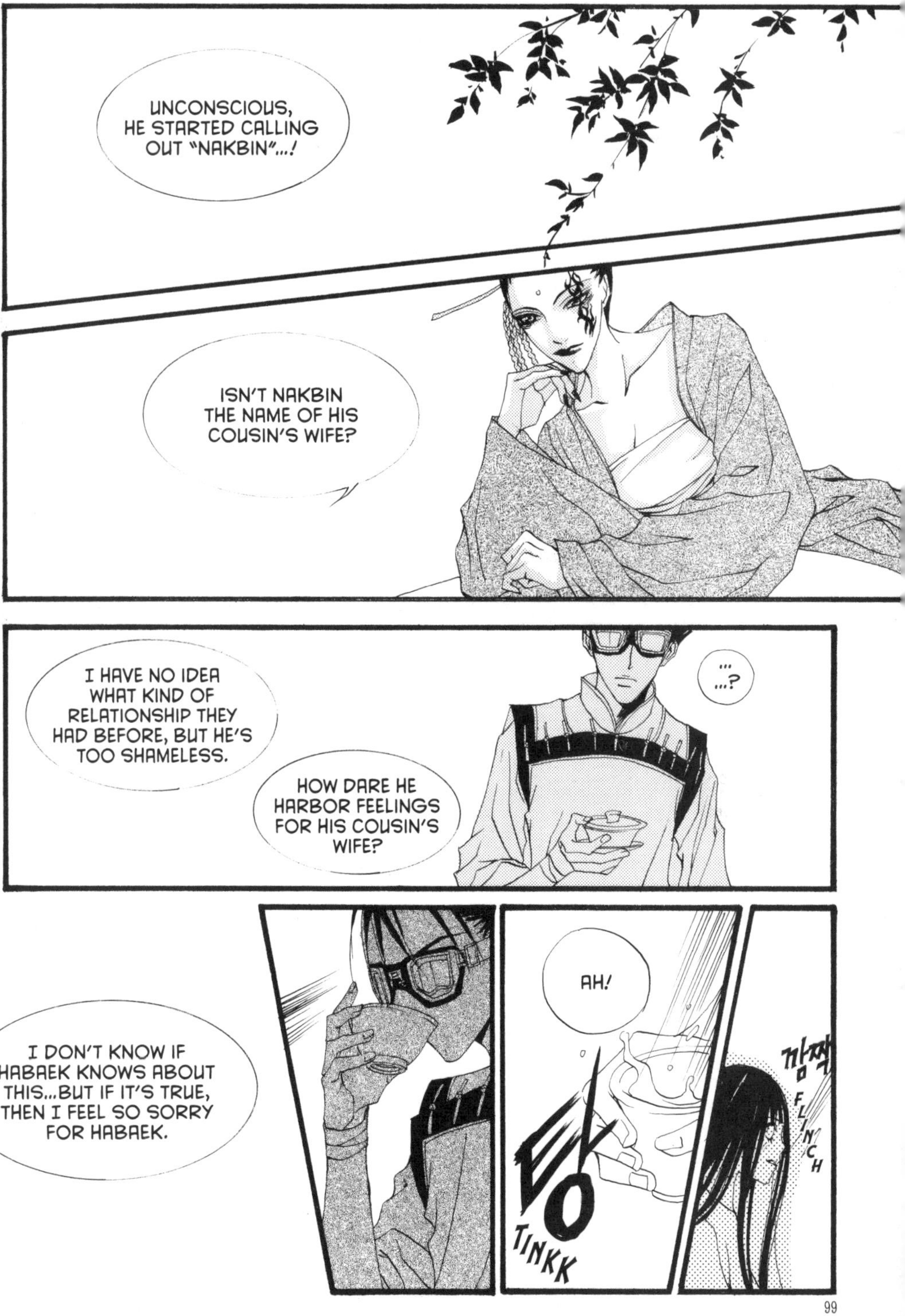
UNCONSCIOUS, HE STARTED CALLING OUT "NAKBIN"...!
ISN'T NAKBIN THE NAME OF HIS COUSIN'S WIFE?
I HAVE NO IDEA WHAT KIND OF RELATIONSHIP THEY HAD BEFORE, BUT HE'S TOO SHAMELESS.
HOW DARE HE HARBOR FEELINGS FOR HIS COUSIN'S WIFE?
... ...?
I DON'T KNOW IF HABAEK KNOWS ABOUT THIS...BUT IF IT'S TRUE, THEN I FEEL SO SORRY FOR HABAEK.
AH!
TINKK
깜짝
FLINCH

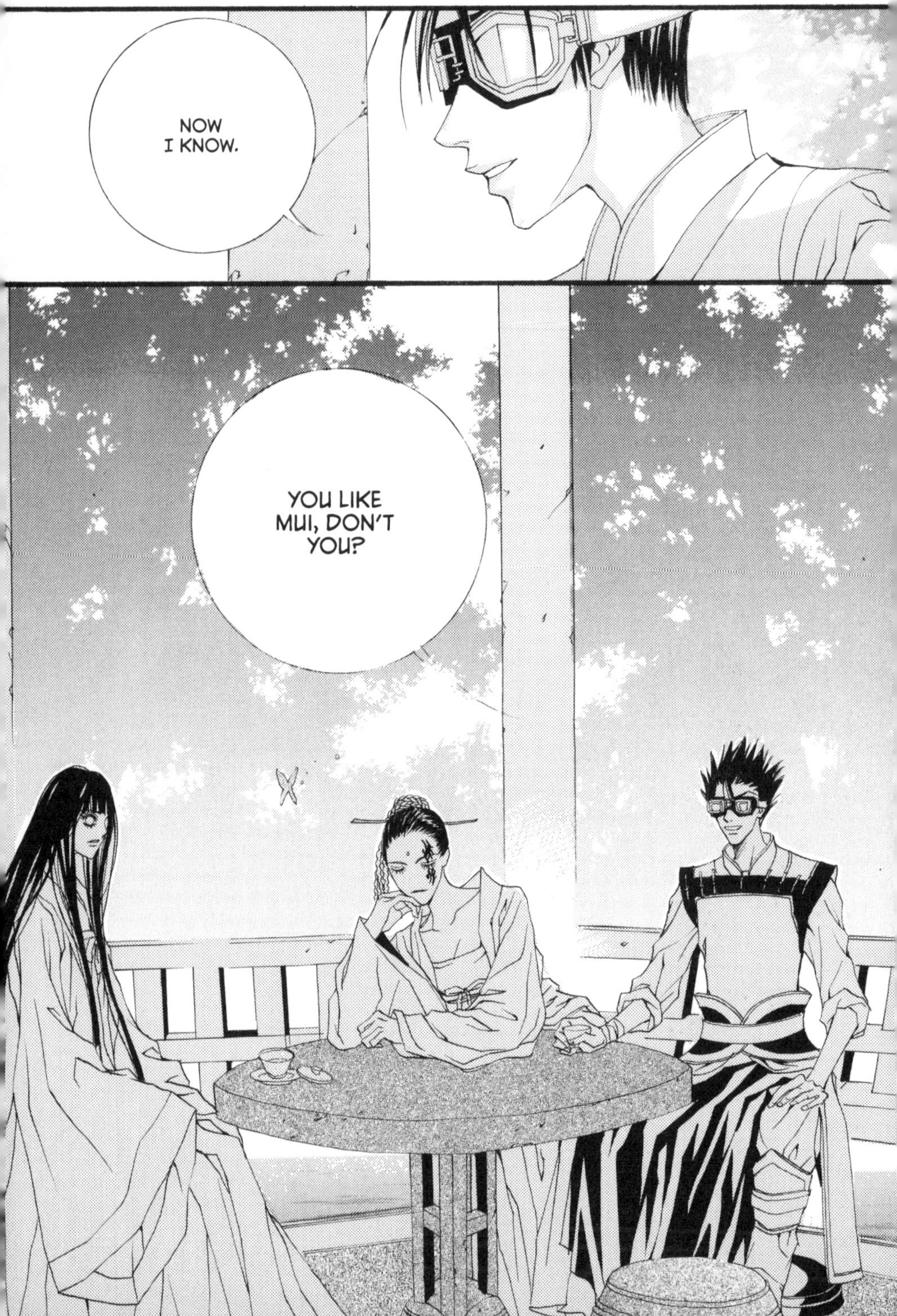
NOW
I KNOW.
YOU LIKE
MUI, DON'T
YOU?

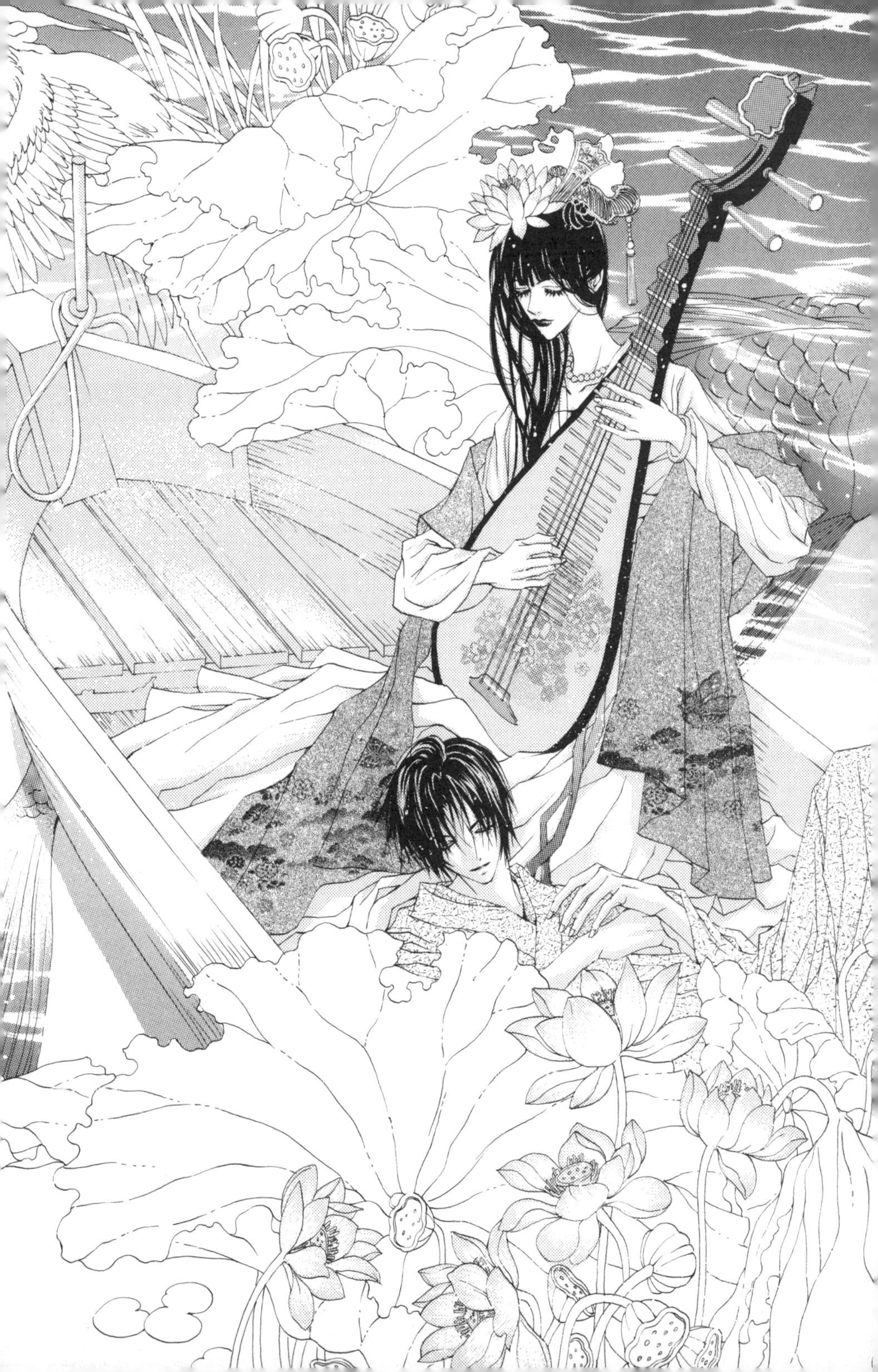

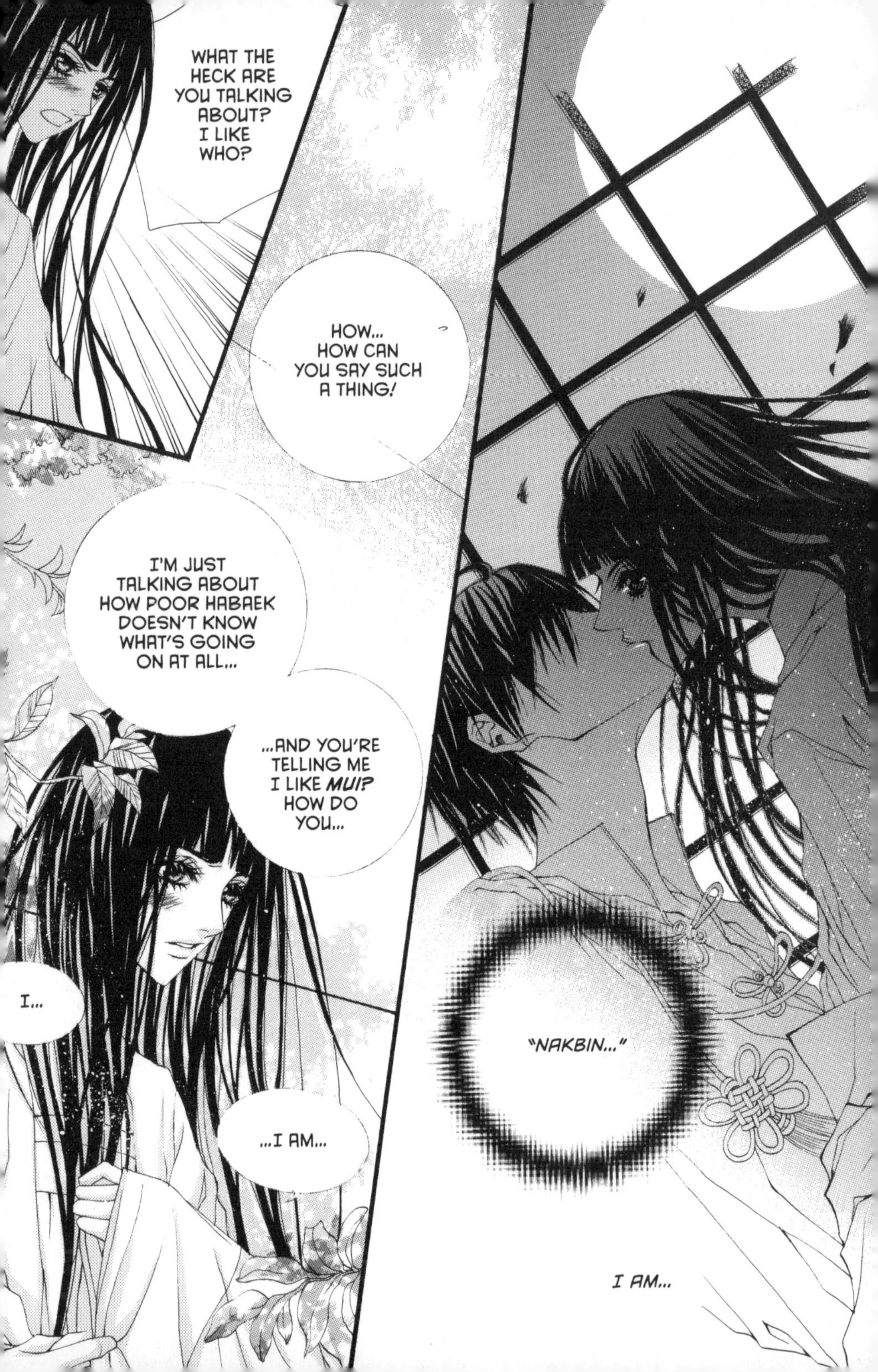
WHAT THE HECK ARE YOU TALKING ABOUT? I LIKE WHO?
HOW... HOW CAN YOU SAY SUCH A THING!
I'M JUST TALKING ABOUT HOW POOR HABAEK DOESN'T KNOW WHAT'S GOING ON AT ALL...
...AND YOU'RE TELLING ME I LIKE *MUI?* HOW DO YOU...
I...
...I AM...
"NAKBIN..."
I AM...

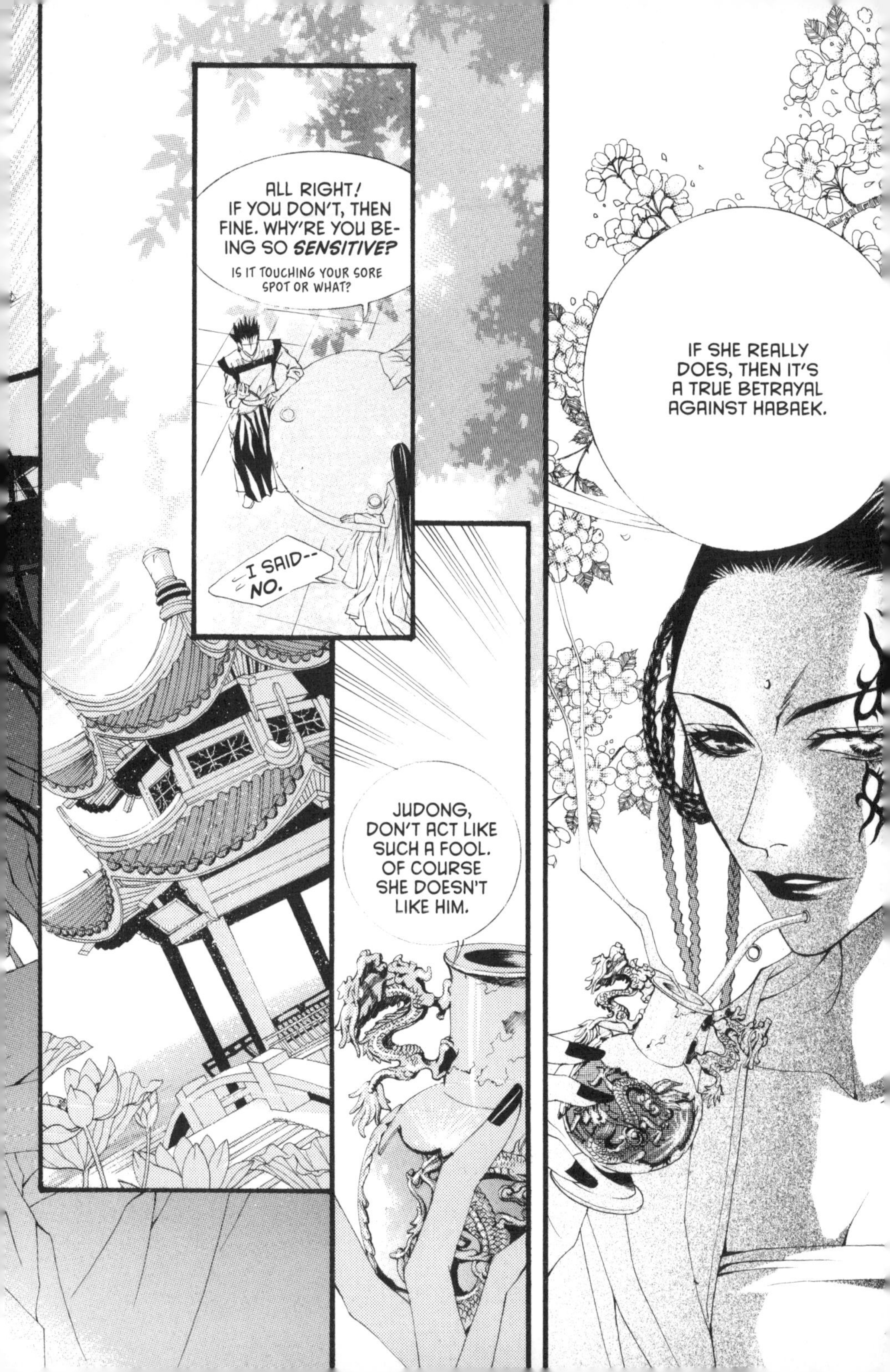
ALL RIGHT! IF YOU DON'T, THEN FINE. WHY'RE YOU BE-ING SO *SENSITIVE?*
IS IT TOUCHING YOUR SORE SPOT OR WHAT?
I SAID-- NO.
JUDONG, DON'T ACT LIKE SUCH A FOOL. OF COURSE SHE DOESN'T LIKE HIM.
IF SHE REALLY DOES, THEN IT'S A TRUE BETRAYAL AGAINST HABAEK.

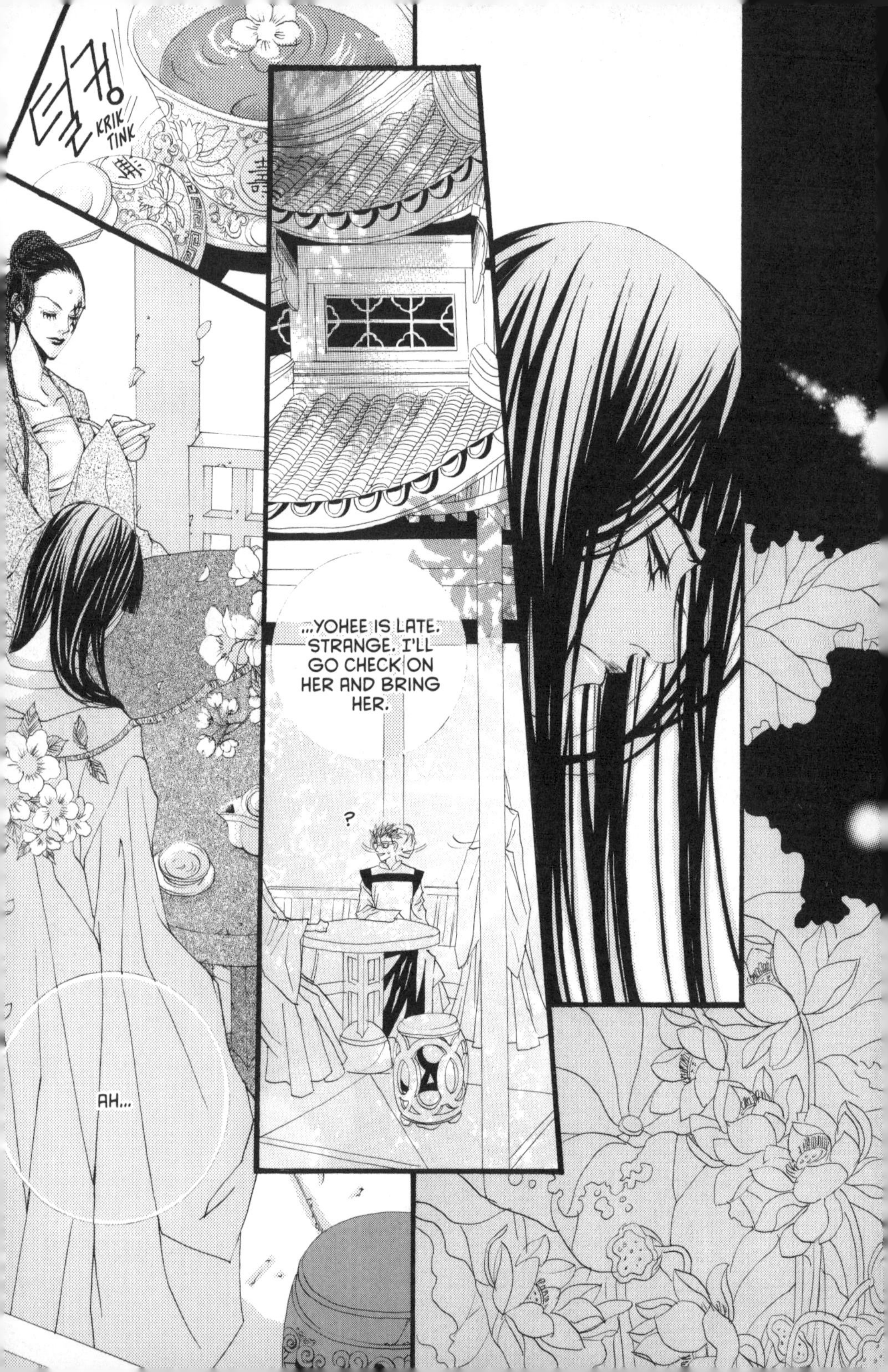

덜컹
KRIK TINK
...YOHEE IS LATE. STRANGE. I'LL GO CHECK ON HER AND BRING HER.
?
AH...

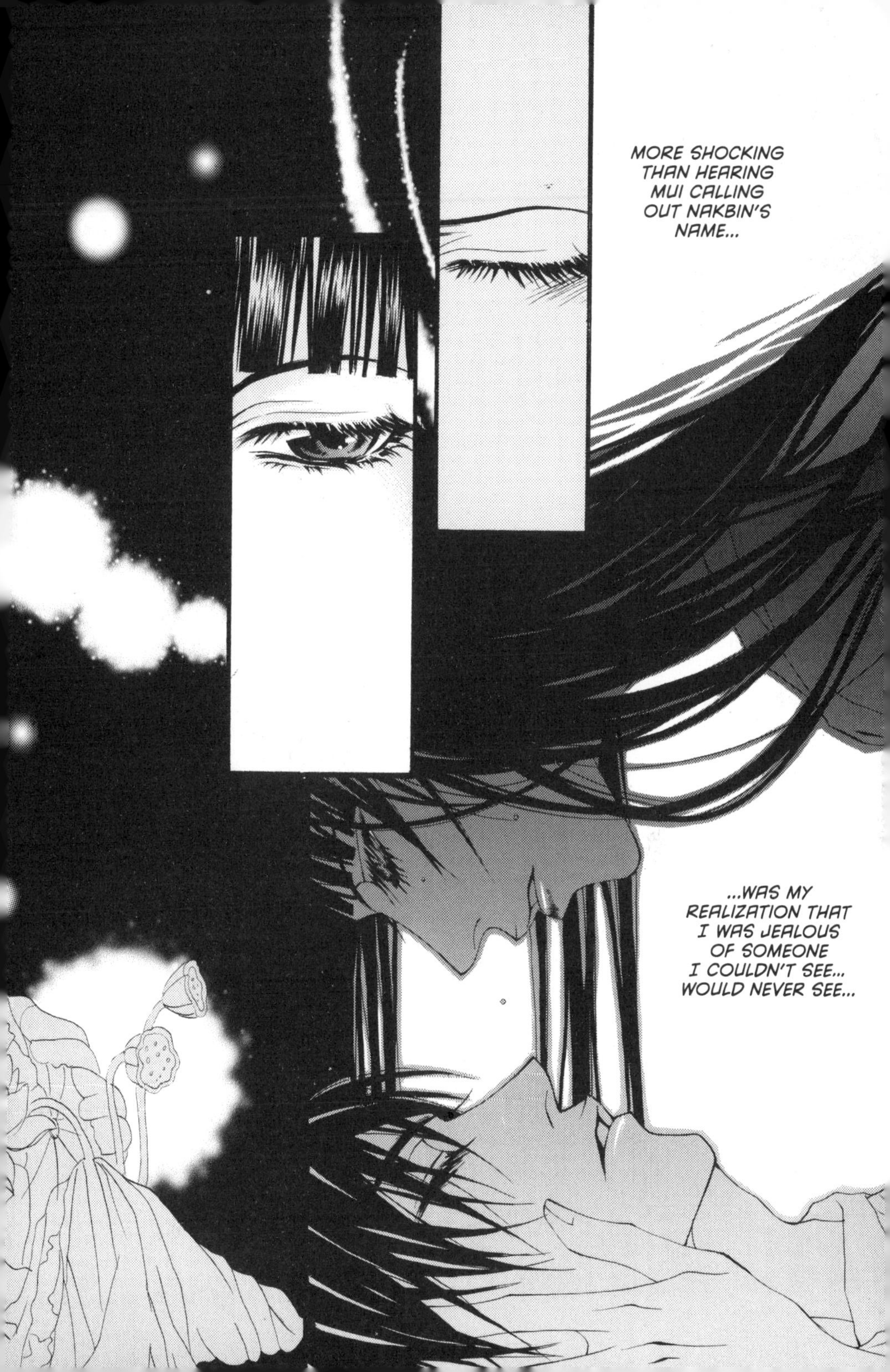
MORE SHOCKING THAN HEARING MUI CALLING OUT NAKBIN'S NAME...
...WAS MY REALIZATION THAT I WAS JEALOUS OF SOMEONE I COULDN'T SEE... WOULD NEVER SEE...

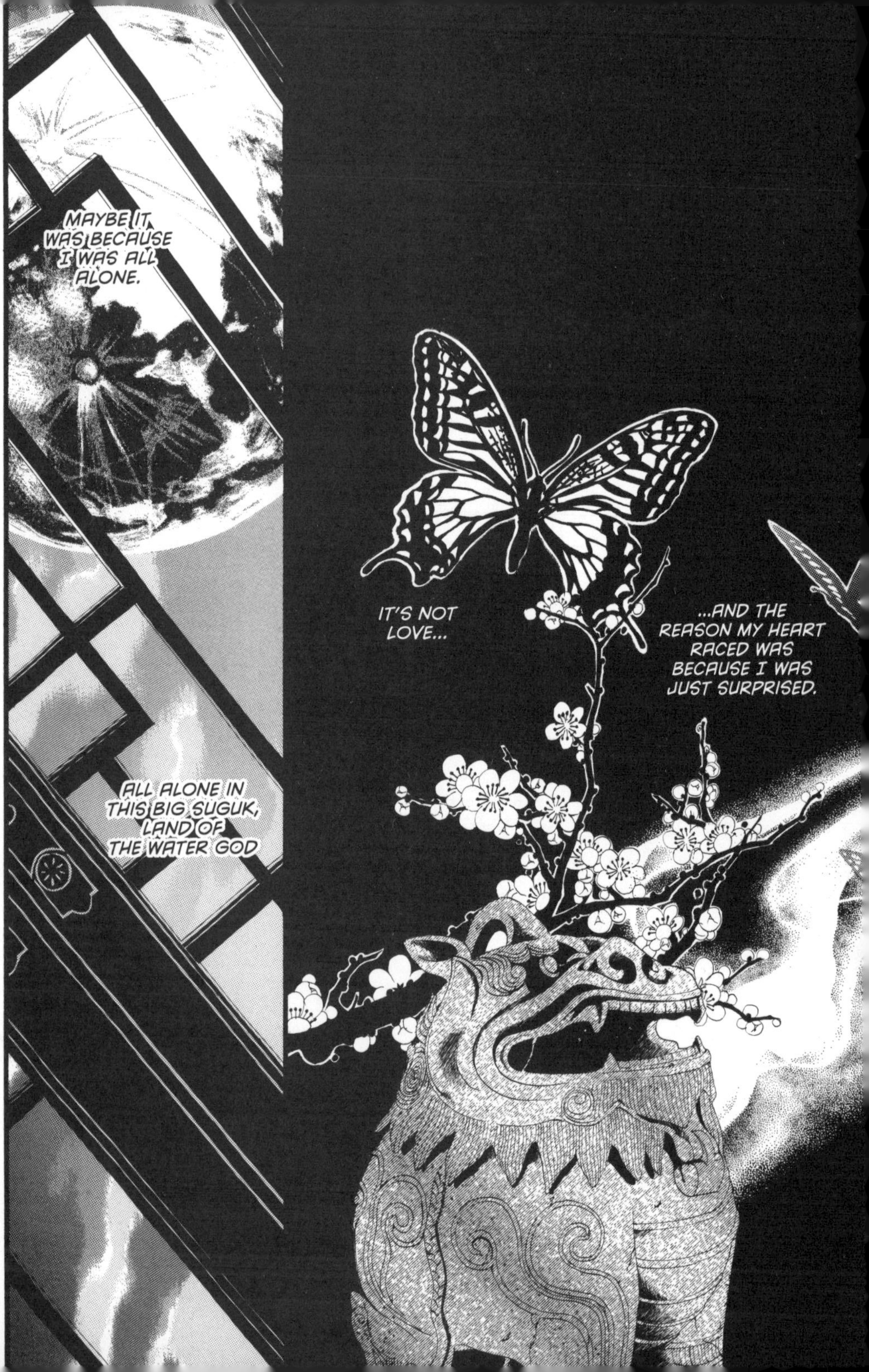
MAYBE IT WAS BECAUSE I WAS ALL ALONE.
ALL ALONE IN THIS BIG SUGUK, LAND OF THE WATER GOD
IT'S NOT LOVE...
...AND THE REASON MY HEART RACED WAS BECAUSE I WAS JUST SURPRISED.

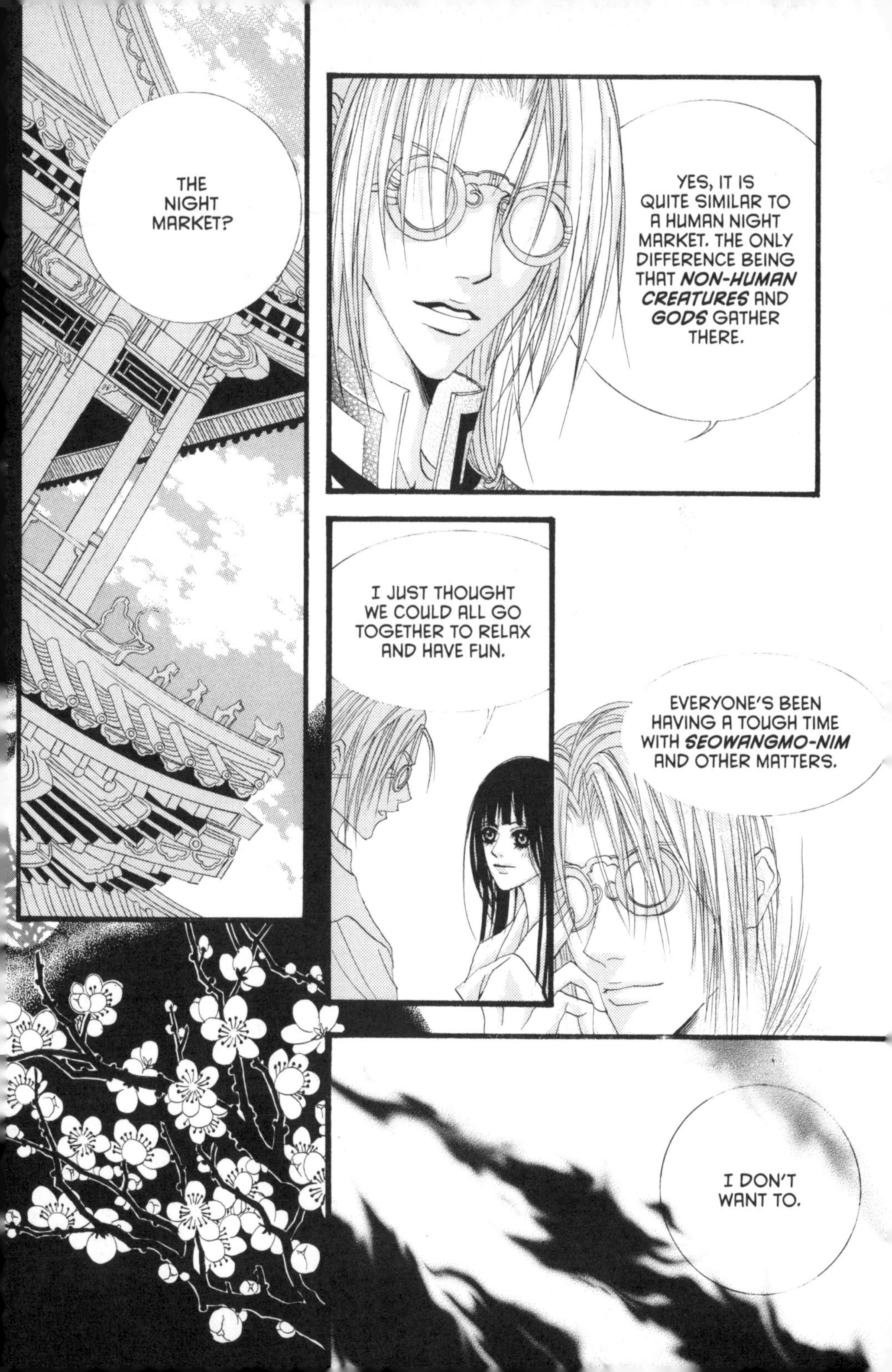

THE NIGHT MARKET?
YES, IT IS QUITE SIMILAR TO A HUMAN NIGHT MARKET. THE ONLY DIFFERENCE BEING THAT *NON-HUMAN CREATURES* AND *GODS* GATHER THERE.
I JUST THOUGHT WE COULD ALL GO TOGETHER TO RELAX AND HAVE FUN.
EVERYONE'S BEEN HAVING A TOUGH TIME WITH *SEOWANGMO-NIM* AND OTHER MATTERS.
I DON'T WANT TO.

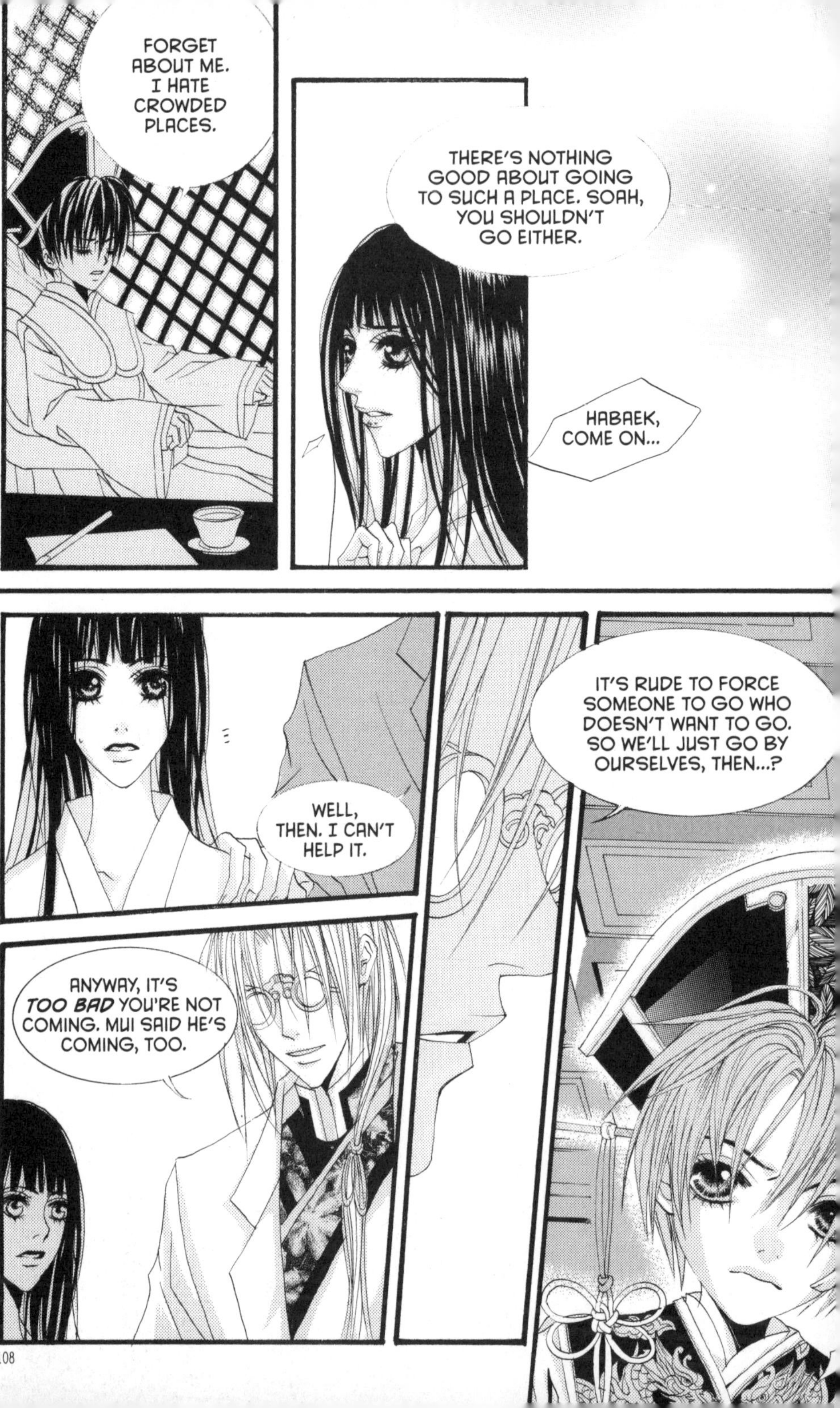
FORGET ABOUT ME. I HATE CROWDED PLACES.
THERE'S NOTHING GOOD ABOUT GOING TO SUCH A PLACE. SOAH, YOU SHOULDN'T GO EITHER.
HABAEK, COME ON...
WELL, THEN. I CAN'T HELP IT.
IT'S RUDE TO FORCE SOMEONE TO GO WHO DOESN'T WANT TO GO. SO WE'LL JUST GO BY OURSELVES, THEN...?
ANYWAY, IT'S TOO BAD YOU'RE NOT COMING. MUI SAID HE'S COMING, TOO.

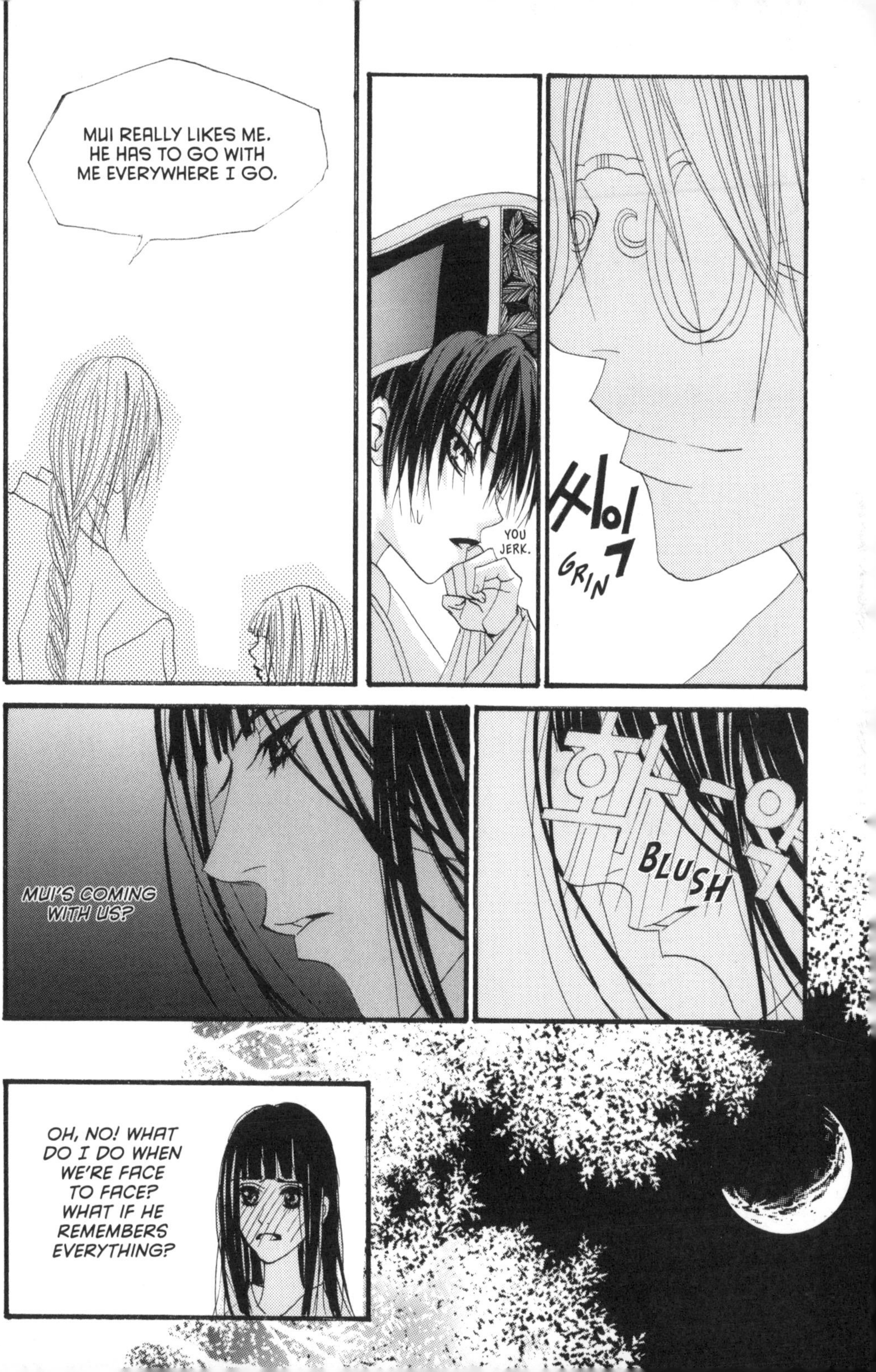
MUI REALLY LIKES ME. HE HAS TO GO WITH ME EVERYWHERE I GO.
YOU JERK.
GRIN
MUI'S COMING WITH US?
BLUSH
OH, NO! WHAT DO I DO WHEN WE'RE FACE TO FACE? WHAT IF HE REMEMBERS EVERYTHING?

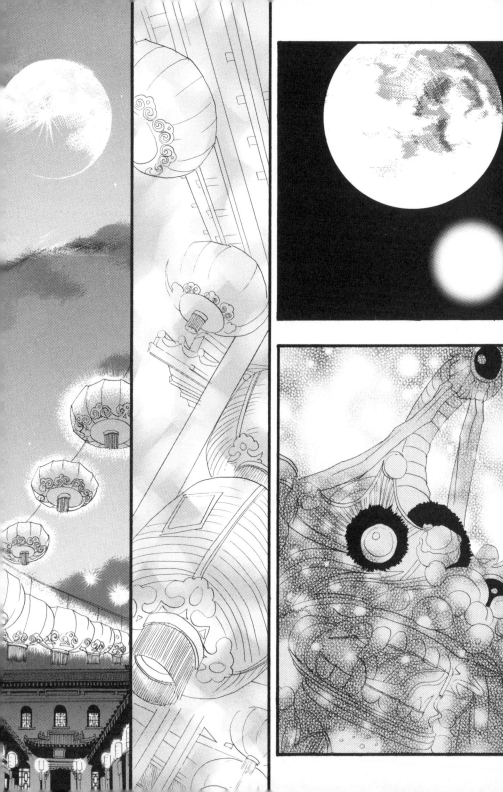

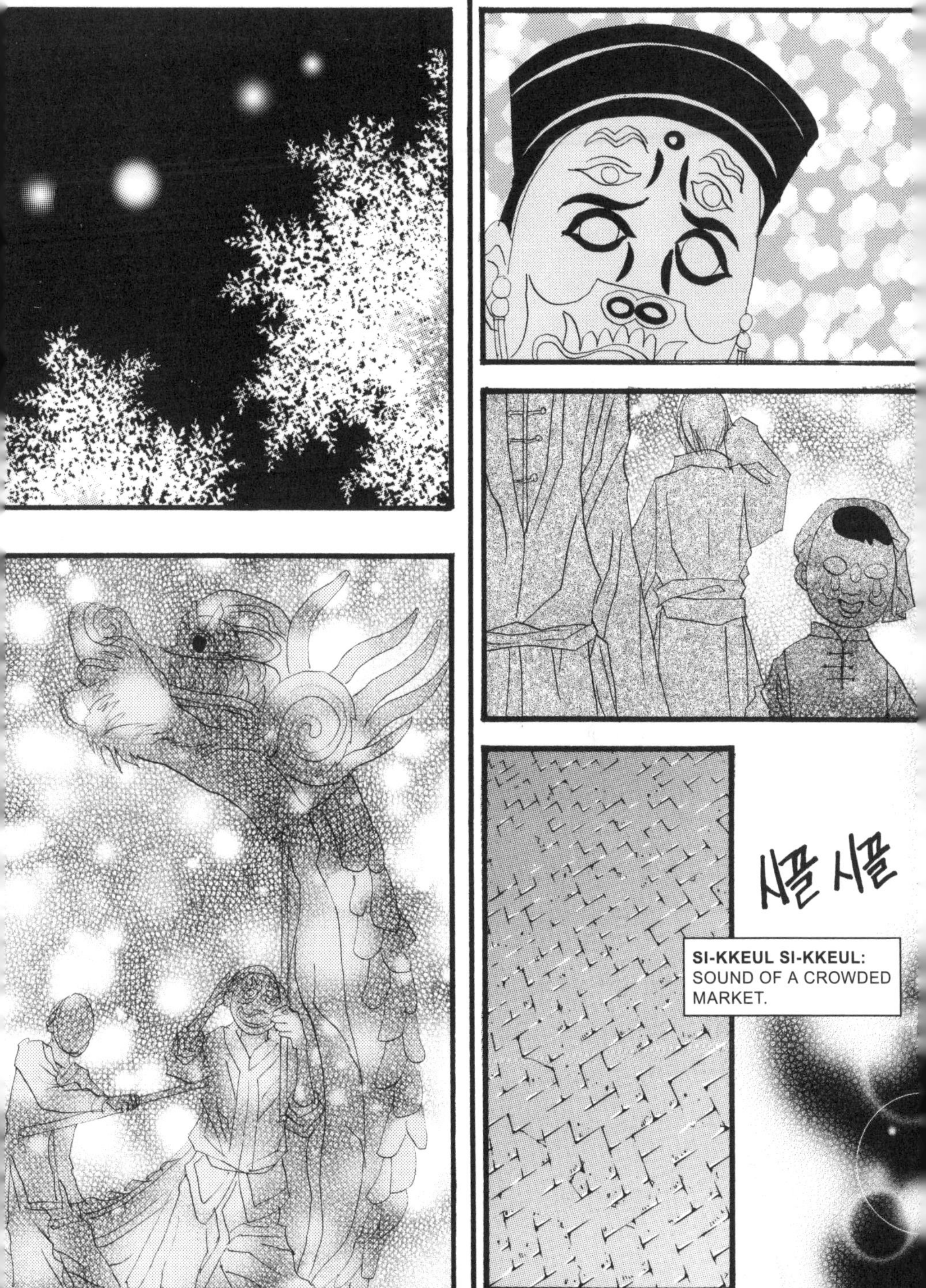
시끌 시끌
SI-KKEUL SI-KKEUL: SOUND OF A CROWDED MARKET.

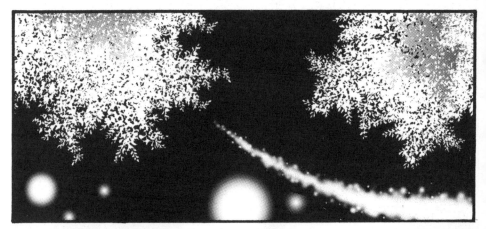

WOW...

HURRY UP, SOAH, OR WE'LL LEAVE YOU!

WHAT'RE *YOU* DOING IN A PLACE LIKE THIS?

OH, WAIT! DON'T LEAVE ME!

AM I MISTAKEN?

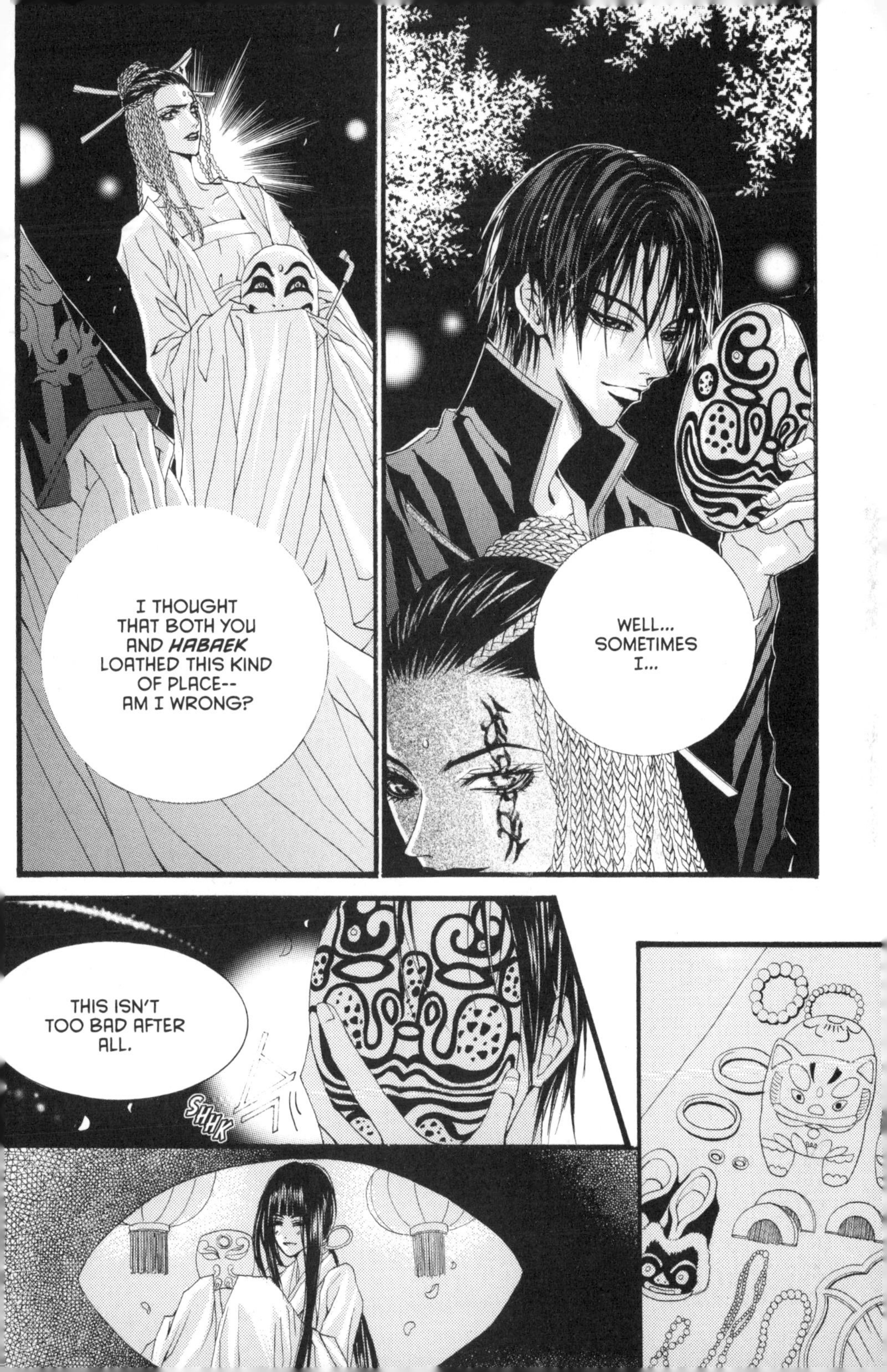
I THOUGHT THAT BOTH YOU AND HABAEK LOATHED THIS KIND OF PLACE-- AM I WRONG?
WELL... SOMETIMES I...
THIS ISN'T TOO BAD AFTER ALL.
SHHK

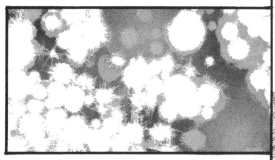

HOLD YOUR
HANDS OUT
FOR ME.

HUH?

IT'S A LITTLE LATE,
BUT THIS IS A
WELCOMING GIFT
FOR YOUR ARRIVAL
TO SUGUK.

?

TK

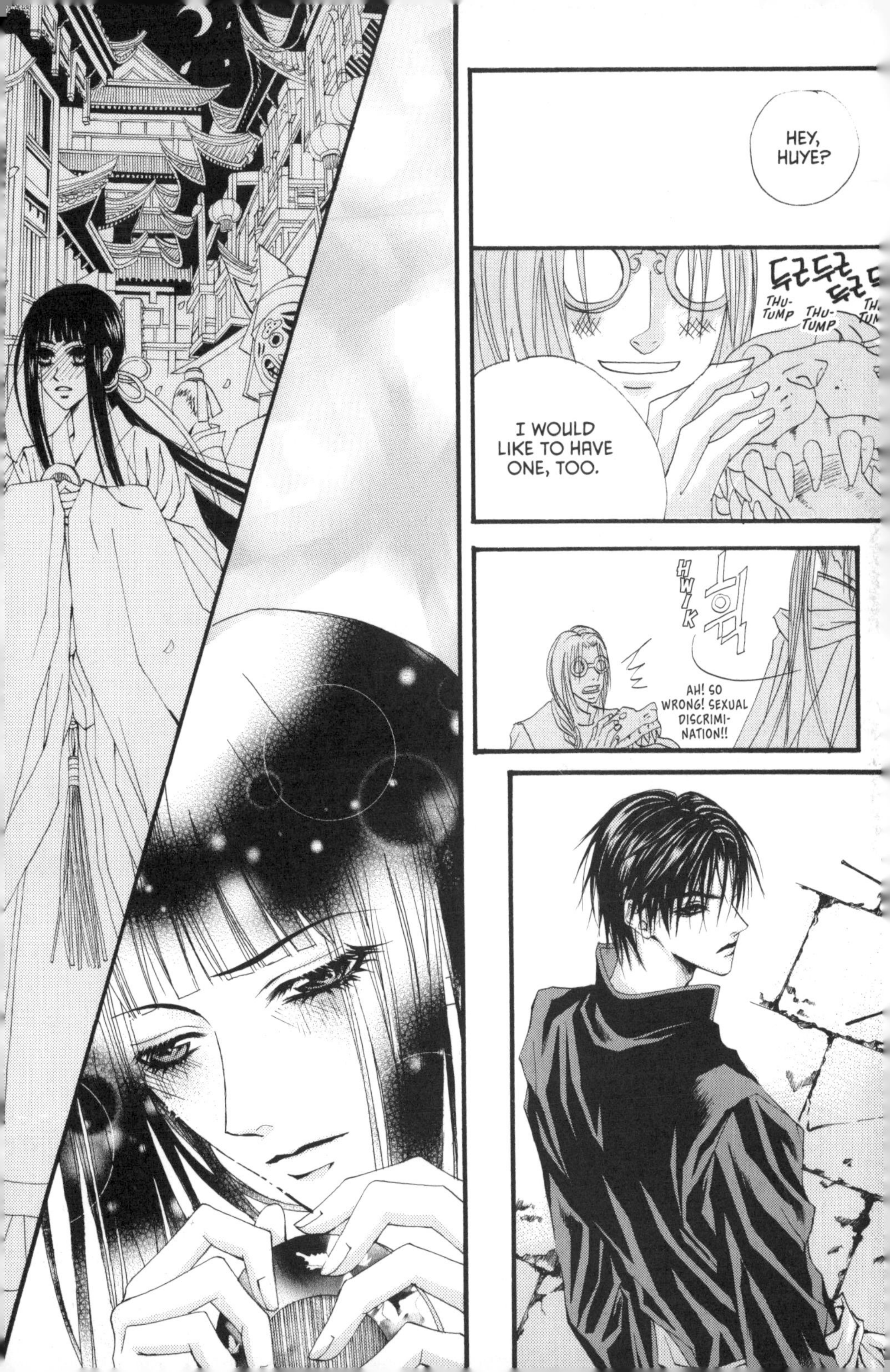
HEY, HUYE?
두근두근 두근 두
THU-TUMP THU-TUMP THU-TUMP
I WOULD LIKE TO HAVE ONE, TOO.
HWIK
헉
AH! SO WRONG! SEXUAL DISCRIMI-NATION!!

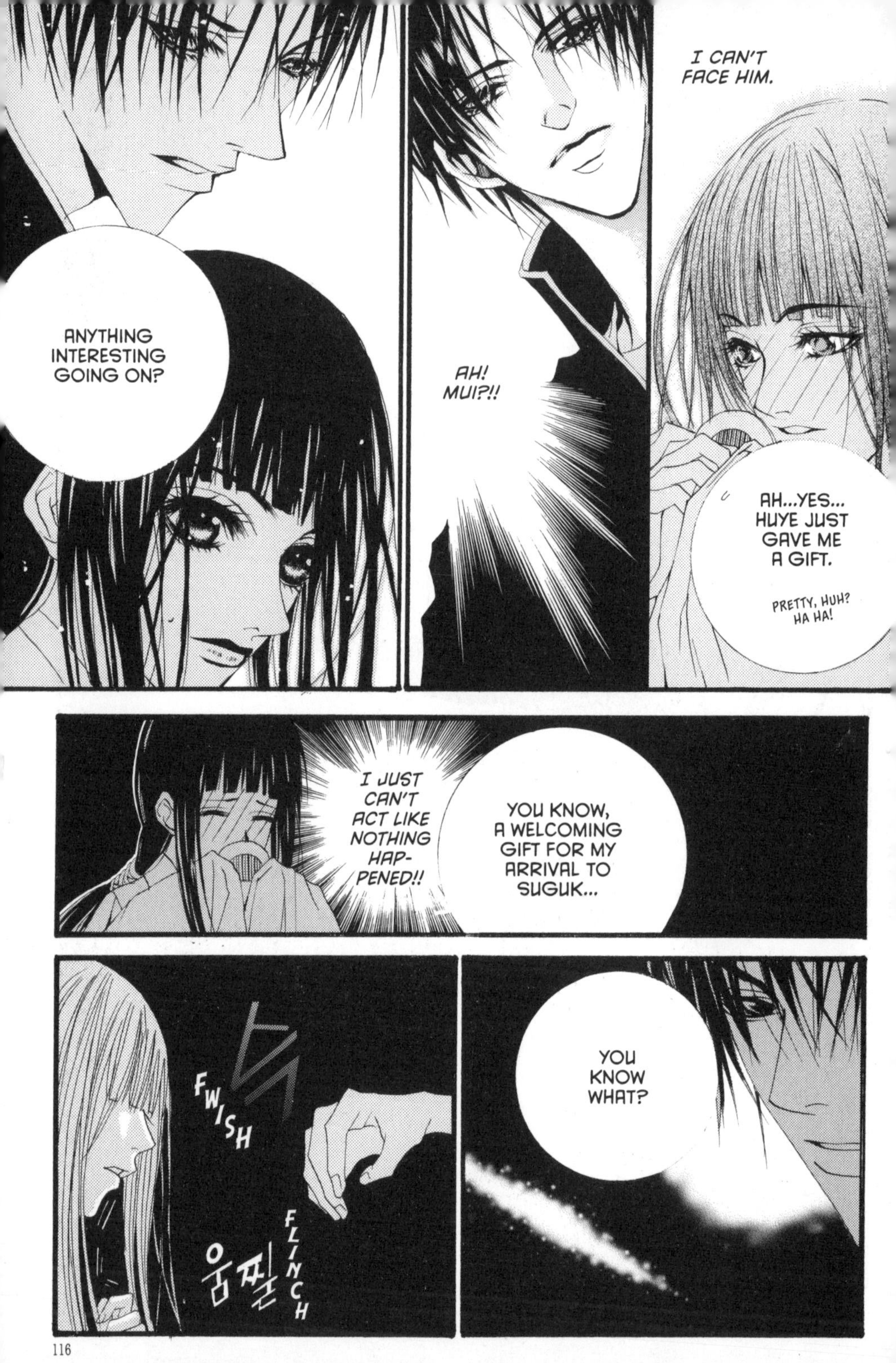
ANYTHING INTERESTING GOING ON?
AH! MUI?!!
I CAN'T FACE HIM.
AH...YES... HUYE JUST GAVE ME A GIFT.
PRETTY, HUH? HA HA!
I JUST CAN'T ACT LIKE NOTHING HAP-PENED!!
YOU KNOW, A WELCOMING GIFT FOR MY ARRIVAL TO SUGUK...
FWISH
움찔
FLINCH
YOU KNOW WHAT?

"A MAN GIVING A LADY A COMB AS A GIFT MEANS HE'S PROPOSING FOR MARRIAGE."

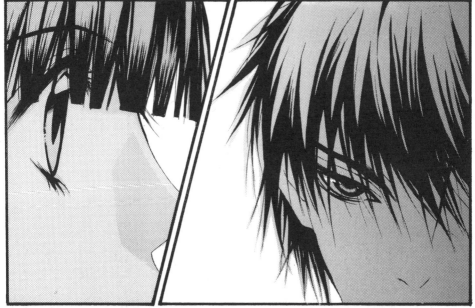

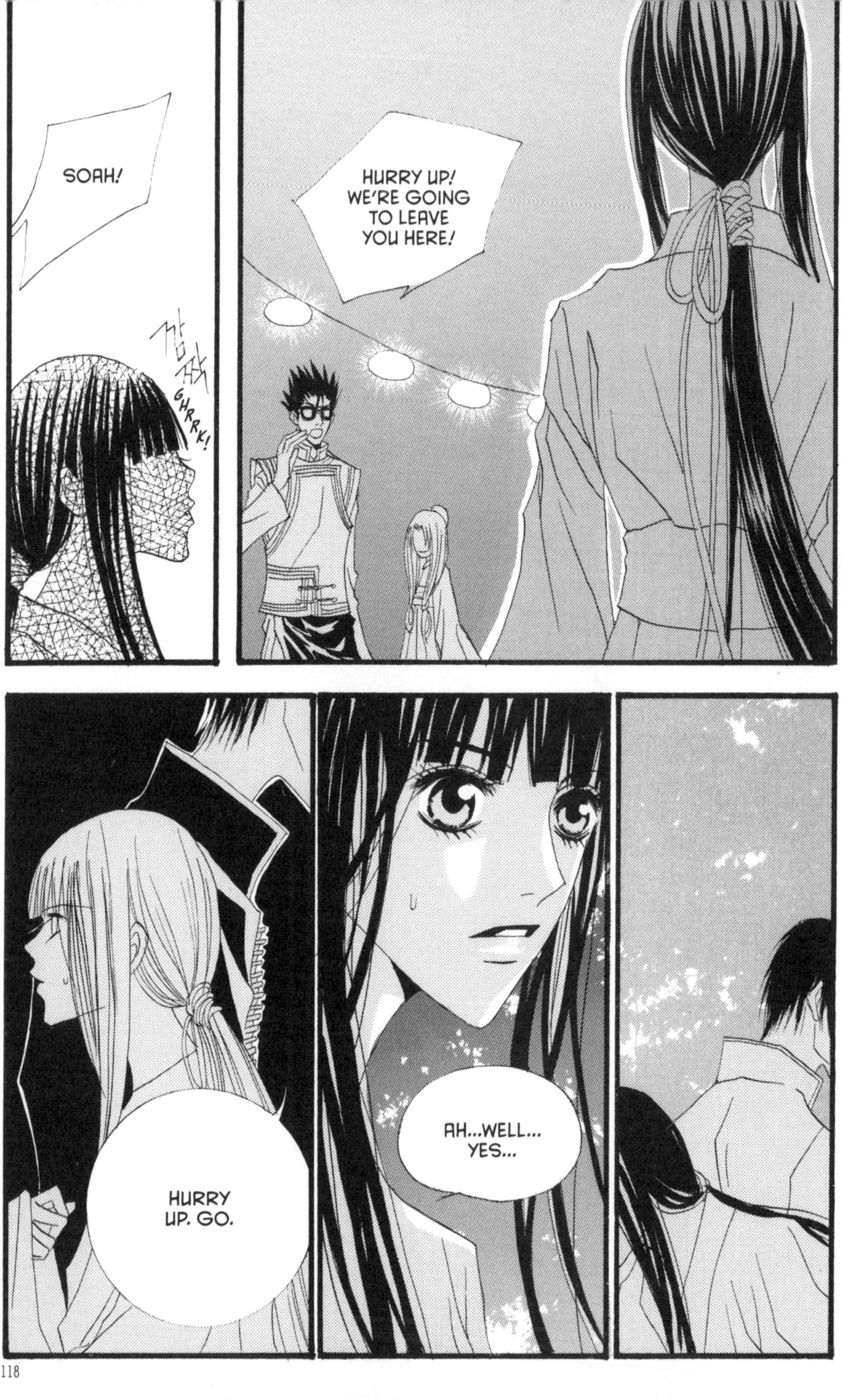
SOAH!
깜짝
GHRRK!
HURRY UP! WE'RE GOING TO LEAVE YOU HERE!
HURRY UP. GO.
AH...WELL... YES...

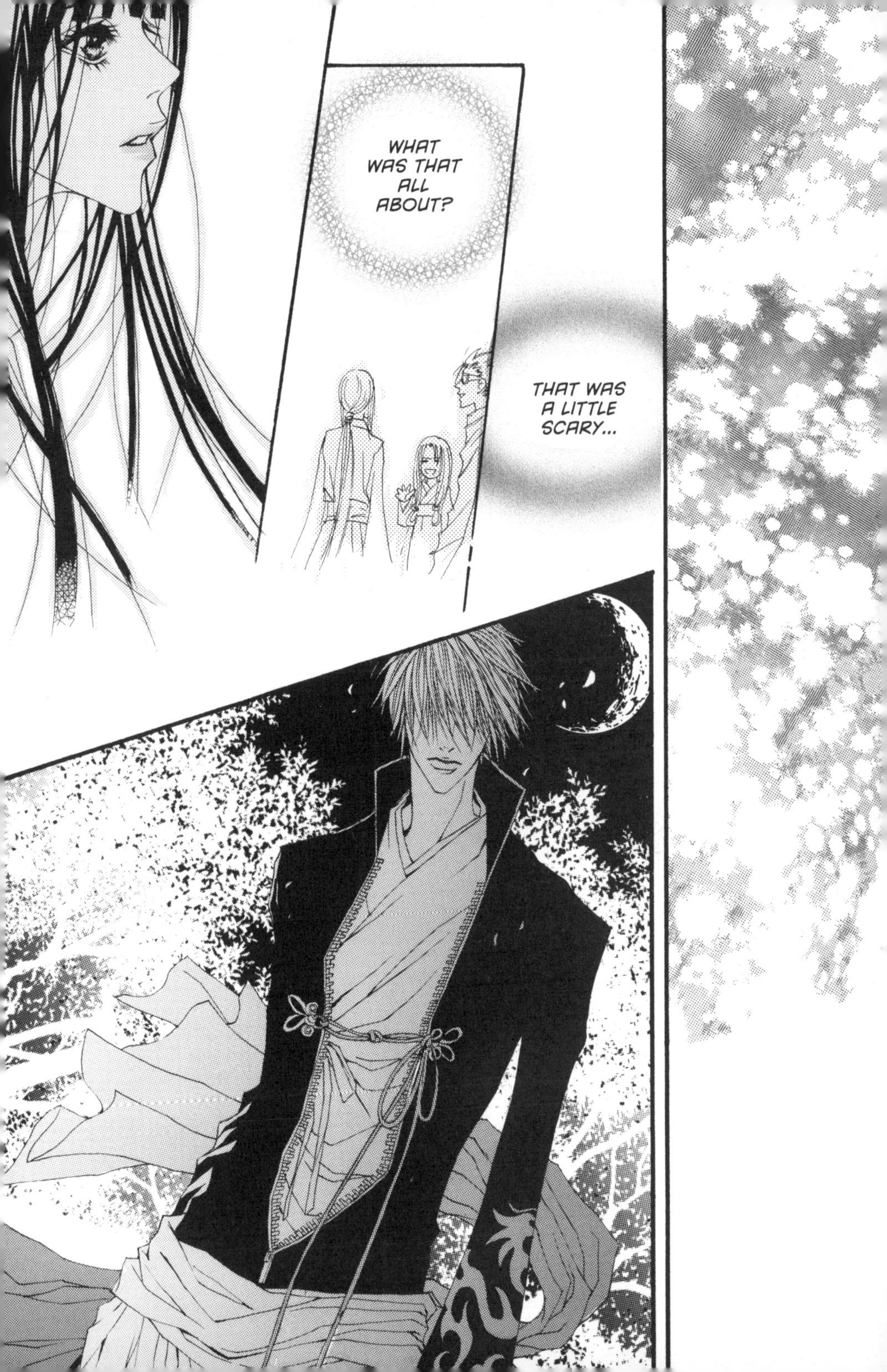
THAT WAS A LITTLE SCARY...
WHAT WAS THAT ALL ABOUT?

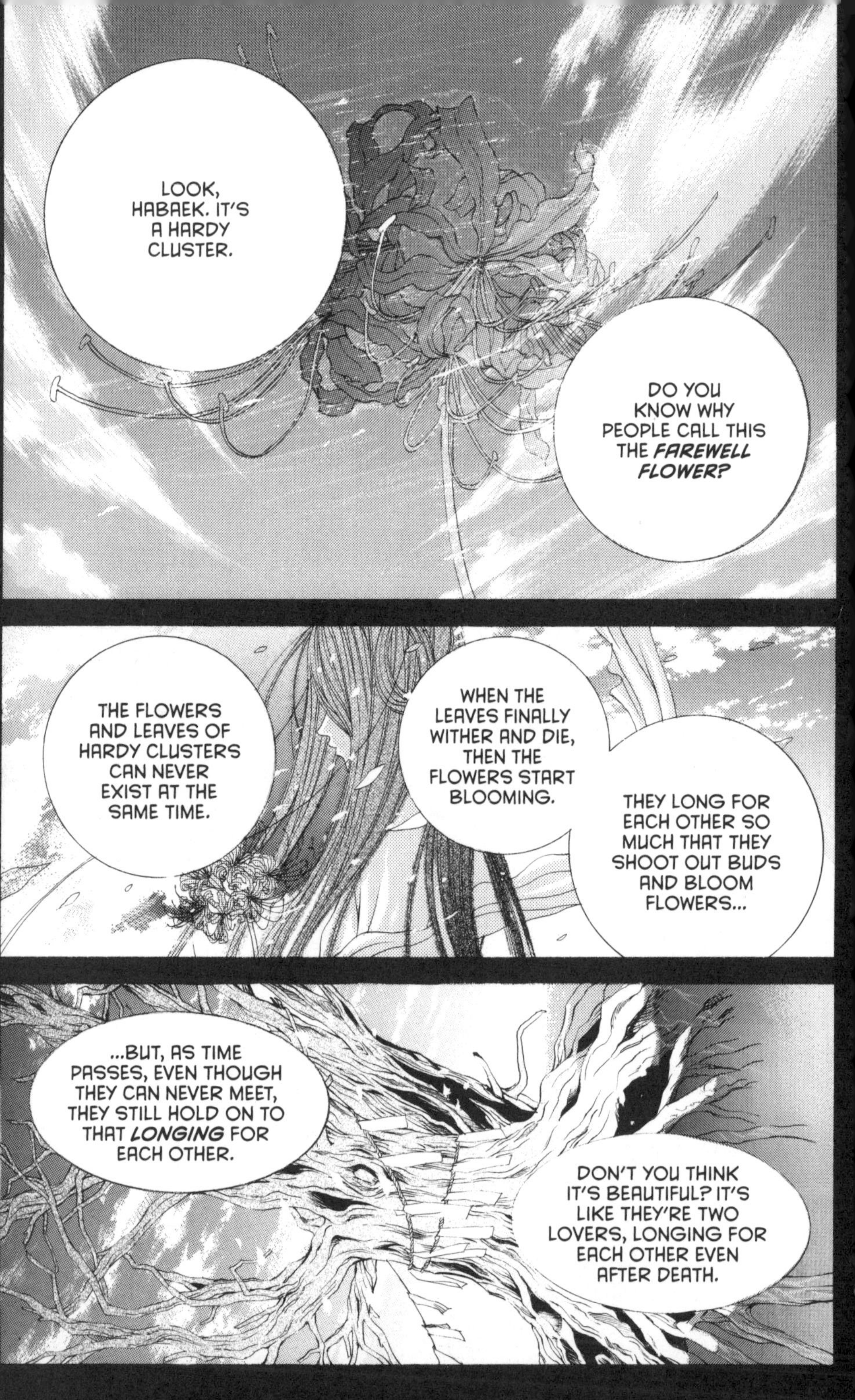
LOOK, HABAEK. IT'S A HARDY CLUSTER.
DO YOU KNOW WHY PEOPLE CALL THIS THE *FAREWELL FLOWER?*
THE FLOWERS AND LEAVES OF HARDY CLUSTERS CAN NEVER EXIST AT THE SAME TIME.
WHEN THE LEAVES FINALLY WITHER AND DIE, THEN THE FLOWERS START BLOOMING.
THEY LONG FOR EACH OTHER SO MUCH THAT THEY SHOOT OUT BUDS AND BLOOM FLOWERS...
...BUT, AS TIME PASSES, EVEN THOUGH THEY CAN NEVER MEET, THEY STILL HOLD ON TO THAT *LONGING* FOR EACH OTHER.
DON'T YOU THINK IT'S BEAUTIFUL? IT'S LIKE THEY'RE TWO LOVERS, LONGING FOR EACH OTHER EVEN AFTER DEATH.

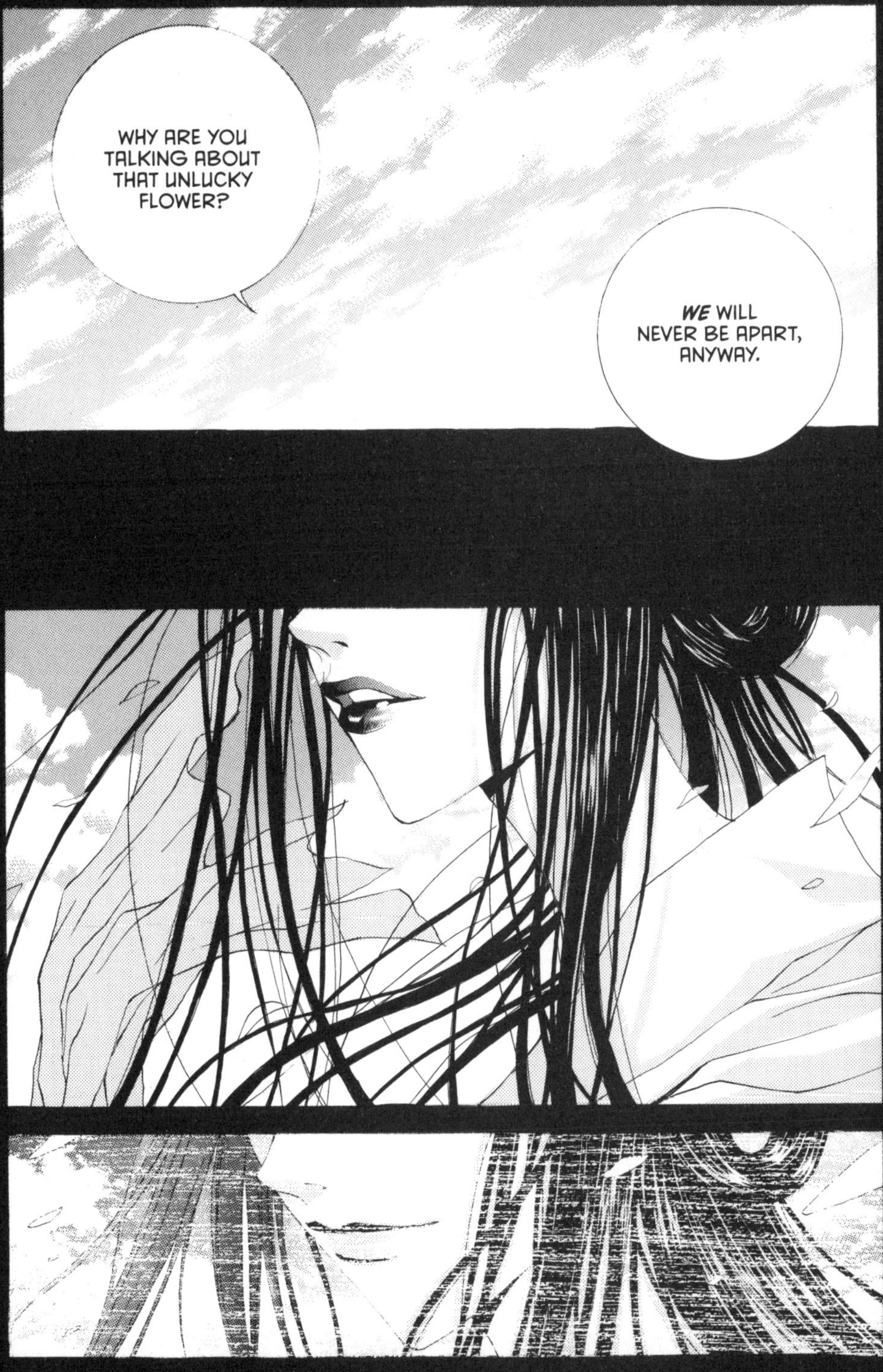

WHY ARE YOU TALKING ABOUT THAT UNLUCKY FLOWER?
WE WILL NEVER BE APART, ANYWAY.

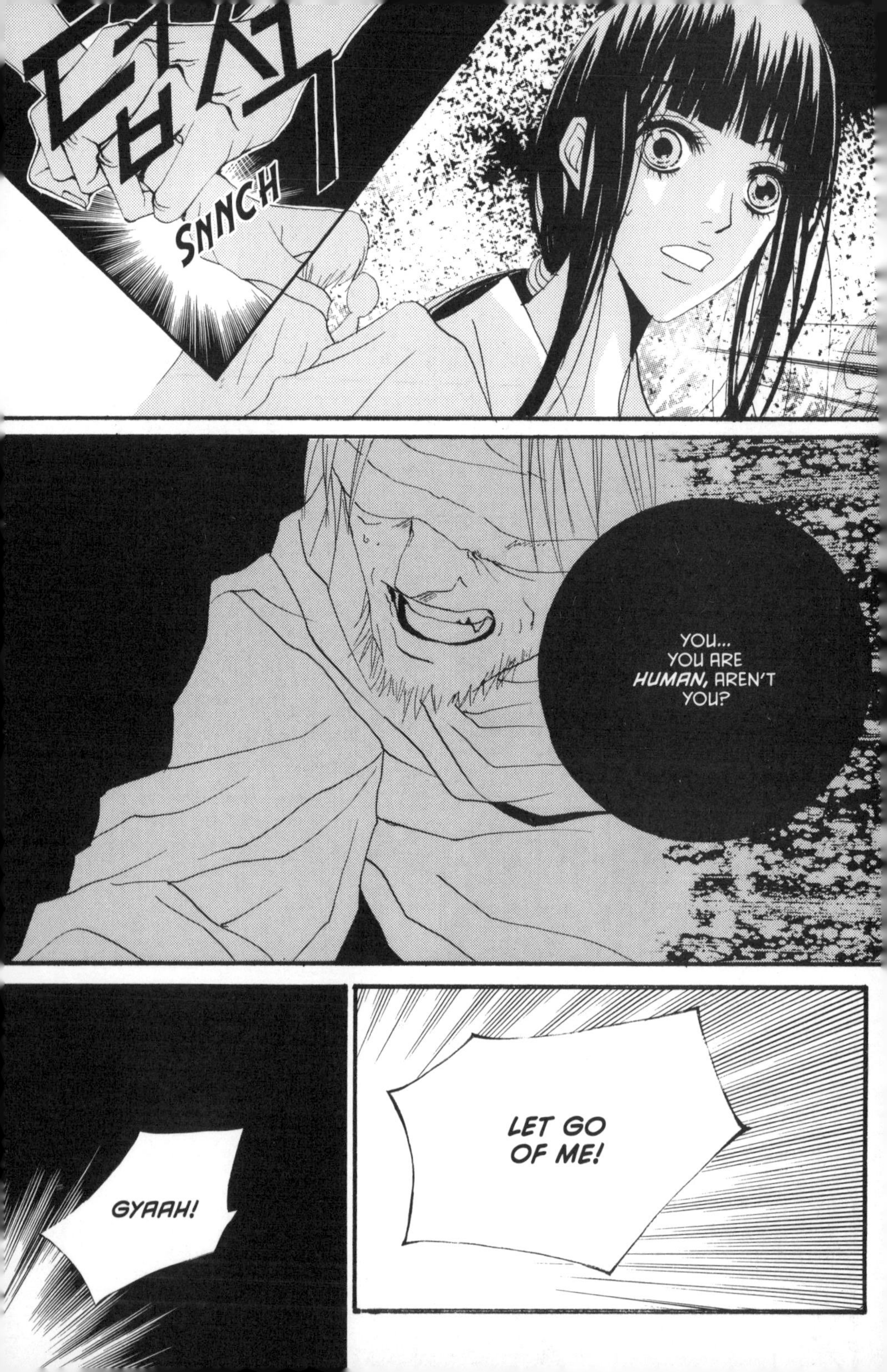

SNNCH
YOU... YOU ARE HUMAN, AREN'T YOU?
LET GO OF ME!
GYAAH!

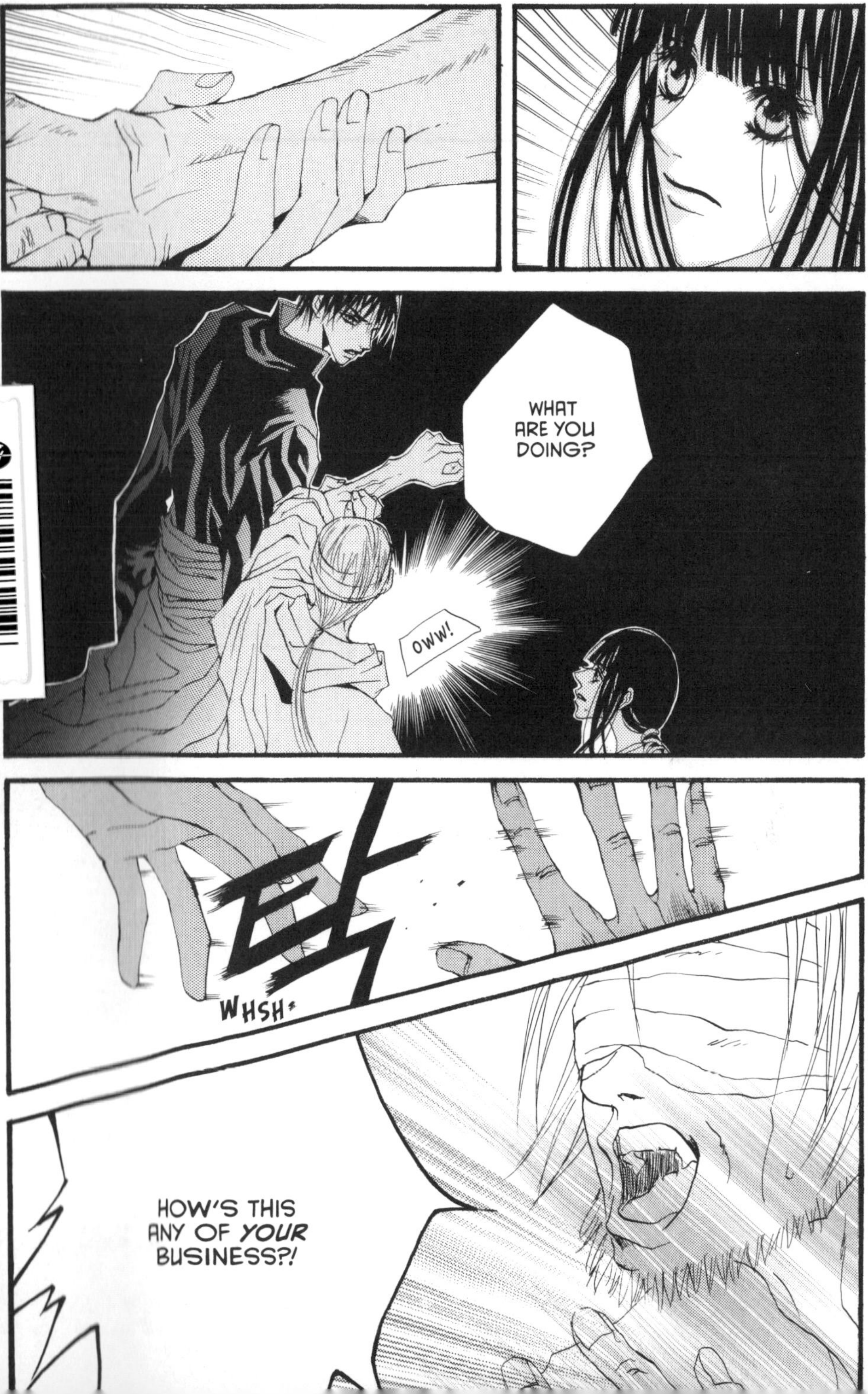
WHAT ARE YOU DOING?
OWW!
WHSH
HOW'S THIS ANY OF *YOUR* BUSINESS?!

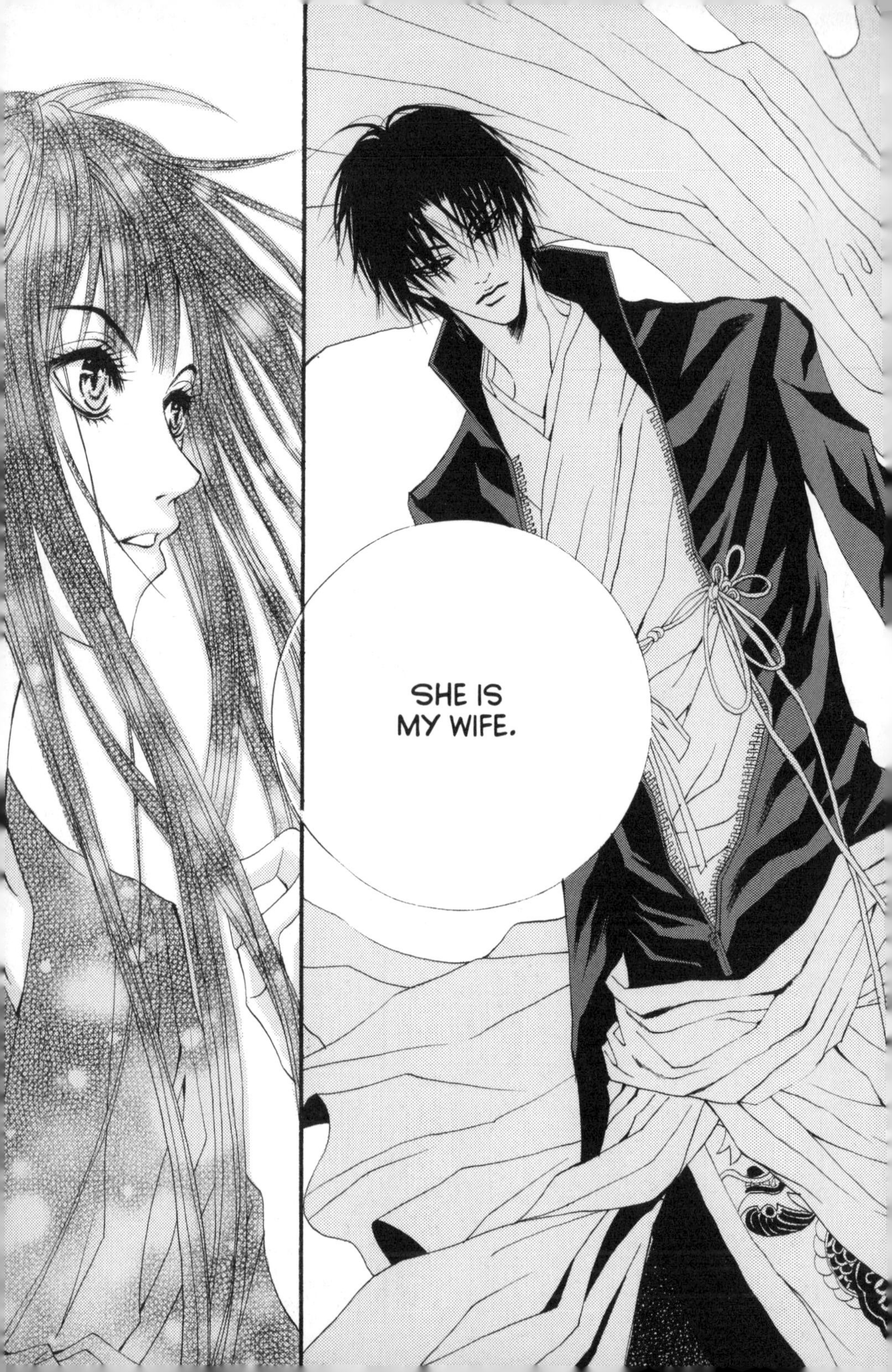
SHE IS MY WIFE.

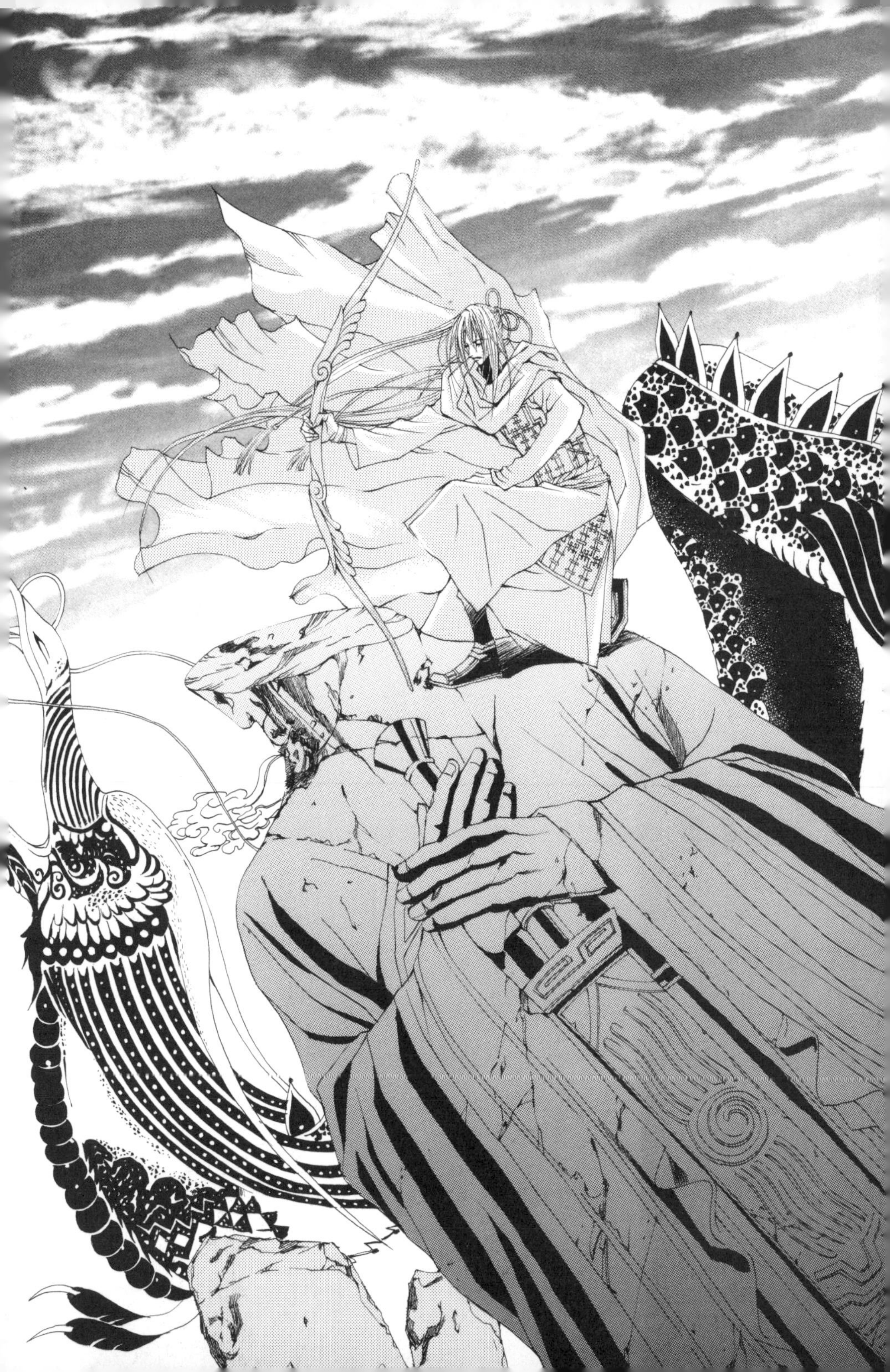

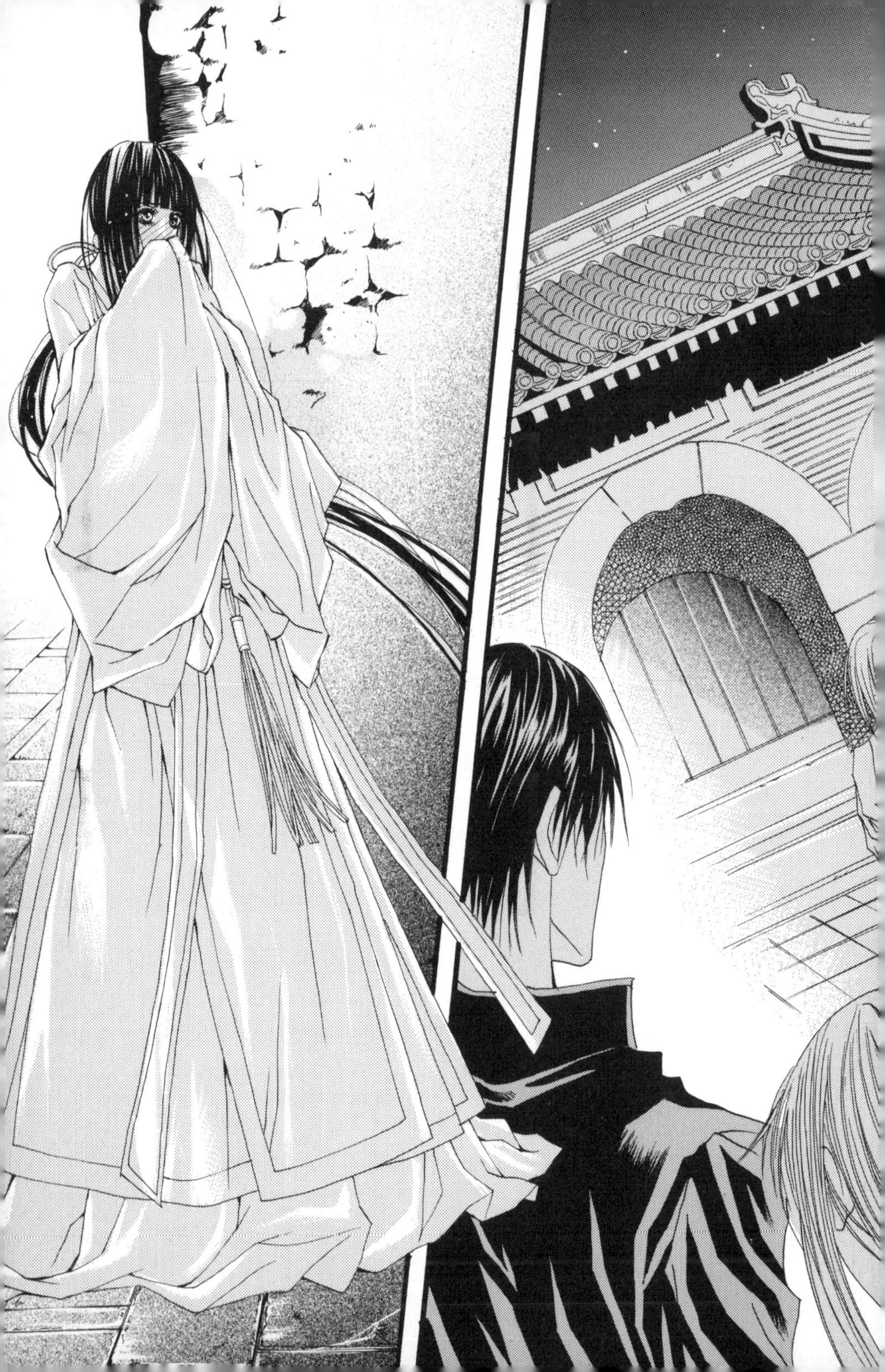

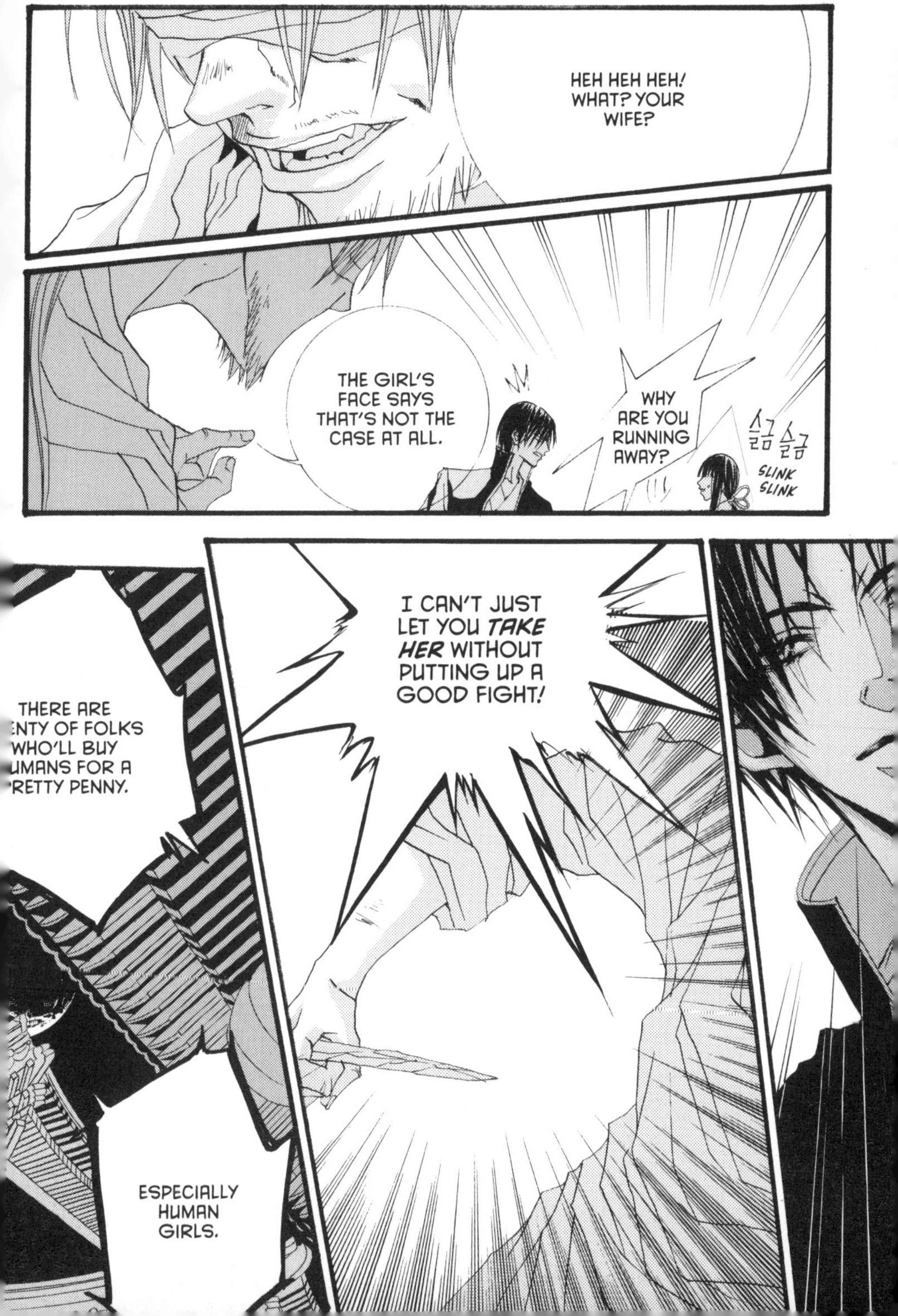

HEH HEH HEH! WHAT? YOUR WIFE?
THE GIRL'S FACE SAYS THAT'S NOT THE CASE AT ALL.
WHY ARE YOU RUNNING AWAY?
슬금 슬금
SLINK SLINK
THERE ARE ENTY OF FOLKS WHO'LL BUY UMANS FOR A RETTY PENNY.
ESPECIALLY HUMAN GIRLS.
I CAN'T JUST LET YOU *TAKE HER* WITHOUT PUTTING UP A GOOD FIGHT!

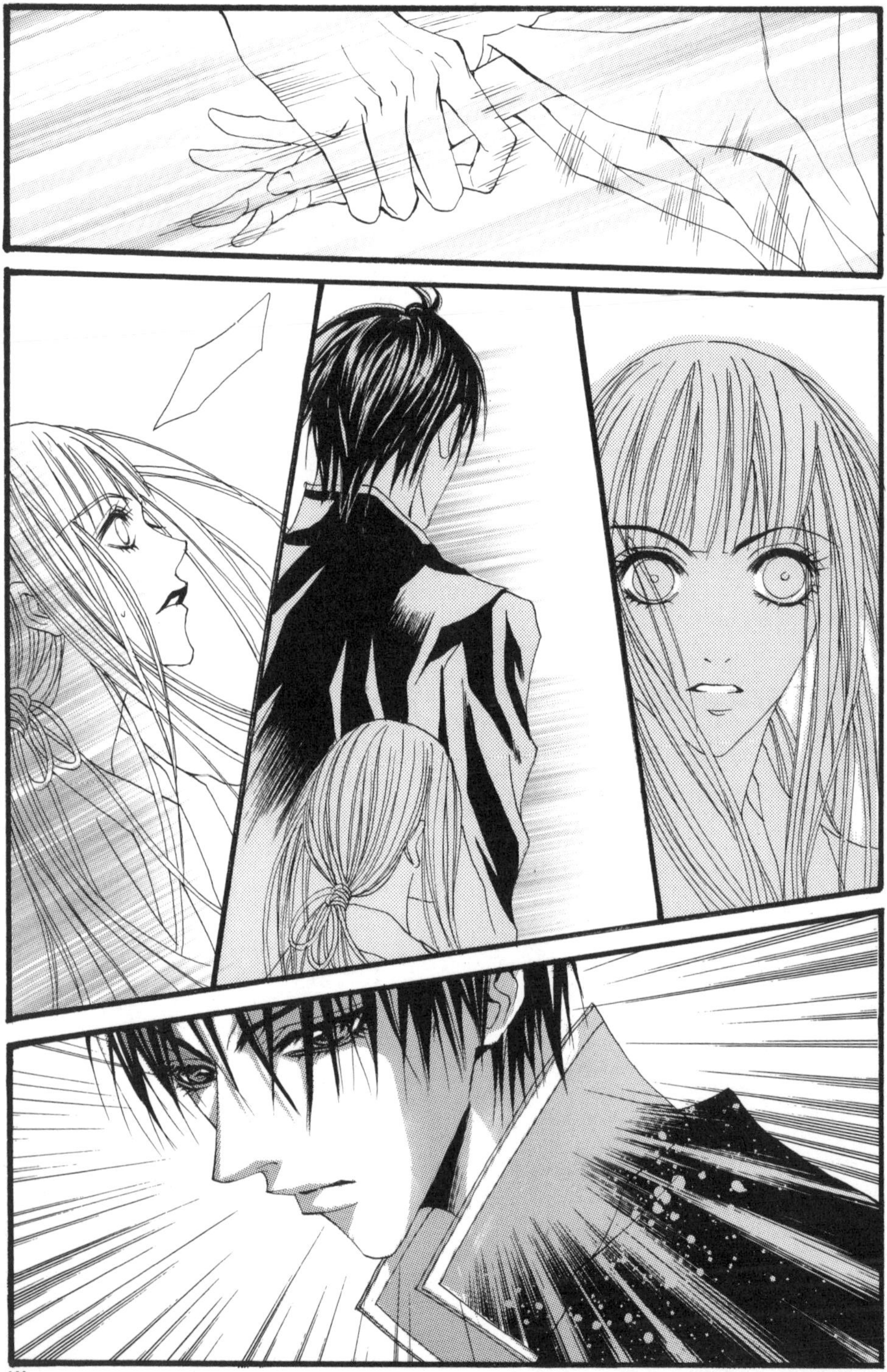

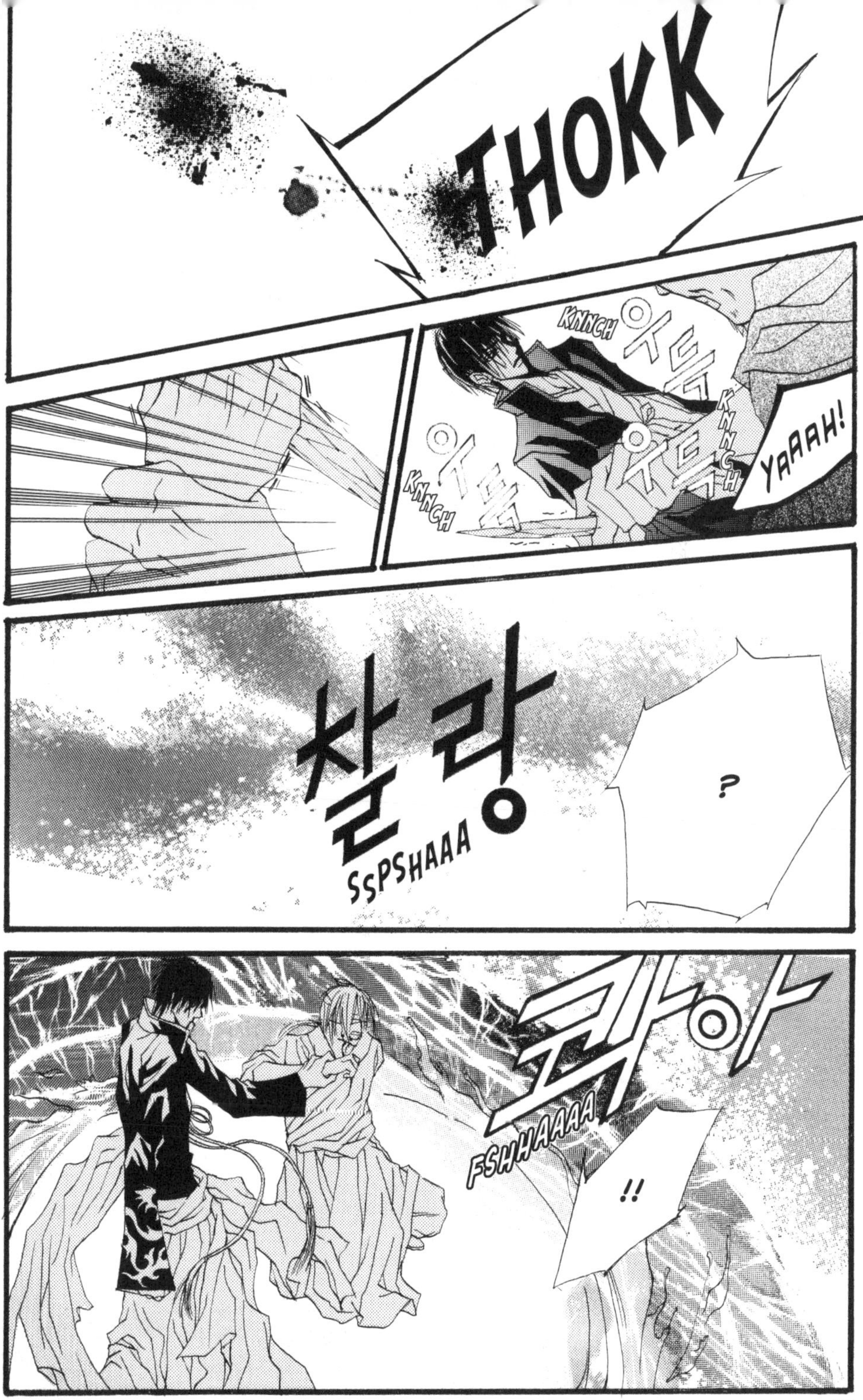
THOKK
KNNCH
KNNCH
KNNCH
YAAAH!
찰랑
SSPSHAAA
?
FSHHAAAA
!!

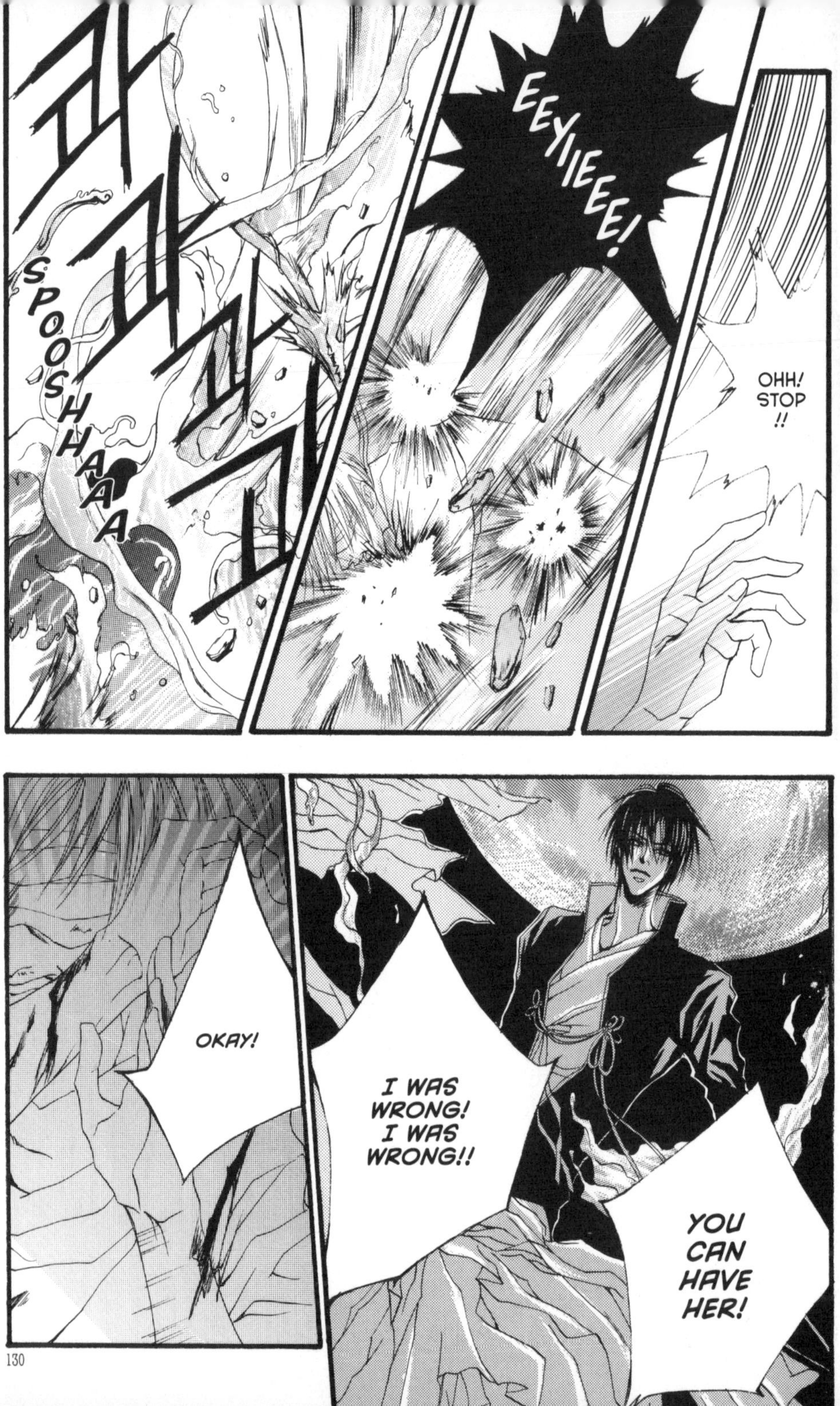
OHH! STOP !!
EEYIIEEEE!
SPOOSHHAAAA
YOU CAN HAVE HER!
I WAS WRONG! I WAS WRONG!!
OKAY!

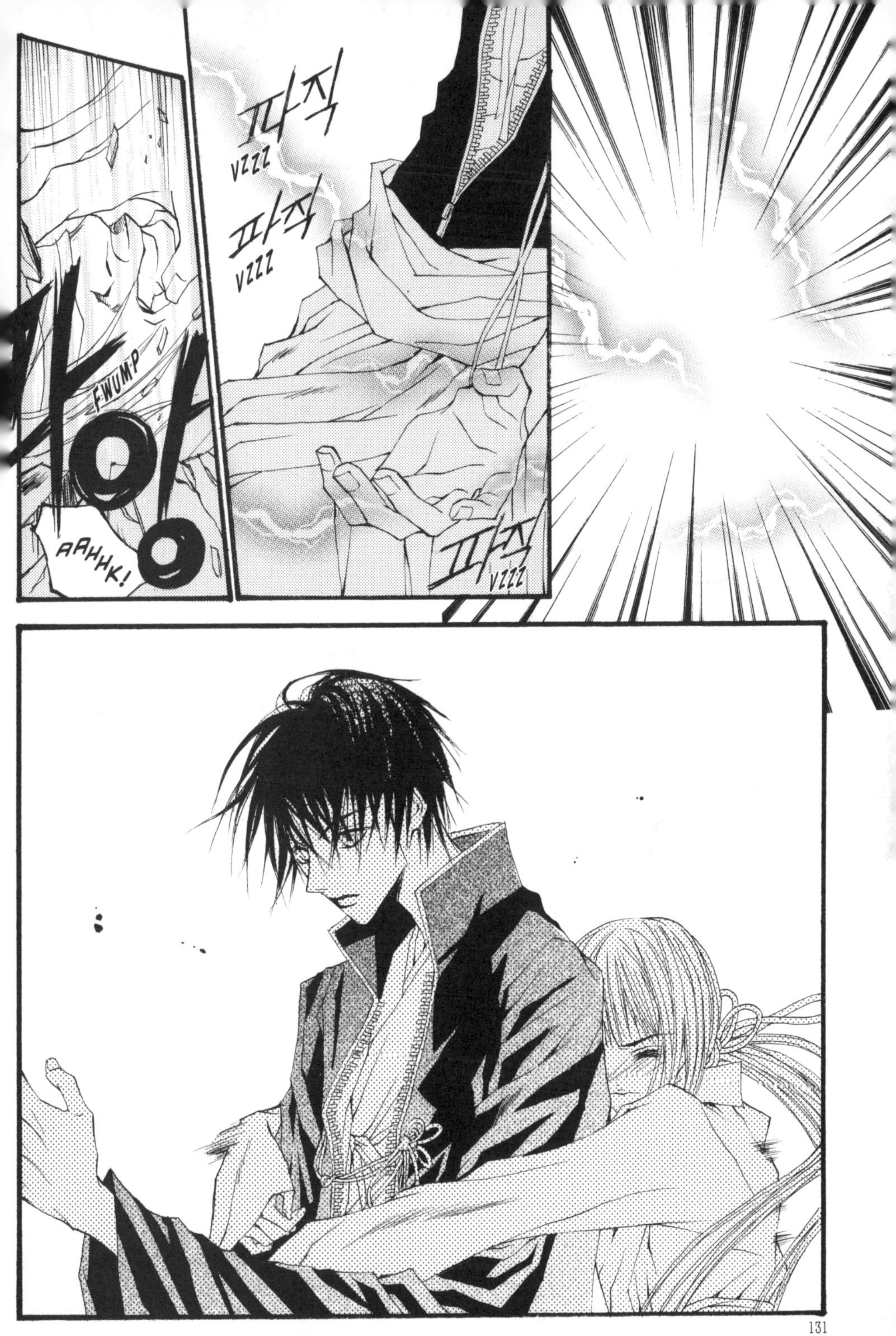
파직
VZZZ
파직
VZZZ
파직
VZZZ
FWUMP
AAHHK!

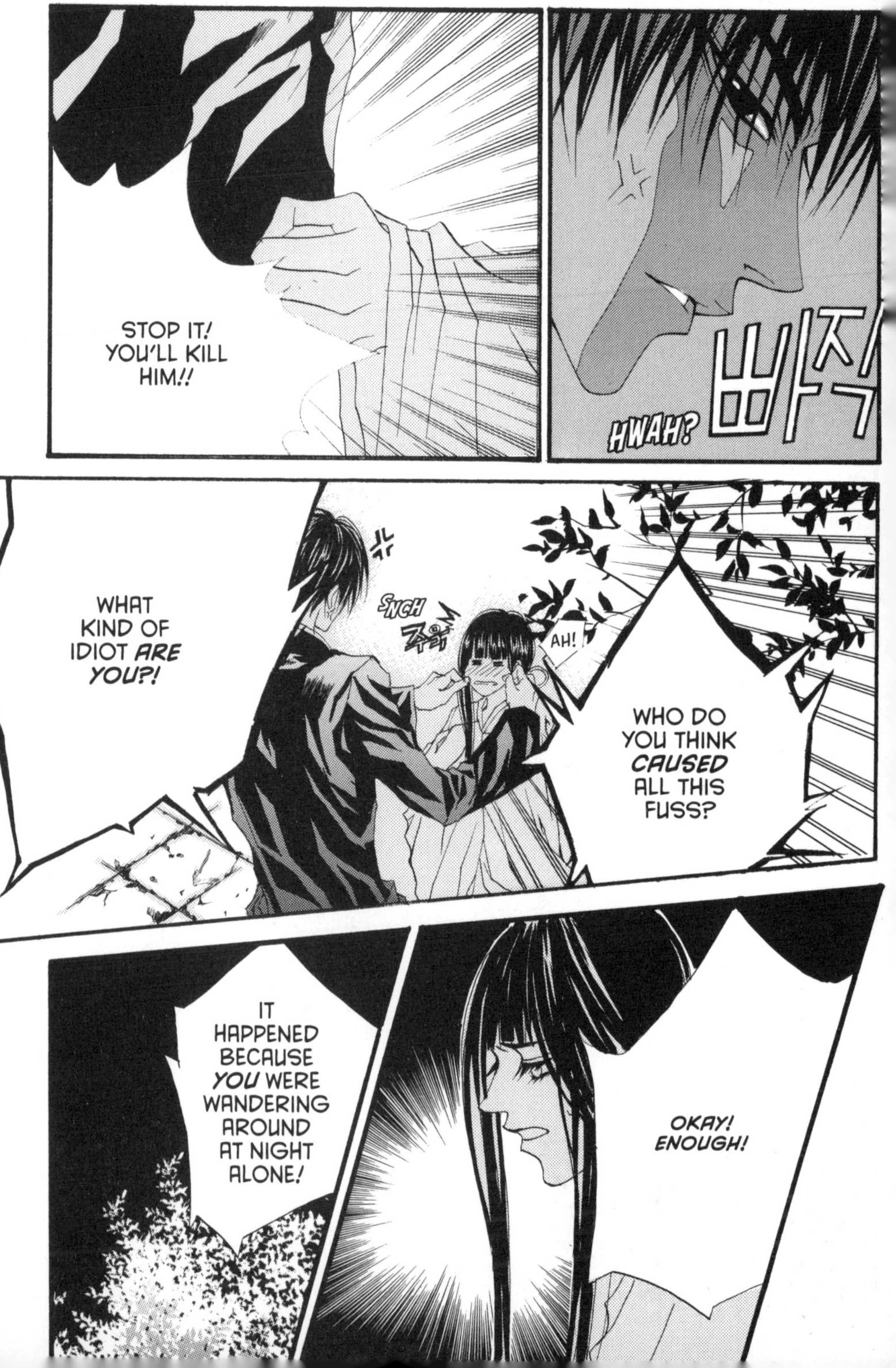

STOP IT! YOU'LL KILL HIM!!
HWAH?
빠직
WHAT KIND OF IDIOT *ARE YOU?!*
SNCH
주욱
AH!
WHO DO YOU THINK *CAUSED* ALL THIS FUSS?
IT HAPPENED BECAUSE *YOU* WERE WANDERING AROUND AT NIGHT ALONE!
OKAY! ENOUGH!

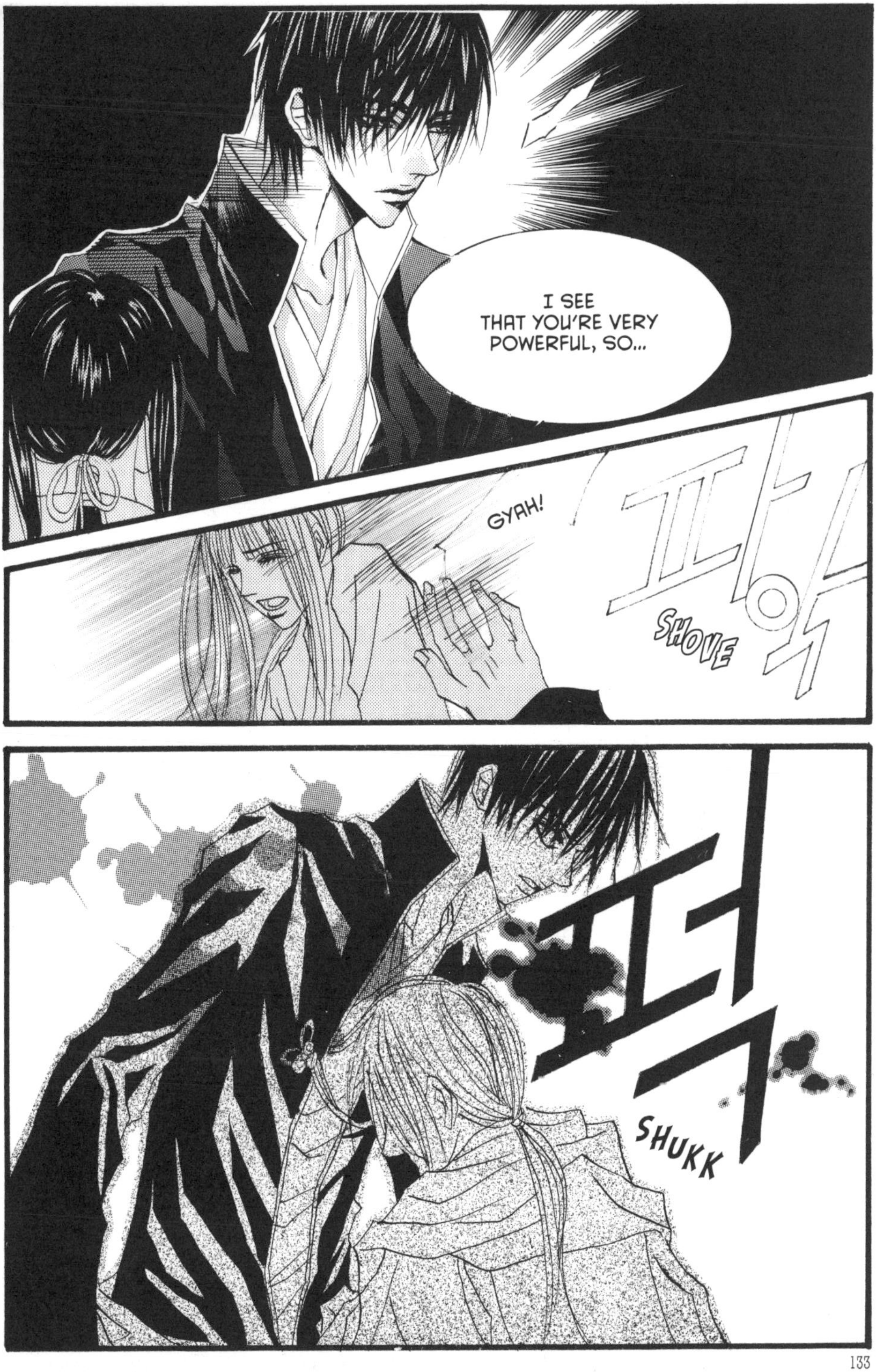
I SEE THAT YOU'RE VERY POWERFUL, SO...
GYAH!
SHOVE
SHUKK

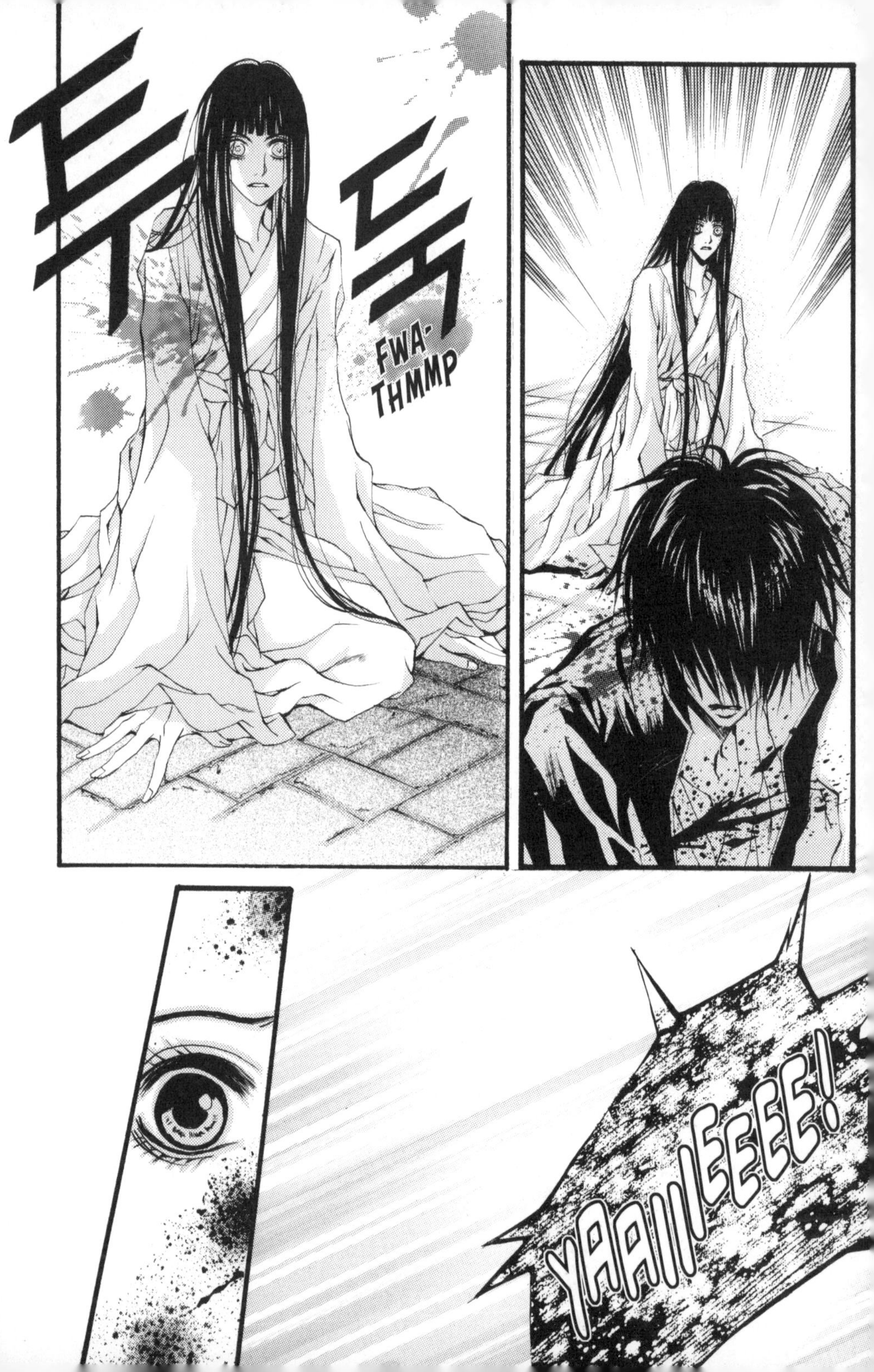
FWA-
THMMP
YAAIIEEEE!

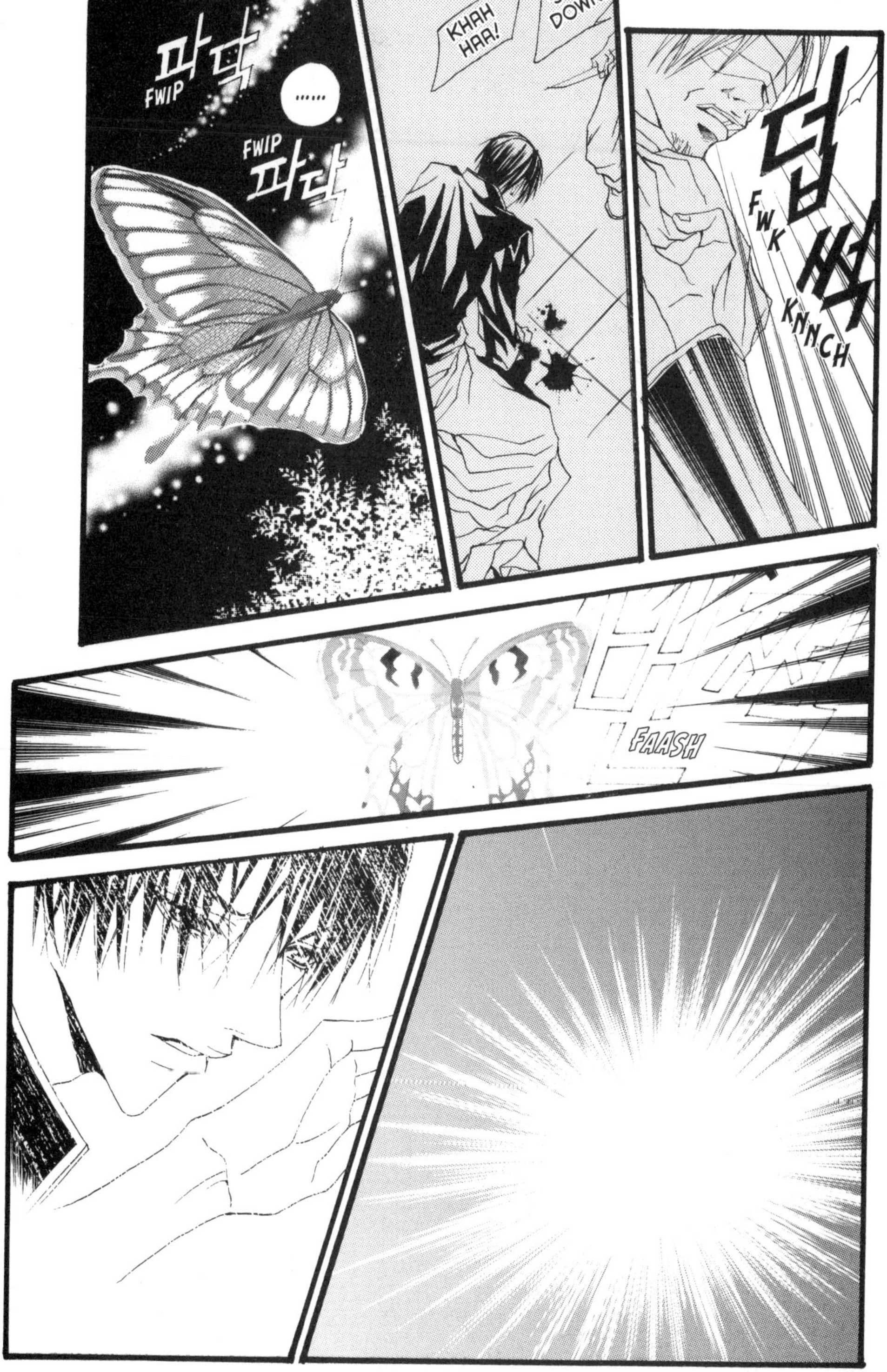
파닥
FWIP
......
FWIP
파닥
KHAH HAA!
STAY DOWN!
FWK
KNNCH
FAASH

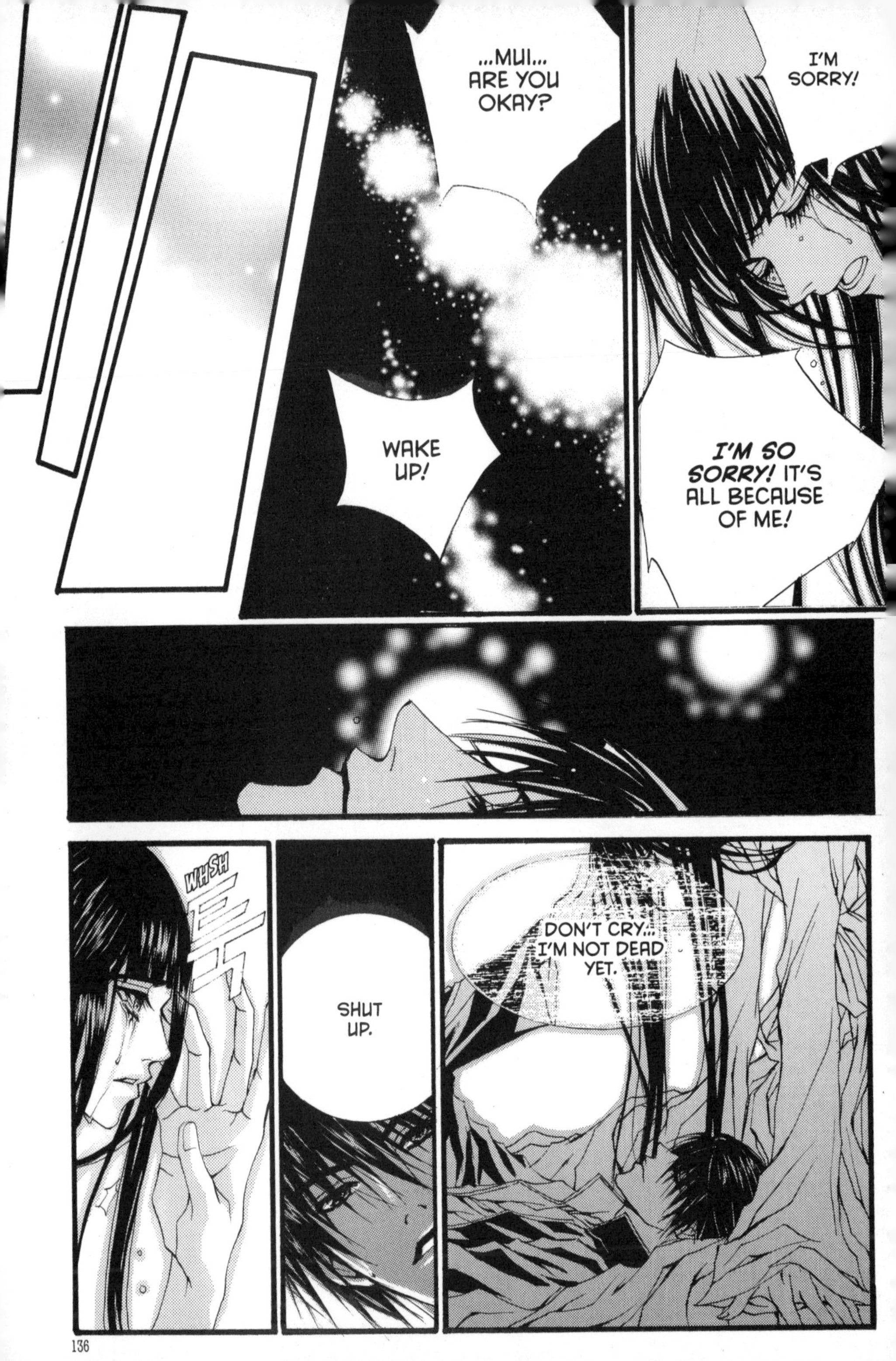

I'M SORRY!
I'M SO SORRY! IT'S ALL BECAUSE OF ME!
...MUI... ARE YOU OKAY?
WAKE UP!
DON'T CRY... I'M NOT DEAD YET.
SHUT UP.
WHSH

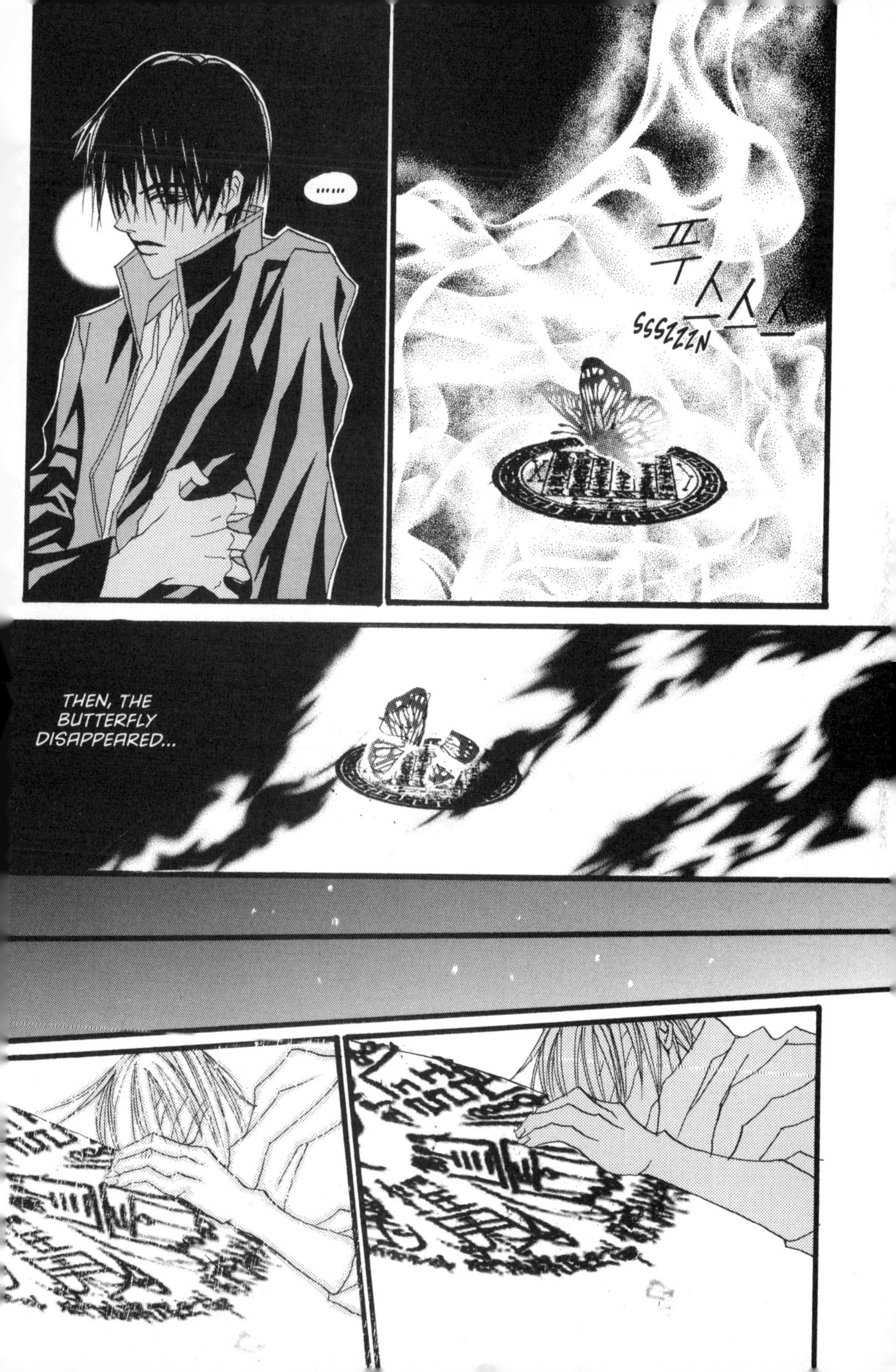
......
프스스스
SSSZZZN
THEN, THE BUTTERFLY DISAPPEARED...

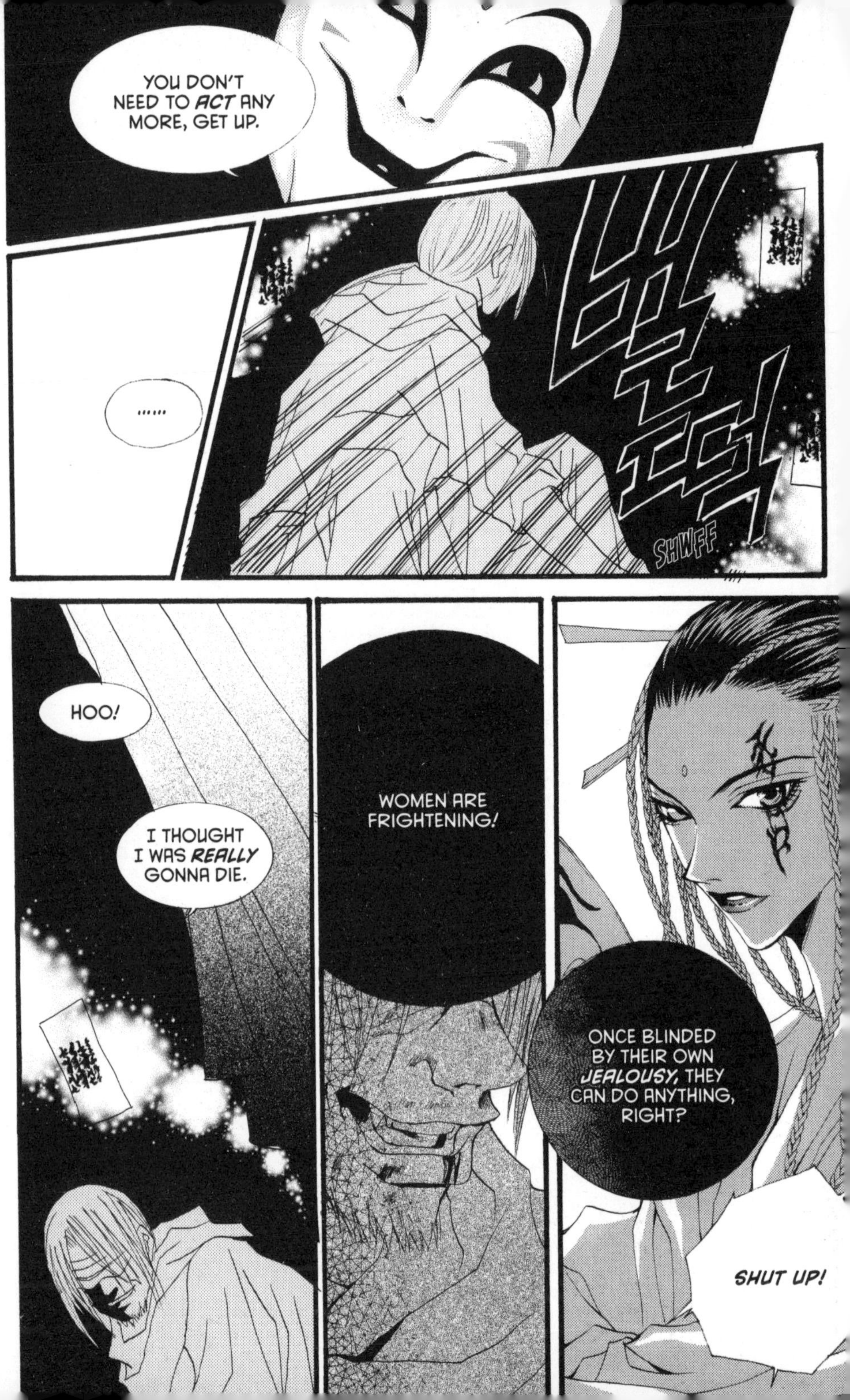

YOU DON'T NEED TO *ACT* ANY MORE, GET UP.
......
SHWFF
HOO!
I THOUGHT I WAS *REALLY* GONNA DIE.
WOMEN ARE FRIGHTENING!
ONCE BLINDED BY THEIR OWN *JEALOUSY,* THEY CAN DO ANYTHING, RIGHT?
SHUT UP!

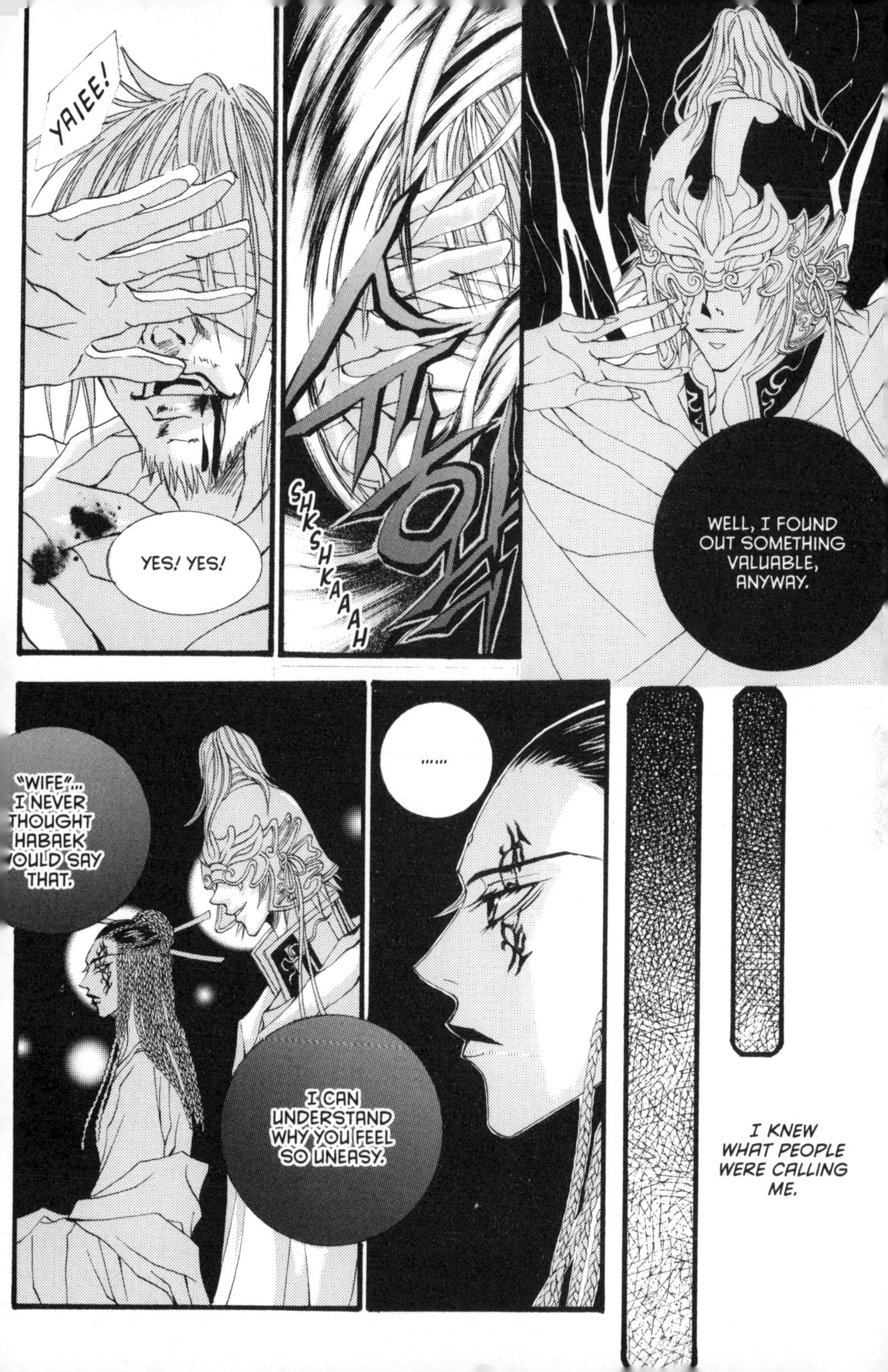
YAIEE!
YES! YES!
SHKSHKAAAAH
WELL, I FOUND OUT SOMETHING VALUABLE, ANYWAY.
"WIFE"... I NEVER THOUGHT HABAEK WOULD SAY THAT.
I CAN UNDERSTAND WHY YOU FEEL SO UNEASY.
......
I KNEW WHAT PEOPLE WERE CALLING ME.

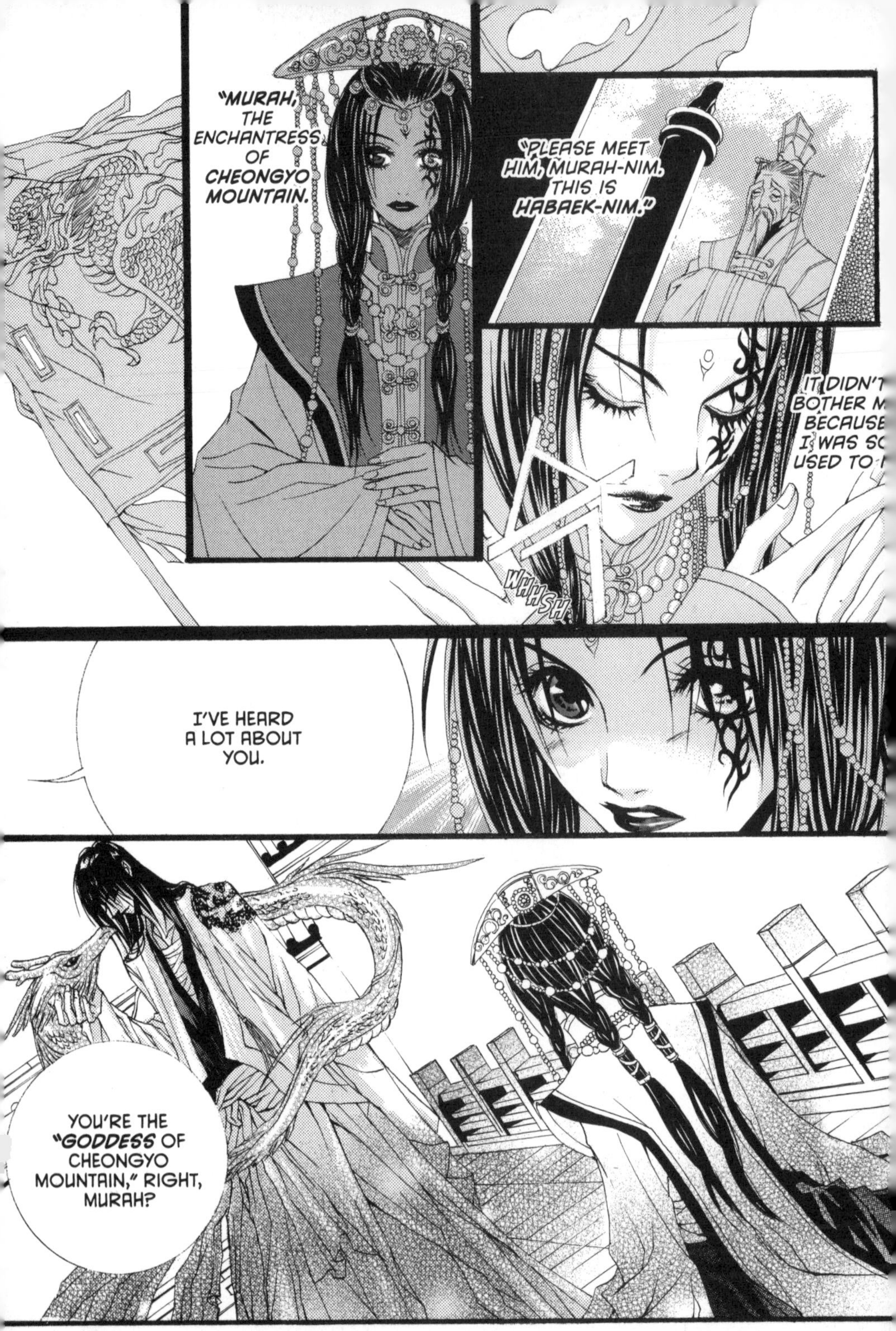
"MURAH, THE ENCHANTRESS OF CHEONGYO MOUNTAIN.
"PLEASE MEET HIM, MURAH-NIM. THIS IS HABAEK-NIM."
IT DIDN'T BOTHER M BECAUSE I WAS SO USED TO
WHHSH
I'VE HEARD A LOT ABOUT YOU.
YOU'RE THE "GODDESS OF CHEONGYO MOUNTAIN," RIGHT, MURAH?

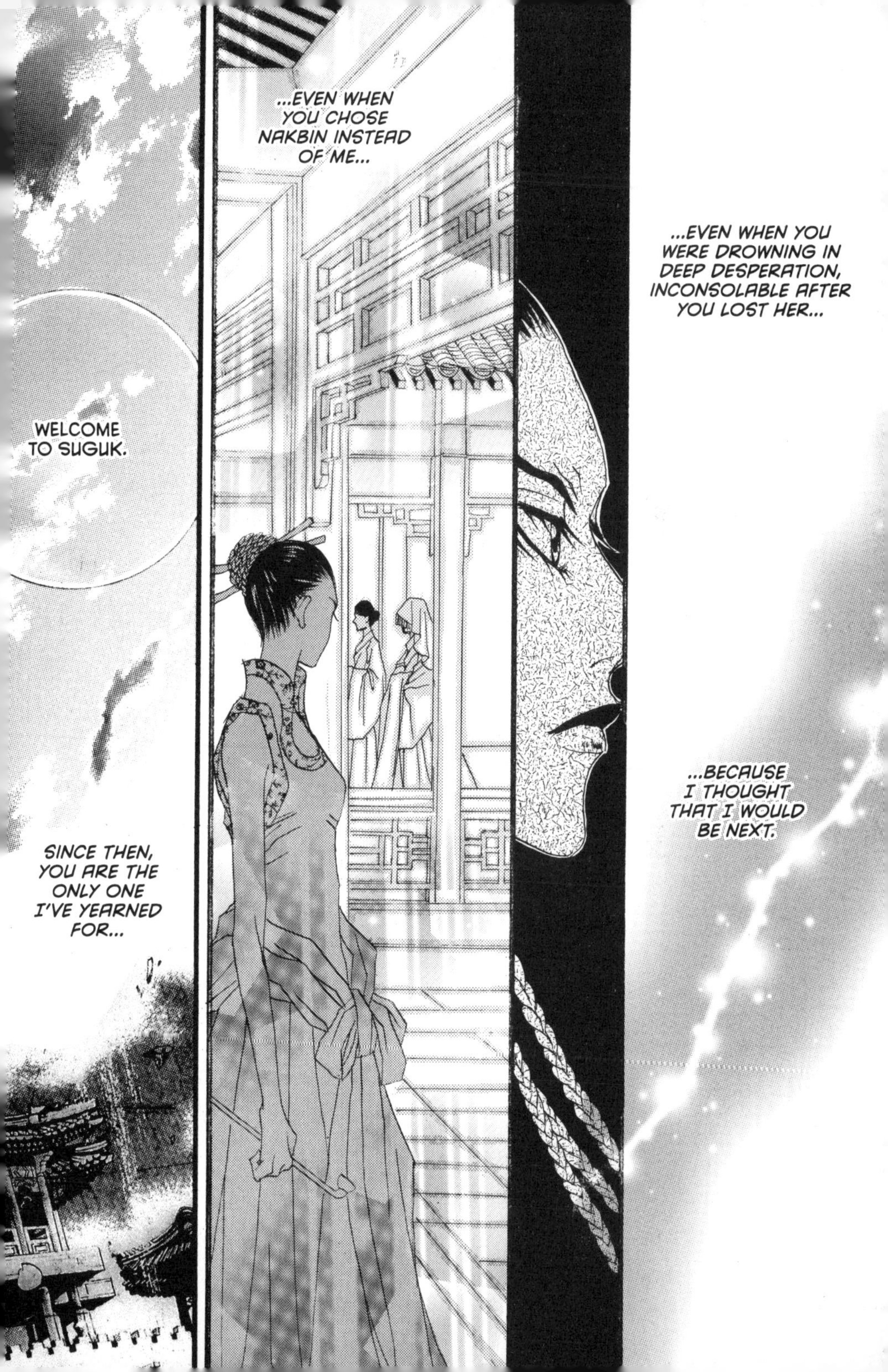
WELCOME TO SUGUK.
SINCE THEN, YOU ARE THE ONLY ONE I'VE YEARNED FOR...
...EVEN WHEN YOU CHOSE NAKBIN INSTEAD OF ME...
...EVEN WHEN YOU WERE DROWNING IN DEEP DESPERATION, INCONSOLABLE AFTER YOU LOST HER...
...BECAUSE I THOUGHT THAT I WOULD BE NEXT.

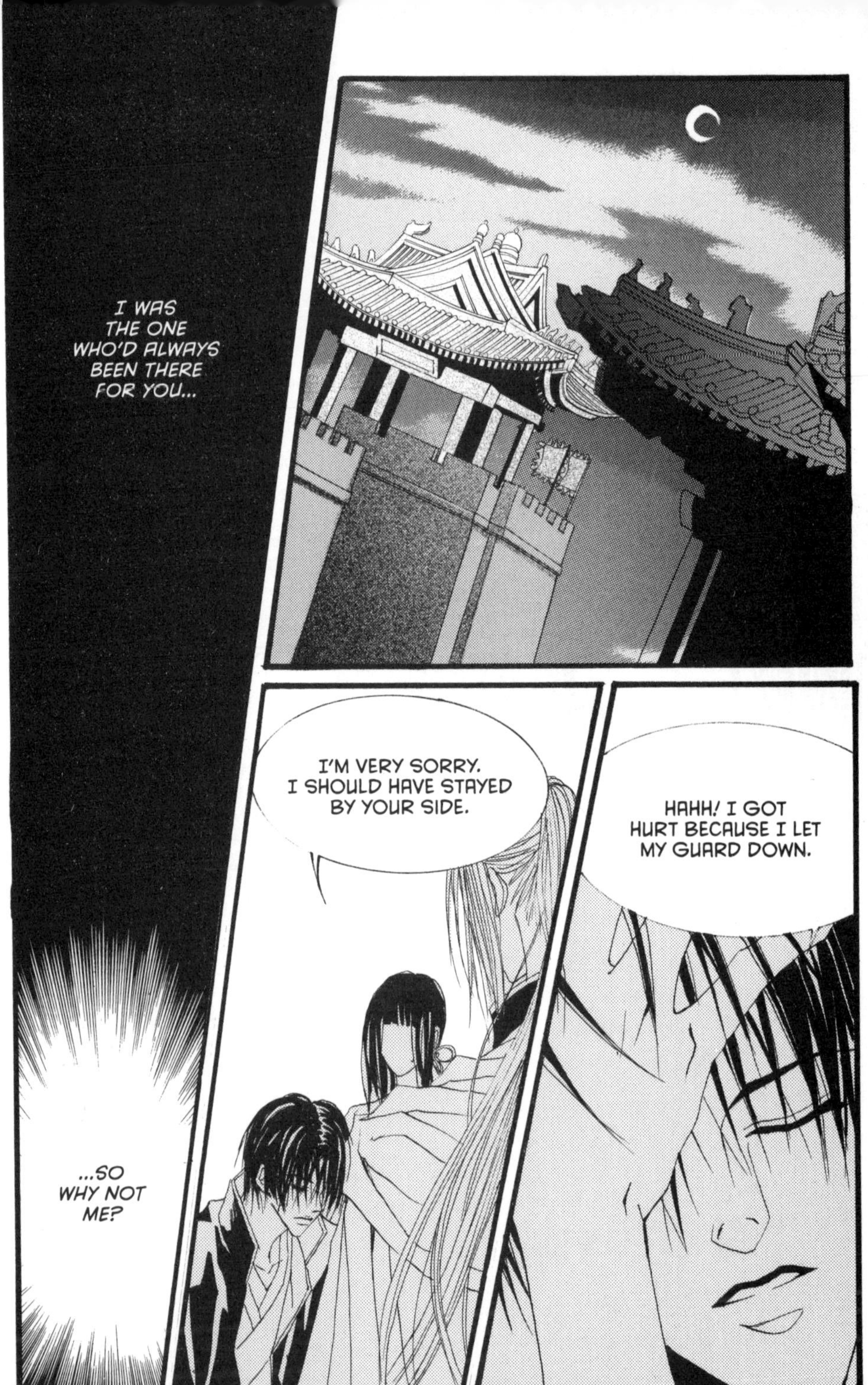
I WAS THE ONE WHO'D ALWAYS BEEN THERE FOR YOU...
I'M VERY SORRY. I SHOULD HAVE STAYED BY YOUR SIDE.
HAHH! I GOT HURT BECAUSE I LET MY GUARD DOWN.
...SO WHY NOT ME?

ARE YOU OKAY, SOAH-NIM?

AH, YES...I'M FINE. THANK YOU VERY MUCH FOR ASKING, HUYE...

WE'D BETTER BE CAREFUL HERE.

YES...?

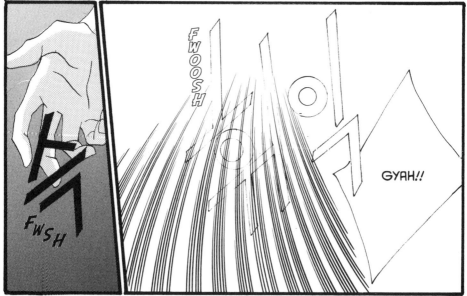

FWOOSH

FWSH

GYAH!!

143

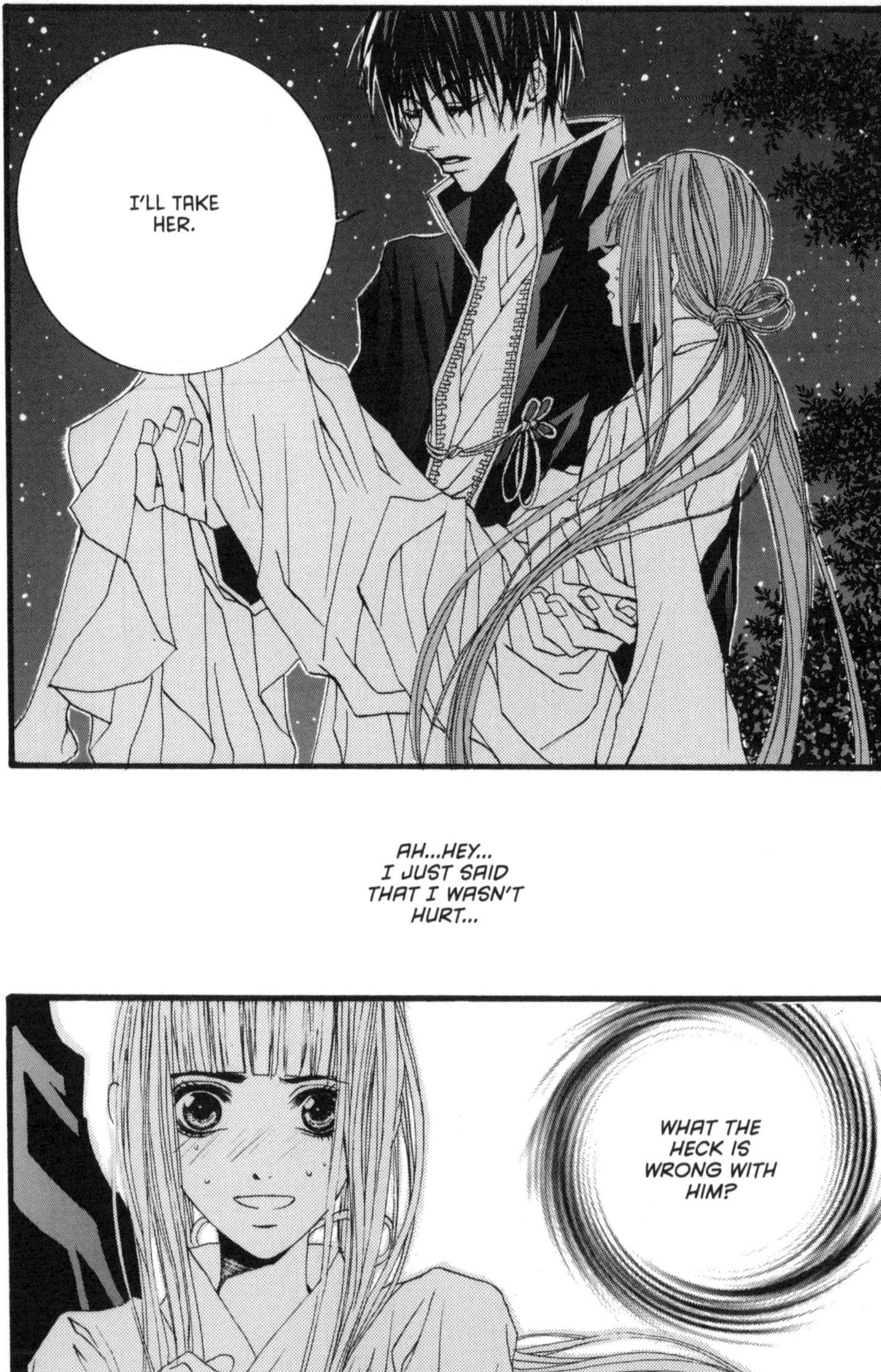
I'LL TAKE HER.
AH...HEY... I JUST SAID THAT I WASN'T HURT...
WHAT THE HECK IS WRONG WITH HIM?

BRIDE of the WATER GOD

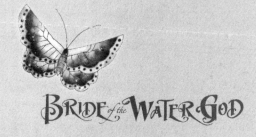

*"Mui mistook
me for Nakbin?"*

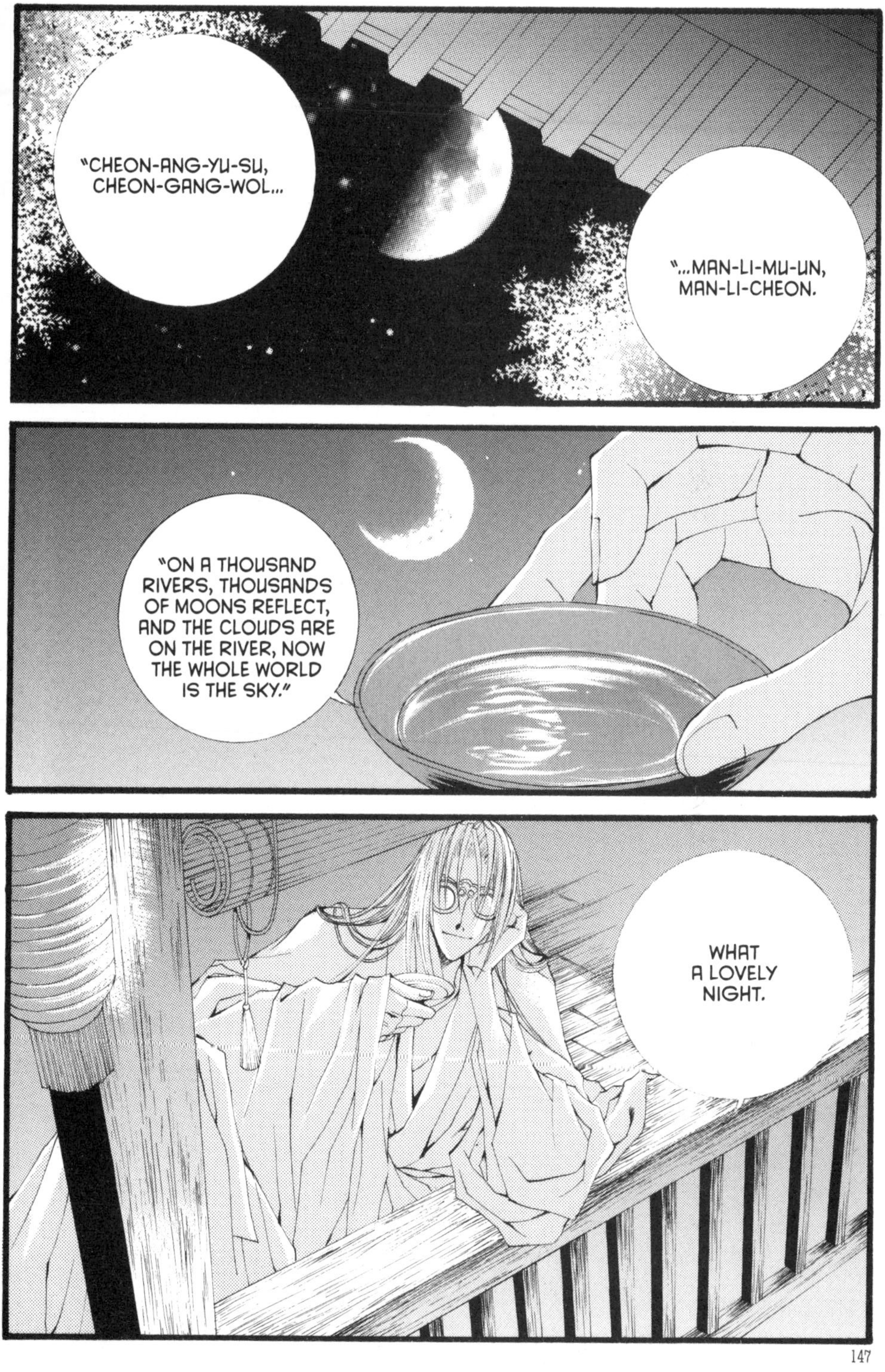
"CHEON-ANG-YU-SU, CHEON-GANG-WOL...
"...MAN-LI-MU-UN, MAN-LI-CHEON.
"ON A THOUSAND RIVERS, THOUSANDS OF MOONS REFLECT, AND THE CLOUDS ARE ON THE RIVER, NOW THE WHOLE WORLD IS THE SKY."
WHAT A LOVELY NIGHT.

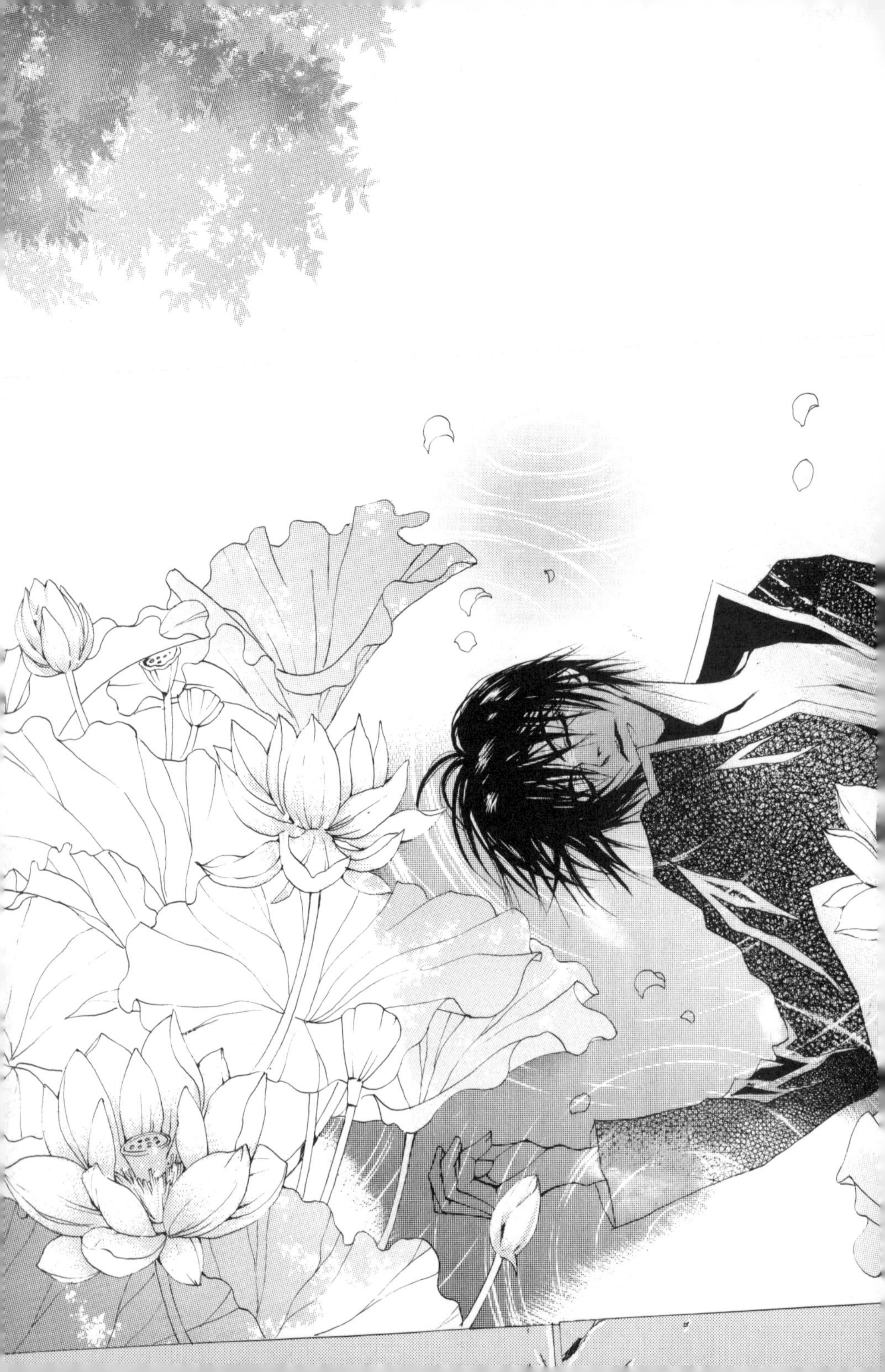

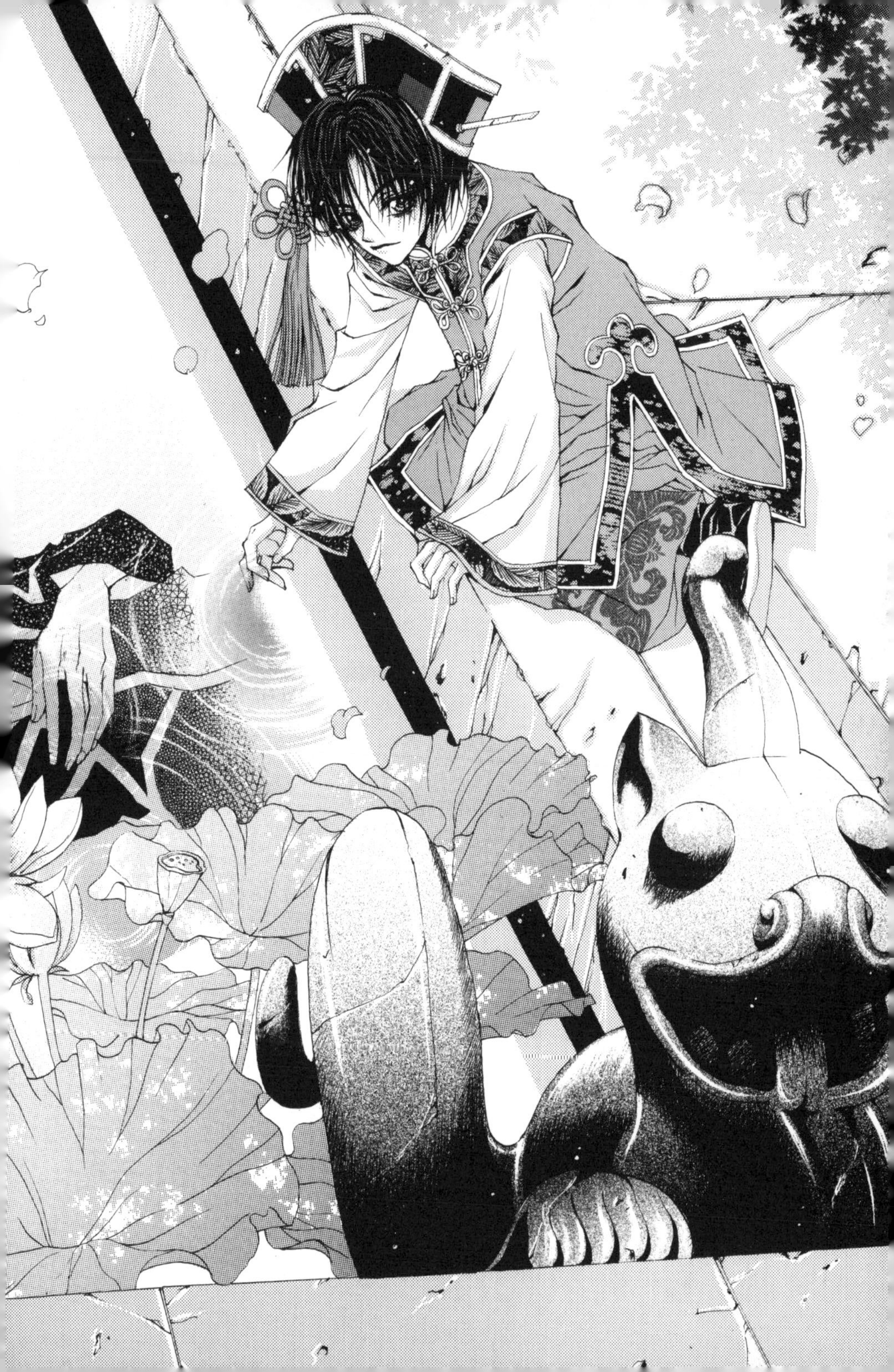

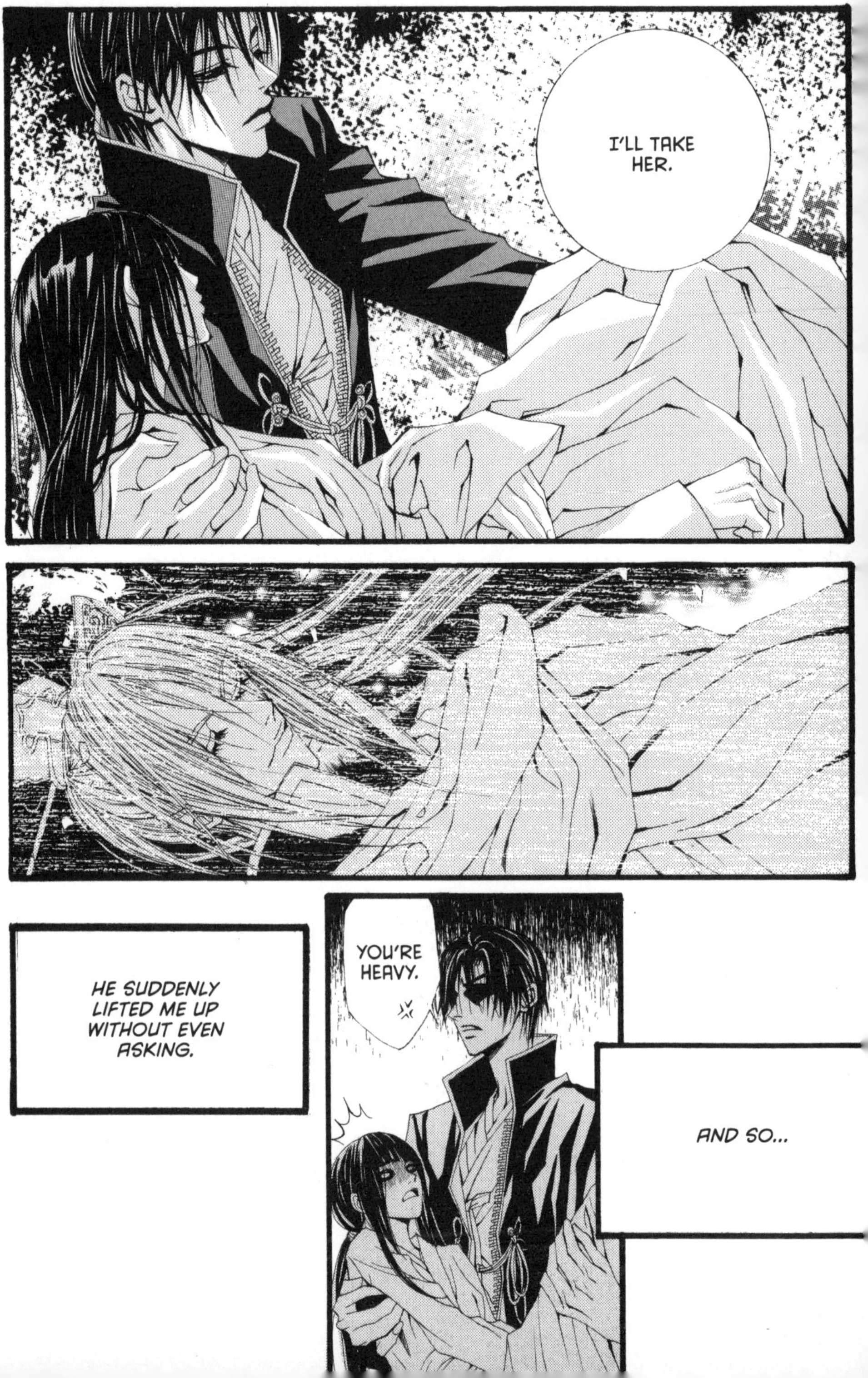
I'LL TAKE HER.
HE SUDDENLY LIFTED ME UP WITHOUT EVEN ASKING.
YOU'RE HEAVY.
AND SO...

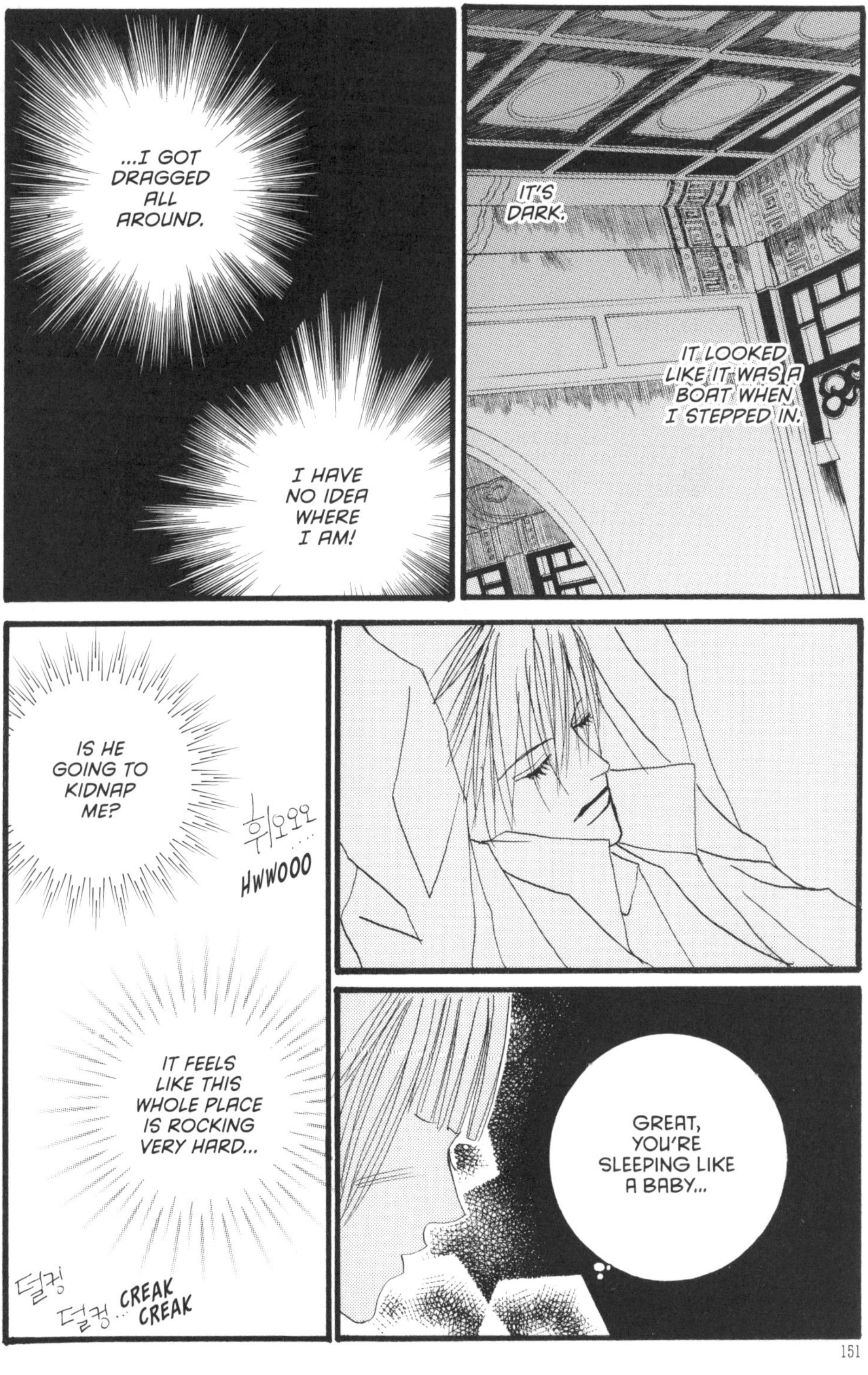
...I GOT DRAGGED ALL AROUND.
I HAVE NO IDEA WHERE I AM!
IT'S DARK.
IT LOOKED LIKE IT WAS A BOAT WHEN I STEPPED IN.
IS HE GOING TO KIDNAP ME?
휘오오오...
HWWOOO
IT FEELS LIKE THIS WHOLE PLACE IS ROCKING VERY HARD...
덜컹 덜컹...
CREAK CREAK
GREAT, YOU'RE SLEEPING LIKE A BABY...

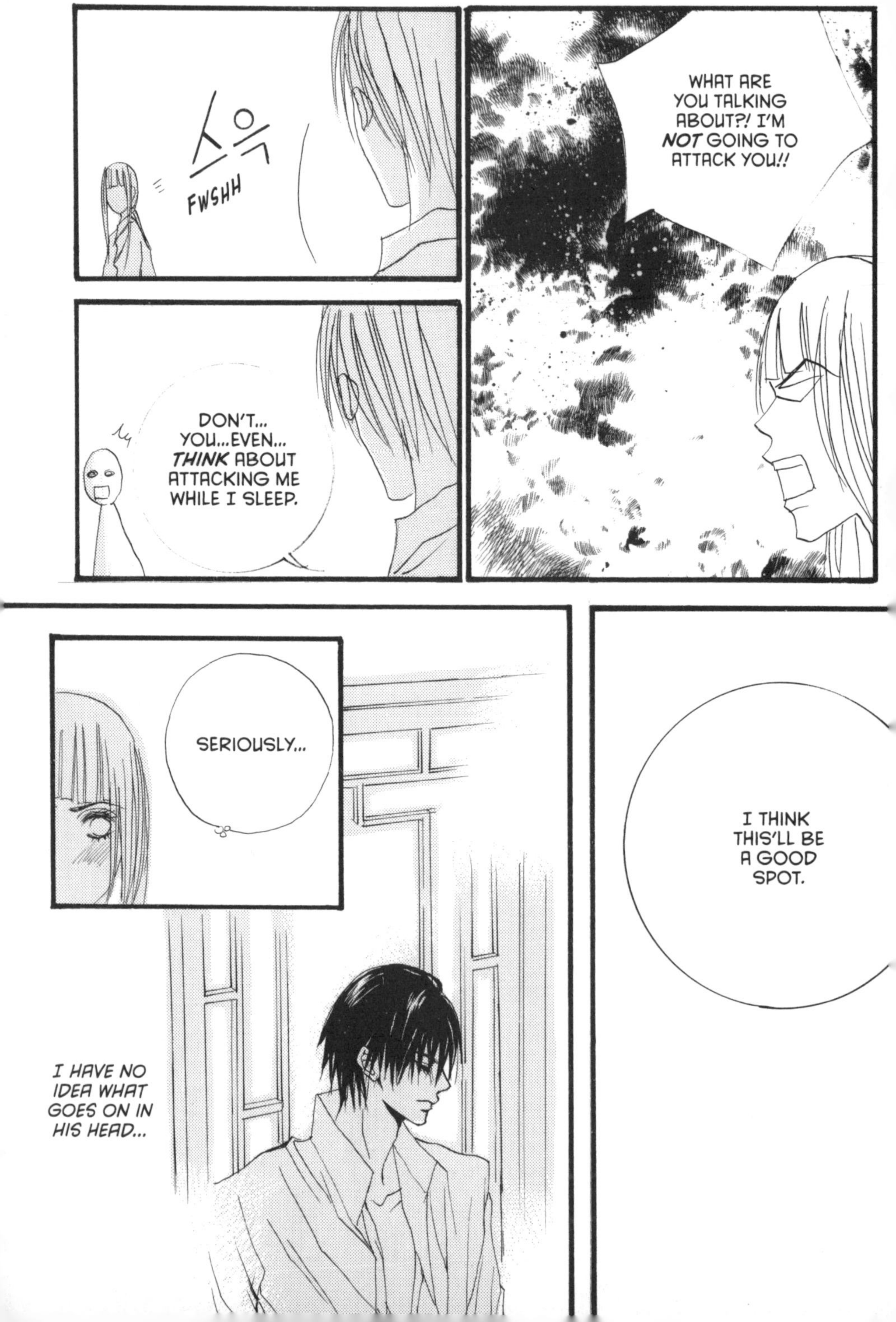
스윽
FWSHH
DON'T... YOU...EVEN... THINK ABOUT ATTACKING ME WHILE I SLEEP.
WHAT ARE YOU TALKING ABOUT?! I'M NOT GOING TO ATTACK YOU!!
SERIOUSLY...
I HAVE NO IDEA WHAT GOES ON IN HIS HEAD...
I THINK THIS'LL BE A GOOD SPOT.

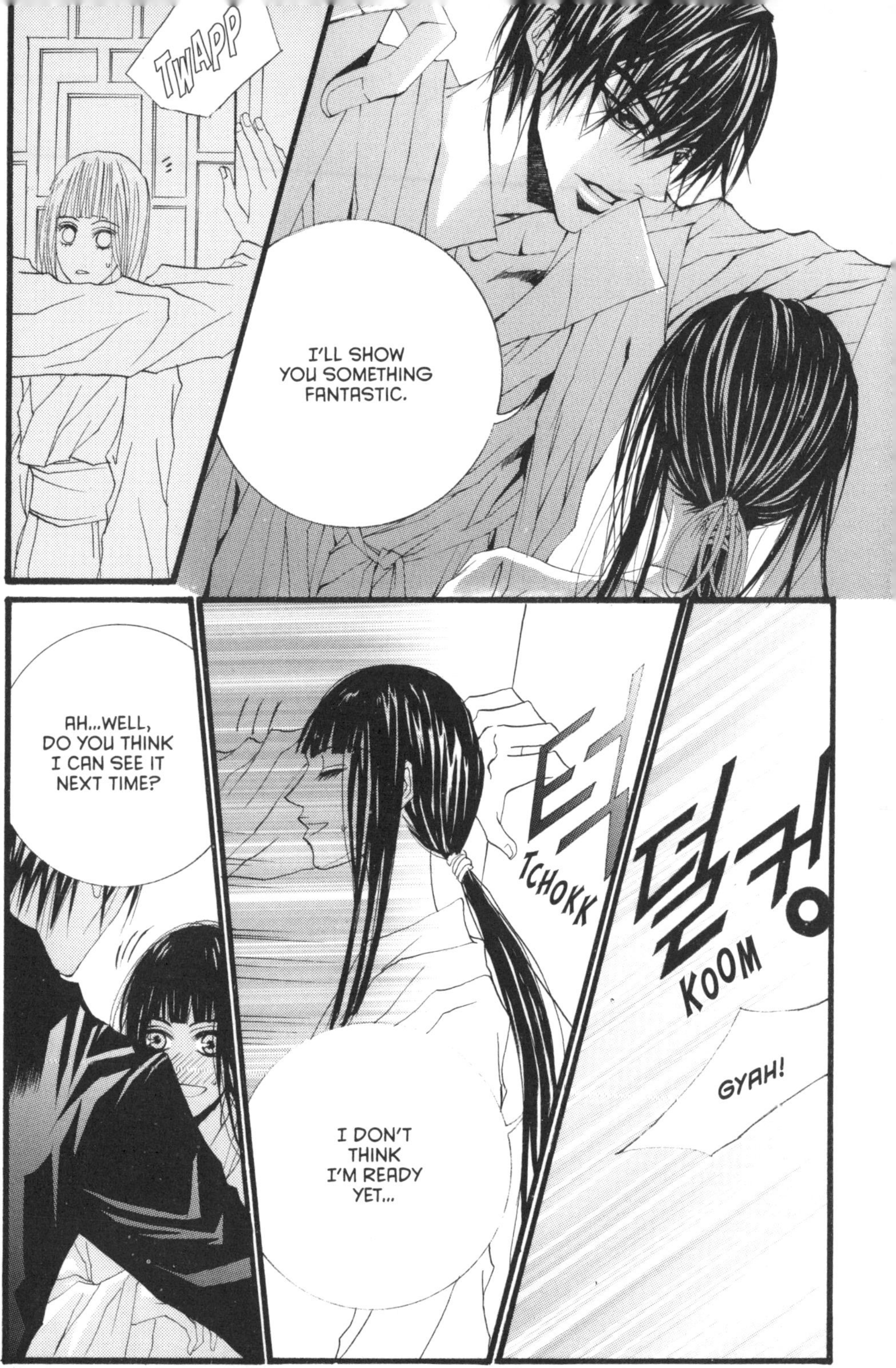
TWAPP
I'LL SHOW YOU SOMETHING FANTASTIC.
AH...WELL, DO YOU THINK I CAN SEE IT NEXT TIME?
I DON'T THINK I'M READY YET...
TCHOKK
KOOM
GYAH!

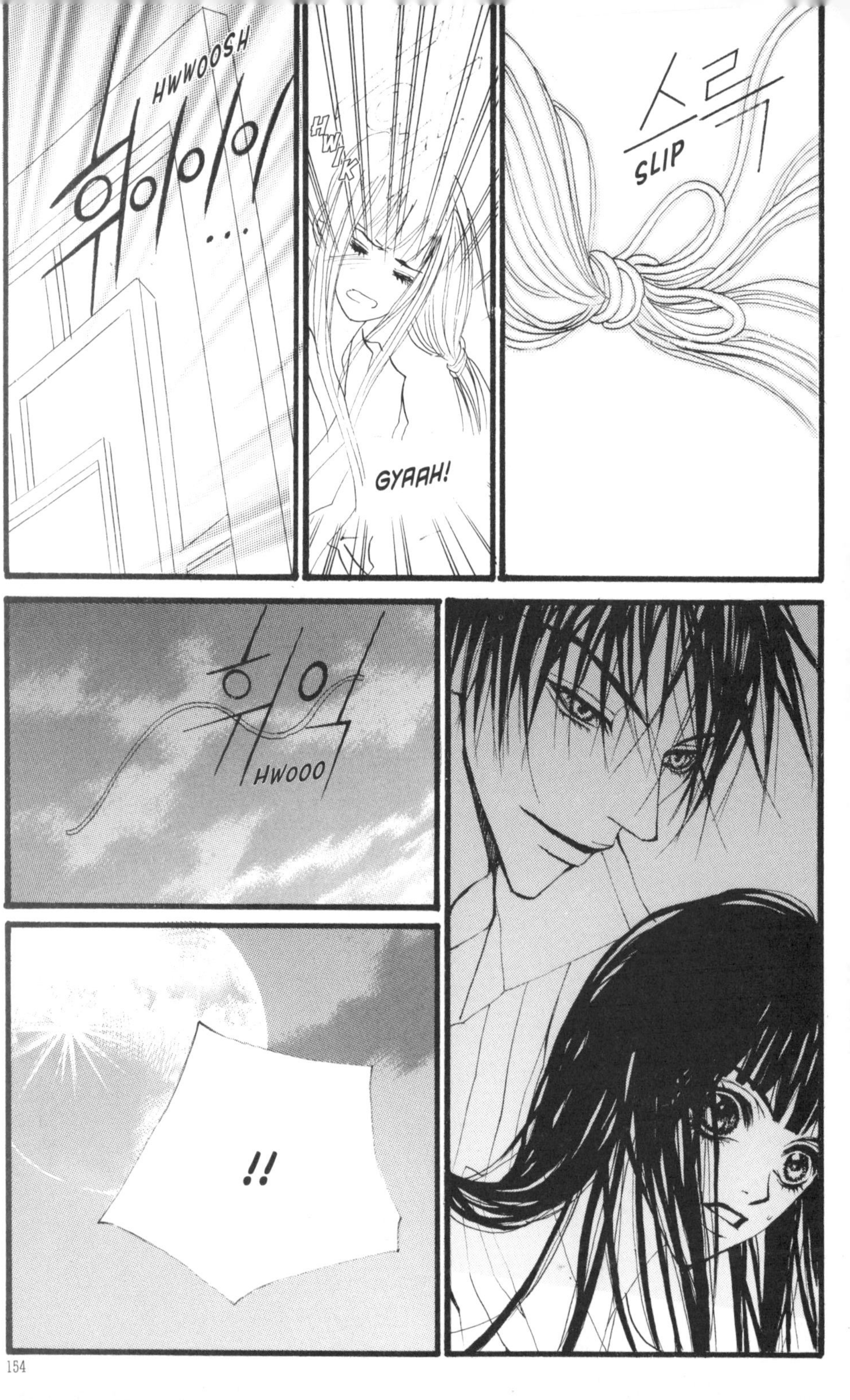
HWWOOSH
...
HWIK
GYAAH!
스륵
SLIP
휘익
HWOOO
!!

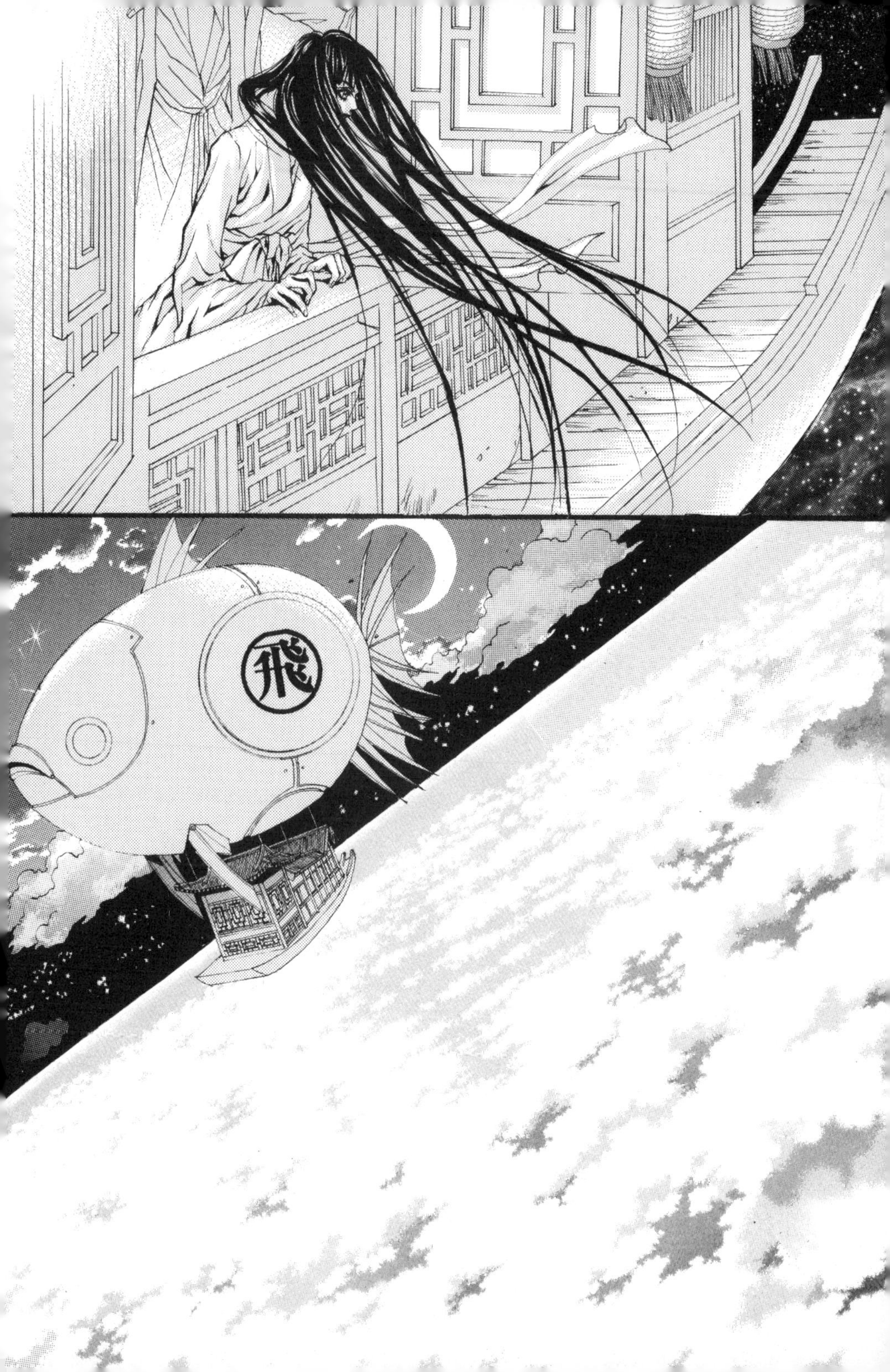
飛

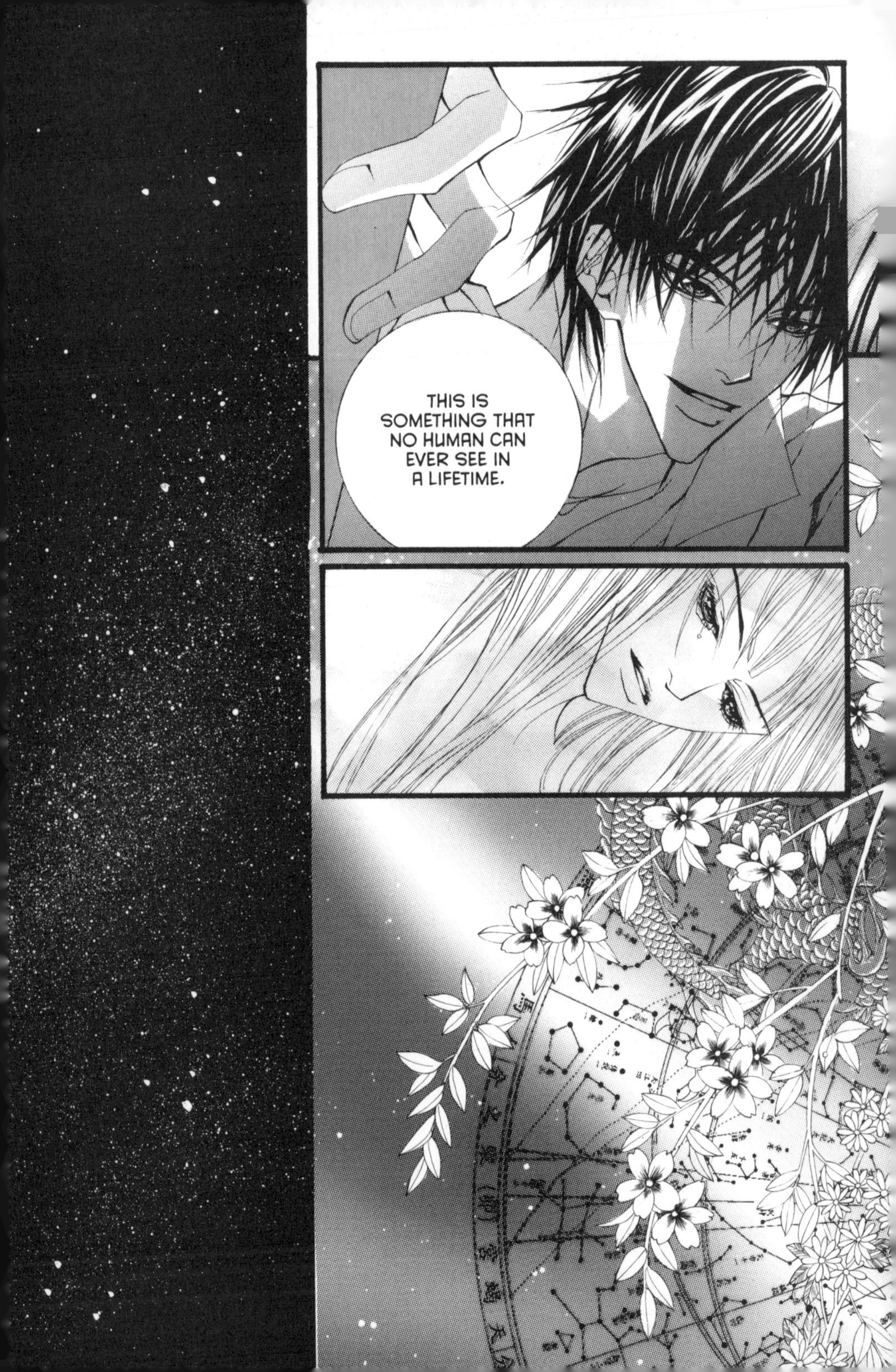
THIS IS SOMETHING THAT NO HUMAN CAN EVER SEE IN A LIFETIME.

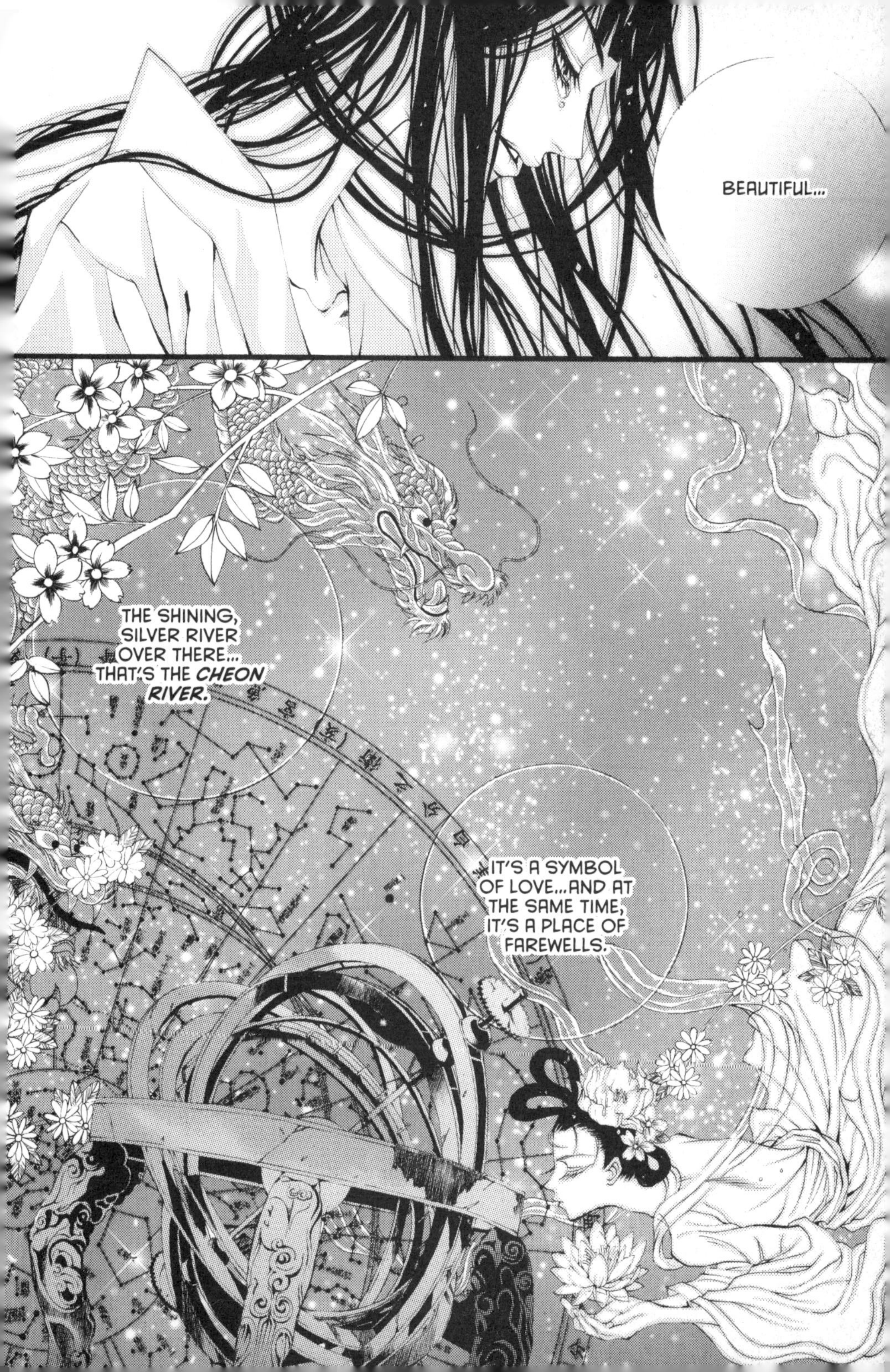
BEAUTIFUL...
THE SHINING, SILVER RIVER OVER THERE... THAT'S THE *CHEON RIVER.*
IT'S A SYMBOL OF LOVE...AND AT THE SAME TIME, IT'S A PLACE OF FAREWELLS.

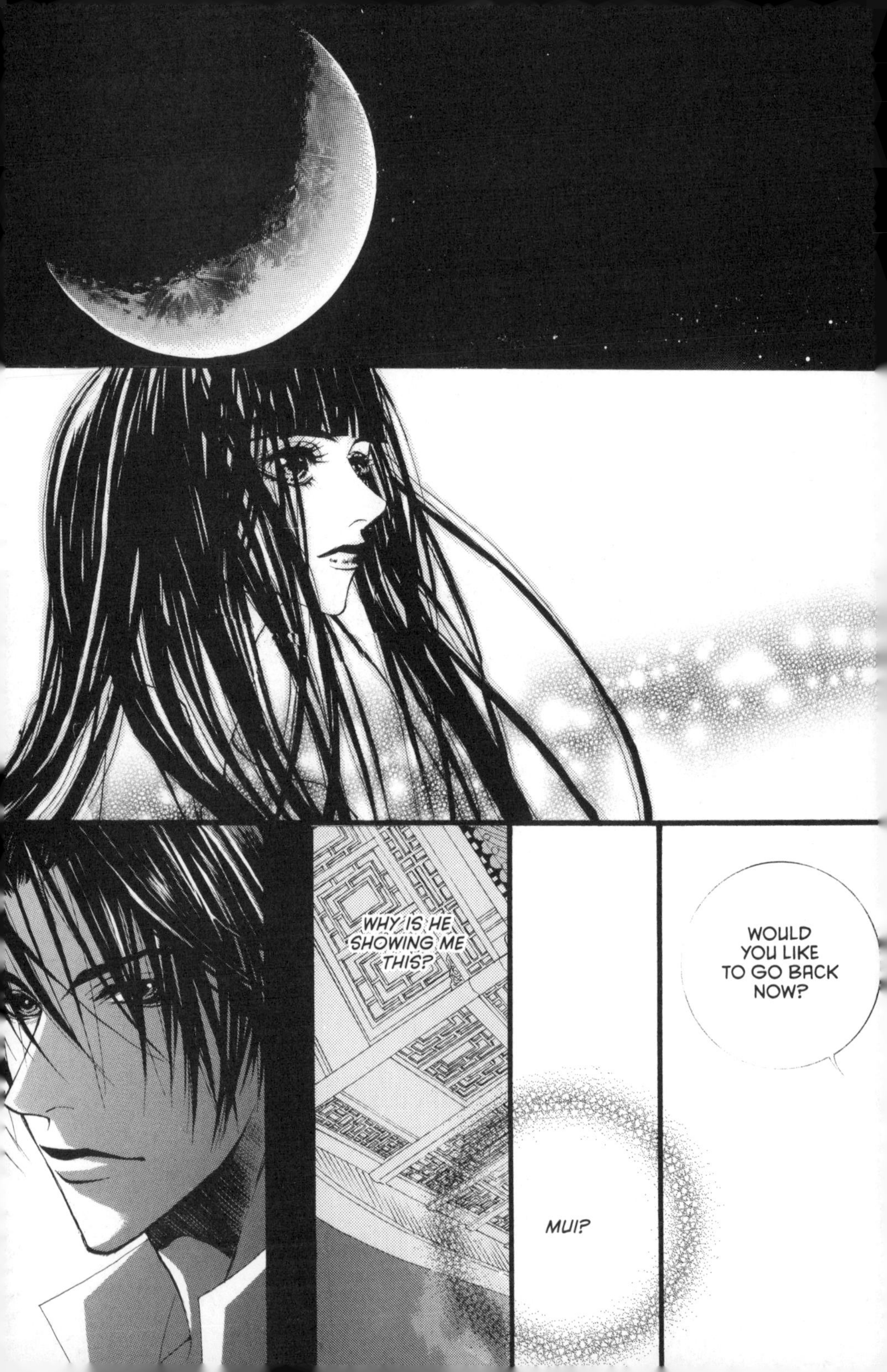
WOULD YOU LIKE TO GO BACK NOW?
MUI?
WHY IS HE SHOWING ME THIS?

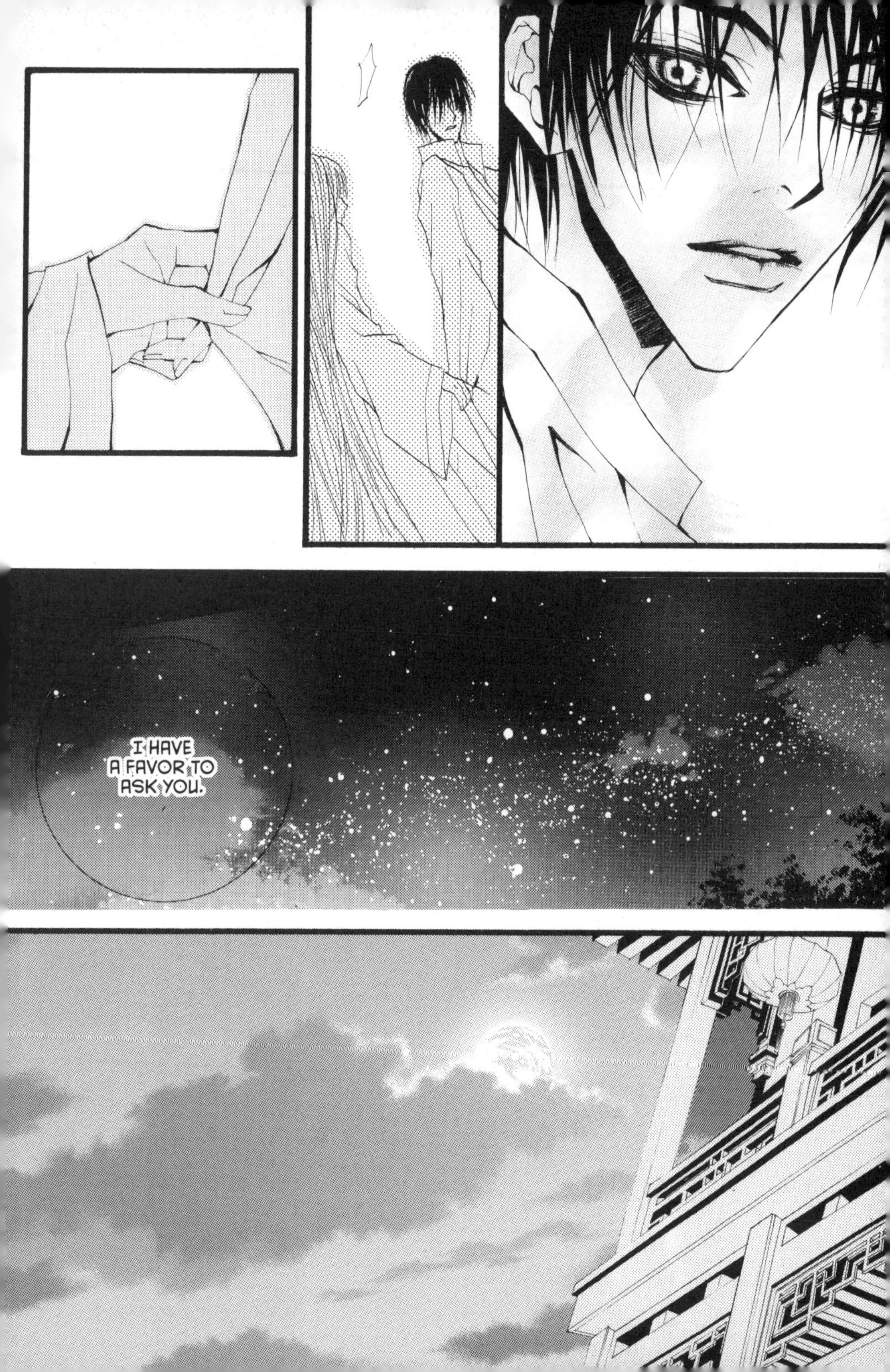
I HAVE A FAVOR TO ASK YOU.

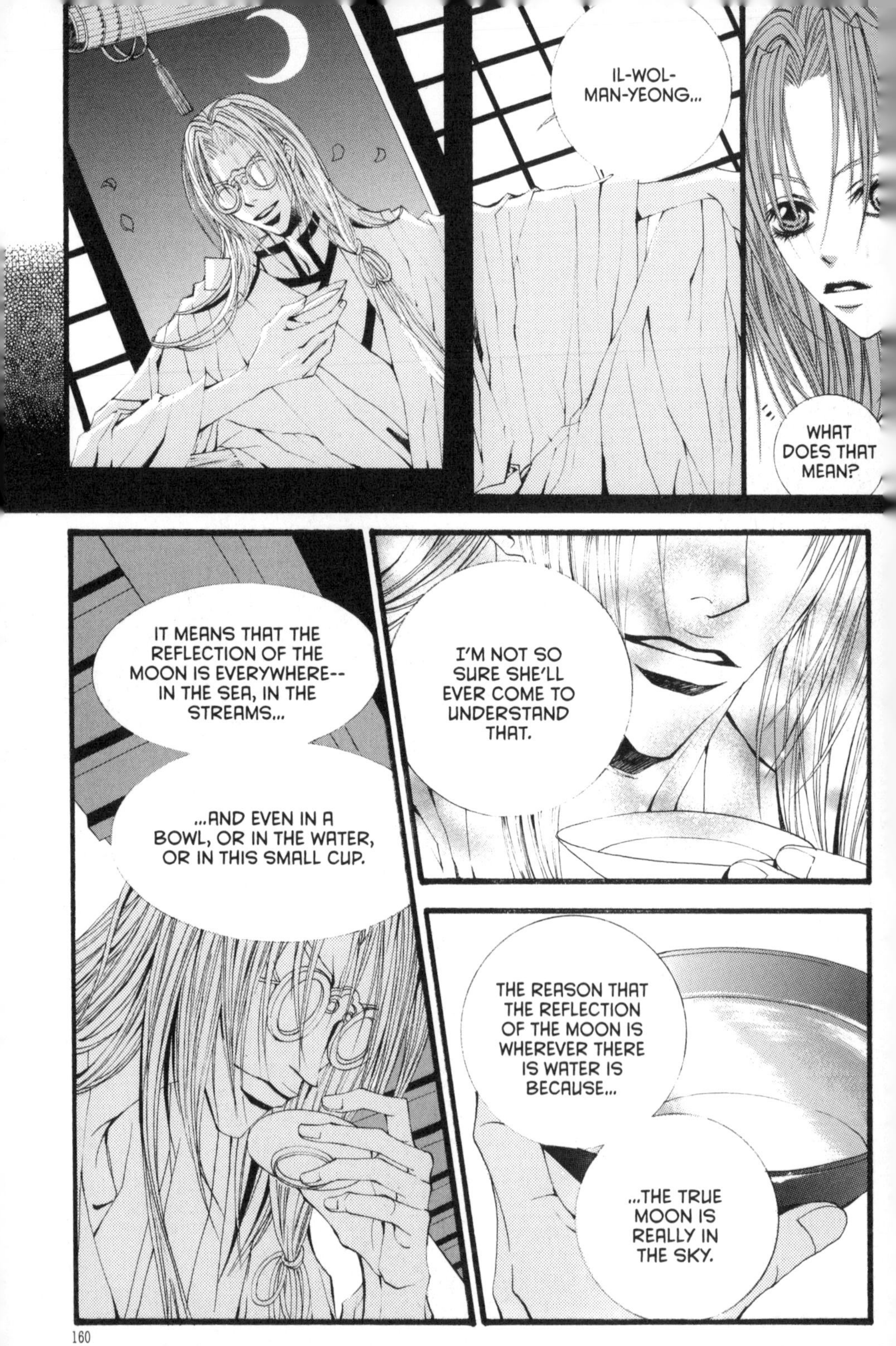
IL-WOL-MAN-YEONG...
WHAT DOES THAT MEAN?
IT MEANS THAT THE REFLECTION OF THE MOON IS EVERYWHERE-- IN THE SEA, IN THE STREAMS...
...AND EVEN IN A BOWL, OR IN THE WATER, OR IN THIS SMALL CUP.
I'M NOT SO SURE SHE'LL EVER COME TO UNDERSTAND THAT.
THE REASON THAT THE REFLECTION OF THE MOON IS WHEREVER THERE IS WATER IS BECAUSE...
...THE TRUE MOON IS REALLY IN THE SKY.

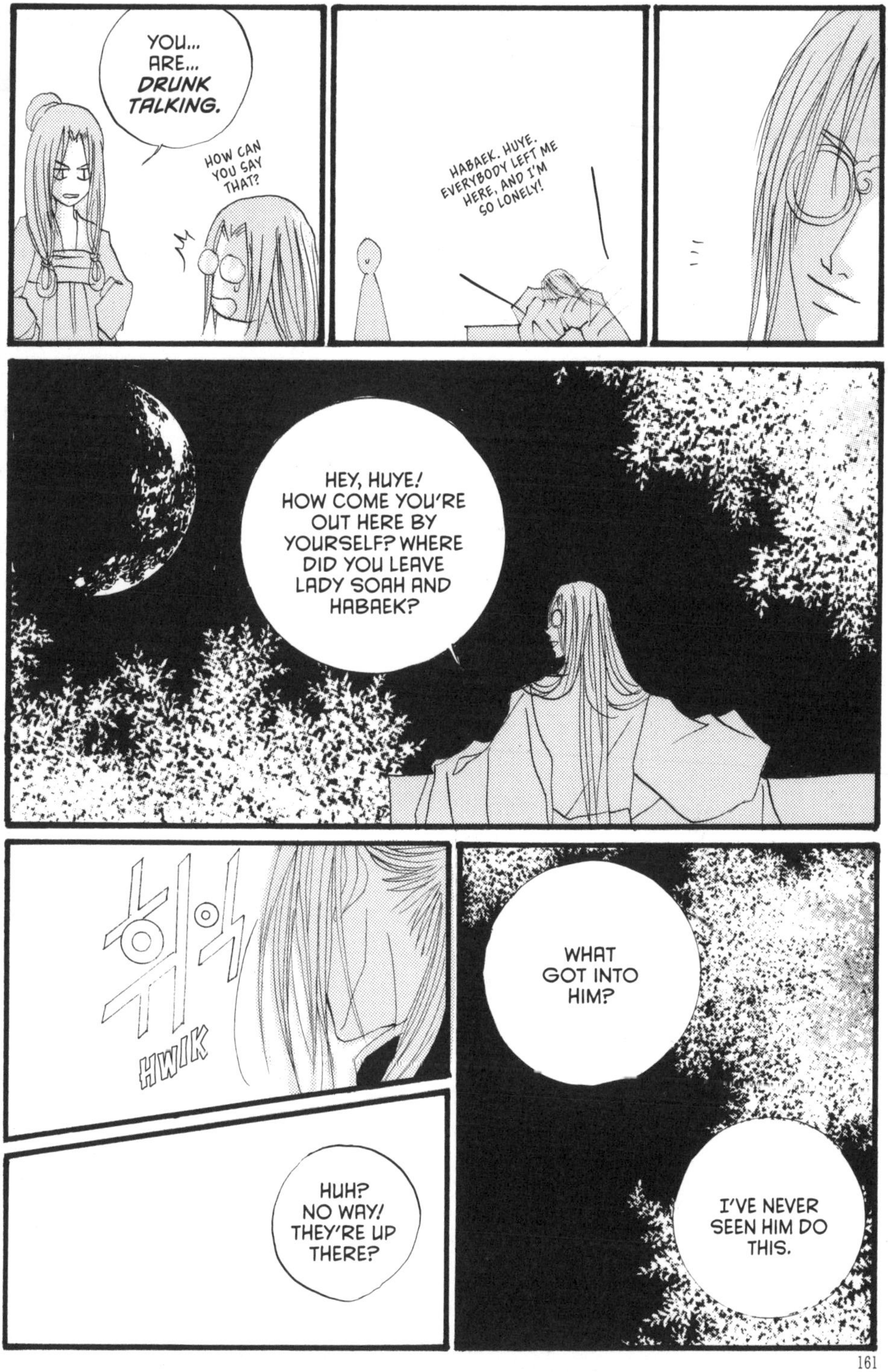
YOU... ARE... DRUNK TALKING.
HOW CAN YOU SAY THAT?
HABAEK. HUYE. EVERYBODY LEFT ME HERE, AND I'M SO LONELY!
HEY, HUYE! HOW COME YOU'RE OUT HERE BY YOURSELF? WHERE DID YOU LEAVE LADY SOAH AND HABAEK?
휘익
HWIK
WHAT GOT INTO HIM?
HUH? NO WAY! THEY'RE UP THERE?
I'VE NEVER SEEN HIM DO THIS.

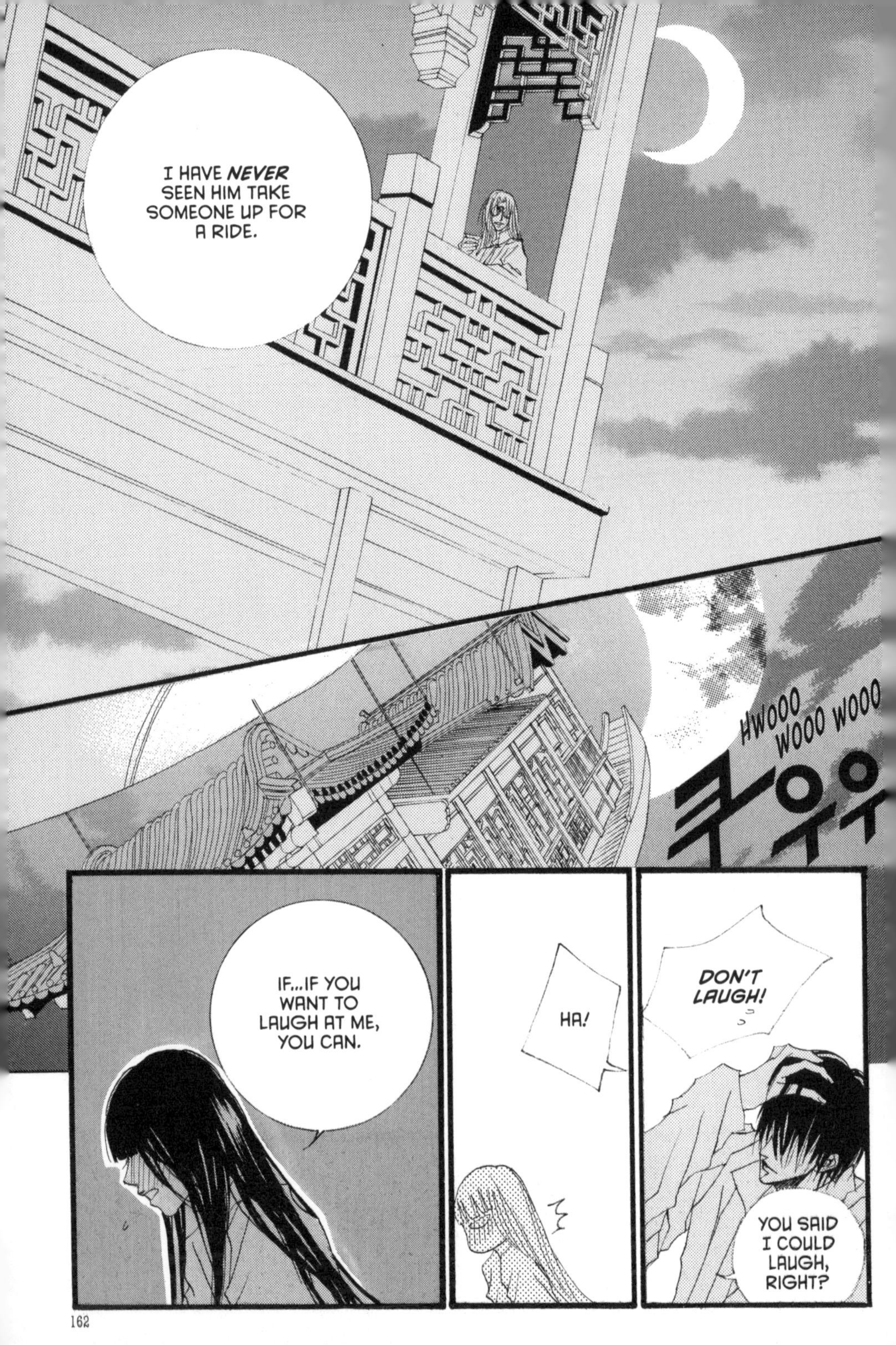
I HAVE *NEVER* SEEN HIM TAKE SOMEONE UP FOR A RIDE.
HWOOO WOOO WOOO
IF...IF YOU WANT TO LAUGH AT ME, YOU CAN.
HA!
DON'T LAUGH!
YOU SAID I COULD LAUGH, RIGHT?

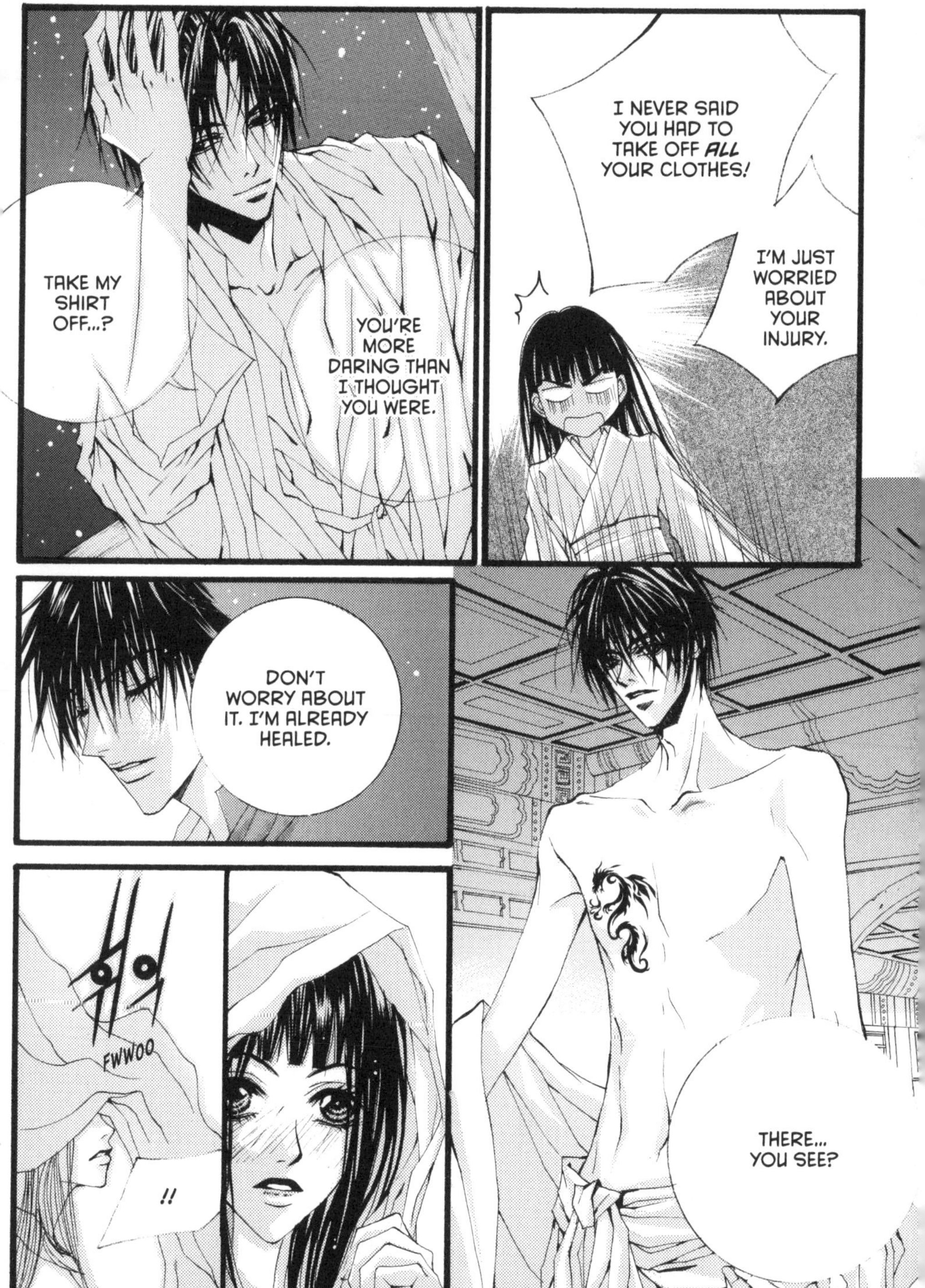

TAKE MY SHIRT OFF...?
YOU'RE MORE DARING THAN I THOUGHT YOU WERE.
I NEVER SAID YOU HAD TO TAKE OFF *ALL* YOUR CLOTHES!
I'M JUST WORRIED ABOUT YOUR INJURY.
DON'T WORRY ABOUT IT. I'M ALREADY HEALED.
THERE... YOU SEE?
FWWOO
!!

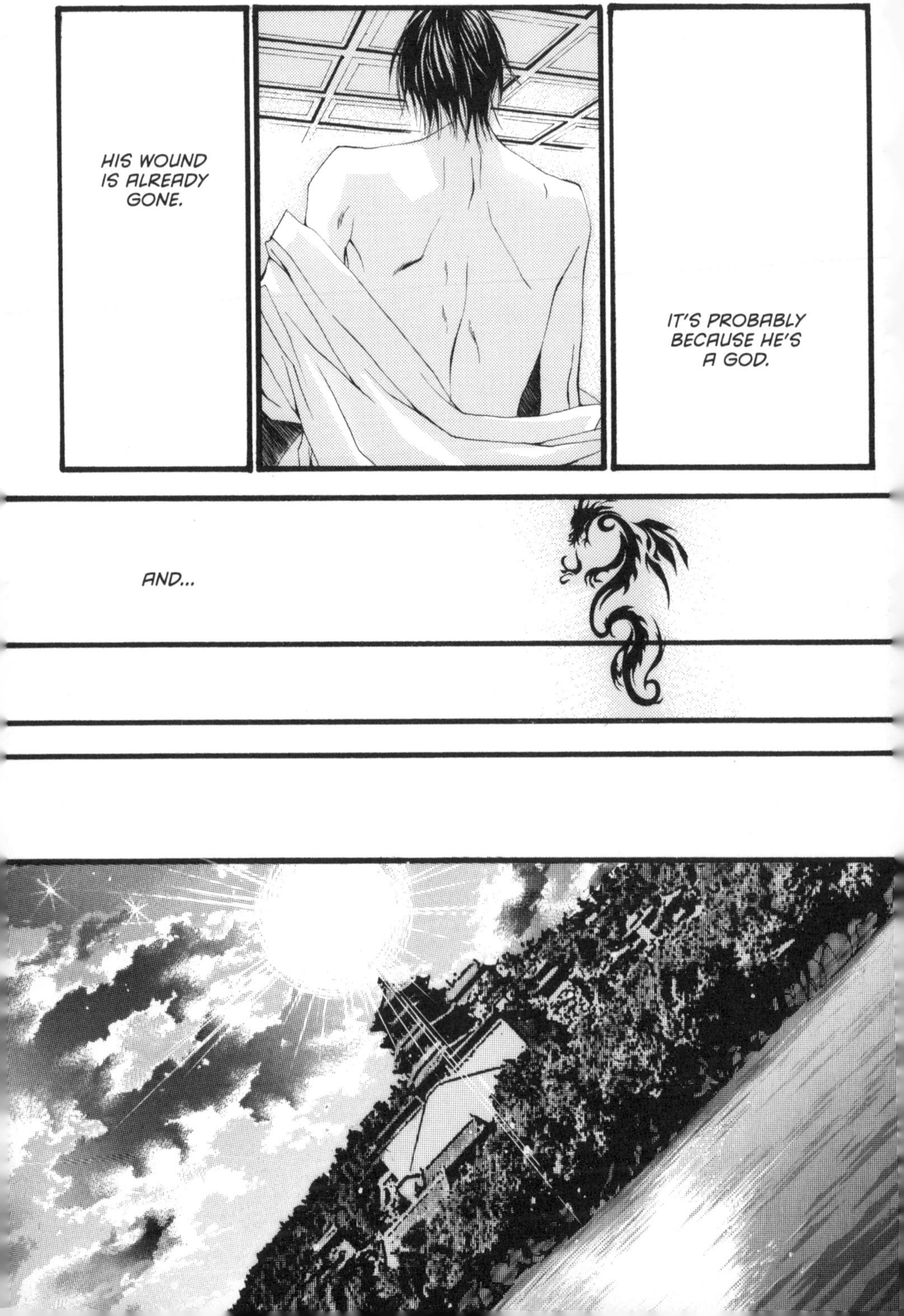

IT'S PROBABLY BECAUSE HE'S A GOD.
HIS WOUND IS ALREADY GONE.
AND...

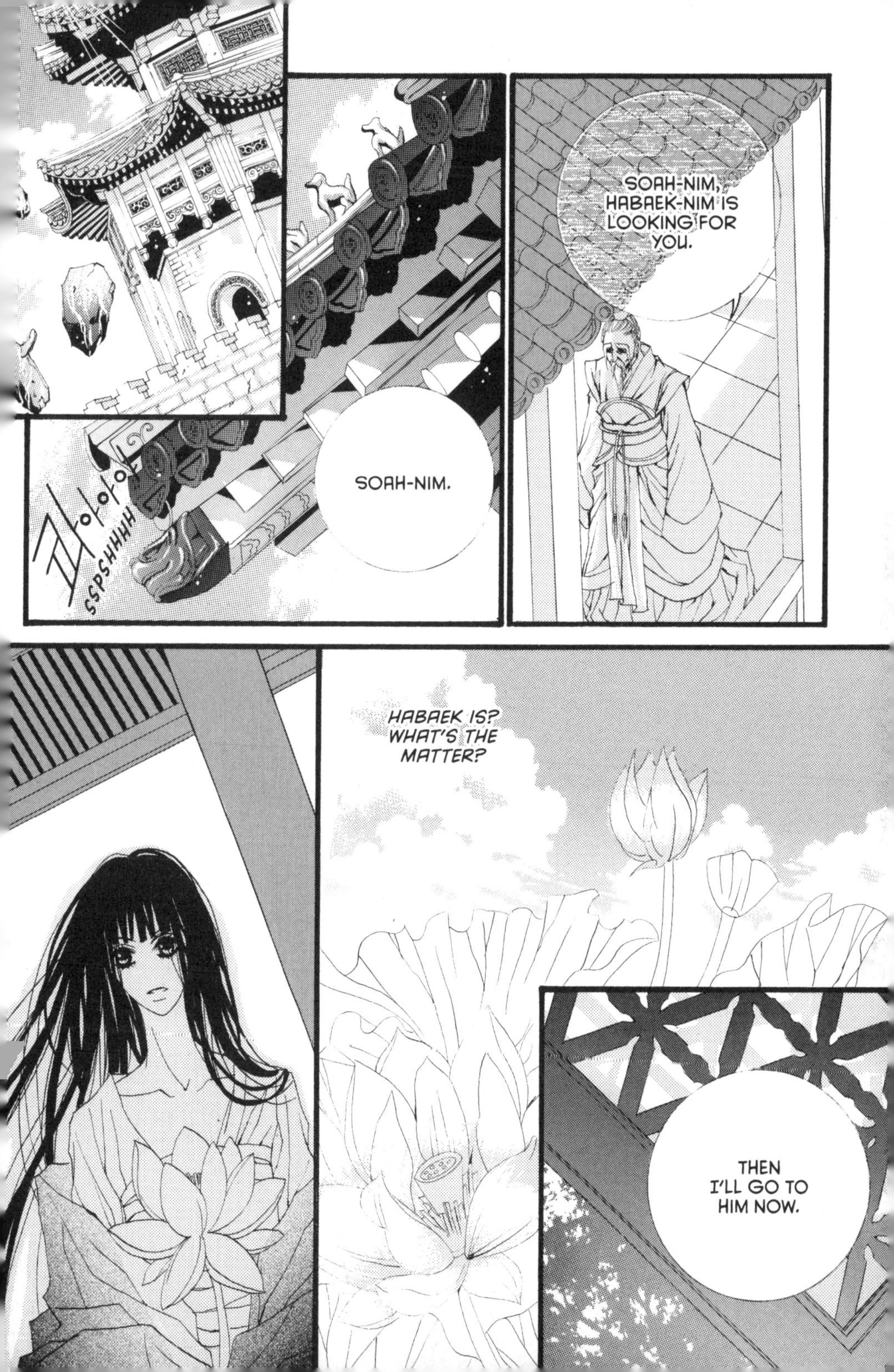
SSPSHHHH
SOAH-NIM.
SOAH-NIM, HABAEK-NIM IS LOOKING FOR YOU.
HABAEK IS? WHAT'S THE MATTER?
THEN I'LL GO TO HIM NOW.

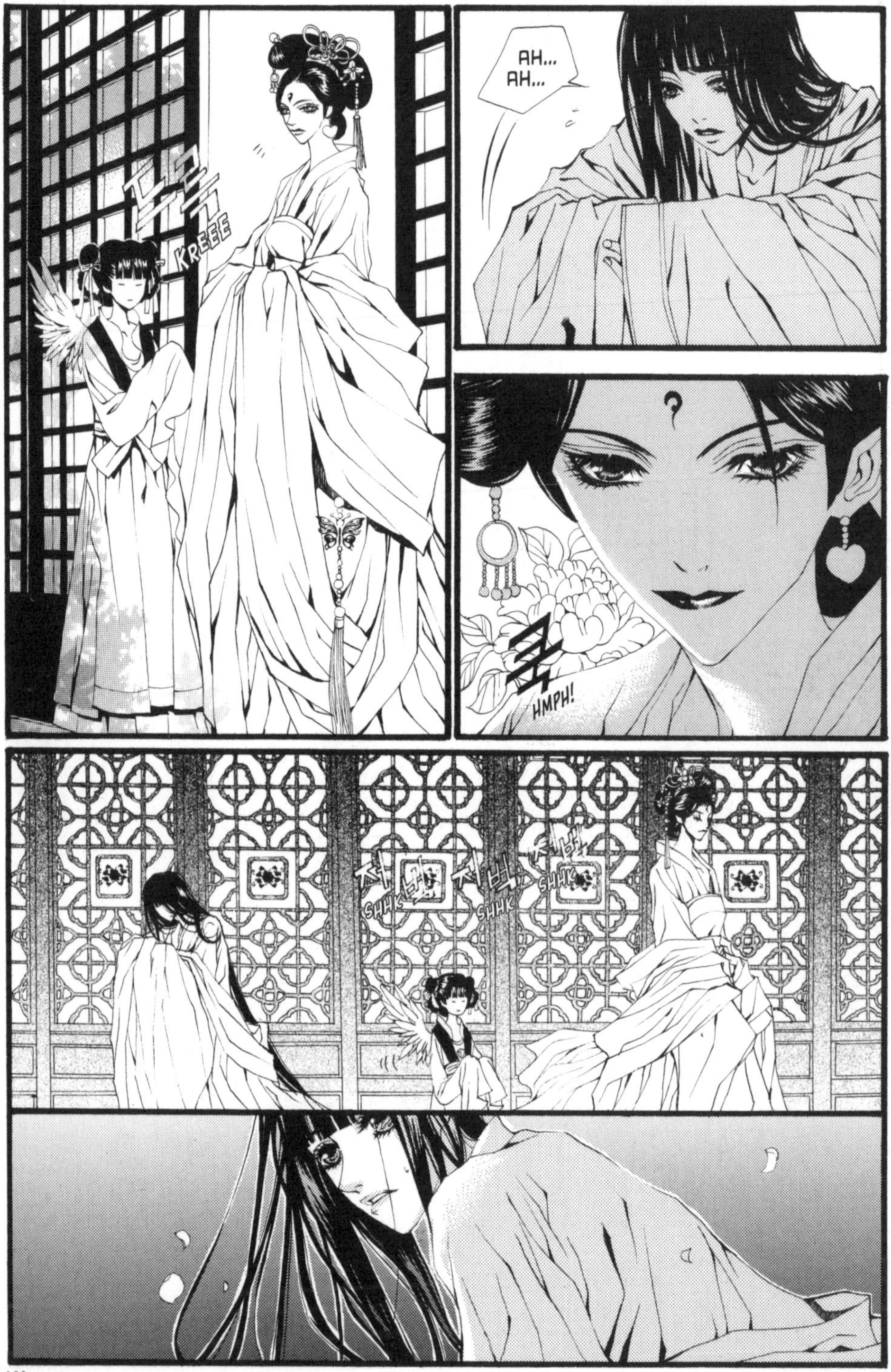
KREEE
AH... AH...
HMPH!
SHHK
SHHK
SHHK

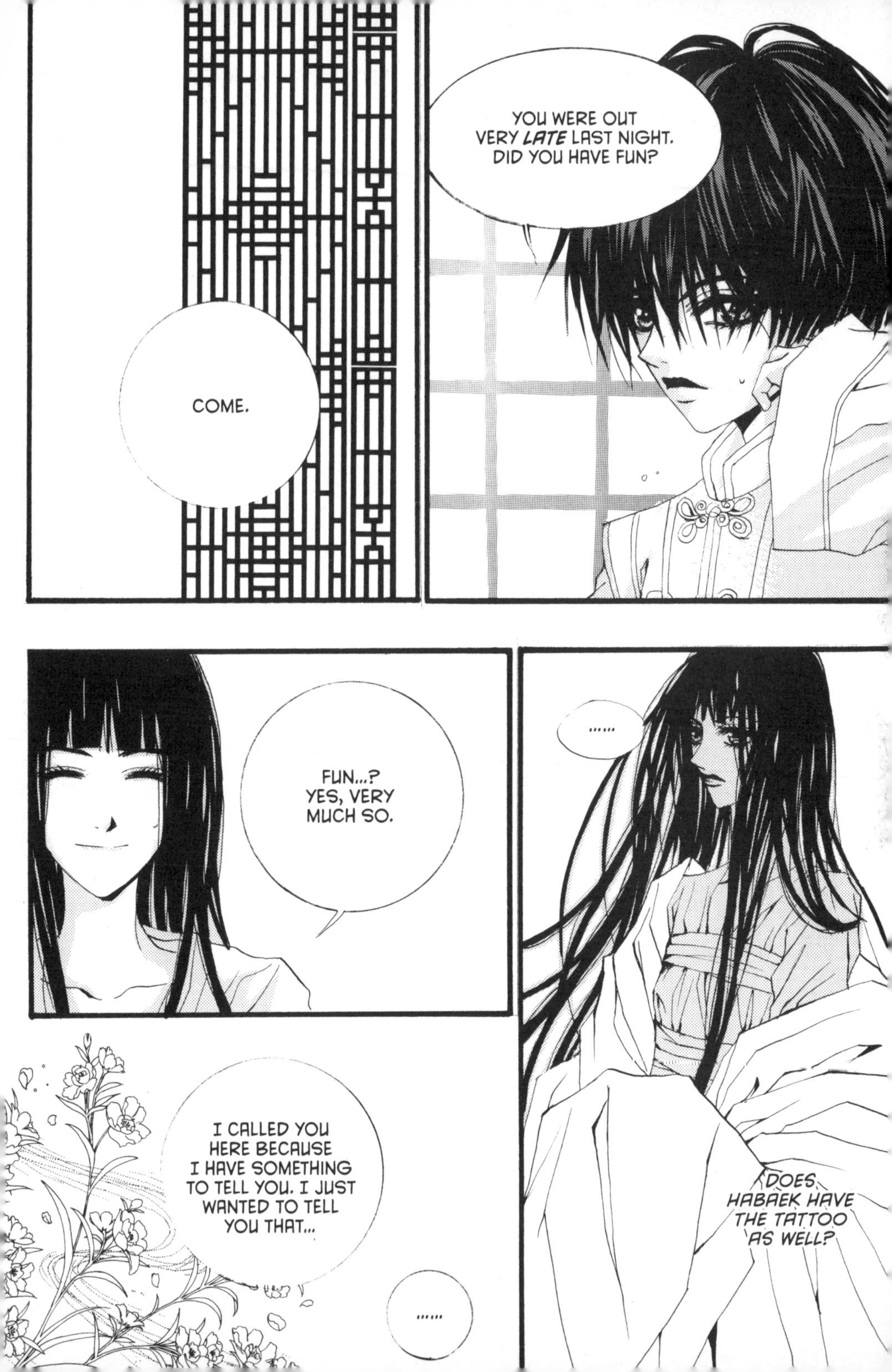
COME.
YOU WERE OUT VERY LATE LAST NIGHT. DID YOU HAVE FUN?
FUN...? YES, VERY MUCH SO.
......
I CALLED YOU HERE BECAUSE I HAVE SOMETHING TO TELL YOU. I JUST WANTED TO TELL YOU THAT...
......
DOES HABAEK HAVE THE TATTOO AS WELL?

SOAH! ARE YOU LISTENING TO ME?

AH...

I'M SORRY, I WAS JUST THINKING ABOUT SOMETHING ELSE.

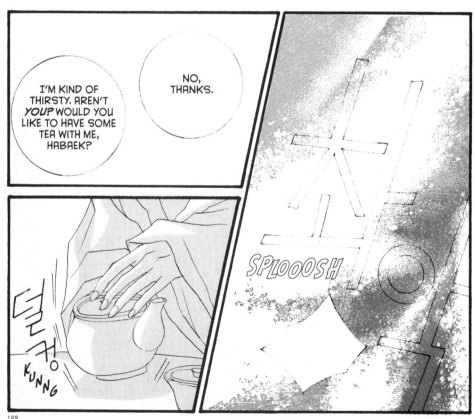

I'M KIND OF THIRSTY. AREN'T *YOU?* WOULD YOU LIKE TO HAVE SOME TEA WITH ME, HABAEK?

NO, THANKS.

SPLOOOSH

KUNNG

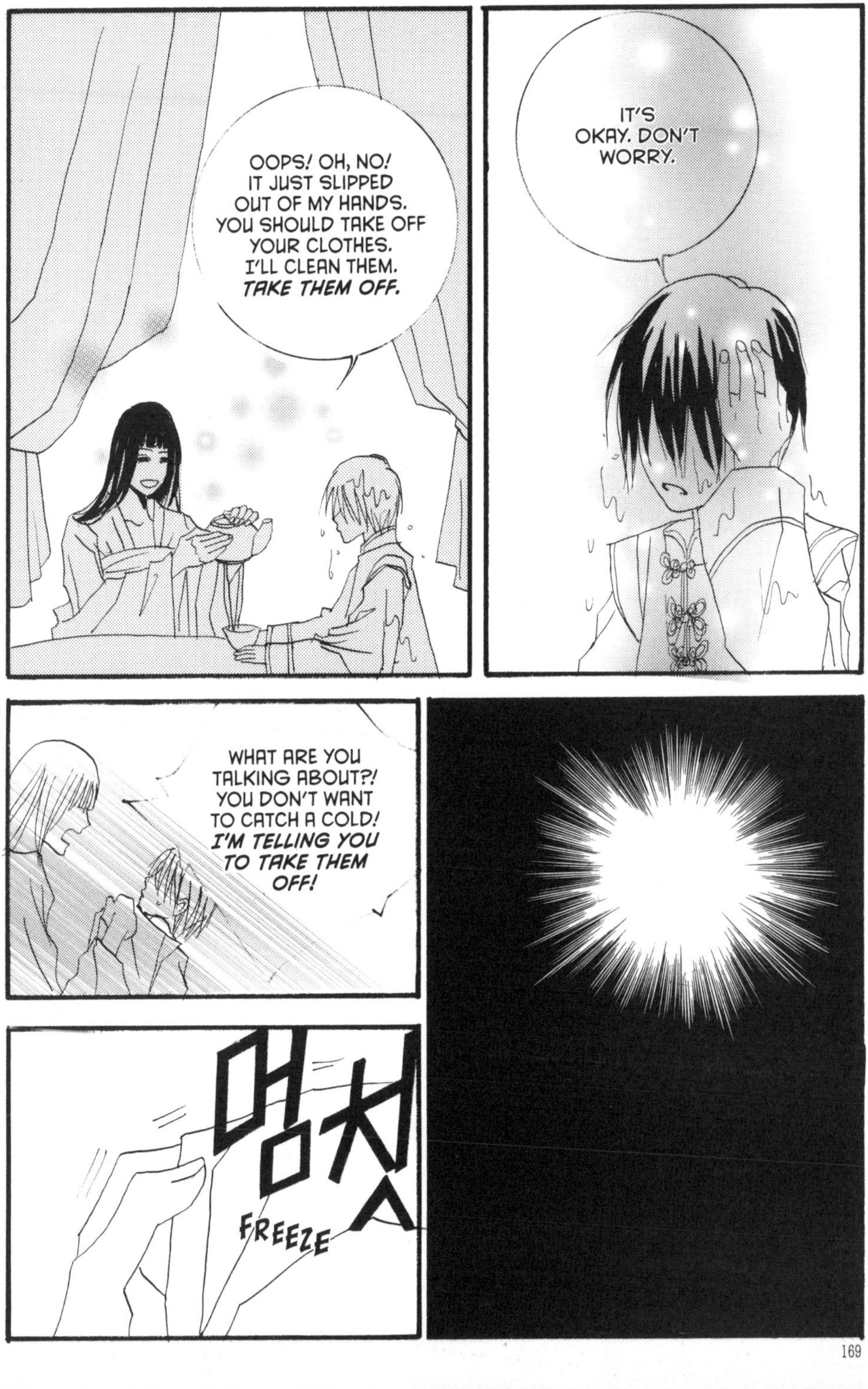
OOPS! OH, NO! IT JUST SLIPPED OUT OF MY HANDS. YOU SHOULD TAKE OFF YOUR CLOTHES. I'LL CLEAN THEM. *TAKE THEM OFF.*
IT'S OKAY. DON'T WORRY.
WHAT ARE YOU TALKING ABOUT?! YOU DON'T WANT TO CATCH A COLD! *I'M TELLING YOU TO TAKE THEM OFF!*
멈칫
FREEZE

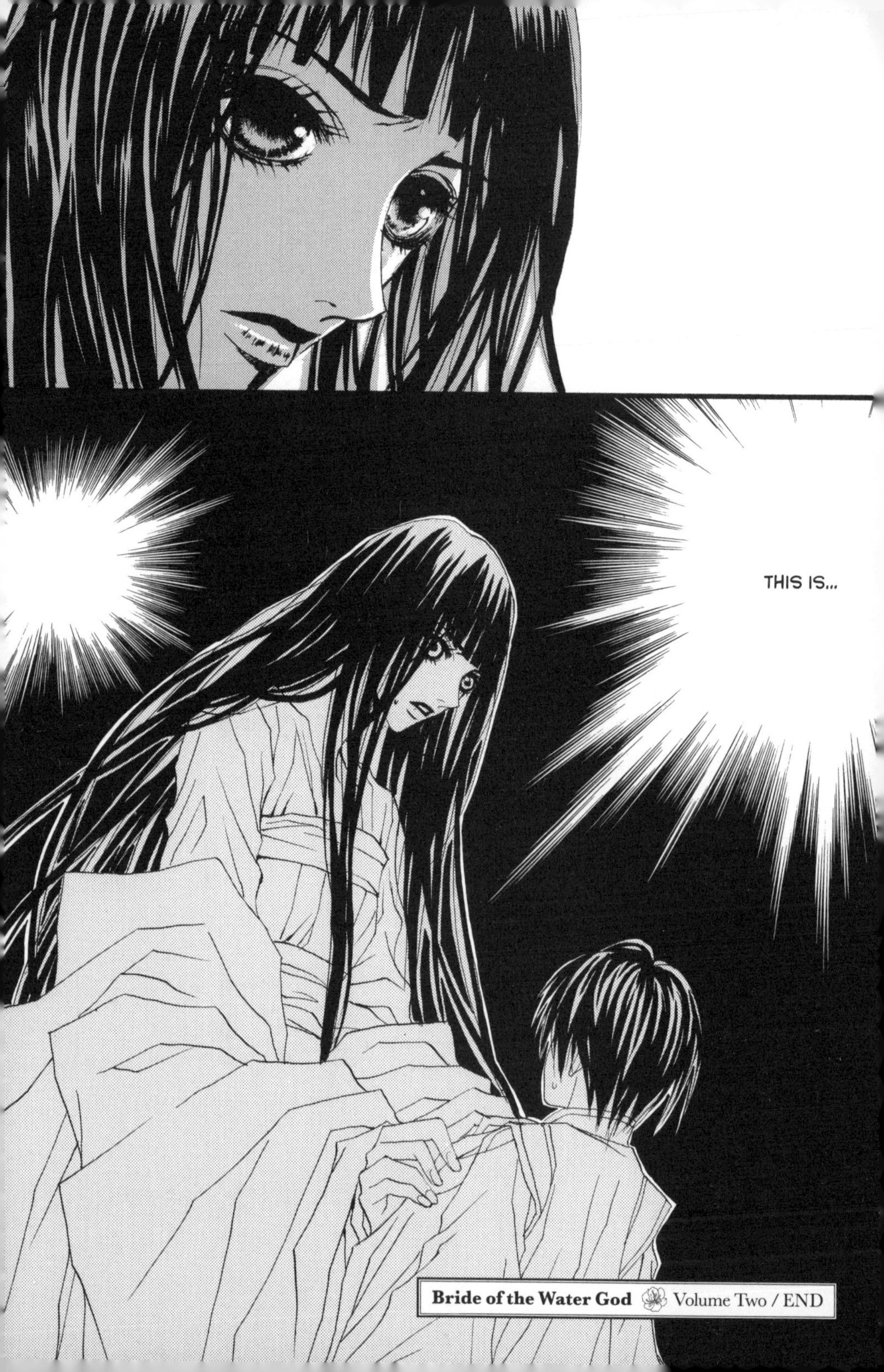
THIS IS...
Bride of the Water God Volume Two / END

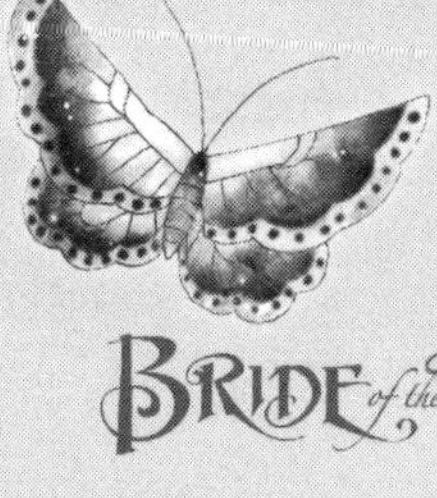

BRIDE of the WATER GOD

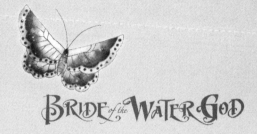

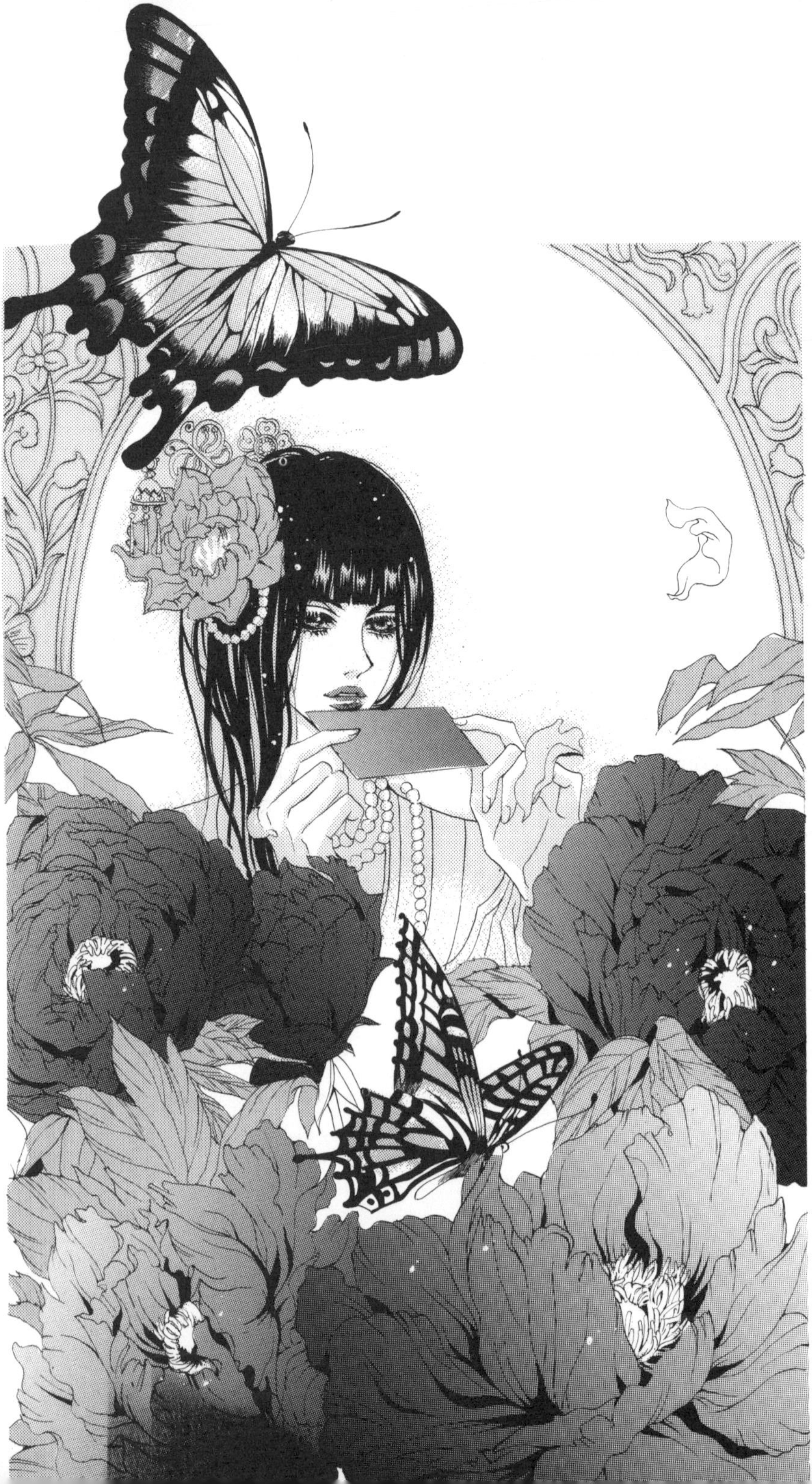

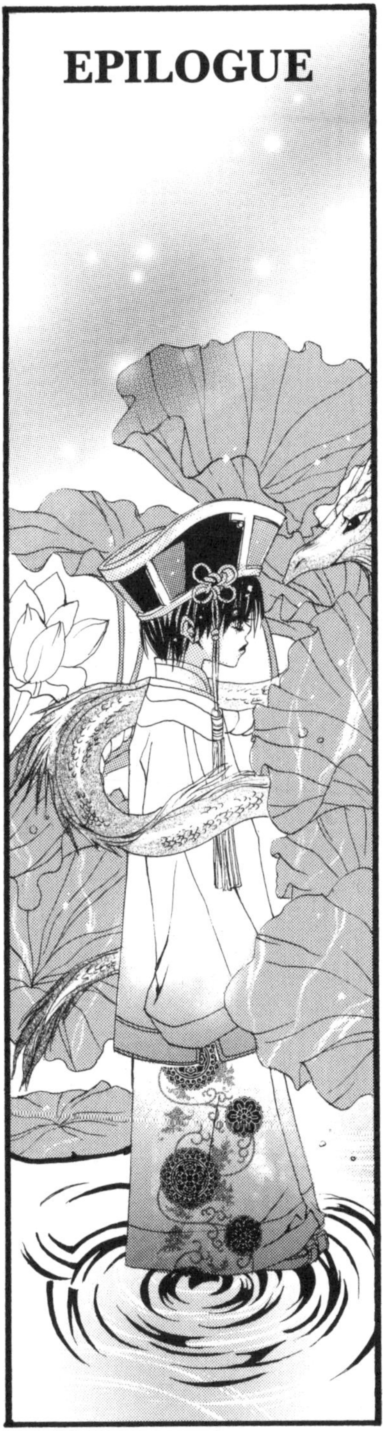
EPILOGUE

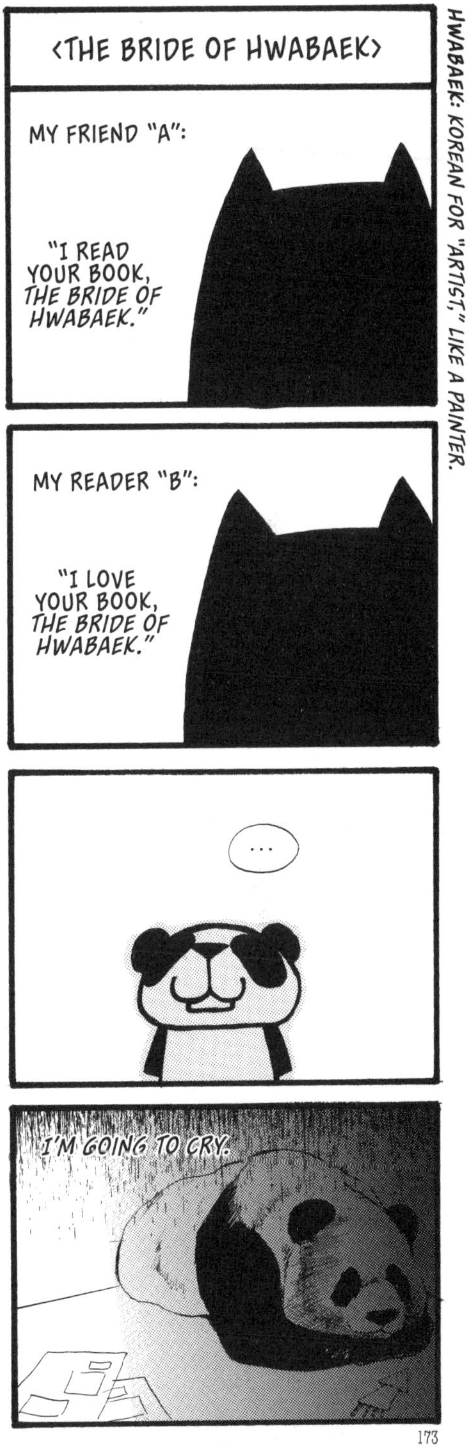
<THE BRIDE OF HWABAEK>
MY FRIEND "A":
"I READ YOUR BOOK, THE BRIDE OF HWABAEK."
MY READER "B":
"I LOVE YOUR BOOK, THE BRIDE OF HWABAEK."
...
I'M GOING TO CRY.

HWABAEK: KOREAN FOR "ARTIST," LIKE A PAINTER.

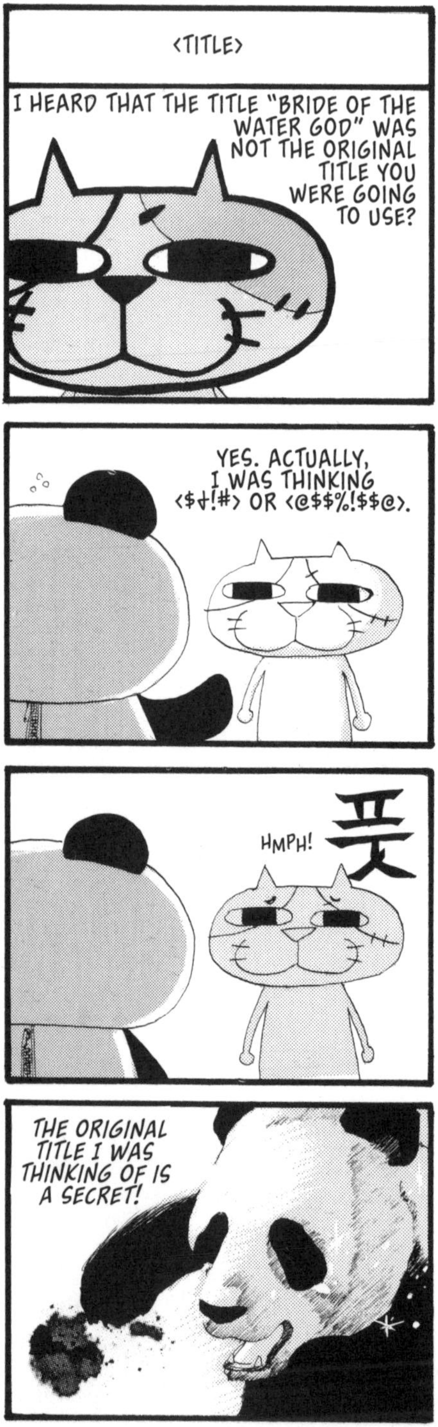
<TITLE>
I HEARD THAT THE TITLE "BRIDE OF THE WATER GOD" WAS NOT THE ORIGINAL TITLE YOU WERE GOING TO USE?
YES. ACTUALLY, I WAS THINKING <$ɟ!#> OR <@$$%!$$@>.
HMPH!
THE ORIGINAL TITLE I WAS THINKING OF IS A SECRET!

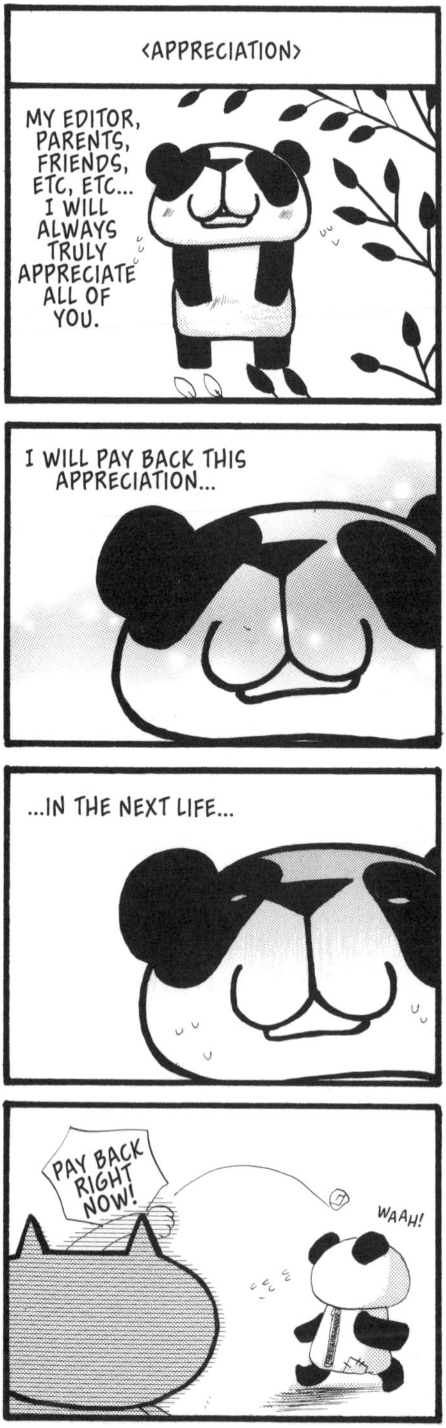
<APPRECIATION>
MY EDITOR, PARENTS, FRIENDS, ETC, ETC... I WILL ALWAYS TRULY APPRECIATE ALL OF YOU.
I WILL PAY BACK THIS APPRECIATION...
...IN THE NEXT LIFE...
PAY BACK RIGHT NOW!
WAAH!

publisher
Mike Richardson

editor
Philip Simon

digital production
Ryan Hill

collection designer
David Nestelle

art director
Lia Ribacchi

Special thanks to Tina Alessi, Davey Estrada, Michael Gombos, Julia Kwon, and Cara Niece.

English-language version produced by DARK HORSE COMICS.

BRIDE OF THE WATER GOD Volume 2

Dark Horse Manhwa
A division of Dark Horse Comics, Inc.
10956 SE Main Street
Milwaukie OR 97222

darkhorse.com

To find a comics shop in your area, call the
Comic Shop Locator Service toll-free at 1-888-266-4226

First edition January 2008
ISBN 978-1-59307-883-6

3 5 7 9 10 8 6 4 2
Printed at Lebonfon Printing, Inc., Val-d'Or, QC, Canada

I'm very happy to have so many good people around me.

I thank my parents who always watch over me, my editor who has to work doubly hard because of my shortcomings, my older sister who even goes to the publisher's office with me for deadlines, my younger sibling who seems to have grown up before I did, my fans at Wink Mi-Kyung Fan Café who always encourage me greatly, Ms. Yuni who always comes from so far away for me for deadlines, my best friend who inspires and encourages me even from far away, and finally all the readers of this book.

I wish all of you great happiness!

—*Mi-Kyung Yun*

CREATOR PROFILE

Born on October 14, 1980. Majored in Animation at Mokwon University.

Received the silver medal for Seoul Media Group's "Shin-in-gong-mo-jeon" ("New Artist Debut Competition") for *Na-eu Ji-gu Bang-moon-gi* (*The Journey of My Earth Visit*) in 2003.

Received a "Shin-in-sang" ("Best New Artist") award from the Dokja-manhwa-daesang organization for *Railroad* in 2004.

Currently publishing *Bride of the Water God* serially in the Korean comics magazine *Wink*.

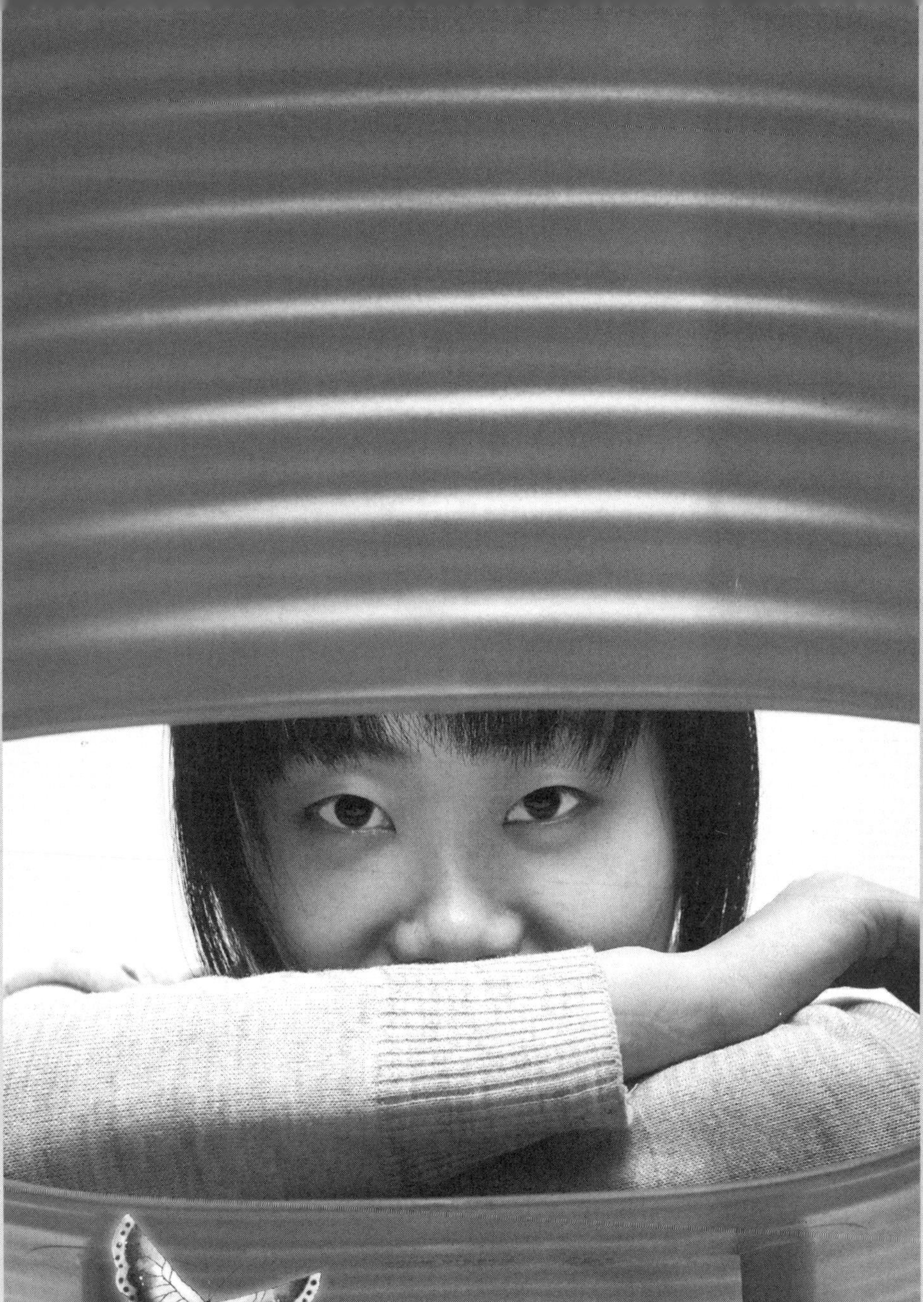

Creator photo gallery

Mi-Kyung Yun and her Korean publisher, Seoul Cultural Publishers, Inc., were kind enough to send us some promotional photographs of the creator, and a shot of one of her workstations.

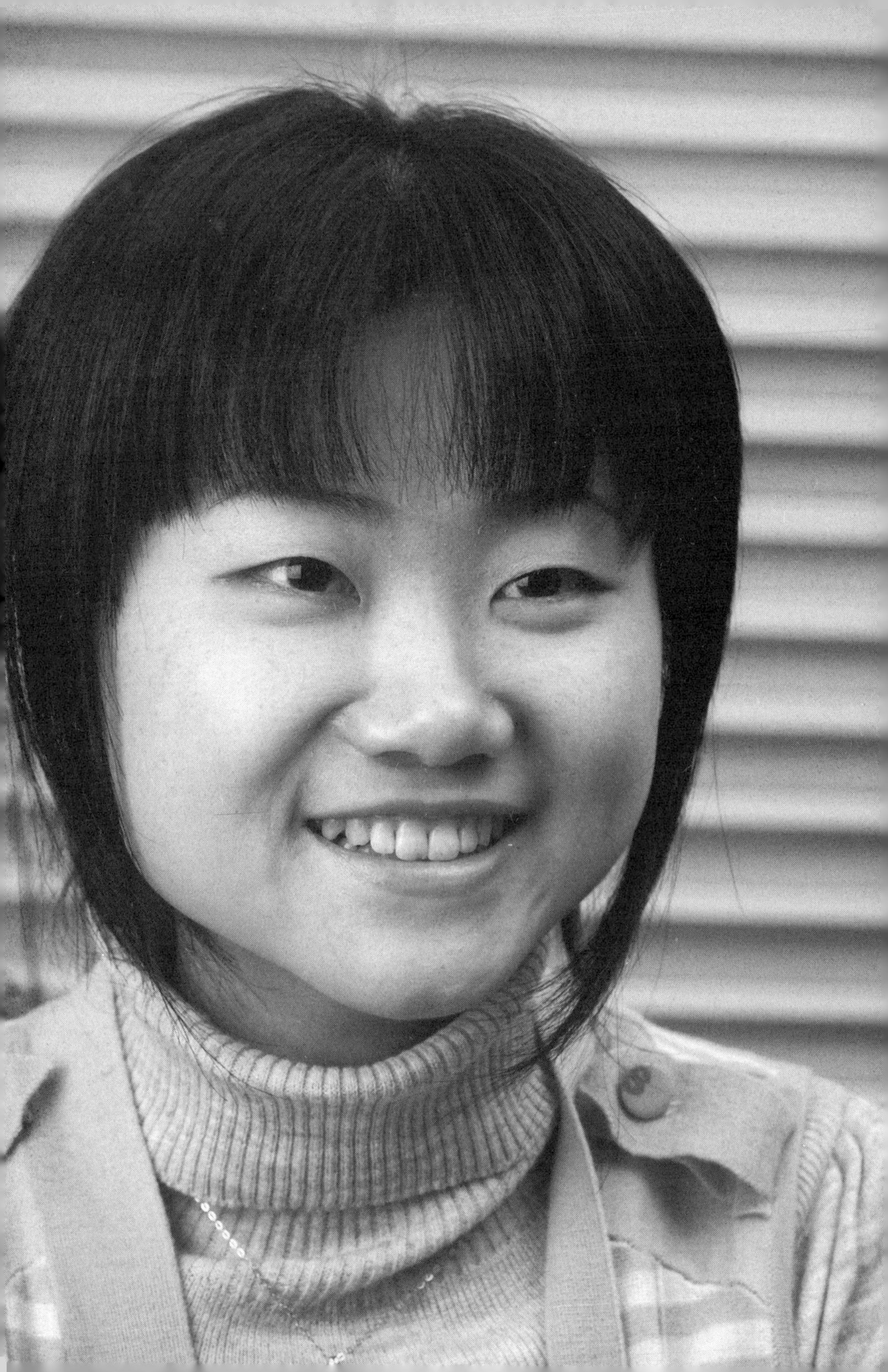

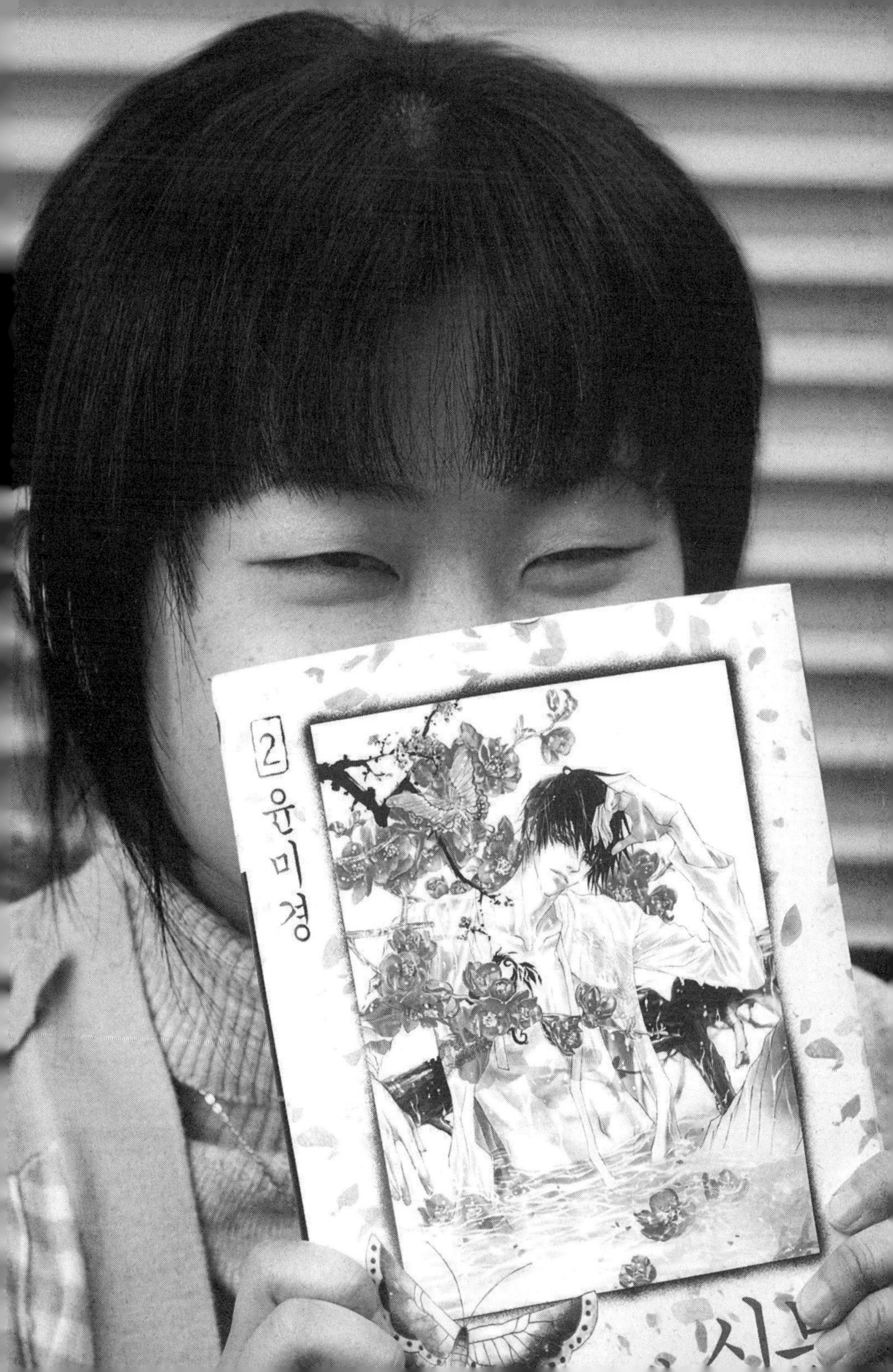
2
윤미경

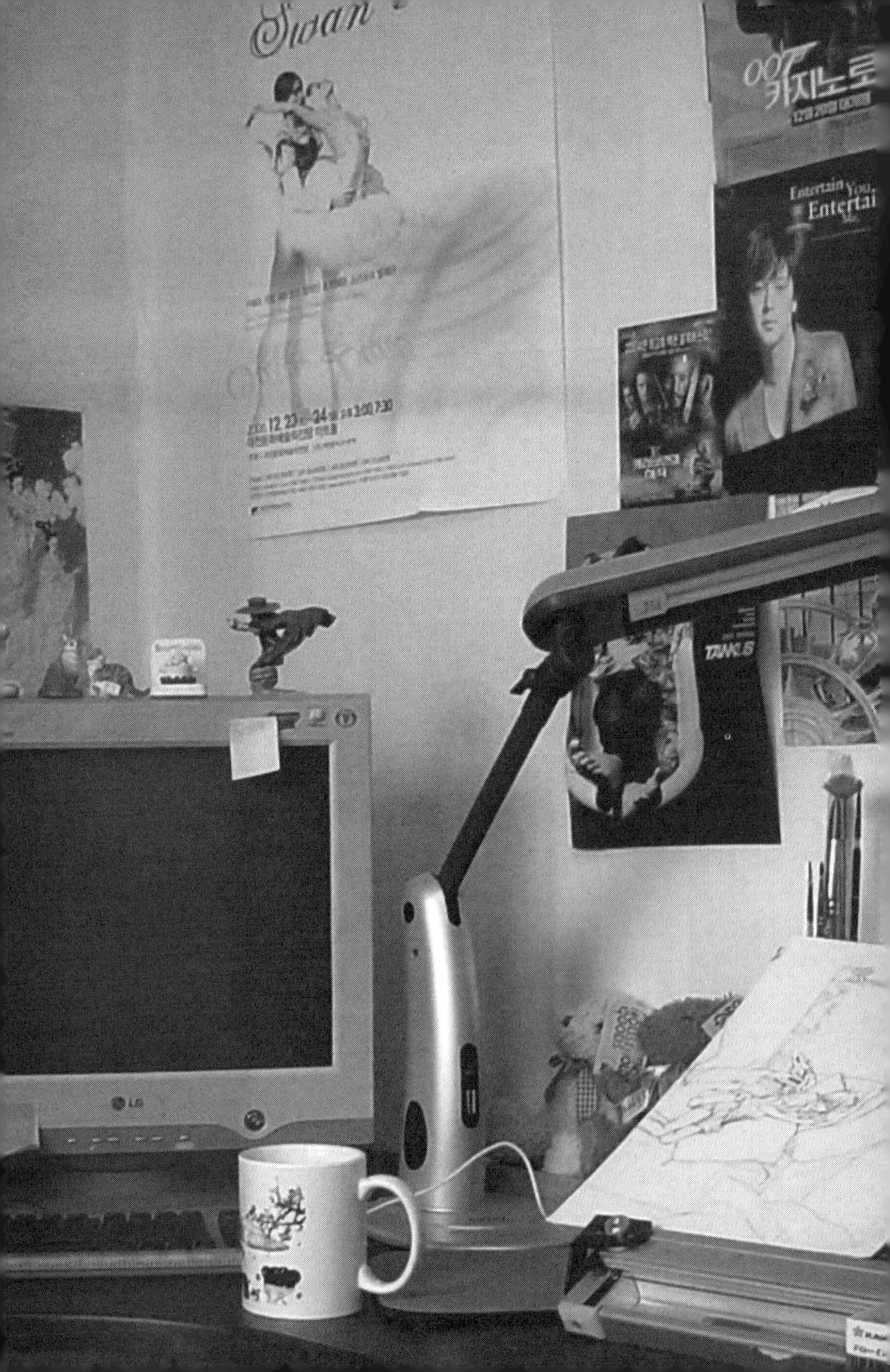
007
Entertain
LG

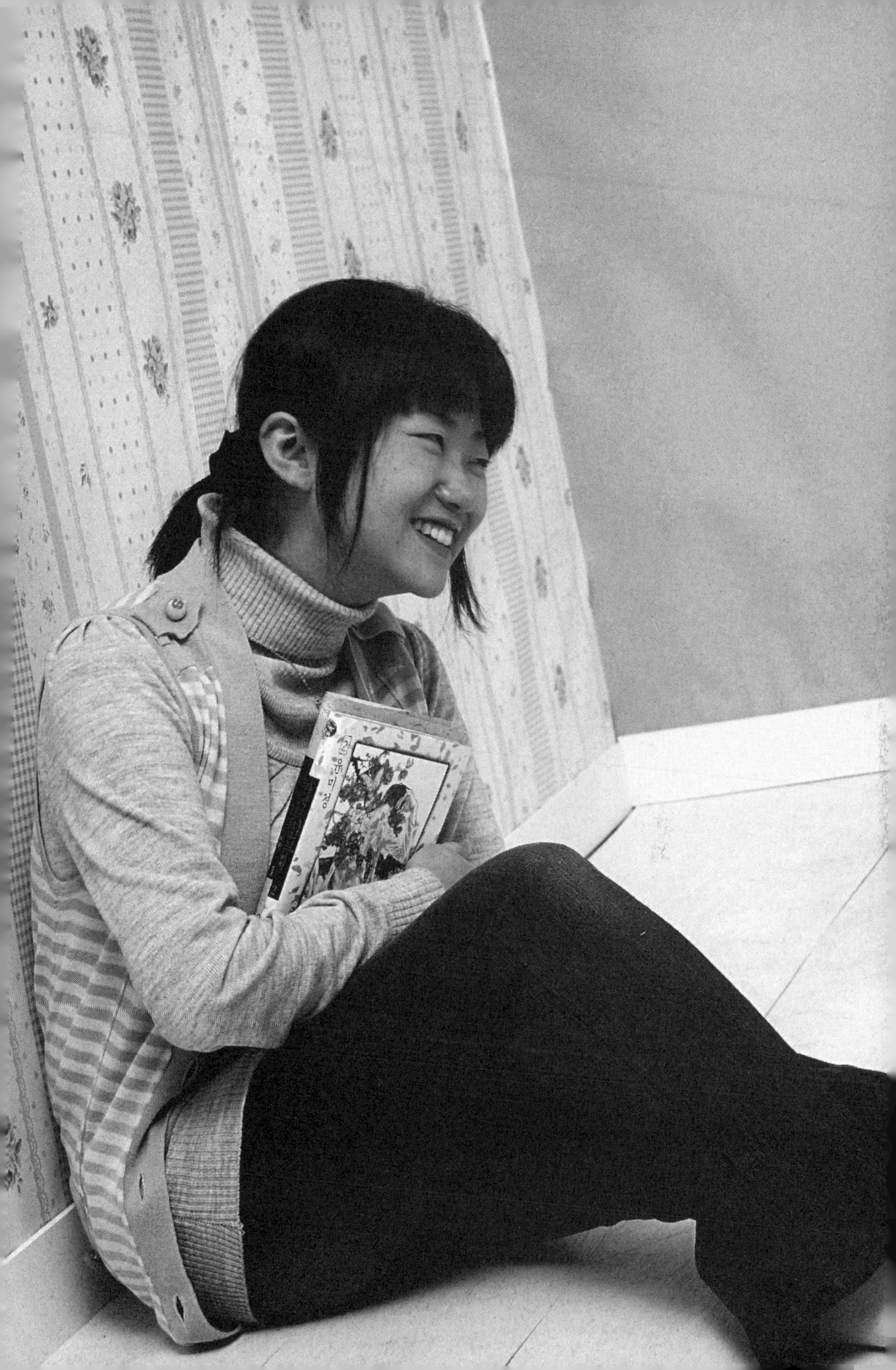
2
유미정

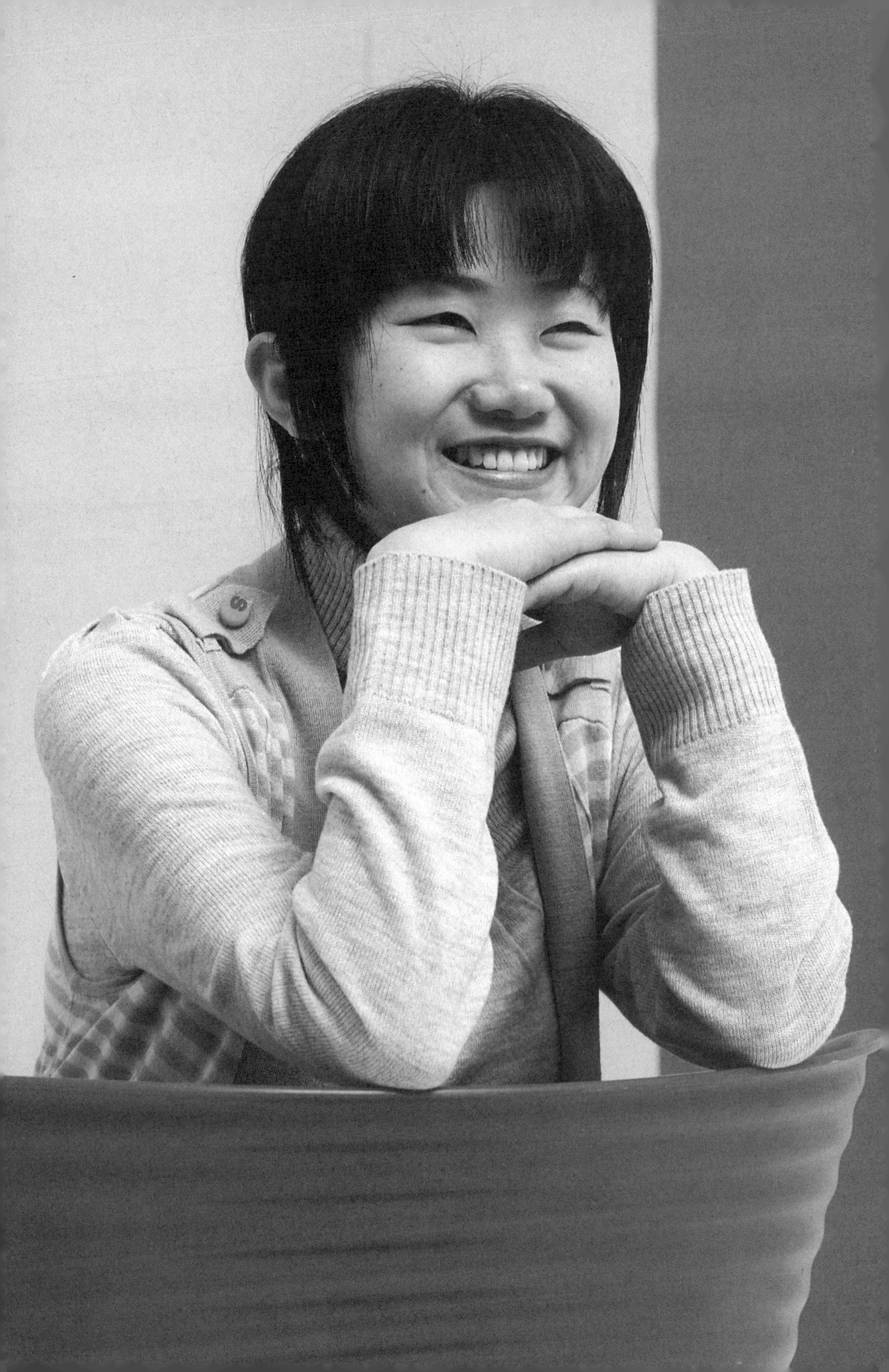

BRIDE of the WATER GOD

When Soah's impoverished, desperate village decides to sacrifice her to the Water God Habaek to end a long drought, they believe that drowning one beautiful girl will save their entire community and bring much-needed rain. Not only is Soah surprised to be *rescued* by the Water God instead of killed; she never imagined she'd be a welcomed guest in Habaek's magical kingdom, where an exciting new life awaits her! Most surprising, however, is the Water God himself, and how very different he is from the monster Soah imagined . . .

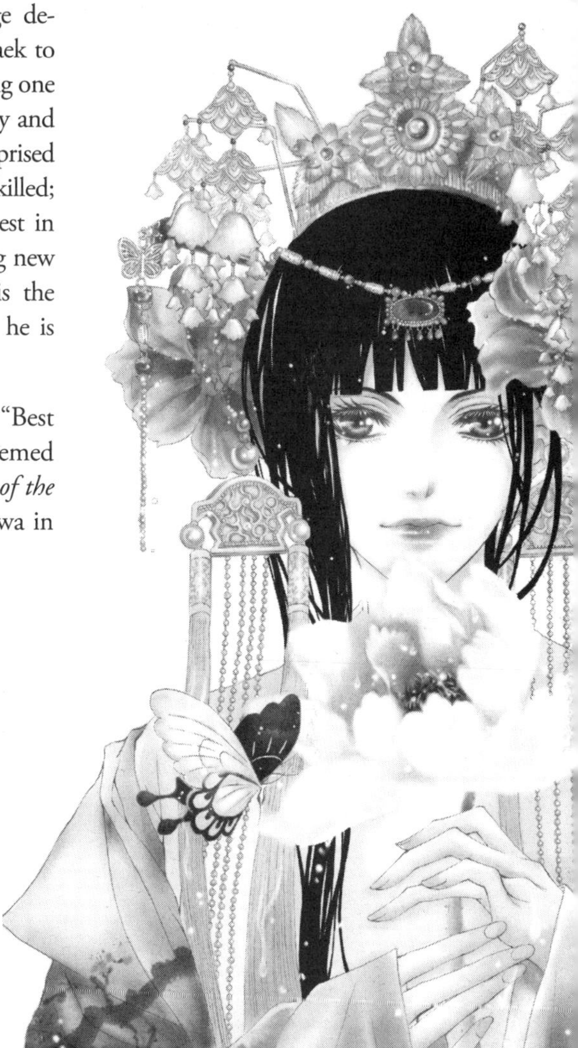

Created by Mi-Kyung Yun, who received the "Best New Artist" award in 2004 from the esteemed *Dokja-manhwa-daesang* organization, *Bride of the Water God* was the top-selling *shoujo* manhwa in Korea in 2006!

Volume 1
ISBN 978-1-59307-849-2

Volume 2
ISBN 978-1-59307-883-6

Volume 3
ISBN 978-1-59582-305-2

Volume 4
ISBN 978-1-59582-378-6

Volume 5
ISBN 978-1-59582-445-5

$19.99 each

Previews for *BRIDE OF THE WATER GOD* and other DARK HORSE MANHWA titles can be found at darkhorse.com!

DARK HORSE MANHWA

AVAILABLE AT YOUR LOCAL COMICS SHOP OR BOOKSTORE! TO FIND A COMICS SHOP IN YOUR AREA, CALL 1-888-266-4226.

For more information or to order direct visit darkhorse.com or call 1-800-862-0052 Mon.–Fri. 9 AM to 5 PM Pacific Time.
*Prices and availability subject to change without notice.

【ㄥ ㄸ ﾍ ㄈ ≋ ━ ㄗ ㄥ ㄥ】
translucent

Can you see right through her?

By Kazuhiro Okamoto

Shizuka is an introverted girl dealing with schoolwork, boys, and a medical condition that has begun to turn her invisible! She finds support with Mamoru, a boy who is falling for Shizuka despite her condition, and with Keiko, a woman who suffers from the same illness and has finally turned *completely* invisible! *Translucent's* exploration of what people see, what people think they see, and what people wish to see in themselves, and others, makes for an emotionally sensitive manga peppered with moments of surprising humor, heartbreak, and drama.

VOLUME 1
ISBN 978-1-59307-647-4

VOLUME 2
ISBN 978-1-59307-677-1

VOLUME 3
ISBN 978-1-59307-679-5

VOLUME 4
ISBN 978-1-59582-218-5

$9.95 Each!

**Previews for *TRANSLUCENT* and other
DARK HORSE MANGA titles can be found
at darkhorse.com!**

AVAILABLE AT YOUR LOCAL COMICS SHOP OR BOOKSTORE
To find a comics shop in your area, call 1-888-266-4226. For more information or
to order direct: • On the web: darkhorse.com • E-mail: mailorder@darkhorse.com
• Phone: 1-800-862-0052 Mon.–Fri. 9 AM to 5 PM Pacific Time.

DARK
HORSE
MANGA

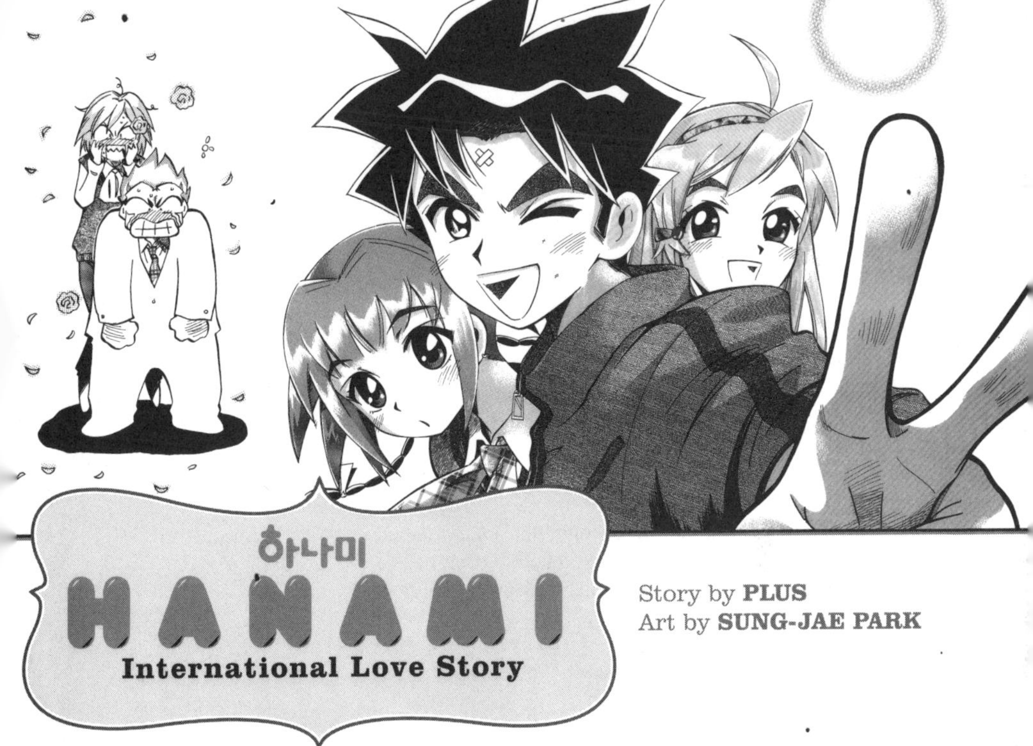

하나미

HANAMI

International Love Story

Story by **PLUS**
Art by **SUNG-JAE PARK**

Seventeen-year-old Joonho Suk just had the best day of his life. He finally asked out his big crush, and she said yes. But after floating home on cloud nine, he found his family packing up to move to Seoul! Now tossed into a big new city and lovesick for the girl still in Suwon, Joonho runs into weird characters at every turn. Girl troubles and crazy adventures abound! Discover one of the most popular comics Korea has to offer!

VOLUME 1
ISBN 978-1-59307-737-2

VOLUME 2
ISBN 978-59307-738-9

VOLUME 3
ISBN 978-1-59307-739-6

$9.95 each!

Previews for *Hanami: International Love Story* and other Dark Horse Manhwa titles can be found at darkhorse.com!

AVAILABLE AT YOUR LOCAL COMICS SHOP OR BOOKSTORE. To find a comics shop in your area, call 1-888-266-4226. For more information or to order direct: On the web: darkhorse.com. E-mail: mailorder@darkhorse.com. Phone: 1-800-862-0052 Mon.–Fri. 9 AM to 5 PM Pacific Time.

Red String

Volume 1
ISBN 978-1-59307-624-5

Volume 2
ISBN 978-1-59307-884-3

Volume 3
ISBN 978-1-59307-958-1

$9.95 each!

When first-year high-school student Miharu Ogawa gets a call from her parents, telling her to come straight home from school, she prepares herself for the worst, but nothing she could ever have imagined could have prepared her for their "great news" . . . Miharu is getting married! How's a spirited and independent teenager who has never even kissed a boy supposed to deal with suddenly having a fiancé she's never even met? And how will her feelings change when she finds out that there are other boys out there vying for her affection, and other girls ready and willing to take away the man she's not even sure she's ready for?

Check out the collected volumes of this hit webcomic by Gina Biggs, which deals with all forms of love: parental, romantic, heterosexual, homosexual, platonic, unrequited, heartbreaking, dishonest, and all stops in between!

DARK HORSE BOOKS

AVAILABLE AT YOUR LOCAL COMICS SHOP OR BOOKSTORE! TO FIND A COMICS SHOP IN YOUR AREA, CALL 1-888-266-4226.

For more information or to order direct visit darkhorse.com or call 1-800-862-0052 Mon.-Fri. 9 A.M. to 5 P.M. Pacific Time. *Prices and availability subject to change without notice.